An Introduction to Vygotsky

In an attempt to provide an account of the social formation of the mind, Lev Vygotsky endowed the twentieth century with an enticing mix of intellectual traditions. His legacy is an exciting but at times chaotic fusion of ideas. Combining reprints of key journal and text articles with editorial commentary and helpful suggestions for further reading, this book offers the reader an accessible introduction to Vygotsky's work and the controversies which surround it.

This thoroughly revised second edition includes newly selected articles to provide a fully up-to-date introduction to Vygotsky's theories and the multidisciplinary contribution he has made to twentieth-century intellectual life. Major elements discussed include the use of the 'culture' concept in social development theory and the implications of Vygotsky's theories for teaching, learning and assessment. Academics and students at all levels will find this an essential source of information about one of the twentieth century's most influential theorists.

Harry Daniels is Professor of Education: Culture and Pedagogy in the Department of Education at the University of Bath, UK.

An Introduction to Vygotsky

Second Edition

Edited by Harry Daniels

Routledge
Taylor & Francis Group

LONDON AND NEW YORK

First published 2005 by Routledge
27 Church Road, Hove, East Sussex BN3 2FA

Simultaneously published in the USA and Canada
by Routledge
270 Madison Avenue, New York, NY 10016

Routledge is an imprint of the Taylor & Francis Group

© 2005 Selection and editorial matter, Harry Daniels; individual
chapters, the contributors

Typeset in Times by RefineCatch Limited, Bungay, Suffolk
Printed and bound in Great Britain by
TJ International Ltd, Padstow, Cornwall
Paperback cover design by Anú Design

This publication has been produced with paper manufactured to strict
environmental standards and with pulp derived from sustainable
forests.

British Library Cataloguing in Publication Data
A catalogue record for this book is available from the British Library

Library of Congress Cataloging in Publication Data
A catalogue record for this book has been requested

ISBN 0–415–32812–8 (hbk)
ISBN 0–415–32813–6 (pbk)

Contents

vi   *Contents*

Figures

Sources

Chapter 1

Minick, N.J. (1987) The development of Vygotsky's thought: an introduction to *Thinking and Speech*, New York: Plenum (edited and translated by N. Minick), pp. 17–35. Reprinted with permission.

Chapter 2

Wertsch, J.V. and Tulviste, P.E. (1992) L.S. Vygotsky and contemporary developmental psychology, *Developmental Psychology*, 28, 4: 548–57. Copyright © 1992 by the American Psychological Association. Reprinted with permission.

Chapter 3

Valsiner, J. and van der Veer, R. (1988) On the social nature of human cognition: an analysis of the shared intellectual roots of George Herbert Mead and Lev Vygotsky, *Journal for the Theory of Social Behaviour*, 18, 117–36. Reprinted by permission of Blackwell Publishing.

Chapter 4

Kozulin, A. (1986) The concept of activity in Soviet psychology: Vygotsky, his disciples and critics, *American Psychologist*, 41, 3: 264–74. Copyright © 1986 by the American Psychological Association. Reprinted with permission.

Chapter 5

Cheyne, J.A. and Tarulli, D. (1999) Dialogue, difference and voice in the Zone of Proximal Development, *Theory and Psychology*, 9: 5–28. Copyright © Sage Publications, 1999. Reproduced with permission.

Chapter 6

Lave, J. and Wenger, E. (1991) Practice, person, social world, Chapter 2 in *Situated Learning: Legitimate Peripheral Participation*, Cambridge:

Cambridge University Press, pp. 45–58. © Cambridge University Press, reprinted with permission.

Chapter 7

Engeström, Y. (1991) *Non scolae sed vitae discimus*: toward overcoming the encapsulation of school learning, *Learning and Instruction*, 1: 243–59. © Copyright 1991. Reprinted with permission from Elsevier.

Chapter 8

Bakhurst, D. (1990) Social memory in Soviet thought, in D. Middleton and D. Edwards (eds) *Collective Remembering*, London: Sage, pp. 203–26. Reprinted by permission of Sage Publishing Ltd.

Chapter 9

Cole, M. (1996) Putting culture in the middle, Chapter 5 in *Cultural Psychology: A Once and Future Discipline*, Cambridge, MA: Harvard University Press, pp. 116–45. Reprinted by permission of the publisher. Copyright © 1996 by the President and Fellows of Harvard College.

Chapter 10

Hedegaard, M. (1990) The zone of proximal development as basis for instruction, in L.C. Moll (ed.) (1991) *Vygotsky and Education*, London: Cambridge University Press, pp. 349–71. © Cambridge University Press, reprinted with permission.

Chapter 11

Lee, C.D. (2000) Signifying in the zone of proximal development in C.D. Lee and P. Smagorinsky (eds) *Vygotskian Perspectives on Literacy Research: Constructing Meaning through Collaborative Inquiry*, Cambridge: Cambridge University Press, pp. 191–225. © Cambridge University Press, reprinted with permission.

Chapter 12

Sullivan Palincsar, A. (1998) Social constructivist perspectives on teaching and learning, *Annual Review of Psychology*, 49: 345–75. Reprinted with permission, from the *Annual Review of Psychology*, Volume 49, © 1998 by Annual Reviews www.annualreviews.org.

Contributors

David Bakhurst, Department of Philosophy, Queens University, Ontario, Canada.

J. Allan Cheyne, University of Waterloo, Waterloo, Ontario, Canada.

Michael Cole, Laboratory for Comparative Human Cognition, University of California, San Diego, 9500 Gilman Drive, La Jolla, CA 92093–050, USA.

Yrjö Engeström, Laboratory of Comparative Human Cognition, University of California, San Diego, La Jolla, CA 92093–0092 and Centre for Activity Research & Developmental Work Research, University of Helsinki, PO Box 47, Fin–00014, Finland.

Mariane Hedegaard, Institute of Psychology, University of Copenhagen, Njalsgade 88, 2300 Copenhagen S, Denmark.

Alex Kozulin, The International Centre for the Enhancement of Learning Potential, 47 Markiss St., PO Box 7755, Jerusalem, 91077, Israel.

Jean Lave, Social and Cultural Studies, Graduate School of Education, 1500 Tollman Hall, University of California, Berkeley, CA 94720, USA.

Carol D. Lee, Northwestern University, School of Education and Social Policy, Program in Learning Sciences, Evanston, IL 60208, USA.

Norris Minick, Programme in Learning Disabilities, Department of Communication Sciences and Disorders, Northwestern University, Evanston, IL 60208, USA.

Annemarie Sullivan Palincsar, University of Michigan, Ann Arbor, 4204c SEB, 610 E University, Ann Arbor, MI 48109, USA.

Donato Tarulli, University of Waterloo, Waterloo, Ontario, Canada.

Peeter Tulviste, Department of Psychology, University of Tartu, Tartu, Estonia.

Jaan Valsiner, Professor and Chair, Department of Psychology, Clark University, Worcester, MA 01610–1477, USA.

René van der Veer, Department of Education, Leiden University, Wassenaarseweg 52, PO Box 9555, 2300 RB Leiden, The Netherlands.

Etienne Wenger, Institute for Research on Learning, 2550 Hanover Street, Palo Alto, CA 94043, USA.

James V. Wertsch, Department of Education, Campus Box 1183, Washington University, One Brookings Drive, St. Louis, MO 63130–4899, USA.

Acknowledgement

I am grateful to all the staff and student members of the Centre for Socio-cultural and Activity Theory Research at the Universities of Bath and Birmingham for the lively discussions that gave rise to the changes in my thinking reflected in this second edition. My thanks are due to them.

Introduction

Harry Daniels

It is a pleasure to be given the opportunity of re-editing this book some eight years after its first publication. As I said at the time, the chapters in this book were selected to provide an introduction to some of the issues that have arisen in the development of the cultural historical schools which have sought inspiration from the work of the Russian scholar L. S. Vygotsky. I wish to emphasize the phrase 'an introduction' because through the use of this phrase I wish to signify that it is one of a range of possible introductions. This text seeks to provide the reader, already familiar with the basic tenets of the theory, with a range of readings which point to particular theoretical and empirical areas of contestation and thus potential development. It is not a basic introduction to the work: rather, it intends to introduce some of the dilemmas that the development of the theory has raised.

As with almost all attempts to sketch the influence of this early twentieth-century writer, it is partial. The main focus is on that part of the development of the analysis of the relationship between the social and the psychological which is concerned with development and learning. This introduction will consider the emergence of Vygotsky's work and what are taken to be some of the key elements of his overall thesis. The general theme of the development of the operational notion of the term 'social' will be pursued against a background of familiar concepts such as the 'zone of proximal development'.

All the chapters in this collection have been published elsewhere. The original idea for such a collection came from the experience of running a short series of lectures for Master's students. As university libraries struggle to maintain broad and balanced collections of journals and books, students often experience particular difficulty in accessing some of the articles reproduced here. The changes that have been introduced in this second edition arose from discussions in seminars and workshops held in the Centre for Sociocultural and Activity Theory Research at the Universities of Bath and Birmingham.

This introduction draws heavily on a number of texts which make a significant contribution to the debates surrounding Vygotsky's work.

THE EMERGENCE OF VYGOTSKY'S WORK

Just as the collection is inevitably partial, it is also concerned with the differences that have emerged in the developments of the original thesis. Not that the original body of writing can be considered coherent and unified. As Minick shows in Chapter 1, the stages and phases of Vygotsky's work were marked by some profound shifts in orientation, albeit with a common frame of reference. There is a sense in which one can feel Vygotsky 'talking his way in' to a thesis that was never finished. This image of an obviously hugely talented thinker grappling with disciplines such as psychology, in which he was, like Piaget, to a large part untrained, carries with it a sense of excitement and verve. His free-ranging cross/multi-disciplinary contribution to twentieth-century intellectual life was supported by his own interpretation of both fellow Russian and European thinkers. Just as he drew on a range of disciplines so did he embed much of his own reading of European philosophical, psycho-logical, sociological and political thought in his writing. This creative fusion and development of many perspectives and persuasions was cast adrift in the tragedy that befell the Soviet Union under Stalin. It was selectively moulded, transformed, developed and, in no small part, suppressed for many years. Although the texts themselves did achieve some small notoriety in *zamisdat* (underground publication) form, both in the Soviet Union and the West, they only really became known in the West in the 1970s. Translation and 'judicious' editing took their toll.

Burmenskaya (1992), a developmental psychologist working in the department of developmental psychology that Gal'perin used to lead, argues that many Western attempts to interpret Vygotsky have been marked more by enthusiasm for Western pedagogical preoccupations than by concern to understand the range and depth of his arguments. This has been compounded by a marked tendency to ignore the work of more recent Russian writers (for a recent exception, see Kozulin *et al.* 2003). Valsiner (1988) analysed the dissemination of Vygotsky's ideas through citations made in journal articles and books. He refers to the 'canalized nature' of references to Vygotsky's writing. Of the 1373 citations he identified, 1129 were made to either *Thought and Language* (*Thinking and Speech*) or *Mind in Society*. Both these texts, he argues, suffer from translation difficulties and, in the case of the original trans-lation of *Thought and Language*, severe truncation. For example, almost all references to Marx were expunged from the first English language translation of *Thought and Language*. As a consequence the version of neo-Vygotskian psychology that is being developed in the West is regarded as, at best, partial if not inaccurate by those concerned with developmental psychology in present-day Russia. Yaroshevsky (1989 and 1990) and Petrovsky (1990) do provide English-language versions of Russian views of the history of psychology in general and of Vygotsky's work in particular. Chaiklin (2003) has delved into some of the more obscure elements of the Vygotskian opus to produce a signifi-cant challenge to much of the received understanding of the much-bowdlerized concept of the 'zone of proximal development'. A key element of his argument is that Western interpretations have subsumed the original intentions within their own culturally-situated academic priorities.

Tulviste (1988), an Estonian, argues that there has been relatively little interchange between psychology in the Soviet Union and the rest of the world. He also cautions against the Western 'one-sided glorification of Vygotsky'. In a consideration of the prospects for the development of Vygotskian psychology Asmolov warns of this process of glorification.

> The canonization of the basic principles of a theory entails much greater dangers than any criticism from within or without. Theories never are killed by criticism; they die in the hands of jealous disciples who are in a hurry to canonize them and then sit back in their easy chairs. Throughout the history of science in each of its stages, disciples have performed one and the same operation, that of raising principles to the rank of postulates requiring no proof.
>
> (Asmolov 1986: 100)

As I have argued elsewhere one may 'read' the particular local official interpretation of Vygotsky, that arises within cultures as well as within disciplines, as relays of more general ideological positions (Daniels 1993 and 2001). This process of 'reading' may be evidenced in the following extract from a review of Wertsch (1985b) by a cognitive psychologist.

> Modern Vygotskians must come to terms with the impact of computation on conceptions of the mind. They must offer an explicit theory that can be modelled in a computer programme in the same way that one can model, say, the economy, or the weather, or quantum electrodynamics. No Marxist psychology is likely to meet this demand, and Vygotsky's grand theory will probably not be followed by another in the foreseeable future.
>
> (Johnson Laird 1986: 879)

The Vygotsky of the 1970s in the West was certainly not the Vygotsky of the 1920s and 1930s in the Soviet Union. That is not to say that all was well with the original thesis. It was composed some 70 years ago by a writer who was both ill and working on the edges of disciplines with which he was only partially familiar. As Johnson Laird (1986) notes, from his own perspective, Vygotsky's work was ill-informed on some crucial matters and he lacked the conceptual/linguistic tools with which to articulate his intended theory.

> He failed to formulate a proper theory of elementary mental processes; he overlooked the role of syntax in language; he proposed a radical discontinuity between evolutionary and cultural processes that is incompatible with anthropological evidence. Vygotsky was an artist trying

to construct a scientific psychology in an era when the only language for theories was the vernacular.

(Johnson Laird 1986: 879)

More recently, and from a much more sympathetic position, Hasan (2004) has argued that although within Vygotskian theory speech is supposedly the primary means of semiotic mediation, the social functioning of language is under-theorized. In an account of the social formation of mind she argues that there is a requirement for theory which relates meanings to interpersonal relations. The emphasis on representational/experiential meaning, and the absence of an account of the ways in which language serves to regulate interpersonal relations and how its specificity is in turn produced through specific patterns of interpersonal relation and thus social regulation, constitute a serious weakness (Hasan 2004).

The 'Vygotskies' who are being created in the early years of the twenty-first century in the West as well as in post-Soviet Russia are diverse and must be seen in their own cultural context. This political, social and historical filtering, selection, transformation and assimilation of the original texts could be used as justification for a revival of some form of Vygotskian fundamentalism searching for the author's true meaning and message. This is not the intention here. Rather, the concern is to offer the reader some flavour of the developing range of tensions and dilemmas associated with the emergent cultural historical schools[1] with which Vygotsky's work is associated.

THE INTERACTIONAL AND THE SOCIAL IN VYGOTSKY'S WORK

Attempts to link the social and the psychological levels of analysis have reverberated throughout the twentieth century. Those which espouse a Vygotskian root may be typified in terms of two important dimensions: first with respect to the way in which the connection between that which is seen to be social and that which is seen to be individual and psychological is discussed, and second with respect to the way in which the social world is theorized, described and, indeed, operationally arranged in the course of academic study. These two dimensions have driven the selection of chapters presented here. These elements are underpinned by two famous propositions: the so-called 'zone of proximal development' and the 'general genetic law of cultural development'.

---

1   The plural term 'schools' is used here to emphasize the diversity in the field. This diversity is amplified by the relative isolation of some groups. For example the important publication edited by Forman *et al.* (1993) contains no reference to the substantial and influential writings of Kozulin (e.g., 1990).

The zone of proximal development

Vygotsky defined the concept of the zone of proximal development (ZPD) as the distance between a child's 'actual developmental level as determined by independent problem solving' and their higher level of 'potential development as determined through problem solving under adult guidance or in collaboration with more capable peers' (Vygotsky 1978: 86).

This statement signals Vygotsky's view of the roles of instruction and assessment. His interest was in assessing the ways in which learners make progress (see Griffin and Cole 1984). The focus on process as well as product in assessment has become embedded in the range of techniques now called 'dynamic assessment'. There are stark differences in the ways in which an idea which has at least some root in Vygotskian theory becomes embedded in other psychological traditions.

The general orientation of dynamic assessment is either explicitly or tacitly inspired by the work of Vygotsky. This contrasts sharply with practices which theorize a lag of learning behind development (as in the case of Piaget), or which theorize learning as development (as in the case of Skinner). Vygotsky clarified his own position with respect to assessment with the following example.

> Suppose I investigate two children upon entrance into school, both of whom are twelve years old chronologically and eight years old in terms of mental development. Can I say that they are the same age mentally? Of course. What does this mean? It means that they can independently deal with tasks up to the degree of difficulty that has been standardized for the eight-year-old level. If I stop at this point, people would imagine that the subsequent course of development and of school learning of these children will be the same, because it depends on their intellect. . . . Now imagine that I do not terminate my study at this point, but only begin it. . . . Suppose I show . . . [that these children] have various ways of dealing with a task . . . that the children solve the problem with my assistance. Under these circumstances it turns out that the first child can deal with problems up to a twelve-year-old's level. The second up to a nine-year-old's. Now are these children mentally the same?
>
> When it was first shown that the capability of children with equal levels of mental development to learn under a teacher's guidance varied to a high degree, it became apparent that those children were not mentally the same and that the subsequent course of their learning would obviously be different. This difference between twelve and eight, or between nine and eight, is what we call the zone of proximal development.
>
> (Vygotsky 1978: 85–86)

Lave and Wenger (1991) argue in Chapter 6 that the operational definition of ZPD has itself undergone many differing interpretations. These differences may be seen to reveal the more general theoretical drift towards a broader, more cultural and historical view of the social, which is theorized as being progressively more intimately a part of the individual. Thus Lave and Wenger (1991) distinguish between a 'scaffolding', a 'cultural' and a 'collectivist' or 'societal' interpretation of the original formulation of the ZPD.

The scaffolding interpretation is one in which a distinction is made between support for the initial performance of tasks and subsequent performance without assistance: 'the distance between problem-solving abilities exhibited by a learner working alone and that learner's problem-solving abilities when assisted by or collaborating with more-experienced people' (Vygotsky 1978: 86).

The cultural interpretation is based on Vygotsky's distinction between scientific and everyday concepts. It is argued that a mature concept is achieved when the scientific and everyday versions have merged. However, as Lave and Wenger (1991) note, no account is taken of

> the place of learning in the broader context of the structure in the social world . . . the distance between the cultural knowledge provided by the socio-historical context – usually made accessible through instruction – and the everyday experience of individuals (Davydov and Markova 1983). Hedegaard (1988) calls this the distance between understood knowledge, as provided by instruction, and active knowledge, as owned by individuals.
>
> (Lave and Wenger 1991: 48)

Taking the collectivist or societal perspective, Engeström defines the zone of proximal development as the 'distance between the everyday actions of individuals and the historically new form of the societal activity that can be collectively generated' (Engeström 1987: 174). Lave and Wenger (1991) argue that under such societal interpretations of the concept of the ZPD researchers tend to concentrate on processes of social transformation. 'This involves the study of learning beyond the context of pedagogical structuring, including the structure of the social world in the analysis, and taking into account in a central way the conflictual nature of social practice' (Lave and Wenger 1991: 48–49).

These types of definition carry with them different implications for schooling and instruction. Chapters 6, 7, 10, 11 and 12 embody differing views of the teaching–learning process. In Chapter 6 Lave and Wenger 'contrast learning as internalisation with learning as increasing participation in communities of practice'. Theirs is a broadly-based social view of instruction. In Chapter 7 Engeström grapples with the process in relation to learning in everyday circumstances and learning at school. He makes comparisons between the work of Lave and Wenger (1991) and Davydov's theory of ascending from the abstract to the concrete in learning and instruction. In Chapter 10 Hedegaard describes a form of schooling which integrates Vygotsky's work with that of other Soviet educational psychologists such as Davydov (1990). She uses a broadly-based definition of ZPD and retains a focus on motivation. Both these chapters have been reproduced here in order to illustrate the differing ways in which views of the social condition suggestions for our understanding of learning in the ZPD. As Chaiklin (2003) reminds us, the reference made by Vygotsky was to instruction that is designed to support the development of psychological functions as they are transformed and reconfigured through particular age periods. Chaiklin suggests that much of what has been discussed under the rubric of the ZPD misses the central insistence on instruction leading *development*. The distinction between microgenesis and ontogenesis is missed in what, for Chaiklin, are misinterpretations of the original formulation of ZPD in its instructional frame of reference. He suggests that terms such as scaffolding should be reserved for practices designed to teach specific skills and subject matter concepts as against instruction designed to serve explicitly developmental purposes.

Another approach to analysing the range of perspectives on teaching and learning is given in Chapter 12, in which Annemarie Sullivan Palincsar discusses different approaches to the theorization of the interdependence of social and individual processes in the co-construction of knowledge. She presents an overview of empirical research which operates at the institutional, interpersonal and discursive levels of analysis, which is subsequently discussed in the context of contemporary educational dilemmas.

The general genetic law of cultural development

The general genetic law of cultural development theorizes the social in connection with the psychological. It lies at the heart of a thesis which is concerned with the social formation of mind.

> Any function in the child's cultural development appears twice, or on two planes. First it appears on the social plane, and then on the psychological plane. First it appears between people as an interpsychological category, and then within the child as an intrapsychological category. This is equally true with regard to voluntary attention, logical memory, the formation of concepts, and the development of volition. We may consider this position as a law in the full sense of the work, but it goes without saying that internalization transforms the process itself and changes its structure and functions. Social relations or relations among people genetically underlie all higher functions and their relationships.
>
> (Vygotsky 1981: 163)

The general genetic law of cultural development underpins much of the subsequent and allied conceptual map which Vygotsky constructed. The ZPD provides the setting in which the social and the individual are brought together. It is in the ZPD that the so-called 'psychological tools' (particularly speech) and signs have a mediational function.

PSYCHOLOGICAL TOOLS AND MEDIATION

Vygotsky distinguished between psychological and other tools:

> The most essential feature distinguishing the psychological tool from the technical tool, is that it directs the mind and behaviour whereas the technical tool, which is also inserted as an intermediate link between human activity and the external object, is directed toward producing one or other set of changes in the object itself.
>
> (Vygotsky 1981: 140)

The very idea of mediation carries with it a number of significant implications concerning control. In that the concept denies the possibility of total control through external or internal forces, it carries with it an intellectual baggage which is potentially highly charged, especially in the political context in which these ideas were promulgated.

> Because this auxiliary stimulus possesses the specific function of reverse action, it transfers the psychological operation to higher and qualitatively new forms and permits the humans, by the aid of extrinsic stimuli, to control their behaviour from the outside.
>
> (Vygotsky 1978: 40)

As noted already, Vygotsky was stating that humans master themselves from the 'outside' through symbolic, cultural systems. What needs to be stressed here is his position that it is not the tools or signs, in and of themselves, which are important for thought development but the *meaning* encoded in them. Theoretically, then, the *type* of symbolic system should not matter, as long as meaning is retained. All systems (Braille for the blind and for the deaf, dactylology or finger spelling, mimicry or a natural gesticulated sign language) are tools embedded in action and give rise to meaning as such. They allow a child to internalise language and develop those higher mental functions for which language serves as a basis. In actuality, qualitatively different mediational means may result in qualitatively different forms of higher mental functioning.

> (Knox and Stevens 1993: 15)

Kozulin (1990) argues that Vygotsky envisaged a theoretical programme which accounted for three types of mediator: signs and symbols; individual activities; and interpersonal relations. The development of Vygotsky's work has involved different degrees of emphasis on these three types or classes of mediational means. In Chapter 4 Kozulin (1986) provides an illuminating discussion of the social history of Vygotsky's psychology. The core of his argument is that the Kharkov group of psychologists lead by Leontiev developed what became known as 'activity theory' as a response to immediate political circumstances. In Kozulin's view they were attempting to locate the analysis of mediation through activity in such a way that it would become acceptable to the dominant interpretation of Marx that arose in the latter part of the 1930s in the Soviet Union.

> While Vygotsky (and Leontiev in earlier works) focused on the mediational role of signs and symbols, the Kharkovites devoted their entire attention to activities, thus bringing them closer to the Piagetian programme with its emphasis on the internalisation of sensory-motor schemas (this rather obvious affinity, however, was played down by the Kharkovites). As a result the notion of symbolic psychological tools, and the role of culture embodied in them, became underrepresented in Soviet psychology starting in the mid-1930s. The issue of the mediating effect of interpersonal relations was taken up only in the 1960s.
>
> (Kozulin 1990: 247)

Analysis of semiotic mediation was certainly diminished in Soviet psychology in the period 1935–1939. The activity theorists of this period suggested that the structure of cognitive processes mirrored the structure of external activity and operations. Practical activity became the mediator of the macro rather than semiotic means. It was argued that practical action should predominate in psychological analysis. In crude terms, collective activity would give rise to a collectivist consciousness. What Lysenko provided with a theory of the inheritance of acquired characteristics was complemented by mid-century activity theory in its raw form. Such theoretical positions suggested that the state could organize labour activities that would give rise to specific forms of individual consciousness that in turn would be transmitted to subsequent generations. The children of active revolutionaries would be revolutionaries. The theoretical apparatus of determinism by and from the state was at hand (Daniels *et al.* 1995).

Davydov and Radzikhovskii (1985), amongst others, subsequently attempted to resolve the implicit opposition to semiotic mediation of mental functions within an activity-oriented approach.

> The concept of sign creates one of the interesting paths of activity. . . . The fact that studies of the sign mediated nature of mental functions have not developed further in the activity oriented approach can be considered a weakness that can be overcome in the near future.
>
> (Davydov and Radzikhovskii 1985: 57)

The original Vygotskian model is distanced from the suggestion that the social context of development is simply the objective environment. There are dialectical relations between social and individual levels which allow for levels of explanation without direct reduction of one to another. In Chapter 3 Jaan Valsiner and René van der Veer explore the roots of the sociogenetic view of human cognition and personality through a consideration of the ways in which the writings of James Baldwin, Josiah Royce, and Pierre Janet influenced George Herbert Mead and Vygotsky. Their emphasis is on the dynamic, dialectical nature of the development and functioning of the self in social context. They link Mead with Royce rather than Baldwin who they associate with Vygotsky. Mead's concern with the interaction with the self and its social roles is contrasted with Vygotsky's concern with the social ontogeny of cognition. The authors argue that there is much to be gained from the development of the core ideas which they share.

There has been a marked reluctance on the part of some theorists to apply the dialectical logic that underpins Vygotsky's work to the development of the theory itself. Interestingly, while attempts to develop Vygotsky's work in Russia have not foregrounded semiotic mediation but have foregrounded the analysis of social transmission in activity settings, much of the work in the West has tended to ignore the social beyond the interactional and to celebrate the individual and mediational processes at the expense of a consideration of socio-institutional, cultural and historical factors. Ideological differences between the West and the East have given rise to differences in theoretical development and of course pedagogical application. According to Davydov (1988), the emphasis on transmission in the former Soviet system of schooling subverted the original requirement for responsive instructional dialogues. Conversely, the emphasis on interpersonal interpretation and interaction as a setting for the facilitation of developmental processes has removed the instructional invective from many Western 'Vygotskian' pedagogies. Thus it would seem that the processes of both interpretation and implementation of Vygotskian ideas must be understood in their specific social contexts. Engeström, who has done much to bring together the three types of account of mediation into a unified model, mounts a defence of the work of Leontiev, claiming that he has suffered at the hands of many Western interpreters.

A careful reading of Leontiev's work reveals that both mediation by signs and subject–subject relations do play an important role in his theory. Proponents of the cultural–historical school repeatedly point out that communication is an inherent aspect of all object-related activities. Leontiev's (1981 pp. 219–220) account of the emergence of speech and language emphasises the original unity of labour actions and social intercourse. . . . So, there is a curious discrepancy between the ways Leontiev is read by critics and those sympathetic to his ideas.

(Engeström 1990: 7)

Within the analysis of the semiotic mode of mediation, speech – the most powerful and pervasive of semiotic devices – functions as a psychological tool in the construction of individual consciousness. The social becomes individual not through a process of simple transmission. Individuals construct their own sense from socially available meanings. Inner speech is the result of a constructive process whereby speech from and with others has become speech for the self. Egocentric speech, rather than being a form of thinking aloud as in the Piagetian thesis, is a transitional phase between ordinary communicative speech and inner speech. The social voice becomes the inner voice. Changes in social circumstances (particularly patterns of communication) give rise to changes in the patterns of construction.

CONCEPT DEVELOPMENT

Vygotsky studied the way in which concepts developed and interacted. His methods were innovative but not without their limitations.

> Vygotsky devised a simple task which revealed some interesting differences between adults' and children's concepts. Wooden blocks differing in shape, colour, size and thickness are laid out on a table, and one of them is turned over to reveal a nonsense label, such as 'MUR', stuck beneath it. The child (or adult) who is being tested then has to sort together all those blocks likely to have the same label. Very young children tend to lump together an unorganised heap of blocks, often on the basis of subjective criteria or because they make a nice pattern. At a later stage, children make their selections on the basis of objective criteria but not in a stable way: one block suggests another in a chain of responses highly dependent on context. Children next grasp the reference of the concept and sort together an appropriate set of objects, but they have yet to master its sense, ie, its stable relations to other concepts independent of context. Hence, when the experimenter turns over one of the blocks that they have selected revealing that it does not have the label 'MUR', they remove it from the pile but do nothing about other similarly offending selections. Only by interacting with adults, Vygotsky claimed, do children finally infer the sense of a concept. His semiotics yields a plausible account of how children master sense and reference. What modern research has shown is that matters are not quite so uniform as he imagined. George Miller and his colleagues have discovered, for example, that children's grasp of the reference of colour terms does not properly stabilise until they have worked out the basic contrastive relations among the terms.
>
> (Johnson Laird 1986: 879)

Using a method which has become known as 'double stimulation', he examined the ways in which subjects used verbal and non-verbal functions to approach problem solving using these blocks.

As detailed in Chapters 5 and 6 of *Thought and Language*, Shif (1935) performed studies on concept formation under the supervision of Vygotsky. She compared causal (because) and adversative (but, although) relations in everyday and school-based situations. Children were asked to complete sentences which were concerned either with everyday situations or with social science themes in school. This work was designed to assist the development of Vygotsky's distinction between scientific and everyday concepts. The major outcome of Shif's work was the finding that the development of scientific concepts appeared to precede the development of everyday concepts. Thus education/schooling served to operate *ahead* of the development of everyday concepts (see Nelson 1995).

Vygotsky argued that these two forms of conceptual development were both important in the formation of what he termed mature concepts. Scientific concepts are formed on the basis of systematic, organized and hierarchical thinking, as distinct from everyday concepts which were seen to be tightly linked to particular contexts and lacking in an overall system. The latter are seen to bring the embedded richness and detailed patterns of signification of everyday thinking into the systematic and organized structure of scientific concepts. As they meld with everyday referents, scientific concepts come to life and find a broad range of applications.

> Vygotsky made it a point to argue that scientific concepts, far from being assimilated in a ready made form, actually undergo substantial development which essentially depends on the existing level of a child's general ability to form concepts. This level of comprehension in its turn is connected with the development of spontaneous concepts. Spontaneous concepts, in working their way upward toward greater abstractness, clear a path for scientific concepts in their downwards development toward greater concreteness.
>
> (Kozulin 1987: xxxiv)

> The essential property of scientific concepts is their structure, the fact that they are organised in hierarchical systems (other possible systems would include 'networks', 'groups', 'genealogical trees', etc). When children interiorise a hierarchical structure this enables them to carry out a series of intellectual operations (different types of definition, logical quantification operations etc). . . . The assimilation of systems of scientific concepts is made possible by systematic education of the type received at school. Organised systematic education is essential for this, unlike oral language acquisition in which teaching has a constructive role but requires no more than the presence of adults with a command of the language to act as partners in shared activities.
>
> (Ivic 1989: 431)

Ivic (1989) argues that Vygotsky was ultimately concerned with the metacognitive dimension of learning in relation to development. Braten (1991) provides a contemporary review which relates Vygotsky's work to metacognitive theory. From this perspective, there is a very real sense in which education cannot be reduced to the acquisition of a body of information.

> The fact is that the assimilation of knowledge systems based on such a degree of generalisation, the interdependence of concepts within a network which smoothes the transition from one concept to another and simplifies the execution of intellectual operations, and the existence of external models (in books or demonstrated by the teacher) for the conduct of these operations, all facilitate the individual's realisation (in Russian, osoznanie) and command (ovladenie) of their cognitive processes.
>
> (Ivic 1989: 432)

There is a level of analysis concerned with particular pedagogic moves within the ZPD. This may be thought of as a particular example of the way in which social circumstances are arranged to meet particular educational imperatives. In Chapter 11 Carol Lee engages with the debates about the nature of scientific and spontaneous (or everyday) concepts. This is undertaken in the context of a discussion concerning a form of talk deployed in the African American Vernacular English (AAVE) speech community. Lee presents an analysis of the role of the spontaneous concepts implicit in this signifying talk in the development of the scientific concepts to be found in literary analysis. She presents a cultural analysis of movement within the ZPD in which she invokes interpersonal and personal/individual analyses of transformation.

Vygotsky himself rarely refers to the kind of instructional and/or collaborative interactions that are appropriate within the ZPD.[2] Tharp (1993) has provided a summary of the types of teaching which have been seen to help 'bring the performance of the learner through the ZPD into an independent capacity' where the 'means of assistance are woven into a meaningful dialogue' (p. 271).

The seven means of assisting performance and facilitating learning identified by Tharp (1993) are as follows:

1 Modelling: offering behaviour for imitation. Modelling assists by giving the learner information and a remembered image that can serve as a performance standard.

2 Feedback: the process of providing information on a performance as it compares to a standard. Feedback is essential in assisting performance because it allows the performance to be compared to the standard and thus allows self-correction. Feedback assists

---

2 Newman *et al.* (1988) and Nunes *et al.* (1993) offer valuable contributions to the literature on pedagogic developments which affiliate, to differing degrees, to a post-Vygotskian model. Tudge (1992) provides a useful discussion of the consequences of peer collaboration.

performance in every domain from tennis to nuclear physics. Ensuring feedback is the most common and single most effective form of self-assistance.

3   Contingency management: application of the principles of reinforcement and punishment to behaviour.

4   Instructing: requesting specific action. It assists by selecting the correct response and by providing clarity, information and decision making. It is most useful when the learner can perform some segments of the task but cannot yet analyse the entire performance or make judgements about the elements to choose.

5   Questioning: a request for a verbal response that assists by producing a mental operation the learner cannot or would not produce alone. This interaction assists further by giving the assistor information about the learner's developing understanding.

6   Cognitive structuring: 'explanations'. Cognitive structuring assists by providing explanatory and belief structures that organise and justify new learning and perceptions and allow the creation of new or modified schemata.

7   Task structuring: chunking, segregating, sequencing or otherwise structuring a task into or from components. It assists learners by modifying the task itself, so the units presented to the learner fit into the ZPD when the entire unstructured task is beyond that zone.

(Tharp 1993: 271–272)

There is another level of analysis which is concerned with an extended view of social arrangement in processes of cultural transmission in schooling. Here is a concrete example of the way in which the general genetic law of cultural development may impact at different levels of analysis. If the social in teaching and learning is constrained to a view of particular teaching technologies and procedures, then the analysis of schooling is both truncated and partial. If the social in schooling is considered in socio-institutional terms then the gaze of the analysis of the outcomes is altered and/or extended.

Vygotsky seemed to be coming to recognise this issue near the end of his life. It is reflected in the difference between Chapters 5 and 6 of *Thinking and Speech* (1987). Both chapters deal with the ontogenetic transition from 'complexes' to 'genuine', or 'scientific' concepts. However, the two chapters differ markedly in what they see as relevant developmental forces. In Chapter 5 (based on research with Shif (1935) and written during the early 1930s), concept development is treated primarily in terms of intra-mental processes, that is, children's conceptual development as they move from 'unorganised heaps' to 'complexes' to 'concepts'.

In Chapter 6 (written in 1934), there is an essential shift in the way Vygotsky approaches these issues. He clearly continued to be interested in intramental functioning, but he shifted to approaching concept development from the perspective of how it emerges in institutionally situated activity. Specifically, he was concerned with how the forms of discourse encountered in the social institution of formal schooling provide a framework for the development of conceptual thinking. He did it by the teacher–child intermental functioning found in this setting.

(Wertsch et al. 1993: 344)

Here is a position which seeks a form of analysis which preserves the integral nature of the individual acting in context. Reductionism of the individual to the pawn of social forces or the social to the individual constitution alone fails to provide ways of understanding the processes of social formation and individual participation.

NATURAL CAUSES?

Tudge and Winterhoff (1993) explore this theme in the context of a critical review of Vygotsky's views on biological influences. On the one hand it would seem that some accounts deny individual difference. Tudge and Winterhoff (1993) remind their readers of the way in which biological factors come into play with cultural factors.

> [T]he child's system of activity is determined at each specific stage both by the child's degree of organic development and by his or her degree of mastery in the use of tools.
>
> (Vygotsky 1978: 21, quoted in Tudge and Winterhoff 1993: 66)

> A normal child's socialisation is usually fused with the process of his maturation. Both series of changes converge, mutually penetrating each other to form, in essence, a single series of formative socio-biological influences on the personality.
>
> (Vygotsky 1983: 22, quoted in Tudge and Winterhoff 1993: 66)

Van der Veer and Van Ijzendoorn (1985) argue that what is often considered to be the problem of a sharp distinction drawn by Vygotsky between higher and lower psychological processes may be resolved through recent studies in activity theory which consider the possibility of demonstrating that 'natural' processes may be influenced by direction and instruction/training.

It is inescapable that Vygotsky did account for biological factors and individual differences. In his work on 'defectology' he insists that individual differences in patterns of communication give rise to differences in patterns of social mediation and hence development.

> A bodily defect is, first of all, a social and not an organic abnormality of

behaviour. A bodily defect in a person causes a certain attitude towards that person among the people around him. It is this attitude, and not the defect in itself, that affects the character of psychological relations to a child with impaired sense organs.

(Yaroshevsky 1989: 107)

However it is in the manner of social engagement that differences may arise and form their own dynamic.

Whatever the anticipated outcome, always and in all circumstances, development, complicated by a defect, represents a creative (physical and psychological) process: the creation and re-creation of a child's personality based upon the restructuring of all the adaptive functions and upon the formation of new processes – overarching, substituting, equalising – generated by the handicap, and creating new, roundabout paths for development.

(quoted in Knox and Stevens 1993: 17)

Similarly he was concerned that social responses to such matters should not create problems of their own.

In principle, Vygotsky's book addresses today's problem of mainstreaming: his view that handicapped children must not be socially cut-off or outcast from the mainstream of society, but must be accepted as full productive members of society, speaks to the question of mainstreaming.

(Knox and Stevens 1993: 22)

However, it is important to remember that in his original writings he most certainly did not subscribe to the extreme relativism with which he has been popularly associated.

We said that in collaboration the child can always do more than he can independently. We must add the stipulation that he cannot do infinitely more. What collaboration contributes to the child's performance is restricted to limits which are determined by the state of his development and his intellectual potential.

(Vygotsky 1987: 209)

PIAGET AND VYGOTSKY

Discussions of the relative merits of Piaget and Vygotsky often seek refuge in dimensions of difference which are cast in terms of causation (biological versus social) or locational/contextual (Swiss versus Russian) factors. Bidell (1992) moves beyond such analyses in his consideration of the issues which serve to distinguish between Piaget's stage theory and Vygotsky's socio-historical theory. In an attempt to draw on the strengths of both writers he suggests that the differences are to be found in the extent to which the social dimension of development is refined and also how *relations* between the social and the personal are conceptualized. His suggestion is that much is to be gained by making an initial distinction between Piaget's stage theory of development and Piaget's constructivist theory of knowledge:

> Piaget's *stage theory* of development tacitly reflects the ideology of individualism. The stage theory is based on an interactionist metaphor in which the relation between the person and the social world is conceived as an individual standing apart from and interacting with a social environment. Piaget's *constructivist theory* of knowledge, in contrast, rejects the Cartesian tradition of reductionism (in both nativist and empiricist versions), affirming a relational and even dialectical view of development.
>
> (Bidell 1992: 307)

Bidell's is an important contribution in that it moves the Vygotsky versus Piaget debate beyond the somewhat sterile opposition that has been re-iterated many times over the last 15 years. Bidell argues that the internal inconsistency within the Piagetian thesis opens the door to powerful theoretical developments. Such developments might entail in the practical integration of Piaget's constructivism with Vygotsky's dialectical method. He suggests that

> Piaget's constructivism implicity supports a contextualist approach to knowledge development and stands in contradiction to the individualism and interactionism of his stage theory. . . . Vygotsky presents a dialectical conception of the relations between personal and social that differs diametrically from reductionist views. . . . dimensions of reality such as the social and the personal are not separate and self-contained but have a shared existence as differing tendencies united within real developing systems. . . . the reductionist metaphor of separation and interaction [is replaced] with the dialectical metaphor of *participation*.
>
> (Bidell 1992: 307)

Readers are referred to Bidell (1988) as an easily accessible point of engagement with this body of work. Smith (1989) provides a useful critique from the Piagetian side of the debate.

Just as post-Vygotskian researchers sometimes have to remind themselves that a biological account is not absent in the dialectical model initiated by Vygotsky, so too do they seek to refine some of the earlier socially determined models of internalization. Bruner (1984) was keen to point out that the concept of mediation allowed for an account of the social formation of mind which was not overly determined.

It is a means of conceiving the action of human beings as something not completely dominated by material and historical forces.

(Bruner 1984: 96)

THEORETICAL DEVELOPMENTS AND UNITS OF ANALYSIS

There has been a persistent reluctance on the part of many psychologists to consider the social world beyond interpersonal interaction in particular settings. A major trend in many recent publications has been to attempt to theorize relations between the social and psychological in such a way that cultural and socio-institutional matters are removed from the 'error term' and introduced as key elements in a unified thesis. Minick *et al.* (1993) provide a recent example of such an approach. This body of writing may in itself also be seen as a development of the two important books produced by James Wertsch in 1985 (Wertsch 1985a and 1985b). Wertsch (1985b) proposed that Vygotsky's theoretical approach can be understood in terms of three major themes: a reliance on a genetic or developmental method; the claim that higher mental functioning in the individual has its origins in social life; and the claim that an adequate account of human mental functioning must be grounded in an analysis of the tools and signs that mediate it. This position has gradually been refined and developed in the course of his work. These and other developments will be discussed during the course of this book. Minick *et al.* (1993) see their work as following in the wake of researchers such as Cole and Scribner (1974), who challenged contemporary notions about mental development by suggesting that cognitive functioning is bound to specific contexts of social practice and that development is based on mastery of defined modes of speaking, thinking and acting (Minick *et al.* 1993). They also connect their analysis with the research tradition concerned with children in collaboration with adults. They propose a four-element conception of development in post-Vygotskian research:

1   The culturally-specific nature of schools demands close attention to the way in which they structure interactions between people and artefacts such as books.
2   Rather than language being understood as a 'generalised or abstract system that mediates activity, interaction and thought' it should be treated as 'a multitude of distinct speech genres and semiotic devices that are tightly linked with particular social institutions and practices'. In schools 'there are many speech genres that mediate specific forms of social and psychological life in distinct ways'.
3   '[E]ducationally significant human interactions do not involve abstract bearers of cognitive structures but real people who develop a variety of

interpersonal relationships with one another in the course of their shared activity in a given institutional context.'

4 '[M]odes of thinking evolve as integral systems of motives, goals, values, and beliefs that are closely tied to concrete forms of social practice.'

(after Minick *et al.* 1993: 6)

Vygotsky saw the psychological characteristics of the scientific concept as inseparable from the unique use of words in the social interaction that occurs between teachers and pupils in formal school instruction (Minick 1985: 107). Institutions such as schools, which are predicated on the need to organize knowledge and provide an induction into a systematic account of a particular academic culture, are concerned with the development of scientific concepts. They embody communicative practices about systems of words and concepts which have their own abstract and formal coherence. These scientific concepts are distinct from the everyday concepts which arise in the richness of everyday life. That is not to say that all forms of schooling give rise to the formation of scientific concepts or that scientific concepts cannot arise outside schooling. These Vygotskian concepts about concepts relate to his understanding of the role of instruction in leading development.

UNITS OF ANALYSIS

Within contemporary debates there is concern about the development of an appropriate unit of analysis. In the most recent translation of Chapter 6 of *Thinking and Speech* Vygotsky claims a particular function of speech in instruction within schooling.

> The instruction of the child in systems of scientific knowledge in school involves a unique form of communication in which the word assumes a function which is quite different from that characteristic of other forms of communication. . . .
>
> 1 The child learns word meanings in certain forms of school instruction not as a means of communication but as part of a system of knowledge.
> 2 This learning occurs not through direct experience with things or phenomena but through other words.
>
> (Rieber and Carton 1987: 27)

This extract reveals Vygotsky's emphasis on 'word meaning' as the unit of analysis. The original Vygotskian thesis has been seen to be in need of a more sophisticated theory of language as well as a general theory of social organization. This suggestion is in line with the theoretical move being developed by researchers such as Tudge and Winterhoff (1993), Wertsch (1991) and

Rogoff (1990). Their work shares a concern with moving the unit of analysis within post-Vygotskian studies away from the original focus on word meaning (Vygotsky, 1987). Bidell (1992) also argues that Rogoff (1990) is developing a theory of social constructivism that goes beyond the interpersonal.

> [They] direct attention to the ways in which activity is structured differently across contexts. If cognitive development proceeds through the construction of meaning from activity, an understanding of the cultural structuring of activity is crucial to an understanding of the ways in which meanings evolve differently in different contexts. Interpersonal interactions, as a unit of analysis, cannot provide insight into the sources of variation in developmental pathways unless they are themselves embedded in a cultural level of analysis that addresses the specific cross-contextual differences in terms of which interpersonal relations vary.
>
> (Bidell 1992: 313)

Wertsch (1991) is one of many writers who have turned to some notion of the use of psychological tools, such as language, in particular contexts as the unit of analysis. Terms such as 'tool-mediated action' or 'goal-directed action' are deployed as potential successors to 'word meaning'. They embody an understanding of the need to study the use of means of mediation in social contexts.

> Meanings, tools and goals all necessarily relate the individual and the social world of which the individual is part, for they are all formed in socio-cultural context. Understanding the use of tools (psychological or physical) is jointly constructed by the developing child and by the culture in which the child is developing, with the assistance of those who are already more competent in the use of those tools and in culturally appropriate goals. These units of analysis therefore integrate the micro-social contexts of interaction with the broader social, cultural and historical contexts that encompass them.
>
> (Tudge and Winterhoff 1993: 67)

INTERNALIZATION: BAKHTIN'S INFLUENCE

Along with the development and refinement of the unit of analysis, recent years have witnessed a return to the original Vygotskian rejection of dualism. Vygotsky went in search of a philosophical base which moved the debate away from Cartesian dualism into some form of monistic account. Some 70 years later the notion of internalization within Vygotsky's work is under scrutiny.

The issue is not whether one should begin with the cultural tools or with the individual. Instead, it is one of understanding the fundamental, irreducible tension between these two aspects of mediated action which are analytically distinct but inextricably connected in reality. On the one hand, cultural tools cannot play any role in human action if they are not appropriated by concrete individuals acting in unique contexts. On the other hand, we cannot act as humans without invoking cultural tools.

(Wertsch 1993: 170)

In turn this approach demands a view of the nature of language which in itself relates concepts of text and context. In Chapter 8, David Bakhurst discusses the social nature of memory and in doing so attempts to reintegrate the notion of semiotic mediation into an account which does not, in his view, compromise the 'integrity of the Soviet Marxist tradition'. He also provides a valuable discussion of the 'mind as text' from Voloshinov/Bakhtin and the Soviet philosopher Il'enkov's work on the 'ideal' (eg. 1977 and 1982). Wertsch (1991) also turns to Bakhtin (1986), whose writing along with that of Voloshinov (1983) introduces concepts such as 'intertextuality', 'ideologically based communication', 'dialogism' and 'speech genre'. The concept of 'speech genre' is of particular interest.

All the diverse areas of human activity involve the use of language. . . . Language is realised in the form of individual concrete utterances (oral and written) by participants in the various areas of human activity. These utterances reflect the specific conditions and goals of each area . . . thematic content, style, and compositional structure are inseparably linked to the whole of the utterance and are equally determined by the specific nature of the particular sphere of communication. Each separate utterance is individual, of course, but each sphere in which language is used develops its own relatively stable types of utterances. These we may call speech genres.

(Bakhtin 1986: 60)

Context and utterance are linked in activity in this definition of genre. It thus serves as a vehicle for the development of an analytical approach that accords with the requirements of recent developments in Vygotskian theory. However it is difficult to see how the notion of speech genre, as it stands, can serve to promote empirical investigation. There is no way in which the social situation can be described in terms that can be related to the structure and or content of genres. Voloshinov (1983: 21) argues that 'the forms of signs are conditioned above all by the social organisation of the participants involved and also by the immediate conditions of their interaction'. However, this notion does lead to a way of articulating the nature of the social organization that is of interest. This vagueness in what is undoubtedly an important body of writing leaves itself open to a great variety of interpretations. What is absent in Bakhtin is the very language of the organizational form. The same absence is to be found in the work of Vygotsky. As a consequence it is difficult to distinguish between contexts. Also absent in the original works of Vygotsky is the possibility of investigating the suggestion that schools may differ and that these differences may assume some social, semiotic and psychological significance. That speech differences *between* genres *within* schools assume semiotic proportions is asserted by Lemke.

> Social semiotics begins from a very simple principle: that all meaning is *made* by specific human social practices. When we say that the mastery of physics or literary criticism means being able to talk physics like a physicist or write analyses like a critic, we are talking about *making the meanings* of physics and literary criticism using the resources of spoken and written language. Talking physics and writing criticism are *social practices*. They are parts of larger social activities. They are learned socially, function socially, and are socially meaningful. Spoken and written language are social resources for making social meaning. And the specific *genres* and *semantic patterns* of physics, or of literary criticism, are institutionalized social formations, patterns of language *use*, and patterns of *deployment* of the social resources of language in particular communities and subcommittees.
>
> (Lemke 1988: 82)

Clearly, schooling constitutes a form of collective social activity with specific forms of interpersonal communication. Furthermore, within schools and between schools there are differences in the content, structure and function of interpersonal communication. Schooling is often thought of as a generic activity, as if it were a social institution which is uniform in its psychological effects. This is certainly true within the Russian tradition where, following Elkonin and Davydov (1966), schooling is seen to constitute a qualitatively distinct social stage in development yet variation between schools is not accounted for. Perhaps this is a manifestation of a 'psychological consciousness' born of centralized planning systems designed to ensure uniformity across institutions.

Foley (1991) discusses research that has considered the distribution of *written* genres within schools but not differences in the distribution of these genres between schools.

> The shifts in learning activities, spread over the day, are themselves encoded in shifts of behavioural patterns and these are reflected in the language. These shifts in language Christie refers to as *curriculum genre*, 'that is the genres produced orally together by teachers and students'. Christie analysed a number of curriculum genres and demonstrated that patterns of interaction between teacher and student are reflected in the written genres produced by the children. The finding that children use particular written genres because of the context in which they are learning

means that even when teachers are not conscious of what they are doing, they are having a powerful effect, not only on the children's writing development, but on the kind of knowledge being constructed in the classroom.

(Foley 1991: 31)

In Chapter 5, J. Allan Cheyne and Donato Tarulli explore the implications of Bakhtin's notion of dialogue and compare it with the implicit understanding of dialogue within Vygotsky's work. Through a consideration of dialogue, otherness and voice they explore the implications of the differences between the two for a view of the ZPD as a site of cultural and historical change as well as individual development. In this way they present a way of rethinking two of the 'dialects' of ZPD which Lave and Wenger outline in Chapter 6.

We know that Vygotsky was concerned with aspects of educational reform which went far beyond the analysis of pedagogy. His work in then so-called 'defectology' was directed towards analysis of the broader social and cultural implications of disability (Knox and Stevens 1993). He was also interested in facilitating the transition from a holistic to a discipline-centred approach in primary schools. These two examples may be taken as indicators of a concern to develop a broadly-based socio-historical analysis of schooling. Within this framework much more than conventional pedagogy is in operation in the ZPD.

Vygotsky attached the greatest importance to the content of educational curricula but placed the emphasis on the structural and instrumental aspects of that content, the significance of which was mentioned in our analysis of the implications of McLuhan's phrase 'the medium is the message'. In this connection it must be said that Vygotsky did not take these fruitful ideas far enough. In this approach it is quite possible to regard the school itself as a 'message', that is, a fundamental factor of education, because, as an institution and quite apart from the content of its teaching, it implies a certain structuring of time and space and is based on a system of social relations (between pupils and teacher, between the pupils themselves, between the school and it surroundings, and so on).

(Ivic 1989: 434)

This statement calls for a radical extension in the scope of the empirical investigation that has been undertaken in the name of Vygotsky. Taken together with the development of units of analysis that conceptually integrate person and context, these moves may be seen to represent a desire to create an account of person formed in and forming culture and society.

CULTURE IN PSYCHOLOGY AND PSYCHOLOGY
IN CULTURE

One clear danger is that enthusiasm for such a project would lead to a down-playing of history on the one hand and biology on the other. While it is true that aspects of a historical legacy may be avoided or amplified in specific circumstances, in the same way that specific biological deficits may be compensated for, it is hard to envisage a complete theoretical discourse adequately accounting for the social formation of mind which floats free from the material conditions provided by both history and biology.

Ever since the famed adventure in Uzbekistan in which Luria (1931) sought to investigate the cognitive consequences of different cultural patterns, there has been a lingering unease within the scientific communities concerned with the development of Vygotsky's work (see Cole 1988). If one is to posit a socio-cultural account of development, is one then forced to a position in which one culture may be seen as a potentially more powerful developmental influence than another? In Chapter 2, Wertsch and Tulviste (1992) explore the prospects and problems that may be inherent in the uses of a developmental method and in particular the uses of the concept 'culture'. Clearly, one-dimensional scales of development that may be linked to cultural roots can assume sinister functions. In Chapter 9, Cole distinguishes between the notion of context defined as that which surrounds and the notion of context defined as that which weaves together. In doing so he draws on the legacy of Bronfenbrenner's 1979 book on the ecology of human development which portrayed layers of context in concentric circles. This image of progressive wrapping of the individual in ever-wider context is transformed by Cole into the following position: '[T]he combination of goals, tools and setting . . . constitutes simultaneously the context of behaviours and ways in which cognition can be related to that context' (Cole 1996: 137). Here we have implications of active construction of context in action. The way in which individuals or groups use artefacts in effect transforms the model of contexts that obtain at any one time in a particular setting. Bronfenbrenner's 'onion rings' may be reshaped, transformed, deleted and mutually interpenetrated. Cole suggests a model in which the separation of the analysis of semiotic mediation and activity is both inappropriate and inadequate.

> What most concerns me in the context of this discussion is that culture was treated very much as a package of independent variables rather than as a medium, and was not directly the object of analysis.
>
> (Cole 1994: 84)

The way in which the relationship between the individual and the social is conceptualized was and remains problematic. The reasons for this may be attributed to the historical split between semiotic and activity-based analysis which started at or just before Vygotsky's death. The way out of the difficulty is seen to lie in a model of dialectical relations between social and individual levels, which allows for levels of explanation without direct reduction of one to another.

Bakhurst (1995) suggests that Russian thinking has developed in a culture which embodies a powerful anti-Cartesian element. He contrasts this kind of intellectual environment with that which obtains in many settings in the West, where much effort has been expended conceptualizing the mind as a 'self-contained private realm, set over against the objective, "external" world of material things, and populated by subjective states revealed only to the "self" presiding over them' (Bakhurst 1995: 155–156). The argument is that culture and community are not merely independent factors which discriminate between settings. They are, as it were, the mediational medium with and through which ideas are developed. This argument underpins Cole's model of culture as that which weaves together.

Questions about what is 'primitive' and what is 'advanced' superimposed on some unitary one-dimensional scale serve to distract attention from the differences in modes of reasoning that may arise in particular situations. Engeström throws out the challenge to embed a Vygotskian account in the political world of values.

> It is surely appropriate to avoid rigid, one-dimensional sequences being imposed on social reality. But especially among Anglo-Saxon researchers adhering to the ideas of Vygotsky, the standard alternative seems to be to avoid history altogether. Differences in cognition across cultures, social groups and domains of practice are thus commonly explained without seriously analysing the historical development that has led to those differences. The underlying relativistic notion says that we should not make value judgements concerning whose cognition is 'better' or more 'advanced' – that all kinds of thinking and practice are equally valuable. While this liberal stance may be a comfortable basis for academic discourse, it ignores the reality that in all domains of societal practice those very value judgements and decisions have to be made every day.
>
> (Engeström 1990: 8)

Perhaps it is worth reconsidering the origins of this work. Vygotsky was writing at a time of tremendous social upheaval. A civil war and a revolution had left as many as seven million children in near-destitute conditions. The country had suffered centuries of feudal exploitation. It is not hard to imagine a writer such as Vygotsky having a clear idea of what 'better' meant. The modernizing force of his writing rests a little uneasily with the postmodern confusion of the late twentieth century. Perhaps the Nordic writers such as Engeström and Hedegaard are leading the way when they implicitly announce a new agenda.

To Hedegaard, the ZPD is clearly more than a psychological construct; it is no abstraction. It itself is socially-culturally-politically determined. She has made the interesting claim that values are an integral component of the ZPD: *She writes*

'The ZPD is a very valuable tool. It implies that we have to have some values and an idea of what a good life is if we are to educate children. . . . if you read Vygotsky carefully, you see that the ZPD is not just a general psychological law. The next "zone" for the child is determined by the society in which we are living, the values and customs for the upbringing of youth etc.'

(Newman and Holzman 1993: 82–83)

In that they are working towards a socially expanded model of the ZPD they are perhaps reminding us that Vygotsky was creating a *psychology for social purposes*. This was, and perhaps is, a psychology which can be used as a tool of change rather than a means by which descriptions of an existing order can be developed. This approach is exemplified in much of the output of the Centre for Developmental Work Research in Helsinki (Engeström 1987, 1993, 1995, 1996, 1999a and 1999b; Engeström *et al.* 1995 and 1999; Engeström and Escalante 1996). This body of work is also influenced by recent developments in Actor Network Theory (Latour 1987, 1993 and 1996; Miettinen 1999).

For Vygotsky, the identity of psychology as a science depended on the degree to which it could contribute to the transformation of the object it investigates. Its tasks were not to simply mirror reality but harness reality.

(Bakhurst 1986: 122–123)

Wertsch (1991) argues that the analysis of change within a Vygotskian framework requires the support of concepts derived from the social sciences beyond psychology. He points to notions such as 'cultural capital' and 'patterns of privileging' as developed by Bourdieu (1984) and 'rationality' which he draws from Weber (1968) and Habermas (1984). To this list I would add the general model of cultural transmission being developed by Bernstein (1977 and 1981), which in itself owes much to the work of Mead, Vygotsky, Marx and Durkheim.

If social and psychological change are to be understood in a unified analytical framework then there is much to be done. The development of the Vygotskian thesis towards an ever more social and coherent theory of the formation of mind has some way to go.

REFERENCES

Asmolov, A.G. (1986) Basic principles of a psychological analysis in the theory of activity, *Soviet Psychology* xxv, 2: 78–101.

Bakhtin, M. (1986) *Speech genres and other late essays*, edited by C. Emerson and M. Holquist. Austin: University of Texas Press.

Bakhurst, D. (1995) Lessons from Ilyenkov, *The Communication Review* 1, 2: 155–178.

Bakhurst, D.J. (1986) Thought, speech and the genesis of meaning: On the 50th anniversary of Vygotsky's 'Myshlenie i rech', *Studies in Soviet Thought* 31: 103–129.

Bernstein, B. (1977) *Class, codes and control vol. 3: Towards a theory of educational transmissions* (2nd edn). London: Routledge & Kegan Paul.

Bernstein, B. (1981) Codes, modalities and the process of cultural reproduction: A model, *Language in Society* 10: 327–363.

Bidell, T. (1988) Vygotsky, Piaget and the dialectic of development, *Human Development* 31: 329–348.

Bidell, T.R. (1992) Beyond interactionism in contextualist models of development, *Human Development* 35: 306–315.

Bourdieu, P. (1984) *Distinction: A social critique of the judgement of taste*. trans. R. Nice. Cambridge, MA: Harvard University Press.

Braten, I. (1991) Vygotsky as precursor to metacognitive theory: I. The concept of metacognition and its roots, *Scandinavian Journal of Educational Research* 35, 3:179–192.

Bruner, J. (1984) Vygotsky's Zone of Proximal Development the hidden agenda, in B. Rogoff and J. Wertsch (eds) (1984) *Learning in the "Zone of Proximal Development"* New Directions for Child Development, 23. San Francisco: Jossey-Bass.

Burmenskaya, G. (1992) *The development of Vygotsky's work*. Mimeograph of Seminar at the Department of Developmental Psychology, Moscow Lomonosov State University, March 1992. Cambridge: Cambridge University Press.

Chaiklin, S. (2003) 'The Zone of Proximal Development' in Vygotsky's analysis of learning and instruction, in A. Kozulin, B. Gindis, V. Ageyev and S. Miller (eds) *Vygotsky's educational theory in cultural context*. Cambridge: Cambridge University Press.

Cole, M. (1988) Cross-cultural research in the sociohistorical tradition, *Human Development* 31: 137–151.

Cole, M. (1994) A conception of culture for a communication theory of mind, in D. Vocate (ed.) *Intrapersonal communication: Different voices, different minds*. Mahwah, NJ: Lawrence Erlbaum Associates.

Cole, M. (1996) Putting culture in the middle, chapter 5 in M. Cole (1996) *Cultural psychology: A once and future discipline*. Cambridge, MA: Harvard University Press, pp.116–145.

Cole, M. and Scribner, S. (1974) *Culture and thought: A psychological introduction*. New York: John Wiley & Sons.

Daniels, H. (2001) *Vygotsky and pedagogy*. London: Routledge.

Daniels, H. (ed.) (1993) *Charting the agenda: Educational activity after Vygotsky*. London: Routledge.

Daniels, H., Lucas, N., Totterdell, M. and Fomina, O. (1995) Humanisation in Russian education: A transition between state determinism and individualism, *Educational Studies* 21, 1: 29–39.

Davydov, V.V. (1988) Problems of developmental teaching: The experience of theoretical and experimental psychological research, *Soviet Education* xxx, 8: 3–87; 9: 3–56; 10: 2–42.

Davydov, V.V. (1990) *Types of generalization in instruction: Logical and psychological problems in the structuring of school curricula.* Reston: National Council of Teachers of Mathematics.

Davydov, V. and Markova, A. (1983) A concept of educational activity for school children, *Soviet Psychology* 11, 2: 50–76.

Davydov, V.V. and Radzikhovskii, A. (1985) Vygotsky's theory and the activity oriented approach, in psychology, in J.V. Wertsch (ed.) *Culture, communication and cognition: Vygotskian perspectives.* Cambridge: Cambridge University Press.

Elkonin, D. and Davidov, V. (eds) (1966) *Learning possibilities at different ages.* Moscow: Prosvescenie.

Engeström, Y. (1987) *Learning by expanding: An activity-theoretical approach to developmental research.* Helsinki: Orienta-Konsultit.

Engeström, Y. (1990) *Activity theory and individual and social transformation,* Open address at the Second International Congress for Research on Activity Theory, Lahti, Finland, May 21–25, 1990.

Engeström, Y. (1993) Developmental studies on work as a testbench of activity theory, in S. Chaiklin and J. Lave (eds) *Understanding practice: Perspectives on activity and context.* Cambridge: Cambridge University Press.

Engeström, Y. (1995) Objects, contradictions and collaboration in medical cognition: An activity-theoretical perspective, *Artificial Intelligence in Medicine* 7: 395–412.

Engeström, Y. (1996) Developmental work research as educational research, *Nordisk Pedagogik: Journal of Nordic Educational Research* 16: 131–143.

Engeström, Y. (1999a) Activity theory and individual and social transformation, in Y. Engeström, R. Miettinen and R-L. Punamäki (eds) *Perspectives on activity theory.* Cambridge: Cambridge University Press.

Engeström, Y. (1999b) Innovative learning in work teams: Analyzing cycles of knowledge creation in practice, in Y. Engeström, R. Miettinen and R-L. Punamäki (eds) *Perspectives on activity theory.* Cambridge: Cambridge University Press.

Engeström, Y., Engeström, R. and Kärkkäinen, M. (1995) Polycontextuality and boundary crossing in expert cognition: Learning and problem solving in complex work activities, *Learning and Instruction* 5: 319–336.

Engeström, Y. and Escalante, V. (1996) Mundane tool or object of affection? The rise and fall of the Postal Buddy, in B.A. Nardi (ed.) *Context and consciousness: Activity theory and human-computer interaction.* Cambridge: The MIT Press.

Engeström, Y., Miettinen, R. and Punamäki, R-L. (eds) (1999) *Perspectives on activity theory.* Cambridge: Cambridge University Press.

Foley, J. (1991) Vygotsky, Bernstein and Halliday: Towards a unified theory of L1 and L2 learning, *Language, Culture and Curriculum* 4, 1: 17–42.

Forman, E.A., Minick, N., and Stone, C.A. (eds) (1993) *Contexts for learning: Sociocultural dynamics in children's development.* Oxford: Oxford University Press.

Griffin, P. and Cole. M. (1984) Current activity for the future: The zo-ped, in B. Rogoff and J.V. Wertsch (eds) *Children's learning in the zone of proximal development.* San Francisco: Jossey-Bass.

Habermas, J. (1984) *The theory of communicative action, Vol. 1: Reason and the rationalisation of society,* trans. T. McCarthy. Boston: Beacon Press.

Hasan, R. (2004) The concept of semiotic mediation: Perspectives from Bernstein's sociology, in J. Muller, B. Davies and A. Marais (eds) *Reading Bernstein, researching Bernstein.* London: RoutledgeFalmer, pp. 30–43.

Hedegaard, M. (1988) Situated learning and cognition: Theoretical learning of Cognition. *Mind, Culture and Activity* 5, 2: 114–126.

Il'enkov, E.V. (1977) *Dialectical logic: Essays in its history and theory*. Moscow: Progress.

Il'enkov, E.V. (1982) *The dialectics of the abstract and the concrete in Marx's 'Capital'*. Moscow: Progress.

Ivic, I. (1989) Profiles of educators: Lev S. Vygotsky (1896–1934), *Prospects* xix, 3: 427–435.

Johnson Laird, P.N. (1986) An artist constructs a science, *The Times Literary Supplement*, August 15, 879–880.

Knox, J.E. and Stevens, C. (1993) Vygotsky and Soviet Russian defectology: An introduction to Vygotsky, L.S., in J.E. Knox and C. Stevens (eds) *The collected works of L S Vygotsky. Vol 2. Problems of abnormal psychology and learning disabilities*. New York: Plenum Press.

Kozulin, A. (1986) The concept of activity in soviet psychology: Vygotsky, his disciples and critics, *American Psychologist* 264–274.

Kozulin, A. (1987) Introduction to Vygotsky, L.S., in A Kozulin (ed.) *Thought and Language*. London: MIT Press.

Kozulin, A. (1990) *Vygotsky's psychology: A biography of ideas*. London: Harvester.

Kozulin A., Gindis B., Ageyev V. and Miller S. (eds) (2003) *Vygotsky's educational theory in cultural context*. Cambridge: Cambridge University Press.

Latour, B. (1987) *Science in action: How to follow scientists and engineers through society*. Cambridge, MA: Harvard University Press.

Latour, B. (1993) Ethnography of a "high-tech" case: About Aramis, in P. Lemonnier (ed.), *Technological choices: Transformation in material cultures since the neolithic*. London: Routledge.

Latour, B. (1996) On interobjectivity, *Mind, Culture, and Activity* 3: 228–245.

Lave, J. and Wenger, E. (1991) Practice, person and social world, chapter 2 in *Situated learning: Legitimate peripheral participation*. Cambridge: Cambridge University Press.

Lemke, J.L. (1998) Analysing verbal data: principles, methods and problems, in K. Tobin and B. Fraser (eds) *International handbook of science education*. New York: Kluwer, pp. 213–298.

Leontiev, A.N. (1981) *Problems of the development of mind*. Moscow: Progress.

Luria, A.R. (1931) Psychological expedition to Central Asia, *Science* 74 (1920): 383–384.

Miettinen, R. (1999) The riddle of things: Activity theory and actor network theory as approaches to studying innovations, *Mind, Culture, and Activity* 6: 170–195.

Minick, N. (1985) *L.S. Vygotsky and Soviet activity theory: New perspectives on the relationship between mind and society*. Unpublished PhD dissertation, Northwestern University.

Minick, N., Stone, C.A., and Forman, E.A. (1993) Introduction: Integration of individual, social and institutional processes in accounts of children's learning and development, in E.A. Forman, N. Minick, and C.A. Stone (eds) *Contexts for learning: Sociocultural dynamics in children's development*. Oxford: Oxford University Press.

Nelson, K. (1995) From spontaneous to scientific concepts: Continuities and discontinuities from childhood to adulthood, in L.M.W. Martin, K. Nelson and E. Tobach (eds) *Sociocultural psychology: Theory and practice of knowing and doing*. Cambridge: Cambridge University Press.

Newman, D., Griffin, P. and Cole, M. (1988) *The Construction Zone: Working for cognitive change in schools*. Cambridge: Cambridge University Press.

Newman, F. and Holzman, L. (1993) *Lev Vygotsky: Revolutionary scientist*. London: Routledge.

Nunes, T., Schielmann, A.D., and Carraher, D.W. (1993) *Street mathematics and school mathematics*. Cambridge: Cambridge University Press.

Petrovsky, A. (1990) *Psychology in the Soviet Union: A historical outline*. Moscow: Progress Publishers.

Rieber, R.W. and Carton, A.S. (eds) (1987) *The collected works of L.S. Vygotsky, Vol. 1*. New York: Plenum Press (includes *Thinking and Speech*).

Rogoff, B. (1990) *Apprenticeship in thinking: Cognitive development in social context*. New York: Oxford University Press.

Shif, Z. (1935) *The development of scientific concepts in the school child: The investigation of intellectual development of the school child in social science instruction*. Moscow-Leningrad: Gosudarsttvennoe Uchebno-Pedagogicheskoe Izdatel'stvo.

Smith, L. (1989) Changing perspectives in developmental psychology, in C. Desforges (ed.) *Early childhood education*. BJEP Monograph 4, Scottish Academic Press.

Tharp, R. (1993) Institutional and social context of educational practice and reform, in E.A. Forman, N. Minick, and C.A. Stone (eds*)* *Contexts for learning: Sociocultural dynamics in children's development*. Oxford: Oxford University Press.

Tudge, J.R.H. (1992) Processes and consequences of peer collaboration: A Vygotskian analysis. *Child Development* 63: 1364–1379.

Tudge, J.R.H. and Winterhoff, P.A. (1993) Vygotsky, Piaget, and Bandura: Perspectives on the relations between the social world and cognitive development, *Human Development* 36: 61 –81.

Tulviste, P. (1988) Some causes of the unsatisfactory state of Soviet psychology, *Voprosy. Psikhologie* 2: 5–18.

Valsiner, J. (1988) *Developmental psychology in the Soviet Union: The developing body and mind, No. 6*. Brighton: Harvester Press.

Van der Veer, R. and Van Ijzendoorn, M.H. (1985) Vygotsky's theory of the higher psychological processes: Some criticisms, *Human Development* 28: 1–9.

Voloshinov, V.N. (1983) *Marxism and the philosophy of language*, trans. L. Matejka and I.R. Titunik. New York: Seminar Press.

Vygotsky, L.S. (1978) *Mind in society: The development of higher psychological processes*. Cambridge, MA: Harvard University Press.

Vygotsky, L.S. (1981) The genesis of higher mental functions, in J.V. Wertsch (ed.) *The concept of activity in Soviet psychology*. Armonk, NY: M.E. Sharpe.

Vygotsky, L.S. (1983) From the notebooks of L.S. Vygotsky, *Soviet Psychology* xxi, 3: 3–17.

Vygotsky, L.S. (1987) Thinking and speech, in R. Rieber and A. Carton (eds) *L.S. Vygotsky, collected works, vol. 1*, trans. N. Minick. New York: Plenum, pp. 39–285.

Weber, J. (1968) *On charisma and institution building: Selected papers*, S.N. Eisenstadt (ed.). Chicago: University of Chicago Press.

Wertsch, J.V. (1985a) *Culture, communication and cognition: Vygotskian perspectives*. New York: Cambridge University Press, pp. 94–118.

Wertsch, J.V. (1985b) *Vygotsky and the social formation of mind*. Cambridge, MA: Harvard University Press.

Wertsch, J.V. (1991) *Voices of the mind: A sociocultural approach to mediated action*. Cambridge, MA.: Harvard University Press.

Wertsch, J.V. (1993) Commentary, *Human Development* 36: 168–171.

Wertsch, J.V. and Tul'viste, P. (1992) L.S. Vygotsky and contemporary developmental psychology, *Developmental Psychology* 28, 4: 548–557.

Wertsch, J.V., Tul'viste, P. and Hagstrom, F. (1993) A sociocultural approach to agency, in E.A. Forman, N. Minick, and C.A. Stone (eds) *Contexts for learning: Sociocultural dynamics in children's development*. Oxford: Oxford University Press.

Yaroshevsky, M. (1989) *Lev Vygotsky*. Moscow: Progress Publishers.

Yaroshevsky, M. (1990) *A history of psychology*. Moscow: Progress Publishers.

1 The development of Vygotsky's thought

An introduction to *Thinking and Speech*

Norris Minick

PREAMBLE

In 1932, Vygotsky delivered a series of lectures in Leningrad and in 1934 his classic monograph *Thinking and Speech* was first published in Russian. In addition to differences in subject matter and style, these two works are separated by an important conceptual shift in Vygotsky's thinking which occurred in 1932 and 1933. Indeed, since several chapters of *Thinking and Speech* were written prior to 1933, the papers which constitute that volume also span this conceptual shift in the development of Vygotsky's thought. As a consequence, if we are to understand these works, their relationship to one another, or their significance as part of the broader Vygotskian corpus, it is critical to consider the major changes that emerged in Vygotsky's thinking as his perspectives developed between 1924 and 1934.[1]

Three major phases in the development of Vygotsky's thought can be identified by focusing on the constructs that served as his analytic units and explanatory principles. The first two phases have been discussed by several Soviet scholars (Bozhovich 1977; Elkonin 1984; Leont'ev 1982a; Radzikhovskii 1979). The third phase has not, perhaps in part because many of the papers representing that period are being published for the first time as part of the collected works.

Between 1925 and 1930, Vygotsky focused on an analytic unit that he called the "instrumental act," a unit of activity mediated by signs that are used as tools or instruments to control behavior. During this phase of his career, the assumption that the stimulus-response unit provides the common foundation for learning and behavior in both humans and animals was fundamental to Vygotsky's theory. He argued, however, that speech and other historically developed sign systems provide humans with a unique form of stimuli that they can use to influence or control their own behavior. He saw the use of signs in the mediation of behavior as the foundation for the development of volitional forms of behavior that cannot be fully understood in terms of stimulus-response laws. Noting that the initial function of signs is communication, Vygotsky sought the explanation of the phylogenetic, historical, and ontogenetic development of these forms of behavior in verbally mediated social interaction.

In a lecture delivered in October of 1930, Vygotsky (1982a) shifted the focus of his research to an analytic unit that he called the "psychological system." In this lecture, Vygotsky argued that psychological research must focus not on the development of individual mental functions but on the development of new relationships between mental functions, on the development of psychological systems that incorporate two or more distinct functions. Thus, where Vygotsky had once argued that the use of the word as a sign-stimulus provides the foundation for a more advanced, mediated form of memory, he now argued that this use of the word constitutes the formation of a new functional relationship between memory and speech, the formation of a new psychological system. Conspicuously absent in Vygotsky's work between 1930 and 1932, however, was any systematic attempt to explain how or why new psychological systems develop.

A third phase in the development of Vygotsky's thinking is reflected in papers and lectures written in 1933 and 1934. The most obvious change in Vygotsky's conceptual framework during this period was associated not with his unit of analysis but with his explanatory principle. During this period, Vygotsky attempted to explain psychological development in terms of the differentiation and development of social systems of interaction and action in which the individual participates. In parallel with this change in his explanatory principle, Vygotsky reduced his emphasis on the relationship between specific mental functions in psychological systems. Rather, he began to develop a system of psychological constructs that would facilitate the analysis of psychological processes in connection with the individual's concrete actions and interactions.

It is important to emphasize at the outset that there is a great deal of continuity between these three phases in the development of Vygotsky's theoretical framework. First, as we shall see, the attempt to study the development of consciousness in connection with the development of behavior was fundamental to nearly all Vygotsky's work. Second, Vygotsky consistently emphasized several concepts, including the importance of the mediation of psychological processes by speech and the socio-historical nature of certain psychological processes in humans (Wertsch 1981, 1985). Indeed, Vygotsky rarely abandoned concepts that had been central to his work as his thinking developed. He tended, rather, to redefine useful concepts and integrate them into the more general and powerful conceptual frameworks he was developing.

MEDIATION AND THE HIGHER MENTAL FUNCTIONS (1925–1930)

As Davydov and Radzikhovskii (1985) have argued, there were three major groups of psychologists in the Soviet Union when Vygotsky began his work in the early 1920s: (1) a small non-influential group led by Chelpanov who continued the traditional focus on consciousness as the object of psychological research: (2) a much larger and clearly dominant group led by Pavlov and Bekhterev who eschewed the study of subjective phenomena and defined psychology as the science of behavior, reflexes, or reaction: and (3) a group led by Kornilov who argued for a synthesis of these two perspectives.[2] Vygotsky's rejection of all three of these positions is reflected in papers written in 1924 and 1925 that initiated his rise to national prominence as a psychologist in the Soviet Union (Vygotsky, 1982b, 1982c).

The central thrust of the argument developed in these papers was quite simple. Vygotsky argued that the conceptual isolation of mind and consciousness from behavior that had been characteristic of the traditional introspective psychologies championed by Chelpanov had led to a false definition of the object of psychological research. The study of behavior – and for Vygotsky human behavior was inherently socially and culturally organized behavior – was fundamental to the development of any adequate psychological theory. However, far from simply accepting the redefinition of the object of psychological research offered by American behaviorism or its Soviet counterparts, Vygotsky argued that these perspectives had retained the conceptual isolation of mind and behavior, effectively extending the conceptual limitations of traditional psychology to the study of behavior (Vygotsky 1982b, 1982c). Referring to the behaviorist approaches, he wrote:

> This is the other half of the same dualism. Previously we had mind without behavior. Now we have behavior without mind. In both cases, we have "mind" and "behavior" understood as two distinct and separate phenomena.
>
> (Vygotsky, 1982c, p. 81)

The final sentence of this statement was extremely important to Vygotsky. Like the group of Soviet psychologists led by Kornilov, Vygotsky had insisted that consciousness and behavior are both proper objects of psychological research. However, Vygotsky differentiated himself from Kornilov and his colleagues by rejecting the notion that a unified psychology could be created through an integration of subjectivist and behaviorist theories and constructs. In Vygotsky's view, the conceptual isolation of consciousness and behavior that had been initiated by the subjectivists and extended by the behaviorists had led to a fundamental misconceptualization of both consciousness and behavior. To achieve a truly unified psychological science, he insisted that a new system of concepts and theories would have to be developed which would overcome the conceptual isolation of behavior and consciousness that was so fundamental to existing theoretical frameworks. In his 1924 and 1925 papers, he suggested that consciousness is "a problem of the structure of behavior," "a feature of human labor activity." More generally, he argued that the development of a psychological theory adequate to its subject required the development of psychological constructs that would allow consciousness and behavior to be conceptualized as aspects of a unified whole.

In these papers, however, Vygotsky was stating a problem for which he had no clearly developed solution. In an important sense, the entire history of the Vygotskian school, including the contemporary development of what is known as the "theory of activity" (Leont'ev 1978; Minick 1985; Wertsch 1981, 1985), must be understood as an attempt to solve the conceptual problem that Vygotsky outlined in these articles. Still, while Vygotsky did not resolve this problem in these early works, he did introduce several concepts that were fundamental to the research carried out by the Vygotskian school between 1925 and 1930.

Like many of his contemporaries, Vygotsky differentiated humans and animals by arguing that consciousness and thinking are characteristic only of the former. Emphasizing the need to explain rather than merely describe psychological processes that are unique to human beings, Vygotsky argued that they have their source not in biological structures or the learning of the isolated individual but in historically developed socio-cultural experience. Suggesting that the mechanisms governing the development of innate behaviors had been identified by Darwin and that those governing individual learning had been identified by Pavlov, Vygotsky emphasized the need to identify the mechanism that allows the development of psychological processes in the individual through the acquisition of social and cultural experience. In these early articles, Vygotsky identified speech and the social interaction that it mediates as the key to this problem, arguing that speech is the mechanism common to both social behavior and the psychological processes that are unique to human beings.

In these early articles, Vygotsky did not provide any clear definition of the aspects of consciousness, thinking, or mind that differentiate humans from animals nor did he specify the mechanisms through which speech and social interaction contribute to their development. These articles are nonetheless fundamental to any attempt to understand the subsequent development of the Vygotskian paradigm because they indicate an important motivation for Vygotsky's concern with the connection between verbally mediated social interaction and the development of psychological functions. Specifically, it was here that Vygotsky first saw the potential for a system of theoretical constructs which would allow him to retain the connection between the organization of behavior (again, for Vygotsky this always meant socially and culturally defined behavior) and the organization of mind that he found lacking in extant psychological theories.

In the research that Vygotsky and his colleagues carried out between 1926 and 1930, they focused on a relatively narrow range of psychological processes and developed a fairly sophisticated theoretical framework in their attempt to demonstrate that speech and social interaction underlie the development of these processes. During this period, the research of the Vygotskian school focused on what were called the higher mental functions, functions such as voluntary attention, voluntary memory, and rational, volitional, goal-directed thought. Vygotsky argued that the fundamental difference between the mental processes of humans and animals is the presence of these volitional higher mental functions in humans. Having accepted the concept that the common foundation for psychological development and psychological functioning in both humans and animals is the stimulus-response unit, the central problem Vygotsky faced was that of explaining the origin of these volitional processes.

Vygotsky's explanation of the origin of the higher mental functions included two components. First, he argued that the higher mental functions rely on the mediation of behavior by signs and sign systems, the most important of which is speech. Vygotsky saw signs as a special type of stimuli that are used as "psychological tools," tools that are "directed towards the mastery or control of behavioral processes – either someone else's or one's own – just as technical means are directed towards the control of nature" (1981a, p. 137), With its inclusion in behavior, "the psychological tools alters the entire flow and structure of the mental functions . . . . by determining the structure of the new instrumental act, just as a technical tool alters the process of natural adaptation by determining the form of labor operations" (1981a, p. 137). Vygotsky described the psychological mechanism that provides the foundation for this restructuring of behavior through psychological tools in the following way:

> In natural memory, the direct (conditioned reflex) associative connection A-B is established between two stimuli, A and B. In artificial, mnemotechnical memory . . . . two new connections A-X and B-X are established with the help of the psychological tool X (e.g., a knot in a handkerchief, a string on one's finger, a mnemonic scheme). As is true of the connection A-B, each of these two new connections is based on the natural conditioned response process and is instantiated by the properties of the brain. What is novel, artificial, and instrumental about the new connection is the fact . . . . (that an) artificial direction is given to the natural process . . . . by means of an instrument.
>
> (Vygotsky 1981a, p. 138)

Vygotsky called this basic unit of the higher mental functions the "instrumental act."

Second, to explain the historical and ontogenetic development of mediated or instrumental forms of behavior, Vygotsky turned to the primary function of speech as a means of social interaction and communication. Vygotsky argued that the higher voluntary forms of human behavior have their roots in social interaction, in the individual's participation in social behaviors that are mediated by speech. It is in social interaction, in behavior that is being carried out by more than one individual, that signs first function as psychological tools in behavior. The individual participates in social activity mediated by speech, by psychological tools that others use to influence his behavior and that he uses to influence the behavior of others. Subsequently, the individual "begins to apply to himself the same forms of behavior that were initially applied to him by others" (Vygotsky 1960a: 192).[3]

In this way, both the organization and the means of social activity are taken over entirely by the individual and ultimately internalized, leading to the development of mediated, voluntary, historically developed mental functions that are based on stimulus-response components but cannot be reduced to them. It was these psychological processes that Vygotsky referred to as the "higher mental functions." Vygotsky formulated the general principle underlying the development of the higher mental functions in the following way:

> Any higher mental function was external (and) social before it was internal. It was once a social relationship between two people. . . . We can formulate the general genetic law of cultural development in the following way: Any function in the child's cultural development appears twice or on two planes. . . . It appears first between people as an intermental category, and then within the child as an intramental category. This is equally true of voluntary attention, logical memory, the formation of concepts, and the development of will.[4]
>
> (1960a, pp. 197–198)

Thus, Vygotsky saw the higher mental functions as "social" in two senses. First, like other aspects of culture, their development is part of the development of the socio-cultural system and their existence is dependent on transmission from one generation to the next through learning. Second, they are nothing other than the organization and means of *actual social behavior* that has been taken over by the individual and internalized (1960a: 198).

Wertsch has made what I consider an extraordinarily important contribution to our understanding of Vygotsky's thinking by emphasizing the significance of this second point (1985, chap. 3). Frequently, psychologists tend to represent society and culture as macrovariables associated with variation in the amount of various kinds of experience available for individual learning rather than with qualitatively unique learning mechanisms or psychological processes. In contrast, research traditions such as social learning theory or cognitive anthropology are based on the concept that there are important mechanisms of learning and development that are inherently social. Vygotsky took this perspective one step further, linking the social not only with unique mechanisms of psychological development such as social interaction and internalization but with types of mental processes that are themselves inherently social, specifically, the higher psychological functions.

This perspective on the higher mental functions and their development provided Vygotsky with a conceptual link between an important aspect of human consciousness and an important aspect of human social behavior. By adapting the mediational means and the modes of organization involved in carrying out certain actions as a social or "intermental" plane and using them to mediate activity, the individual develops not only new means of carrying out specific actions but qualitatively new kinds of mental functions. Significantly, these mental functions were seen as developing not merely through the individual's experience in social interaction but through the transformation of social behavior from the intermental to the intramental plane. As reflected in Vygotsky's use of the terms "intermental" and "intramental," this representation of psychological development allowed Vygotsky to overcome the conceptual isolation of behavior and consciousness that he had earlier rejected. Thus, it was in these constructs that Vygotsky first found a means of reconceptualizing consciousness and behavior as aspects of an integral system.

Between 1926 and 1930, Vygotsky and his colleagues carried out two types of research. First, they collected material on the use of rudimentary external sign systems in the mediation of behavior. For example, they discussed the use of knots or notched sticks in remembering, the use of fingers and other external devices in counting, and the use of practices such as drawing straws and casting lots in decision making (1960c). Vygotsky saw these rudimentary sign-means as evidence of the historical transition from natural to mediated forms of behavior, forms of behavior in which "man himself determines his behavior with the help of an artificially created stimulus means" (1960a, p. 101). Second, Vygotsky and his colleagues conducted extensive experimental research in which they attempted to demonstrate how the child's behavior is restructured through the introduction of external sign-means and to explore how this behavior is internalized (Vygotsky 1929, 1981b; Leont'ev 1931).

Noticeably absent in this work was any attempt to carry out empirical research on the development of mental processes in social interaction.[5] Two factors would seem to account for the absence of this kind of research.

First, it is important to recognize that the central purpose of this research was simply to demonstrate that the structure and origin of the higher mental functions differs from that of behavior based on instinct or conditioned reflexes. Just as Pavlov had used simple experiments on salivation to demonstrate the unique characteristics of the conditioned reflex, the historical and empirical research carried out by Vygotsky and his colleagues during this period was an attempt to demonstrate the socio-historical roots of the higher mental functions and the differences between these functions and instinctive or conditioned reflex behaviors.

However, a second factor should be mentioned here if we want to understand the forces that led to subsequent developments in Vygotsky's thinking. Vygotsky had been interested in semiotics, semantics, and the role of speech in social interaction long before his career as a professional psychologist began. He had long been familiar with some of the most advanced thinking on these issues both inside and outside the Soviet Union (Radzikhovskii 1979; Wertsch 1985, Chapter 1). While simple sign-means such as a notched stick used as an aid in memory could be analyzed within a framework in which signs were conceptualized as "stimuli," to conceptualize speech in this way would have resulted in the kind of simplistic notions characteristic of Watson's attempts to deal with the role of speech in human behavior. To apply his profound understanding of speech and communication to the analysis of the mental processes and their development, Vygotsky had to abandon the concept that speech functions as a simple stimulus in human behavior. This required the rejection of the assumption that the stimulus-response unit is the basic building block of behavior.

INTERFUNCTIONAL RELATIONS AND THE DEVELOPMENT OF WORD MEANING (1930–1932)

By 1929 Vygotsky had begun to abandon this assumption. This shift in Vygotsky's perspective, and some of its immediate implications, are apparent in Vygotsky's 1929 paper, "The Genetic Roots of Thinking and Speech" (Chapter 4 of *Thinking and Speech*).

A useful index of the shift that occurred in Vygotsky's thinking during this period are his citations of Kohler's research on the intelligence of the higher apes. Where earlier references to this research had emphasized the chimpanzee's use of tools as an embryonic form of mediated behavior (Vygotsky 1929, 1960b), Vygotsky began to argue in this paper that:

> Kohler's experiments demonstrate clearly that the rudiments of intellect or thinking appear in animals independent of the development of speech and absolutely unconnected with the level of speech development. The "inventions" of the higher apes, their preparation and use of tools, and their use of indirect paths in the solution of problems, clearly constitute an initial *pre-speech* phase in the development of thinking, a *pre-speech* phase its development.
>
> (Vygotsky, 1934: 101)

Beginning 1929, then, Vygotsky's writings no longer reflect the assumption that all animal behavior is restricted to systems constructed on the basis of stimulus-response units. Rather, Vygotsky had begun to argue that certain primitive forms of intellect are found in animals and young children independent of any functional connection with speech.

Vygotsky did not, however, abandon his view that the functional relationship between speech and thinking was an extremely important factor in the psychological development of human beings. Rather, he argued that speech – like intellect – has developmental roots in the higher apes and very young children which are independent of intellect, citing in this connection indicative gestures and emotional expressions (i.e., means of communication that do not involve the naming of objects or events, the relating of words and object). However, citing Buhler's notion that there is a time in the child's development when he or she "discovers that every object has its name," he argued that the independent developmental paths of intellect and speech "intersect" here and at other points in the developmental process leading to the emergence of "verbal thinking" and "meaningful speech." Vygotsky saw these as qualitatively new types of mental functions that have developmental dynamics and psychological characteristics not present in either of their precursors.

The new perspective on the relationship between thinking and speech that emerged as Vygotsky abandoned the view that complex behaviors are constructed on the foundation of stimulus-response units liberated Vygotsky from the need to demonstrate how complex and volitional mental functions emerge on the basis of the mediation of behavior by signs. It also allowed him to begin to incorporate his knowledge of semiotics and communication more fully into his analysis of psychological development. Equally significant, however, was the more general conception of psychological development that emerged from this new perspective on the genetic relationship between what Vygotsky now represented as the independent functions of thinking and speech.

This perspective was outlined by Vygotsky in a lecture that he delivered to his students and colleagues in October 1930, a lecture entitled "On Psychological Systems" (1982a). In this lecture, Vygotsky argued that

> In development, and in particular in the historical development of behavior, what changes is not so much the functions as we earlier studied them (this was our mistake) – not so much their structure or the dynamics of their development – as the relationships and connections between them. In development, groupings of psychological functions emerge that were unknown at preceding stages.
>
> (1982a, p. 110)

Thus, in this lecture, Vygotsky extended his insight concerning the emergence of verbal thinking on the basis of the independent functions of thinking and speech to the whole psychological development, arguing that the key to understanding psychological development is the study of the changing "Interfunctional relationships" among the mental functions, the study of the emergence and development of new "psychological systems."

In 1930, then, Vygotsky abandoned the "instrumental act" and the "higher mental functions" as his unit and object of analysis, turning his attention to changes in interfunctional relationships, to the emergence and development of what he called "psychological systems."

Once again, this is not to say that Vygotsky abandoned his interest in the role of speech in psychological development. His interests in the relationship between thinking and speech were reflected in work on the development of verbal thinking, particularly in studies of the development of word meaning (i.e. verbal concepts) and the role of egocentric and inner speech in the mediation of thought. Similarly, his interests in the verbal mediation of memory processes were reflected in discussions of the emergence of logical memory. At the same time, however, Vygotsky was able to extend his analysis of psychological development beyond cognitive processes, including the study of motivation and affect.

Nonetheless, while this shift in Vygotsky's definition of his analytic object was in many respects a positive step in the evolution of his thinking, he failed to adapt his explanatory framework to this new conception of the mental functions and their development. The attempt to explain psychological development in terms of the individual's participation in social interaction was largely abandoned. In several contexts, Vygotsky did discuss relationships between social variables and the development of psychological systems. He noted that dreaming plays an important role in certain decision making processes in some societies but not in others. He cited Piaget's claim that argument is the foundation for the development of logic. He suggested that imagination has its roots in play. Nowhere, however, did he attempt to generalize these ideas into a coherent explanatory framework.

As a consequence, Vygotsky was left with no general explanatory framework, no explanatory principle. He explained the emergence of new psychological systems in terms of the development of new functional relationships between mental processes. On the whole, however, he made little attempt to explain how or why these new functional relationships emerge. Throughout his career, Vygotsky had criticized psychological paradigms that simply described the nature and development of mental functions without trying to explain them. With equal consistency, he criticized paradigms that failed to differentiate the biological and the social in psychological development. Because he was unable to adapt his explanatory principles to his new conception of psychological development, however, Vygotsky's writings were open to precisely these criticisms during this period.

Nowhere was this reflected more clearly than in his attempts to analyze the development of word meaning. Under Vygotsky's direction, L. Sakharov had carried out a series of experiments that resulted in the identification of several stages in the development of word meaning (i.e., complexes, pseudoconcepts, and concepts) (Chapter 5 of *Thinking and Speech*). In important respects, the design and analysis of these experiments reflected features of Vygotsky's conception of psychological systems that separated the second phase in the development of his thought from the first, while connecting it with the third. Vygotsky insisted that the analysis of concept development cannot be divorced from the analysis of the development of word meaning and he insisted that the development of concepts is not the development of the functional relationship between thought and speech in verbal thinking. Conspicuously absent in this work, however, is any explanation of how and why this development occurs.

Both the strengths and weaknesses of Vygotsky's developing perspective are clearly reflected in the psychological constructs utilized by Vygotsky during this second phase in the development of his theoretical framework. First, in concepts such as "psychological system," "verbal thinking," and "word meaning," Vygotsky defined constructs at differing levels of abstraction that allowed him to analyze the integral development of psychological systems, to avoid the conceptual isolation of mental functions that was inherent in his conception of the "higher mental functions." On the other hand, these constructs did not allow Vygotsky to link psychological development with the development of social behavior in the way that his conception of the higher mental functions and their development in social interaction had. Fundamental to the third and final phase of Vygotsky's work was the attempt to develop an explanatory framework and a system of constructs that would permit an analysis of the development of psychological systems in connection with the development of social behavior.

FUNCTIONAL DIFFERENTIATION AND ANALYSIS ACCORDING TO UNITS (1933–1934)

In much the same sense that Vygotsky's 1929 paper on the genetic roots of thinking and speech (Chapter 4 of *Thinking and Speech*) was pivotal to the transition from the first to the second phases in the development of his theory, his 1932 critique of Piaget's work on egocentric speech (Chapter 2 of *Thinking and Speech*) represents an important first step towards the emergence of the explanatory and conceptual framework which constitutes the third and final phase of his work. As early as 1929, Vygotsky had cited Piaget's work on egocentric speech, arguing that the non-communicative speech with which young children often accompany their ongoing activity represents a transitional phase between the intermental and the intramental plane, a transitional phase between speech that functions to mediate social behavior and speech that functions to mediate the behavior of the individual (Chapter 4 of *Thinking and Speech* pp. 113–14, 1984g, pp. 16–23).

In his 1932 critique of Piaget, however, Vygotsky's discussion of the transition from social to inner speech is reformulated in significant ways, with a focus emerging on what he called "functional differentiation." In this paper, Vygotsky moved beyond the simple claim that egocentric speech represents a transitional stage between social and inner speech to argue that the characteristics unique to egocentric and inner speech can be understood in terms of their changing functions in the individual's activity. Specifically, Vygotsky argued that the phonetic and grammatical abbreviation of inner speech as well as its nonvocalized character, emerge in connection with a change in the function of speech from the mediation of social behavior to the mediation of individual behavior. In the same spirit, he argued that the vocalized quality of egocentric speech is a reflection of its inadequate differentiation as a form of "speech for oneself" from communicative speech.[6]

The explanatory framework that emerged in Vygotsky's work in 1933 and

1934 was a direct extension of this notion of functional differentiation. Fundamental to all Vygotsky's work during this period was the notion that psychological processes develop in connection with transformations in behavior, whether these transformations are the consequence of biological maturation (e.g., the emergence of the capacity for locomotion in the infant), the internal development of the child's own activity (e.g., the differentiation of inner speech from communicative speech or the early stages of the development of play), or the inclusion of the child in new forms of social interaction and social practice (e.g., the development of "scientific concepts" in school or the development of written speech). In concluding his critique of Piaget's work, Vygotsky wrote that "what is missing, then, in Piaget's perspective is reality and the child's relationship to that reality. What is missing is the child's practical activity. This is fundamental" (Chapter 2 of *Thinking and Speech*, p. 87). And he continued:

> Conceptualized in this way, development is not self movement but a logic of arbitrary circumstance. And where there is no self movement, there is no place for development in the true sense of the word. Here [i.e., in Piaget's theory – NM] one phenomenon replaces the other, but it does not emerge from the other.
>
> (ibid., p. 29)

In contrast to his perception of Piaget's approach, Vygotsky attempted to analyze what he called the internal development of the child's activity or practice in the final phase of his work, focusing on how one form of practice emerges from another and how new "psychological formations" develop in connection with these newly emerging forms of practice.

Vygotsky's work on the development of word meaning between 1993 and 1934 provides a useful illustration of this emerging explanatory frame-work. In many respects, the empirical data he cites in this work are identical to those he cited in 1931 in his discussion of the Vygotsky–Sakharov studies on concept formation (Chapter 5 of *Thinking and Speech*). Vygotsky used many of the same examples to illustrate the nature of the child's speech at various points in its development in these discussions. Methodologically and conceptually, however, his approach was very different in 1933–1934 than it had been in 1931.

The central premise of Vygotsky's new approach was that the analysis of the development of word meaning must be carried out in connection with the analysis of the development of the function of the word in communication. Fundamental to the experimental design of the Vygotsky–Sakharov studies was an assumption Vygotsky explicated in his discussion of that work, the assumption that the "function" of word meaning is abstraction and generalization (Chapter 5 of *Thinking and Speech*). In contrast, in 1933 and 1934 Vygotsky began to re-emphasize the central function of word meaning as a means of communication, as a critical component of social practice.

Vygotsky's emerging perspective was outlined in the first chapter of *Thinking and Speech* where he wrote that:

> It may be appropriate to view word meaning not only as *a unity of thinking and speech*, but as a *unity of generalization and social interaction, a unity of thinking and communication*.
>
> This statement of the problem has tremendous significance for all issues related to the genesis of thinking and speech . . . . [and] reveals the true potential for a *causal-genetic analysis of thinking and speech*. Only when we learn to see the unity of generalization and social interaction do we begin to understand the actual connection that exists between the child's cognitive and social development.
>
> (1934, p. 49)

Here, Vygotsky argued that one cannot understand the development of word meaning if one begins by divorcing the "communicative function of speech from its intellectual function" (Chapter 1 of *Thinking and Speech*, p. 48). Along similar lines, Vygotsky elsewhere criticized Buhler and Koffka for failing to recognize that the act of naming is not a mental activity but a means of social interaction.

> Child speech is not the personal activity of the child. . . . Only viewing individual speech as part of dialogue, of cooperation and social interaction, can provide the key to understanding its changes.
>
> (1984b, p. 356)

In contrast to the approach he had taken in his earlier work with Sakharov, then, Vygotsky began to insist in 1933 and 1934 that the analysis of the development of word meaning must begin with the analysis of the function of the word in mediating specific types of social interaction and communication, in mediating specific forms of social practice.

The only empirical work on the development of word meaning that Vygotsky and his colleagues were able to complete within this conceptual framework prior to Vygotsky's death in 1934 was the research of Zh.I. Shif on the development of scientific concepts within the context of formal schooling (Shif 1935; Vygotsky 1935, Chapter 6 of *Thinking and Speech*). In discussing this research (Chapter 6 of *Thinking and Speech*), Vygotsky argued that the instruction of the child in systems of scientific knowledge in school involves a unique form of communication in which the word assumes a function which is quite different from that characteristic of other forms of communication. Specifically, he argued: (1) that the child learns word meanings in certain forms of school instruction not as a means of communication but as part of a system of knowledge; and (2) that this learning occurs not through direct experience with things or phenomena but through other words. As it is used in these communicative contexts, then, the word begins to function not only as a means of communication but as the object of communication activity, with the child's attention being directed explicitly toward word meanings and their interrelationships. Consistent with his emerging theoretical framework, Vygotsky argued that this new function of the word in the child's activity leads to the development of a new type of word meaning or concept, what he referred to as the "scientific" or "true" concept. Where in his earlier work he had simply noted the emergence of a new type of concept (Chapter 5 of *Thinking and Speech*), he now linked the emergence of a new type of word meaning to the child's participation in a new form of social practice.

This new approach to the analysis of the development of word meaning is further illustrated by Vygotsky's discussion of word meanings in what he called "autonomous speech" (1984f). In most respects, the characteristics Vygotsky attributed to word meanings in this form of speech are identical to those he had attributed to "complexes" in his earlier discussions of the Vygotsky–Sakharov research (Chapter 5 of *Thinking and Speech*). In fact, he used many of the same examples in the two contexts to illustrate the nature of the child's speech.[7] Once again, however, the conceptual and explanatory frameworks differ in important respects.

In several contexts, Vygotsky had discussed the emergence of the indicative gesture in the infant's interaction with the adult (1960b, 1981b). He argued that when the infant cries or reaches for an object, the adult attributes meaning to that behavior. Though the infant has no communicative intent, these acts nonetheless function to communicate the infant's needs to his caretaker. Here, as in the adult's attempts to interact with the infant, the infant is included in communicative social activity before he has the capacity to use or to respond adequately to communicative devices. Vygotsky argued that this provides the foundation for the transformation of the infant's behaviors into intentional indicative gestures.

In his discussions of autonomous speech, Vygotsky argued that the initial stages in the development of word meaning represent a transitional stage between these indicative gestures and true word meanings. According to Vygotsky, the child uses words in autonomous speech to refer not to a single type or class of objects but to what adults would consider different kinds of objects in different situations. In contrast to his earlier claims that the concept simply has a diffuse or inconsistent content for the child at this stage of development (Chapter 5 of *Thinking and Speech*), Vygotsky now began to argue that – like the indicative gesture – the word in the child's autonomous speech has no meaning outside the concrete context in which it is used. At this stage in its development, the function of the word has an indicative but not a signifying function. In Vygotsky's words, at this stage in the development of the child's speech the word is simply an "oral indicative gesture" (1984f, pp. 332–337). Consistent with his emerging explanatory framework, then, Vygotsky argued that the characteristics of word meaning at this stage – what he had earlier referred to in his discussion of complexes as the instability of word meaning – is a product of the peculiar function of the word in the child's developing communicative activity.

There is no need to speculate about how Vygotsky might have treated other stages in the development of word meaning within this new explanatory framework. The logic of the approach is clear. The characteristics of the word meaning reflect the characteristics of the communicative activity in which it develops. The characteristics of the word as a generalization or abstraction are a reflection of the child's use of the word as a means of communication and social interaction, a reflection of its function in social practice.

> Whatever the form of social interaction, such will be the nature of gener-
> alization. Social interaction and generalization are internally connected.
>
> (Vygotsky 1982d, p. 166)

The analysis of the development of verbal concepts and verbal thought must begin with the analysis of the forms of social interaction and communication that the word mediates.

Given his focus on social interaction and cognitive development in the first phase of his work and his strong emphasis on the centrality of language during the second, it is important to emphasize that Vygotsky extended his explanatory framework beyond social interaction and sign systems in this third phase of the development of his theory. Though implicit in many respects in his critique of Piaget in 1932 (Chapter 2 of *Thinking and Speech*), this effort is perhaps reflected most clearly in a 1933 paper on the development of imagination in play (Vygotsky 1966, 1978c) and in a series of lectures on child development written in 1933 and 1934 (Vygotsky 1984d).

Vygotsky's paper on imagination and play provides a particularly good illustration of the change which characterized the shift from the second to the third phases in the development of his thought. In a variety of papers written in 1931 and 1932 (Vygotsky 1983, p. 325, 1984g, pp. 14–15, 1984b, pp. 347–350), Vygotsky had represented play and imagination as a product of the power of speech to free behavior and thought from the domination of the immediate perceptual field. In his 1933 paper on play,[8] Vygotsky began in much the same way that he had in his earlier papers, arguing that the young child is bound to the perceptual field. Far from invoking language as the force which frees the child from the perceptual field, however, Vygotsky argued here that word meanings are similarly bound to their objects for the young child, with the word and thing fused in the child's consciousness. Reversing his earlier arguments, Vygotsky maintained in this paper that it is through the development of the child's play activity that thought and meanings are liberated from their origins in the perceptual field, providing the foundation for the further development of speech and its role in advanced forms of thinking and imagination.

The earliest forms of play, Vygotsky argued, are the child's attempts to reproduce a situation or action that he has actually experienced. Playing with dolls, for example, the child reproduces the actions of his caretakers. Vygotsky saw this primitive form of play as "more memory in action than a novel imaginary situation" (1978c, p. 103) and represented it as a transitional stage between behavior based on memory and behavior involving developed imagination. To explain how more advanced forms of play could emerge from these more primitive forms, Vygotsky needed a mechanism which would facilitate the child's separation of meaning from object or action.

Vygotsky argued that one such mechanism could be found in what he called a "pivot," an object used to function as another object in the play situation. He represented the nature and function of the pivot in the following way:

> Thought is separated from the thing because a piece of wood begins to play the role of a doll, a stick becomes a horse; action according to rules begins to be defined from thought rather than things themselves. . . . The child doesn't do this suddenly. To tear thought (word meaning) from the thing is a terribly difficult task for the child. Play is a transitional form. At the moment the stick (i.e., the thing) becomes a pivot for tearing the meaning from the real horse . . . . one of the basic psychological structures that defines the child's relationship to reality is change.
>
> The child cannot yet tear the thought from the thing. He must have a pivot in another thing. . . . To think of the horse, he must define his action by this horse in the stick or pivot. . . . I would say that in play the child operates in accordance with meaning that is torn from things but not torn from real actions with real objects. . . . This is the transitional character of play. This is what makes it a middle link between the purely situational connectedness of early childhood and thinking that is removed from the real situation.
>
> (1978c, pp. 69–71)

For Vygotsky, the child's initial substitution of a stick for a horse did not represent a manifestation of symbolic or imaginative capacities. In these early stages in the development of imagination, the child cannot yet use any object to stand for another in the way that the adult does in symbolic activity. For the young child, the object that is substituted for the horse must have characteristics that allow it to act as a functional substitute for the horse in play activity. It is only within the activity of play that the child can substitute one object for another in this way, only within the activity of play that he begins to separate the object's meaning from the object itself by using another object as a pivot. In brief, then, Vygotsky saw the development of the child's play activity as providing the foundation for the emergence of new forms of behavior and for the development of forms of imagination and abstract thought that are connected with them.

Thus, just as he had argued that word meaning develops in connection with the development of communication and social interaction or that inner speech develops through the functional differentiation of social speech,

Vygotsky argued here that imagination develops in connection with the development of play and other forms of socially organized action and interaction. To paraphrase a statement Vygotsky made in his analysis of the development of word meaning (Chapter 1 of *Thinking and Speech*, p. 49), the central premise of his work on play was that "only when we learn to see the unity of imagination and play do we begin to understand the actual connection that exists between the child's cognitive development and his social development." Just as new psychological characteristics of word meaning are connected with kinds of communication that are particularly prevalent in school, Vygotsky saw the rudiments of imagination emerging in connection with particular forms of object play. Indeed, at certain points in development, Vygotsky saw the psychological characteristics of imagination as inseparable from play in the same way that he saw the psychological characteristics of the scientific concept as inseparable from the way that the word is used in certain types of verbally mediated social activity.

As I suggested earlier, in his arguments on the development of imagination in play, Vygotsky had quite consciously moved beyond an explanatory framework in which speech and social interaction were seen as the sole motive force underlying psychological development. In a series of papers and lectures written in 1933 and 1934 (1984d), Vygotsky attempted to outline this more general explanatory framework.

In these papers, Vygotsky identified two tasks as basic to the analysis of the child's psychological development: (1) the analysis of the social situation that defines the child's life; and (2) the analysis of the psychological structures that develop in connection with this mode of life.

> The social situation of development, which is specific to each age, strictly defines the child's entire mode of life, his social existence. . . . Having clarified the social situation of development that forms at the beginning of a given age and defines the relationships between the child and the environment, we must then clarify how the new formations characteristic of this age necessarily arise and develop from the child's life in this social situation.
>
> (1984d, p. 259)[9]

In these papers, Vygotsky applied this general conceptual framework to a broad range of issues. In his analysis of infancy, he emphasized the infant's dependence on the adult, arguing that the development of early forms of speech and mobility in the first year of life radically transform the child's mode of life and his potential for social interaction and that the development of new communicational skills and new needs and motives in the ensuing years lead to continued changes in the social situation of the child's development. At the same time, focusing on changes originating from the side of the social environment, Vygotsky explored the way that the child's introduction to organized games, formal schooling, or work activity changes his mode of life. In each of these cases, he attempted to indicate how new psychological formations emerge in connection with the developing social situation of development, exploring the kinds of connections between the development of social behavior and the development of psychological processes that he had discussed in his work on egocentric speech, scientific concepts, and play.

Fundamental to Vygotsky's efforts to develop this explanatory framework were his attempts to establish criteria for defining psychological constructs. In the first two phases of his work, Vygotsky had developed systems of novel theoretical constructs that allowed him to develop his theory and research. In each of these phases, he carefully defined a construct which represented his general analytic object (i.e., the "higher mental function" or "instrumental act" in the first phase and the "psychological system" in the second). In this third phase in the development of his thought, Vygotsky did not identify a comparable analytic object, but he did initiate a major effort to describe how psychological constructs would have to be conceptualized and defined if they were to facilitate the study of psychological development in connection with social interaction and social practice.[10]

One of Vygotsky's efforts to address this issue is found in his discussion of what he called "analysis according to units" in the first chapter of *Thinking and Speech*. This discussion is extremely important to any understanding of the nature of Vygotsky's theoretical framework during this third and final phase in the development of his thought, though it is important to note that Vygotsky fuses two distinct issues in this particular attempt to address the problem of defining appropriate analytic constructs.

The first aspect of this discussion, which is not particularly relevant to our current concerns, deals with the identification of constructs that are appropriate for the study of mental functions as they are functionally related in psychological systems. Focusing on the problem of the functional relationship between thinking and speech, Vygotsky argued that it is impossible to understand this relationship by first studying the characteristics of speech and thinking in conceptual isolation from one another and then trying to analyze their functional relationships or interactions. As he had in earlier papers, Vygotsky argued that verbal thinking is qualitatively different from the speech and intellect that serve as its precursors, that it is a unique psychological system with its own functional and developmental dynamics. To study this unity, he insisted, one must identify an analytical unit that retains the characteristics of the whole. Vygotsky found this unit in "word meaning," a component of verbal thinking that contains thinking (i.e., generalization) and speech in functional relationship.[11]

The second aspect of this discussion of "analysis according to units" is more relevant to the present discussion, focusing as it does on the relationship between psychological processes and social interaction. Vygotsky argued that "it may be appropriate to view word meaning not only as *a unity of thinking and speech*, but as a *unity of generalization and social interaction, of thinking and communication* (Chapter 1 of *Thinking and Speech*, p. 49). This conception of "word meaning" as a unit of both thinking and social interaction provided the foundation for Vygotsky's analysis of the development of word meaning during this phase of his career, providing the potential for a causal-genetic analysis of the development of word meaning that was lacking in the Vygotsky–Sakharov research discussed in Chapter 5 of *Thinking and Speech* and more generally in all of Vygotsky's work carried out under the "psychological systems" framework.

In the last of the series of lectures he delivered in 1933 and 1934, Vygotsky developed an argument dealing with "analysis according to units" that paralleled this argument on "word meaning" (1984c, pp. 376–385). Focusing on the relationship between the individual and the environment, Vygotsky stated the problem in the following way:

> We have inadequately studied the internal relationship of the child to the people around him. . . . We have recognized in words that we need to study the child's personality and environment as a unity. It is incorrect, however, to represent this problem in such a way that on one side we have the influence of personality while on the other we have the influence of the environment. Though the problem is frequently represented in precisely this way, it is incorrect to represent the two as external forces acting on one another. In the attempt to study the unity, the two are initially torn apart. The attempt is then made to unite them.
>
> (1984c, p. 380)

Vygotsky argued that the fundamental inadequacy of most attempts to study the influence of the environmental on the child's development is the practice of describing the environment in terms of "absolute indices." That is, the problem lies in conceptualizing the environment as it exists in isolation from the child rather than studying it in terms of "what it means for the child," in terms of "the child's relationship to the various aspects of this environment" (1984c, p. 318).

In a manner comparable to his conceptualization of the environment as the "social situation of development," Vygotsky argued that the key is the identification of an analytic unit representing the individual in the individual/environment relationship that maintains the functional relationship between the individual and the environment. He proposed "experience" as an adequate psychological construct in this context, arguing that:

> The child's experience is the kind of simple unit of which it is impossible to say that it is the influence of the environment on the child or a characteristic of the child himself. Experience is a unit of personality and environment as they exist in development. . . . Experience must be understood as the internal relationship of the child as an individual to a given aspect of reality.
>
> (1984c, p. 382)

Of course, by "relationship" Vygotsky meant here not a passive relationship or perceiving or processing incoming stimuli, but a relationship defined by the child's needs and goals, a relationship defined by the forms of social practice that "relate" the child to the objective environ- ment and define what that environment means for the child. Here again, we find the psycho- logical inherently tied to the organization of social practice.

These explicit attempts to develop units of analysis adequate to his emerging conceptual framework were accompanied by the use of a whole series of constructs which maintained the connection between mind and social interaction/action that Vygotsky had called for in his discussion of "units of analysis." This connection was maintained, for example, in Vygotsky's treatment of "imagination" in his work on imagination and play (Vygotsky 1966, 1978c) and in his definition of the concept of the "social situation of development" in his lectures on child development (Vygotsky 1984d). It was further developed and elaborated in other key concepts developed by Vygotsky during this period as well, one of the more significant of which was his concept of the "zone of proximal development" (Minick 1987; Rogoff and Wertsch 1984; Wertsch 1985).

In developing these theoretical constructs, this general approach to the def- inition of constructs in psychological theory, and the explanatory framework which was emerging in his work during this phase in his career, Vygotsky was making some significant strides towards the realization of the goal that he had established in 1924 and 1925, the goal of developing a theoretical per- spective that would allow a unified analysis of behavior and consciousness while recognizing the unique socio-historical nature of the human mind.

CONCLUSION

Vygotsky has had a tremendous impact on the development of Soviet psych- ology, associated primarily with a psychological paradigm developed by Vygotsky's students and associates that is commonly referred to as the "theory of activity" or the "activity approach" (Wertsch 1981, 1985; Leont'ev 1978, 1982b). In the late 1930s and early 1940s, extending what they saw as the central concept in Vygotsky's later work, a group of Vygotsky's associates led by A.N. Leont'ev developed a set of theoretical constructs based on the concept that the phylogenetic, historical, and ontogenetic development of psychological processes in both animals and man is intimately connected with the development of the actions and activities through which the organ- ism is related to the external world. Over the past fifty years, the research paradigm that developed on this foundation has become one of the most influential in Soviet psychology. Significantly, however, it has failed to develop several of Vygotsky's central ideas, in particular, those associated with the significance of social interaction and the development of word meaning in ontogenesis. The publication of Vygotsky's collected works is associated with a movement within this research tradition to develop these aspects of Vygotsky's thinking.

Vygotsky's influence on the development of psychology outside the Soviet Union is much more difficult to characterize (Cole and Wertsch, 1986). Until recently, access to Vygotsky's works in the West has been extremely restricted, due both to the limited amount of translated material and to a lack of understanding of the relationship of that material to the general system of theory, problem, and research that it represents. In the past decade, through the efforts of scholars such as Cole[12] and Wertsch (1981, 1985) in the United States and their counterparts in Europe, we have begun to have access to a much wider selection of translations representing the works of Vygotsky and the Vygotskian school and to develop a much better understanding of the general theoretical framework that these works represent. Of course, psychologists and social scientists in the West who are now incorporating concepts based on the works of the Vygotskian school into their own research differ widely in their interpretation and application of these concepts. What unites them, however, is a shared conviction that Vygotsky and his intellectual descendants in the Soviet Union have developed a conceptual framework that overcomes many limitations of other attempts to represent the relationship between the social and the individual in psychological development.

As a rule, the publication and translation of the works of a scholar such as Vygotsky who lived and worked nearly a half century ago would be carried out because the ideas they contain are perceived in retrospect to have been "ahead of their time" or because they had considerable influence on the subsequent development of science. The Soviet publication of Vygotsky's collected works, and our translation of them, is motivated by different concerns. They are motivated by the conviction of Vygotsky's students in the Soviet Union and in the West that his ideas and insights are in many respects considerably ahead of our time, by the conviction that his influence on the development of psychology and the social sciences has not been nearly as considerable as it must be.

NOTES

1 Vygotsky became a significant force in Soviet psychology following his move to Moscow in 1924. He died of tuberculosis in the spring of 1934. For a translated bibliography of his work, see Vygotsky (1978a, pp. 141–151).

2 For a useful discussion of the early development of Soviet psychology see Kozulin (1984).

3 Vygotsky attributed this general concept to Janet.

4 As Wertsch has noted (1985, p. 235), these terms have commonly been translated as inter/intrapsychological rather than the more literal inter/intramental. I have used the more literal translation in this volume because it seems to highlight Vygotsky's view that mental activity can be attributed to two or more people who are acting cooperatively and that the organization and means of his mental activity is comparable to that of the individual who is acting alone.

5 Studies of the type are not being carried out in the West (e.g., Wertsch 1985; Rogoff and Wertsch 1984).

6 These ideas were developed in much greater detail in Chapter 7 of *Thinking and Speech* (written in 1933–1934), where Vygotsky extended his discussion of the differentiation of speech functions to written speech and poetic speech.

7 In his discussion of autonomous speech, he does not mention Sakharov's research or the scheme of concept development elaborated on the foundation of that research.

8 What follows is based on the version of this article in the original Russian (Vygotsky 1966). These aspects of Vygotsky's discussion of play and imagination emerge less clearly in the edited English translation (Vygotsky 1978c).

9 Vygotsky contrasted his conception of the "social situation of development" with the concept "objective environment," that is, with the environment conceptualized in isolation from the behavior and psychological characteristics of the child. For Vygotsky, when the infant learns to crawl or the toddler learns to speak, the social situation of the child's development changes. Vygotsky defined the social situation of development as "the system of relationships between the child of a given age and social reality" (1984d, p. 260).

10 See Davydov and Radzikhovskii (1985) and Zinchenko (1985) for interesting discussions of Vygotsky's criteria for "analytic units."

11 To illustrate this general concept, Vygotsky argued that the proper unit for the analysis of water is not the atom of hydrogen or oxygen but the molecule of water, since it is only through the analysis of the relationship of these atoms in the molecule that what we know of hydrogen and oxygen can help us to understand the characteristics that are not found in either of its components.

12 In addition to extensive research influenced by the Vygotskian paradigm (e.g., Cole and Scribner (1974) and Scribner and Cole 1981), Cole has played a leading role in facilitating the translation of key works of the Vygotskian school through his editorship of the translation journal *Soivet Psychology* and several important books (e.g., Luria 1976, 1979; Vygotsky 1978a).

REFERENCES

Bozhovich, L.I. (1977). The concept of the cultural-historical development of mind and its prospects. *Soviet Psychology*, 16, 5–22.

Cole, Michael and Sylvia Scribner (1974). *Culture and thought: A psychological introduction*. New York; John Wiley & Sons.

Cole, Michael and James V. Wertsch (1986). Preliminary remarks on the Soviet sociocultural approach to mind and psychological research in the United States. Paper presented at the First International Congress on the Theory of Activity, Berlin, October 1986.

Davydov, V.V. and L.A. Radzikhovskii (1985). Vygotsky's theory and the activity-oriented approach in psychology. In James V. Wertsch (ed.), *Culture, communication and cognition: Vygotskian perspectives* (pp. 35–65). New York: Cambridge University Press.

Elkonin, D.B. (1984). Poleslovie [Afterword]. In L.S. Vygotsky, *Sobranie sochinenie: Detskaia psikhologiia (Tom 4)* [Collected works: Child psychology (Vol. 4)]. Moscow: Pedagogika.

Kozulin, Alex (1984). *Psychology in utopia: Toward a social history of Soviet psychology*. Cambridge, Mass.: MIT.

Leont'ev, A.N. (1931). *Razvitie pamiati: Eksperimental'noe issledovanie vysshykh psikhologicheskikh funktii* [The development of memory: An experimental study of the higher psychological functions]. Moscow: Uchpedgiz.

Leont'ev, A.N. (1978). *Activity, consciousness, and personality*. Englewood Cliffs, New Jersey: Prentice-Hall.

Leont'ev, A.N. (1982a). Vystupitel'naia stat'ia [Introductory article]. In L.S. Vygotsky, *Sobranie sochinenie: Voprosy teori i istorii psikhologii (Tom 1)* [Collected works: Problems of the theory and history of psychology (Vol. 1)]. Moscow: Pedagogika.

Leont'ev, A.N. (1982b). *Problems of the development of mind*. Moscow: Progress Publishers.

Luria, A.R. (1976). *Cognitive development: Its cultural and social foundations*. Cambridge, Mass.: Harvard University Press.

Luria, A.R. (1979). *The making of mind: A personal account of Soviet psychology*. Cambridge, Mass.: Harvard University Press.

Minick, Norris (1985). L.S. Vygotsky and Soviet activity theory: New perspectives on the relationship between mind and society. PhD. Dissertation. Northwestern University, Evanston, Illinois.

Minick, Norris (1987). The zone of proximal development and dynamic assessment. In Carol S. Lidz (ed.), *Dynamic assessment*. New York: Guilford Press.

Radzikhovskii, L.A. (1979). *Osnovnye etapy nauchnogo tvorchestva L.S. Vygotskogo* [The basic stages in the scientific creativity of L.S. Vygotsky]. Candidate's Dissertation. Moscow Federal University, Moscow, USSR.

Rogoff, Barbara and James V. Wertsch (eds.)(1984). *Children's learning in the "zone of proximal development"*. San Francisco: Jossey-Bass.

Scribner, Sylvia and Michael Cole (1981). *The psychology of literacy*. Cambridge, Mass.: Harvard University Press.

Shif, Zh. I. (1935). *Razvitie zhiteiskikh i nauchnykh poniatii* [The development of everyday and scientific concepts]. Moscow: Uchpedgiz.

Vygotsky, L.S. (1929). The problem of the cultural development of the child. *Journal of Genetic Psychology*, *36*, 415–432.

Vygotsky, L.S. (1935). *Umstvennoe razvitie detei v protsesse obucheniia* [The mental development of the child in the process of instruction]. Moscow-Leningrad: Uchpedgiz.

Vygotsky, L.S. (1960a). *Razvitie vysshikh psikhicheskikh funktsii* [The development of the higher mental functions]. Moscow: APN.

Vygotsky, L.S. (1960b). Istoriia razvitiia vysshikh psikhicheskikh funktsii [The history of the development of the higher mental functions]. In L.S. Vygotsky, *Razvitie vysshikh psikhicheskikh funktsii* [The development of the higher mental functions]. Moscow: APN.

Vygotsky, L.S. (1960c). Povedenie zhivotnykh i cheloveka [The Behavior of Animals and Man]. In L.S. Vygotsky, *Razvitie vysshikh psikhicheskikh funktsii* [The development of the higher mental functions]. Moscow: APN.

Vygotsky, L.S. (1966). Igra i ee rol' v psikhicheskom razvitii rebenka [Play and its role in the mental development of the child]. *Voprosy Psikhologii*, No. 6, 62–76.

Vygotsky, L.S. (1978a). *Mind in Society*. Cambridge, Mass.: Harvard University Press.

Vygotsky, L.S. (1978b). Problems of method. In L.S. Vygotsky, *Mind in Society*. Cambridge, Mass.: Harvard University Press.

Vygotsky, L.S. (1978c). The role of play in development. In L.S. Vygotsky, *Mind in Society*. Cambridge, Mass.: Harvard University Press.

Vygotsky, L.S. (1981a). The instrumental method in psychology. In James V. Wertsch (ed.), *The Concept of Activity in Soviet Psychology*. Armonk, New York: M.E. Sharpe.

Vygotsky, L.S. (1981b). The development of the higher forms of attention in childhood. In James V. Wertsch (ed.), *The Concept of Activity in Soviet Psychology*. Armonk, New York: M.E. Sharpe.

Vygotsky, L.S. (1982a). O psikhologicheskikh sistemakh [On psychological systems]. In L.S. Vygotsky *Sobranie sochinenie: Voprosy teorii i istorii psikhologii (Tom 1)* [Collected works: Problems of the theory and history of psychology (Vol. 1)]. Moscow Pedagogika.

Vygotsky, L.S. (1982b). Metodika refleksologicheskogo i psikhologicheskogo issledovaniia [Methods of reflexological and psychological research]. In L.S. Vygotsky, *Sobranie sochinenie: Voprosy teorii i istorii psikhologii* (Tom 1) [Collected works: Problems of the theory and history of psychology (Vol. 1)]. Moscow: Pedagogika.

Vygotsky, L.S. (1982c). Soznanie kak problema psikhologii povedeniia [Consciousness as a problem of the psychology of behavior]. In L.S. Vygotsky, *Sobranie sochinenie: Voprosy teorii i istorii psikhologii (Tom 1)* [Collected works: Problems of the theory and history of psychology (Vol. 1)]. Moscow: Pedagogika.

Vygotsky, L.S. (1982d). Problema soznaniia [The problem of consciousness]. In L.S. Vygotsky, *Sobranie sochinenie: Voprosy teorii i istorii psikhologii (Tom 1)* [Collected works: Problems of the theory and history of psychology (Vol. 1)]. Moscow: Pedagogika.

Vygotsky, L.S. (1982e) *Sobranie sochinenie: Voprosy teorii i istorii psikhologii (Tom 1)* [Collected works: Problems of the theory and history of psychology (Vol. 1)]. Moscow: Pedagogika.

Vygotsky, L.S. (1983). *Sobranie sochinenie: Problemy razvitiia psikhiki (Tom 3)* [Collected works: Problems of the development of mind (Vol. 3)]. Moscow: Pedagogika.

Vygotsky, L.S. (1984a). Pedologiia podrostka [The pedagogy of teenagers]. In L.S. Vygotsky, *Sobranie sochinenie: Detskaia psikhologiia (Tom 4)* [Collected works: Child psychology (Vol. 4)]. Moscow: Pedagogika.

Vygotsky, L.S. (1984b). Ranee detstvo [Early childhood]. In L.S. Vygotsky, *Sobranie sochinenie: Detskaia psikhologiia (Tom 4)* [Collected works: Child psychology (Vol. 4)]. Moscow: Pedagogika.

Vygotsky, L.S. (1984c). Krizis semi let [The crisis of seven years]. In L.S. Vygotsky, *Sobranie sochinenie: Detskaia psikhologiia (Tom 4)* [Collected works: Child psychology (Vol. 4)]. Moscow: Pedagogika.

Vygotsky, L.S. (1984d). Problema vozrasta [The problem of ages]. In L.S. Vygotsky, *Sobranie sochinenie: Detskaia psikhologiia (Tom 4)* [Collected works: Child psychology (Vol. 4)]. Moscow: Pedagogika.

Vygotsky, L.S. (1984e). *Sobranie sochinenie: Detskaia psikhologiia (Tom 4)* [Collected works: Child psychology (Vol. 4)]. Moscow: Pedagogika.

Vygotsky, L.S. (1984f). Krizis pervogo goda zhizni [The crisis of the first year of life]. In L.S. Vygotsky, *Sobranie sochinenie: Detskaia psikhologiia (Tom 4)* [Collected works: Child psychology (Vol. 4)]. Moscow: Pedagogika.

Vygotsky, L.S. (1984g). Orudie i znak v razvitii rebenka [Tool and sign in the development of the child]. In L.S. Vygotsky, *Sobranie sochinenie: Nauchnoe nacledstvo (Tom 6)* [Collected works: Scientific archives (Vol. 6)]. Moscow: Pedagogika.

Wertsch, James V. (ed.) (1981). *The concept of Activity in Soviet Psychology*. Armonk, New York: M.E. Sharpe.

Wertsch, James V. (1985). *Vygotsky and the social formation of mind.* Cambridge, Mass.: Harvard University Press.

Zinchenko, V.P. (1985). Vygotsky's ideas about units for the analysis of mind. In James V. Wertsch (ed.), *Culture, communication, and cognition: Vygotskian perspectives.* New York: Cambridge University Press.

2 L.S. Vygotsky and contemporary developmental psychology

James V. Wertsch and Peeter Tulviste

Over the past decade there has been a major upsurge of interest in the ideas of Lev Semenovich Vygotsky (1896–1934). This is reflected in the dramatic rise in citations of Vygotsky's publications (Belmont, 1988), in the spate of new translations of his writings (Vygotsky, 1978, 1981a, 1981b, 1981c, 1986, 1987 in press, and in several new volumes about his life and work (Kozulin, 1990; A.A. Leont'ev, 1990; Minick, Forman and Stone, in press: Moll, 1990; Puzerei, 1986; Ratner, 1991; van der Veer and Valsiner, in press; Wertsch, 1985a, 1985b, 1991; Yaroshevskii, 1989).

The reasons for the new interest in Vygotsky in the United States are not altogether clear, but several factors seem to have played a role. One of them is the recent publication or republication of most of his writings in Russian (Vygotsky, 1982a, 1982b, 1983a, 1983b, 1984a, 1984b) and the subsequent translation of these items into English (Vygotsky, 1987, in press). Another is that increased scholarly exchanges between the United States and the former Soviet Union and the emigration of several Soviet psychologists to the West have provided a coterie of experts who can deal authoritatively with these writings. Yet a third is the fact that many of Vygotsky's ideas seem directly relevant to issues in education and other applied fields (Moll, 1990). And perhaps the most important factor is that Western scholars, especially those in the United States, have been actively searching for new theoretical frameworks and Vygotsky's ideas seem to address many of the issues that have motivated their quest.

Our goal in this chapter is not to provide a general review of the origins and fate of Vygotsky's ideas. This task has been carried out admirably by authors such as Kozulin (1990) and van der Veer and Valsiner (in press). Instead, our intent is to review a few of Vygotsky's ideas that have particular relevance for contemporary developmental psychology and to see how these ideas can be extended in light of recent theoretical advances in the social sciences and humanities. Our discussion focuses primarily on two points in Vygotsky's theoretical approach: his claim about the social origins and social nature of higher (i.e., uniquely human) mental functioning and his uses of culture. In examining these points we also touch on his use of a developmental method and on his distinction between elementary and higher mental functioning.

SOCIAL ORIGINS OF INDIVIDUAL
MENTAL FUNCTIONING

Perhaps the major reason for Vygotsky's current appeal in the West is his analysis of the social origins of mental processes. This is a theme that has reemerged with considerable force in Western developmental psychology over the past twenty years or so, and Vygotsky's ideas have come to play an important role in this movement.

In Vygotsky's view, mental functioning in the individual can be understood only by examining the social and cultural processes from which it derives. This involves an analytical strategy that may appear to some to be para-doxical at first glance. Namely, it calls on the investigator to begin the analysis of mental functioning in the individual by going outside the individual. As one of Vygotsky's students and colleagues, A.R. Luria, put it:

> In order to explain the highly complex forms of human consciousness one must go beyond the human organism. One must seek the origins of conscious activity . . . . in the external processes of social life, in the social and historical forms of human existence.
>
> (1981, p. 25)

This view stands in marked contrast to the strong individualistic assumptions that underlie the bulk of contemporary Western research in psychology (see Sarason, 1981, for a critique of these assumptions).

Vygotsky's claims about the analytic priority to be given to social processes were in evidence throughout his career as a psychologist (basically the decade before his death of tuberculosis in 1934). For example, in one of his first articles from this period he asserted that "the social dimension of conscious-ness is primary in time and in fact. The individual dimension of conscious-ness is derivative and secondary" (Vygotsky, 1979, p. 30). As Bruner (1962) noted, this aspect of Vygotsky's approach bears a striking resemblance to the ideas of George Herbert Mead. Its actual origins in Vygotsky's writings, however, seem to have been in the writings of Marx (Wertsch, 1985b) and in the ideas of the French psychiatrist and psychologist Pierre Janet (1928; also see van der Veer and Valsiner, 1988), who was in turn strongly influenced by the French sociological school of Emile Durkheim.

Perhaps the most useful general formulation of Vygotsky's claims about the social origins of individual mental functioning can be found in his "general genetic law of cultural development."

> Any function in the child's cultural development appears twice, or on two planes. First it appears on the social plane, and then on the psychological plane. First it appears between people as an interpsychological category, and then within the child as an intrapsychological category. This is equally true with regard to voluntary attention, logical memory, the formation of

concepts, and the development of volition. . . . [I]t goes without saying that internalization transforms the process itself and changes its structure and functions. Social relations or relations among people genetically underlie all higher functions and their relationships.

(Vygotsky, 1981b, p. 163)

There are several aspects of this statement worth noting. The first is that the notion of mental functioning it presupposes differs from that which is typically assumed in contemporary Western psychology. Instead of beginning with the assumption that mental functioning occurs first and foremost, if not only, within the individual, it assumes that one can speak equally appropriately of mental processes as occurring *between* people on the intermental plane.[1] Indeed, it gives analytic priority to such intermental functioning in that intramental functioning is viewed as being derivative, as emerging through the mastery and internalization of social processes.

This fundamental difference in orientation is clearly manifested in how terms are used. In contemporary usage terms such as *cognition, memory*, and *attention* are automatically assumed to apply exclusively to the individual. In order to use these terms when speaking of processes carried out on the social plane, some modifier must be attached. This is the source of recent terms such as *socially shared cognition* (Resnick, Levine and Behrend, 1991), *socially distributed cognition* (Hutchins, 1991), and *collective memory* (Middleton, 1987). The need to use modifiers such as "socially shared" reflects the derivative, or nonbasic, status that mental functioning carried out on the social plane is assumed to have contemporary paradigms.

In contrast to traditions in which individualistic assumptions are built into the very terms used to discuss psychological phenomena, Vygotsky's view was based in his claims about the social origins and "quasi-social nature" (Vygotsky, 1981b, p. 164) of intramental functioning. This orientation reflects an implicit rejection of the primacy given by individual functioning and to the seemingly neat distinction between social and individual processes that characterize many contemporary approaches in psychology. In contrast to such approaches, Vygotsky viewed mental functioning as a kind of action (Wertsch, 1991) that may be carried out by individuals or by dyads and larger groups. Much like that of authors such as Bateson (1972) and Geertz (1973), therefore, this view is one in which mind is understood as "extending beyond skin." Mind, cognition, memory, and so forth are understood not as attributes or properties of the individual, but as functions that may be carried out intermentally or intramentally

Vygotsky's claims about the social origins of individual mental functioning surface in many ways throughout his writings. Two issues that have taken on particular importance in contemporary developmental psychology in the West are the "zone of proximal development" (Vygotsky, 1978, 1987) and "egocentric" and "inner speech" (Vygotsky, 1978, 1987). Each of these phenomena has taken on a sort of life of its own in the contemporary developmental literature, but from a Vygotskian perspective it is essential to remember how they are situated in an overall theoretical framework. In particular, it is important to remember that they are specific instances of more general claims about the social origins of individual mental functioning.

The zone of proximal development has recently received a great deal of attention in the West (e.g., Brown and Ferrara, 1985; Brown and French, 1979; Cole 1985; Rogoff, 1990; Rogoff and Wertsch, 1984; Tharp and Gallimore, 1988). This zone is defined as the distance between a child's "actual developmental level as determined by independent problem solving" and the higher level of "potential development as determined through problem solving under adult guidance or in collaboration with more capable peers" (Vygotsky, 1978, p. 86).

Vygotsky examined the implications of the zone of proximal development for the organization of instruction and for the assessment of intelligence. With regard to the former he argued that instruction should be tied more closely to the level of potential development than to the level of actual development: with regard to the latter he argued that measuring the level of potential development is just as important as measuring the actual developmental level. He used the following example to illustrate his ideas about assessment:

> Imagine that we have examined two children and have determined that the mental age of both is seven years. This means that both children solve tasks accessible to seven-year-olds. However, when we attempt to push these children further in carrying out the tests, there turns out to be an essential difference between them. With the help of leading questions, examples, and demonstrations, one of them easily solves test items taken from two years above the child's level of [actual] development. The other solves test items that are only a half-year above his or her level of [actual] development.
>
> (Vygotsky, 1956, pp. 446–447)

Given this set of circumstances, Vygotsky (1956, p. 447) went on to pose the question, "Is the mental development of these two children the same?" In his view it was not:

> From the point of view of their independent activity they are equivalent, but from the point of view of their immediate potential development they are sharply different. That which the child turns out to be able to do with the help of an adult points us towards the zone of the child's proximal development. This means that with the help of this method, we can take stock not only of today's completed process of development, not only the cycles that are already concluded and done, not only the processes of maturation that are completed; we can also take stock of processes that

are now in the state of coming into being, that are only ripening, or only developing.

(Vygotsky, 1956, pp. 447–448)

In such analyses, it is essential to keep in mind that the actual and potential levels of development correspond with intramental and intermental functioning, respectively. By doing so one can avoid the temptation to view the zone of proximal development simply as formulation for improving the assessment of individual mental functioning. Instead, it can be seen as having powerful implications for how one can *change* intermental, and hence intramental, functioning. This has been the key to intervention programs such as the "reciprocal teaching" outlined by Palincsar and Brown (1984, 1988).

As in the case of the zone of proximal development, Vygotsky's account of egocentric and inner speech reflects his more general concern with the sociocultural origins of individual mental functioning and has given rise to a spate of recent research (e.g., Berk, 1986; Berk and Garvin, 1984; Bivens and Berk, 1990; Bivens and Hagstrom, in press; Diaz and Berk, in press; Emerson, 1983; Kohlberg, Yaeger, and Hjertholm, 1968; Wertsch, 1979a, 1979b, 1985b). Vygotsky claimed that inner speech enables humans to plan and regulate their action and derives from previous participation in verbal social interaction. Egocentric speech is "a [speech] form found in the transition from external to inner speech" (Vygotsky, 1934, p. 46). The appearance of egocentric speech, roughly at the age of 3, reflects the emergence of a new self-regulative function similar to that of inner speech. Its external form reflects the fact that the child has not fully differentiated this new speech function from the function of social contact and social interaction.

As was the case in his account of the zone of proximal development Vygotsky's treatment of egocentric and inner speech is grounded in the assumptions spelled out in his general genetic law of cultural development. This is reflected at several points in his treatment. For example, let us turn once again to the terminology involved. Why did Vygotsky formulate his claims in terms of inner *speech* rather than in terms of *thinking, mental processes*, or some other commonly used label? The answer to this question lies in the assumptions about the social origins and quasi-social nature of intramental functioning. As was the case for other theorists in his milieu (e.g., Potebnya, 1922), Vygotsky's use of the term *speech* here reflects the fact that he viewed individual mental functioning as deriving essentially from the mastery and internalization of social processes.

Vygotsky's emphasis on the social origins of individual mental processes in this case emerges quite clearly in his analysis of the functions of language. He argued that "a sign is always originally a means used for social purposes, a means of influencing others, and only later becomes a means of influencing oneself" (Vygotsky, 1981b, p. 157). And focusing more specifically on the sign system of language, he argued that "the primary function of speech, both for the adult and for the child, is the function of communication, social contact, influencing surrounding individuals" (Vygotsky, 1934, p. 45). With regard to egocentric and inner speech Vygotsky argued that because these forms derive from "communication, social contact, influencing surrounding individuals," it follows that they should reflect certain properties of their intermental precursors, properties such as a dialogic structure. This is precisely what he seems to have had in mind when he asserted that "egocentric speech . . . . grows out of its social foundations by means of transferring social, collaborative forms of behavior to the sphere of the individual's psychological functioning" (Vygotsky, 1934, p. 45). Explications and extensions of this basic argument of how social, dialogic properties of speech characterize inner speech have been made by scholars such as Bibler (1975, 1981), Emerson (1983), and Wertsch (1980, 1985b, 1991).

THE ROLE OF A DEVELOPMENTAL METHOD

A second theme in Vygotsky's work that has made it attractive to contemporary Western psychology is his use of a developmental, or genetic, method. His reliance on this method is reflected in the very title of his "general genetic law of cultural development." The fact that the law is formulated in terms of developmental transitions reflects his assumption that the most adequate way to understand human mental functioning is to trace it back through the developmental changes it has undergone. In his view,

> We need to concentrate not to the *product* of development but on the very *process* by which higher forms are established. . . . To encompass in research the process of a given thing's development in all its phases and changes – from birth to death – fundamentally means to discover its nature, its essence, for "it is only in movement that a body shows what it is." Thus, the historical [that is, in the broadest sense of "history"] study of behavior is not an auxiliary aspect of theoretical study, but rather forms its very base.
>
> (Vygotsky, 1978, pp. 64–65)

Vygotsky's account of a genetic method derived from several theoretical sources. For example, his debt to his contemporaries in psychology is reflected in the distinction he drew between description and explanation in psychology.

> Following Lewin, we can apply [the] distinction between the phenotypic (descriptive) and genotypic (explanatory) viewpoints to psychology. By a developmental study of a problem, I mean the disclosure of its genesis, its causal dynamic basis. By phenotypic I mean the analysis that begins directly with an object's current features and manifestations. It is possible

to furnish many examples from psychology where serious errors have been committed because these viewpoints have been confused.

(Vygotsky, 1978, p. 62)

Unlike many contemporary developmental psychologists, Vygotsky did not limit the application of his genetic analysis to ontogenesis. Instead, he viewed ontogenesis as one of several "genetic domains" (Wertsch, 1985b) that must eventually be taken into consideration in order to provide an adequate account of human mental processes. In addition, he was concerned with phylogenesis, sociocultural history, and microgenesis (Wertsch, 1985b). In his view, an adequate account of human mental functioning could be derived only through understanding how these various genetic domains operate within an integrated system. Vygotsky posited that change in each genetic domain is associated with a distinct set of explanatory principles.

> The use and "invention" of tools in humanlike apes crowns the organic development of behavior in evolution and paves the way for the transition of all development to take place along new paths. It creates *the basic psychological prerequisites for the historical development of behavior*. Labor and the associated development of human speech and other psychological signs with which primitives attempt to master their behavior, signify the beginning of the genuine cultural or historical development of behavior. Finally, in child development, along with processes of organic growth and maturation, a second line of development is clearly distinguished – the cultural growth of behavior. It is based on the mastery of devices and means of cultural behavior and thinking.
>
> (Vygotsky and Luria, 1930, pp. 3–4)

In this view it is misguided to reduce the account of change in one genetic domain to the principles invoked in connection with another, a point associated with Vygotsky's basic antirecapitulationist orientation (Wertsch, 1991).

Vygotsky was particularly interested in "revolutionary," as opposed to evolutionary, shifts in development. For example, in outlining his account of the form of genetic transition involved in phylogenesis, sociocultural history, and ontogenesis, he argued,

> All three of these moments are symptoms of new epochs in the evolution of behavior and indications of a *change in the type of development itself*. In all three instances we have thereby selected turning points or critical steps in the development of behavior. We think that the turning point or critical moment in the behavior of apes is the use of tools; in the behavior of primitives it is labor and the use of psychological signs; in the behavior of the child it is the bifurcation of lines of development into natural-psychological and cultural-psychological development.
>
> (Vygotsky and Luria, 1930, p. 4).

The tenets of Vygotsky's developmental approach provided the basic methodological framework within which all other aspects of his analyses were formulated.

VYGOTSKY'S USES OF CULTURE

Up to this point our comments on the social origins and social nature of individual mental functioning have focused on a particular kind of social process. Specifically, we have concentrated on intermental functioning in the form of dyadic or small group processes and how it fits into Vygotsky's genetic analysis. This was a major focus of Vygotsky's thinking and certainly constitutes one of the ways in which mind may be said to extend beyond the skin in his approach. It has also been the concern of a great deal of Vygotsky-inspired research in contemporary Western psychology (e.g., Rogoff, 1990; Rogoff and Wertsch, 1984; Wertsch, 1979a).

There is a second, equally important sense, however, in which mental functioning may be said to extend beyond the skin in Vygotsky's writings, a sense that draws on his notion of culture. Mind extends beyond the skin in this second sense because human mental functioning, on the intramental as well as intermental plane, involves cultural tools, or mediational means. In contrast to the "unencumbering image of the self" that is presupposed by so much of contemporary psychology (Taylor, 1985; Wertsch, 1991), Vygotsky's account of culture suggests that humans are never as autonomous and as free of outside interference as it might at first appear. Instead, human mental functioning, even when carried out by an individual acting in isolation, is inherently social, or sociocultural, in that it incorporates socially evolved and socially organized cultural tools.

The two senses in which mental functioning may be said to extend beyond the skin are analytically distinct and hence require the use of different theoretical and methodological categories. However, in concrete human action they are inextricably linked, a point that surfaces in many forms throughout Vygotsky's writings. For example, the relationship between intermental functioning and culture is outlined in his statement that

> the word "social" when applied to our subject has great significance. Above all, in the widest sense of the word, it means that everything that is cultural is social. Culture is the product of social life and human social activity. That is why just by raising the question of the cultural development of behavior we are directly introducing the social plane of development.
>
> (Vygotsky, 1981b, p. 164)

From this statement one can see that Vygotsky understood culture as something that comes into concrete existence in social processes, and he viewed these social processes as providing the foundation for the emergence of individual mental processes. However, he did not assume that it is possible to reduce an account of culture to a set of principles that apply to intermental processes.

Despite the clear role that cultural tools played in Vygotsky's approach, his account of the more general category of culture is by no means well developed. Furthermore, the difficulties that arise in understanding his notion of culture are not primarily difficulties that can be resolved by correcting translations or by making more texts available. The fact is that even though the school of psychology he founded came to be called the cultural-historical school in the Soviet Union in the 1930s, neither Vygotsky nor his followers provided extensive accounts of the notion of culture.[2]

An explication of Vygotsky's notion of culture must be based on an analysis of the role that culture played in his overall theoretical system. In this system Vygotsky gave the idea of mediation analytic priority over the notion of culture (as well as other themes, see Wertsch, 1985b). Indeed, his analysis of culture is part of his attempt to elaborate the notion of mediation. In his view, a criterial feature of human action is that it is mediated by tools ("cultural tools") and signs ("psychological tools"). His primary concern was with the latter (what we are here calling "cultural tools"), and for that reason we shall focus primarily on "semantic mediation."

Basic to this perspective is Vygotsky's insight that the inclusion of psychological, or cultural, tools into human functioning fundamentally transforms this functioning. The incorporation of mediational means does not simply facilitate processes that would otherwise have occurred. Instead,

> by being included in the process of behavior, the psychological tool alters the entire flow and structure of mental functions. It does this by determining the structure of a new instrumental act, just as a technical tool alters the process of a natural adaptation by determining the form of labor operations.
>
> (Vygotsky, 1981c, p. 137)

According to Vygotsky (1981c):

> The following can serve as examples of psychological tools and their complex systems: language; various systems for counting; mnemonic techniques; algebraic symbol systems; works of art; writing; schemes, diagrams, maps, and mechanical drawings; all sorts of conventional signs; and so on.
>
> (p. 137)

In all cases, these are mediational means that are the products of sociocultural evolution and are appropriated by groups or individuals as they carry out mental functioning.

Vygotsky's tendency to approach the notion of culture via his account of mediation reflects the fact that he understood culture in terms of sign systems, an understanding that has been considerably elaborated in more recent Soviet cultural analyses (e.g., Lotman, 1973; Lotman and Uspensky, 1978). Vygotsky's semiotic view of culture probably derives from the work of Saussure, which was very influential among Russian linguists in the 1920s (see Matejka, 1973; Voloshinov, 1973). As was the case for Saussure, Vygotsky was primarily interested in one sign system, language. In his studies he focused on psychological processes that make use of natural language and on systems built on natural language – above all, prose and poetry (Vygotsky, cf. 1971). At the same time, he showed a continuing interest in the use of non-verbal signs. For example, he often drew on examples having to do with the use of sign systems from traditional societies, such as tying knots to organize memory, and he was involved in A.N. Leont'ev's (1931) early research on children's and adults' use of pictures to assist performance in memory tasks (see Vygotsky, 1978).

Vygotsky was quite familiar with the general theories of culture that were being developed in his time by scholars in sociology, anthropology, and other disciplines. However, he chose not to incorporate them into his writings in any major way. Indeed, he firmly rejected the basic assumptions of the British evolutionary anthropologist that laws of individual mental functioning (i.e., laws of association) were adequate for explaining the historical development of culture, human behavior, and human thinking. Instead of assuming that human mental functioning remains basically the same across historical epochs, he argues that

> culture creates special forms of behavior, changes the functioning of mind, constructs new stories in the developing system of human behavior. . . . In the course of historical development, social humans change the ways and means of their behavior, transform their natural premises and functions, elaborate and create new, specifically cultural forms of behavior.
>
> (Vygotsky, 1983a, pp. 29–30)

On the issue of the relation between culture and language, Vygotsky's views are quite close to those of the French sociological school of Durkheim (but see Tulviste, 1991, on their differences), and on the issue of the qualitative changes in thinking that occur in the course of historical development, he had much in common with the views of Levy-Bruhl (1923; also see Tulviste, 1987). Furthermore, he often turned to the work of Thurnwald, but this was mainly to find examples of how signs are used in "primitive" cultures or to find support for his claim that changes in humans during sociocultural history are not attributable to changes in brain structure but to changes in other aspects of higher mental processes. Throughout all of his work, however, there is little evidence of any major interest on Vygotsky's part in the general theories of culture being elaborated by evolutionist, French sociologist, or cultural relativists. To the extent that he drew on them, he did so in connection with his interest in the cultural tools used to mediate intermental and intramental functioning.

A first major fact about Vygotsky's notion of culture, then, is that it was motivated primarily by a concern with semiotic mediation and its role in human mental functioning. A second fact is that he held strongly to a evolutionist account of culture (one that was heavily influenced by figures such as Marx, Spencer [1900], and Tylor [1888]). In line with his mediation-based approach to culture, this fact was manifested in his comments on mediational means. These means were viewed as being capable of supporting more "rudimentary" and advanced levels of intermental and intramental functioning. A correlate of this was Vygotsky's concern with more and less developed cultures, primitive and modern cultures, people, minds, and so forth.

This evolutionist approach to culture, which contrasts with approaches being outlined at the time by Boas (1966) and Sapir (1921), carries with it some intellectual baggage that is not widely accepted today. For example, as van der Veer and Valsiner (in press) have noted, it reflects a kind of ethnocentric perspective, namely Eurocentrism, that makes it difficult to interpret some of the most interesting findings generated by cross-cultural studies.

The issue here is not so much the terminology, which was commonplace in his time (Tulviste, 1991; van der Veer and Valsiner, in press), but rather the fact that Vygotsky clearly regarded some cultures as inferior to others. It must be recognized that he believed people in all cultures to be capable of, and indeed in need of, developing. For instance, he argued that education in Soviet Russia should aim at turning all children into "supermen" or "new [Soviet] men." The notion of a superman was of course borrowed from Nietzsche, but in Vygotsky's view, cultural, rather than biological, factors were capable of creating this new kind of human (Vygotsky, 1930).

In addition to their role in the ideological framework within which Vygotsky was operating, his evolutionist ideas were manifested in concrete ways in his empirical research. This is most apparent in his account of conceptual development. As Wertsch (1985b) noted, the "decontextualization of mediational means" (p. 33) serves as a kind of developmental metric in Vygotsky's analysis of sociocultural history and of ontogenesis. While arguing that all humans share a capacity to use language in a variety of ways, Vygotsky's assumption was that only more advanced groups had taken the evolutionary step necessary to use words in abstract, decontextualized ways. This assumption underlay several studies conducted by Luria (1976) in the 1930s in Soviet Central Asia that compared the performance of various cultural groups.

Vygotsky and Luria tended to interpret the results of these studies in terms of whether subjects were from primitive or advanced societies. They proceeded on the assumption that it is possible to characterize individuals and groups generally in terms of whether they use "scientific" versus "everyday" concepts (Vygotsky, 1987), rely on "abstract" versus "situational" thinking (Luria, 1976), and so forth. This is entirely consistent with Vygotsky's evolutionist approach to culture, according to which it is possible to rank cultures on some kind of scale from lower to higher.

In reanalyzing and extending the studies by Luria, authors such as Scribner and Cole (1981) and Tulviste (1986, 1991) argued that it is more accurate to interpret subjects' performance in these studies in terms of the demands of particular task settings than in terms of the general level of subjects' mental functioning or of a culture. Specifically, they demonstrated that the kinds of differences documented in subjects' performances are primarily attributable to differences in experience with the activity of a particular institutional setting, formal schooling. This is the crux of Scribner and Cole's (1981) "practice account of literacy" (p. 235). According to this account, subjects' exposure to the patterns of speaking and reasoning in formal instructional settings gives rise to a particular set of discourse and cognitive skills. Instead of assuming that these skills represent a general measure by which one can classify individuals and groups, Scribner and Cole emphasized that they are a particular form of literacy practice. The form of activity here contrasts, for example, with literacy practices, such as memorizing religious texts, that were found to be associated with other cognitive skills.

Tulviste (1986, 1991) developed a related set of claims in his analysis of the "heterogeneity" of activities in which humans participate. Drawing on the ideas of Vygotsky and Vygotsky's student A.N. Leont'ev (1959, 1981), Tulviste outlined an analysis of "activity relativity" that parallels the ideas about linguistic relativity proposed by the American linguistic anthropologist Whorf (1956). As with Scribner and Cole (1981), a major point of Tulviste's account is that rather than viewing forms and levels of human mental functioning as some kind of general, immutable property of individuals or groups, the key to understanding their mental processes lies in the activity settings in which they are required to function. Furthermore, given the heterogeneity of such settings, we should anticipate a heterogeneity of forms of situationally specific mental processes.

The roots of this explication and extension of Vygotsky's ideas are to be found in the writing of Vygotsky himself. His claims about the situational specificity of mental functioning began to emerge only in the last years of his career, but they are clearly manifested in the differences between Chapter 5 and 6 of *Thinking and Speech* (Vygotsky, 1987). Both chapters deal with the ontogenetic transition from "complexities" to "genuine," or "scientific", concepts. They differ, however, in what Vygotsky sees as relevant developmental forces. In Chapter 5 (based on research with Shif [1935] and written in the early 1930s), concept development is treated primarily in terms of intramental processes, that is, children's conceptual development as they move from "unorganized heaps" to "complexes" to "concepts."

In Chapter 6 (written in 1934) there is an essential shift in the way Vygotsky approached these issues. He clearly continued to be interested in intramental functioning, but he shifted to approaching concept development from the perspective of how it emerges in particular spheres of socioculturally situated activity. Specifically, he was concerned with how the forms of teacher–student intermental functioning encountered in the institutional setting of formal schooling provide a framework for the development of conceptual thinking.

This shift in Vygotsky's focus is an essential shift for two reasons. First, it was a move towards analyzing conceptual thinking in terms of its intermental precursors. This of course is in line with the argument he had used all along in connection with issues such as inner speech, and it follows naturally from his general genetic law of cultural development. Second, and more important for our purposes, it was a move towards recognizing that an account of the social origins of intramental functioning cannot stop with the intermental plane. Instead, the point is that the forms of mediated intermental functioning involved must themselves be recognized as being socioculturally situated with respect to activity settings and associated mediational means.

This transition in Vygotsky's thinking is important because it indicates a direction he was beginning to consider which, among other things, suggests a way out of the quandary of Eurocentrism. It suggests that instead of viewing particular forms of mental functioning as characterizing individuals or groups in a general way, these forms can be viewed as being characteristic of specific settings. As Tulviste (1991) noted, then, it follows that because individuals and groups are exposed to varieties of activity settings, we can expect them to master a heterogeneous set of mediational means and hence a heterogeneous set of mental processes.

PROBLEMS AND PROSPECTS

There is little doubt that the renewed interest in Vygotsky's writings has had a powerful and positive influence on contemporary studies in developmental psychology. However, this by no means should be taken to indicate that there are no weaknesses in his approach or that revision and extension are not in order. In this final section, we touch on a few of these weaknesses and outline some ways in which they can be addressed.

The first of these concerns Vygotsky's Eurocentrism. In our opinion, Vygotsky made some major contributions to the discussion of historical differences in mental functioning, an issue that has seldom been addressed satisfactorily in psychology since his time. However, we believe that he tended to use the notion of a developmental hierarchy too broadly when trying to interpret differences in mental functioning. The result was a view in which modern European cultural tools and forms of mental functioning were assumed to be generally superior to the tools and functioning of their peoples. In many instances we believe it is more appropriate to view differences in terms of coexisting but qualitatively distinct ways of approaching a problem rather than as more or less advanced general levels of mental functioning.

As we noted in the preceding section, there are indications that Vygotsky was moving away from a view in which forms of mental functioning are viewed as properties that characterize the general level of individuals' and groups' functioning. In its place he seems to have been suggesting that particular forms of mental functioning are associated with particular institutionally situated activities. An implication of this is that it is more appropriate to characterize the mental functioning of individuals in terms of heterogeneity (Tulviste, 1986, 1991) or a "cultural tool kit" (Wertsch, 1991) of mental processes rather than in terms of a single, general level. This has been the focus of research directly motivated by Vygotsky's writings (e.g., Laboratory of Comparative Human Cognition, 1983; Tulviste, 1991; Wertsch, 1991) as well as of research only indirectly motivated by Vygotsky's ideas (Gardner, 1983).

Reformulating mental functioning in terms of heterogeneity and cultural tool kits helps avoid the often ungrounded assumption that various individuals or groups can generally be ranked as inferior or superior to others. However, it still leaves unresolved the issue of what role developmental progression plays in mental processes. There is little doubt in most people's minds that there has been historical progress in at least certain forms of activities and the mental processes (e.g., reasoning) associated with them. For example, if one considers scientific knowledge about electricity, there is little doubt that the past two centuries have witnessed significant progress. It follows that *within specific domains of knowledge* certain activities, cultural tools, and forms of reasoning may be more advanced than others. One of the major challenges of a Vygotskian approach, then, is how to capture such facts about developmental progression without falling prey to ungrounded assumptions about the general superiority or inferiority of individuals or groups.

A second major issue in Vygotsky's approach that will require further attention emerges in his account of the ontogenetic domain. In formulating his notion of this domain, he argued that two lines of development – the cultural line and the natural line – come into contact and transform one another.

> The growth of the normal child into civilization usually involves a fusion with the processes of organic maturation. Both planes of development – the natural and the cultural – coincide and mingle with one another. The two lines interpenetrate one another and essentially form a single line of sociobiological formation of the child's personality.
>
> (Vygotsky, 1960, p. 47)

Although this general formulation continues to make a great deal of sense, the fact is that Vygotsky said very little and was quite unclear about the natural line of development. At some points he spoke of "organic growth and maturation" (Vygotsky and Luria, 1930, p. 4) when dealing with his line of development. This could refer to everything from the emergence of sensory abilities to motor skills to neurological development, but he did not specify which. In other places he seems to have been concerned with developmental changes that are not attributable directly to organic maturation on the one hand but are not cultural by his definition on the other. For example, he sometimes referred to changes in young children's abilities to use primitive tools, such as those outlined by Piaget (1952) in his account of the sensorimotor development having to do with new means to old ends.

Furthermore, Vygotsky said almost nothing about how the "elementary mental functioning" that grows out of the natural line of development might influence the "higher mental functioning" that derives from the mastery of cultural tools. Instead, he focused almost exclusively on ways in which cultural forces transform the natural line of development. In accordance with such a view, the natural line provides a kind of raw material whose fate is to be transformed by cultural forces.

A further problem with Vygotsky's account of the natural and cultural line in ontogenesis is that he viewed these lines as operating quite independently of one another during early phases of life. Since the time he made these claims, investigators such as Piaget (1952), Bower (1974), and Bruner (1976) have made major research advances that bring this assumption into question, and some of Vygotsky's own followers have taken a critical stance toward it. In reviewing Vygotsky's theoretical approach, A.N. Leont'ev and Luria noted that "after all, even in children at the very earliest ages mental processes are being formed under the influence of verbal social interaction with adults who surround them" (1956, p. 7).

Vygotsky's relatively unsophisticated view of the natural line of development can be traced largely to the dearth of theoretical and empirical research on infants available in the early decades of the twentieth century. However, it also reflects another problematic assumption that underlay his work. This is the assumption that the primary force of development comes from outside the individual. Whereas one of the reasons for Vygotsky's renewed influence in contemporary psychology is that his ideas provide a corrective to the tendency to isolate individuals from their sociocultural milieu, passages such as the following might seem to suggest that ontogenesis is solely a function of environment and leaves little room to consider the role of the active individual.

> The environment appears in child development, namely in the development of personality and specific human qualities, in the role of the source of development. Hence the environment here plays the role not of the situation of development, but of its source.
>
> (Vygotsky, 1934, p. 113)

Such passages in Vygotsky's writing seem to suggest that social and cultural processes almost mechanistically determine individual processes. This view minimizes the contributions made by the active individual. Among other things, it raises the question of how individuals are capable of introducing innovation and creativity into the system.

It is clear that Vygotsky has often been read in ways that make this a major problem. However, we believe that several points in his theoretical approach contradict such a reading. For the most part, these points do not emerge in the form of explicit counterstatements; instead, they surface in the assumptions about human action that underlie the entire framework of Vygotsky's approach. As we have stressed throughout this article, the notion of mediation by cultural tools plays a central role in his approach. This applies nowhere more forcefully than in his account of action. The basic form of action that Vygotsky envisioned was *mediated action* (Wertsch, 1991; Zinchenko, 1985). Such action inherently involves cultural tools, and these tools fundamentally shape it. However, this does not mean that such action can be reduced to or mechanistically determined by these tools and hence by the more general sociocultural setting. Instead, such action always involves an inherent tension between the mediational means and the individual or individuals using them in unique, concrete instances.

In such an approach one cannot derive an adequate account of mediated action by focusing either on the mediational means or on the individual or individuals initiating and carrying out action in isolation. Instead, both components are inherently involved in such a way that agency is defined as "individual(s)-operating-with-mediational-means" (Wertsch 1991; Wertsch, Tulviste, and Hagstrom, in press). This account allows for innovation because each concrete use of mediational means by individuals involves some differences from other uses. Indeed, the individuals use may vary quite radically from previous uses. On the other hand, however, mediated action is always constrained in certain fundamental ways by the fact that existing cultural tools are used. As a result, any creativity that occurs involves the transformation of an existing pattern of action, a new use for an old tool.

It is possible to trace the implications of this claim more concretely as they relate to semiotic mediation by considering the ideas of some of Vygotsky's contemporaries. In particular, the ideas of the Soviet philosopher, semiotician, and literary scholar M.M. Bakhtin (1981, 1984, 1986) on "voice" and "dialogicality" complement those of Vygotsky in many important respects. In Bakhtin's view, speaking always involves a concrete individual in a unique setting using language tools provided by others to create utterances. As outlined by Wertsch (1991), such ideas provide concrete ways for exploring the Vygotskian account of agency as individual(s)-operating-with-mediational-means.

Such analyses should not be taken to suggest, however, that the issue of mediated action has been adequately addressed in the Vygotskian literature. Major attention has been given to the issue of action in Soviet theories of activity (e.g., A.N. Leont'ev, 1959, 1975: Rubinshtein, 1957) and there are complementary ideas to be found in the writings of authors such as Bakhtin. In general, however, it is only recently that the notion of mediated action has ben explored in detail in connection with Vygotsky's writings (Wertsch, 1991; Zinchenko, 1985).

The presentation and critique of Vygotsky we have outlined in this chapter should by no means be assumed to be exhaustive. Much more in the way of background and interpretation can be obtained by consulting the publications we listed in the first section. Furthermore, one should not assume that our interpretation and critique of Vygotsky's ideas are uncontested. Although there is widespread agreement that Vygotsky's ideas are extremely rich and have major implications for contemporary research in developmental psychology, there are also major differences among authors over how these ideas should be understood and applied. Perhaps the one thing that is clear to all, however, is that Vygotsky's writings are of more than historical concern. They are capable of providing the basis for major reformulations in developmental psychology today and hence are again proving their merit as classic texts.

NOTES

1 In this article we use the terms *intermental* and *intramental* rather than *interpsychological* and *intrapsychological*, respectively. This follows the translation practices established in Vygotsky (1987) and contrasts with those found in earlier translated texts (Vygotsky, 1978, 1981b). *Intermental* and *intramental* are translations of the Russian terms *interpsikhicheskii* and *intrapsikhicheskii*, respectively.
2 The second part of the term *cultural-historical* has had better luck, notably in Scribner's (1985) analysis of "Vygotsky's Uses of History," from which we borrowed to formulate the title of the present section.

REFERENCES

Bakhtin, M.M. (1981). *The dialogic imagination: Four essays by M.M. Bakhtin* (M. Holquist, ed.; C. Emerson and M. Holquist, trans.). Austin: University of Texas Press.

Bakhtin, M.M. (1984). *Problems of Dostoevsky's poetics* (C. Emerson, ed. and trans.). Minneapolis: University of Minnesota Press.

Bakhtin, M.M. (1986). *Speech genres and other late essays* (C. Emerson and M. Holquist, eds; V.W. McGee, trans.). Austin: University of Texas Press.

Bateson, G. (1972). *Steps to an ecology of mind: A revolutionary approach to man's understanding of himself.* New York: Ballantine.

Belmont, J.M. (1988). Cognitive strategies and strategic learning: The socio-instructional approach. *American Psychologist*, *44*, 142–148.

Berk, L.E. (1986). Relationship of elementary school children's private speech in behavioral accompaniment to task, attention, and task performance. *Developmental Psychology*, *22*, 671–680.

Berk, L.E. and Garvin, R. (1984). Development of private speech among low-income Appalachian children. *Developmental Psychology*, *20*, 271–286.

Bibler, V.S. (1975). *Myshlenie kak tvorchestvo* [Thinking as creation]. Moscow: Izdatel'stvo Politicheskoi Literatury.

Bibler, V.S. (1981). Vnutrennyaya rech' v ponimanii L.S. Vygotsogo (Eshsche raz o predmete psikhologii) [Inner speech in L.S. Vygotsky's conceptualization (once again on the object of psychology)]. In *Nauchnoe tvorchestvo L.S. Vygotskogo i sovremen-naya psikhologiva*. Tezisy dokladov vsesoyuznoi konferentsii, Moskva, 23–25 iyunya 1981 [The scientific work of L.S. Vygotsky and contemporary psychology. Thesis of the presentations of an all-union conference, Moscow, June 23–25, 1981]. Moscow: Akademiya Pedagogicheskikh Nauk SSSR.

Bivens, J.A. and Berk, L.E. (1990). A longitudinal study of the development of elementary school children's private speech. *Merrill–Palmer Quarterly, 36,* 443–463.

Bivens, J.A. and Hagstrom, F. (in press). The representation of private speech in children's literature. In R.M. Diaz and L.E. Berk (eds), *Private speech: From social interaction to self-regulation*. Hillsdale, NJ: Erlbaum.

Boas, F. (1966). Introduction. In F. Boas (ed.), *Handbook of American Indian Languages*. Lincoln: University of Nebraska Press.

Bower, T.G.R. (1974). *Development in infancy*. San Francisco: Freeman.

Brown, A.L. and Ferrara, R. (1985). Diagnosing zones of proximal development. In J.V. Wertsch (ed.), *Culture, communication, and cognition: Vygotskian perspectives* (pp. 273–305). New York: Cambridge University Press.

Brown, A.L. and French, L.A. (1979). The zone of potential development: Implications for intelligence testing in the year 2000. *Intelligence, 3,* 255–277.

Bruner, J.S. (1962). Introduction to L.S. Vygotsky. In *Thought and language*. Cambridge, MA: MIT Press.

Bruner, J.S. (1976). Early social interaction and language acquisition. In H.R. Schaffer (ed.), *Studies in mother-infant interaction* (pp. 56–78). San Diego, CA: Academic Press.

Cole, M. (1985). The zone of proximal development: Where culture and cognition create each other. In J.V. Wertsch (ed.), *Culture, communication, and cognition: Vygotskian perspectives* (pp. 146–161). New York: Cambridge University Press.

Cole, M. and Scribner, S. (1974). *Culture and thought: A psychological introduction*. New York: Wiley.

Diaz, R.M. and Berk, L.E. (eds), (in press) *Private speech: From social interaction to self-regulation*. Hillsdale, NJ: Erlbaum.

Emerson, C. (1983). The outer word and inner speech: Bakhtin, Vygotsky, and the internalization of language. *Critical Inquiry, 10,* 245–264.

Gardner, H. (1983). *Frames of mind: The theory of multiple intelligences*. New York: Basic Books.

Geertz, C. (1973). *The interpretation of cultures*. New York: Basic Books.

Goudena, P. (1987). The social nature of private speech of preschoolers during problem solving. *International Journal of Behavioral Development, 10,* 187–206.

Hutchins, E. (1991). The social organization of distributed cognition. In L.B. Resnick, J.M. Levine and S.D. Teasley (eds), *Perspectives on socially shared cognition* (pp. 283–307). Washington, DC: American Psychological Association.

Janet, P. (1928). *De l'angoisse à l'extase: Etudes sur les croissances et les sentiments. Vol. 2: Les sentiments fondamentaux* [From anguish to ecstasy: Studies on beliefs and emotions. Vol. 2: The basic emotions]. Paris: Librairie Felix Alcan.

Kohlberg, L., Yaeger, J. and Hjertholm, E. (1968). Private speech: Four studies and a review of theories. *Child Development, 39,* 691–736.

Kozulin, A. (1990). *L.S. Vygotsky*. Brighton, England: Harvester Press. Laboratory of Comparative Human Cognition, University of California, San Diego. (1983).

Culture and cognitive development. In W. Kessen (ed.). *Mussen's handbook of child psychology* (4th edn, Vol. 1). New York: Wiley.

Leont'ev, A.A. (1990). *L.S. Vygotsky*. Moscow: Prosveshchenie.

Leont'ev, A.N. (1931). *Razvitie pamyati: Eksperimental'noe issledovanie vysshikh psikhologicheskikh funktsii* [The development of memory: Experimental research on higher psychological functions]. Moscow–Leningrad: Uchpedgiz.

Leont'ev, A.N. (1959). *Problemy razvitiya psikhiki* [Problems in the development of mind]. Moscow: Izdatel'stvo Moskovskogo Universiteta.

Leont'ev, A.N. (1975). *Deyatel'nost' soznanie, lichnost'* [Activity, consciousness, personality]. Leningrad: Izdatel'stvo Politicheskoi Literaturi.

Leont'ev, A.N. (1981). The problem of activity in psychology. In J.V. Wertsch (ed.), *The concept of activity in Soviet psychology* (pp. 37–71). Armonk, NY: Sharpe.

Leont'ev, A.N. and Luria, A.R. (1956). Mirovozrenie psikhologii L.S. Vygotskogo [L.S. Vygotsky's outlook on psychology]. In L.S. Vygotsky, *Izbrannye psikholog-icheskie issledovaniya* [Selected psychological investigations] (pp. 3–22). Moscow: Izdatel'stvo Akademii Pedagogicheskikh Nauk.

Levy-Bruhl, L. (1923). *Primitive mentality* (L.A. Clare, trans.). London: Allen & Unwin.

Lotman, Yu. M. (1973). Different cultures, different codes. *Times Literary Supplement*, October 12, pp. 1213–1215.

Lotman, Yu. M. and Uspensky, B.A. (1978). On the semiotic mechanism of culture. *New Literary History, 9*, 211–232.

Luria, A.R. (1976). *Cognitive development: Its cultural and social foundation*. Cambridge, MA: Harvard University Press.

Luria, A.R. (1981). *Language and cognition* (J.V. Wertsch, ed.). New York: Wiley Intersciences.

Matejka, L. (1973). On the first Russian prolegomena to semiotics. In V.N. Voloshinov, *Marxism and the philosophy of language* (pp. 161–174). New York: Seminar Press.

Middleton, D. (1987). Collective memory and remembering: Some issues and approaches. *Quarterly Newsletter of the Laboratory of Comparative Human Cognition, 9*, 2–5.

Minick, N.J., Forman, E. and Stone, C.A. (in press). *Education and mind: The integration of institutional, social, and developmental processes*. New York: Oxford University Press.

Moll, L.C. (ed.). (1990). *Vygotsky and education: Instructional implications and applications of sociohistorical psychology*. Cambridge, England: Cambridge University Press.

Palincsar, A.S. and Brown, A.L. (1984). Reciprocal teaching of comprehension-fostering and comprehension-monitoring activities. *Cognition and Instruction, 1*, 117–175.

Palincsar, A.S. and Brown, A.L. (1988). Teaching and practicing thinking skills to promote comprehension in the context of group problem solving. *RASE, 9*, 53–59.

Piaget, J. (1952). *The origins of intelligence in children*. New York: International Universities Press.

Potebnya, A.A. (1922). *Mysl' i yazyk* [Thought and language]. Odessa, Ukraine: Gosudarstvennoe Izdatel'stvo Ukrainy.

Puzerei, A.A. (1986). *Kul'turno-istoricheskaya teoriya L.S. Vygotskogo i sovremennaya psikhologiya* [L.S. Vygotsky's cultural-historical theory and contemporary psychology]. Moscow: Izdatel'stvo Moskovskogo Universiteta.

Ratner, C. (1991). *Vygotsky's sociocultural psychology and its contemporary applications*. New York: Plenum.

Resnick, L.A., Levine, R. and Behrend, A. (1991). *Perspectives on socially shared cognition*. Washington, DC: American Psychological Association.

Rogoff, B. (1990). *Apprenticeship in thinking: Cognitive development in social context*. New York: Oxford University Press.

Rogoff, B. and Wertsch, J.V. (eds). (1984). Children's learning in the "zone of proximal development" (no. 23). In *New directions for child development*. San Francisco: Jossey-Bass.

Rubinstein, S.L. (1957). *Bytie i soznanie* [Being and consciousness]. Moscow: Izdatel'stvo Akademii Nauk, SSSR.

Sapir, E (1921). *Language: An introduction to the study of speech*. New York: Harcourt, Brace, and World.

Sarason, S.B. (1981). An asocial psychology and a misdirected clinical psychology. *American Psychologist, 36*, 827–836.

Scribner, S. (1985). Vygotsky's uses of history. In J.V. Wertsch (ed), *Culture, communication, and cognition: Vygotskian perspectives* (pp. 119–145). New York: Cambridge University Press.

Scribner, S. and Cole, M. (1981). *The psychological consequences of literacy*. Cambridge, MA: Harvard University Press.

Shif, Zh. I. (1935). *Razvitie nauchnykh ponyatii u shkol'nika: Issledovanie k voprosu umstvennogo razvitiya shkol'nika pri obuchenii obshchestvovedeniyu* [The development of scientific concepts in the school child: The investigation of intellectual development of the school child in social science instruction]. Moscow–Leningrad: Gosudarstvennoe Uchebno-Pedagogicheskoe Izdatel'stvo.

Spencer, H. (1900). *The principles of sociology*. New York: Appleton.

Taylor, C. (1985). *Human agency and language. Philosophical papers 1*. Cambridge, England: Cambridge University Press.

Tharp, R.G. and Gallimore, R. (1988). *Rousing minds to life*. New York: Cambridge University Press.

Tulviste, P. (1986). Ob istoricheskoi geterogennosti verbal'nogo myshleniya [The historical heterogeneity of verbal thinking]. In Ya. A. Ponomarev (ed), *Myshlenie, obshchenie, praktika: Sbornik nauchnykh trudov* [Thinking, society, practice: A collection of scientific works] (pp. 19–29). Yaroslavl, USSR: Yaroslavskii Gosudarstvennyi Pedagogicheskii Institut im. K.D. Ushinskogo.

Tulviste, P. (1987). L. Levy-Bruhl and problems of the historical development of thought. *Soviet Psychology, 25*, 3–21.

Tulviste, P. (1991). *Cultural-historical development of verbal thinking: A psychological study*. Commack, NY: Nova Science Publishers.

Tylor, E.B. (1888). *Primitive culture: Researches into the development of mythology, philosophy, religion, language, art, and custom*. New York: Holt.

van der Veer, R. and Valsiner, J. (1988). Lev Vygotsky and Pierre Janet: On the origin of the concept of sociogenesis. *Developmental Review, 8*, 52–65.

van der Veer, R. and Valsiner, J. (in press). *A quest for synthesis: Life and work of Lev Vygotsky*. London: Routledge.

Voloshinov, V.N. (1973). *Marxism and the philosophy of language* (L. Matejka and I.R. Titunik, trans.). New York: Seminar Press.

Vygotsky, L.S. (1930). Sotsialisticheskaya peredelka cheloveka [The socialist transformation of man]. *VARNITSO, 9–10*, 36–44.

Vygotsky, L.S. (1934). *Myshlenie i rech': Psikhologicheskie issledovaniya* [Thinking and speech: Psychological investigations]. Moscow and Leningrad: Gosudarstvennoe Sotsial'no-Ekonomicheskoe Izdatel'stvo.

Vygotsky, L.S. (1956). *Izbrannye psikhologicheskie issledovaniya* [Selected psychological investigations]. Moscow: Izdatel'stvo Akademii Pedagogicheskikh Nauk.

Vygotsky, L.S. (1960). *Razvitie vysshykh psikhicheskikh funktsii* [The development of higher mental functions]. Moscow: Izdatel'stvo Akademii Pedagogicheskikh Nauk.

Vygotsky, L.S. (1971). *The psychology of art*. Cambridge, MA: MIT Press.

Vygotsky, L.S. (1978). *Mind in society: The development of higher psychological processes* (M. Cole, V. John-Steiner, S. Scribner and E. Souberman, eds). Cambridge, MA: Harvard University Press.

Vygotsky, L.S. (1979). Consciousness as a problem in the psychology of behavior. *Soviet Psychology*, *17*, 3–35.

Vygotsky, L.S. (1981a). The development of higher forms of attention in childhood. In J.V. Wertsch (ed.), *The concept of activity in Soviet psychology* (pp. 189–240). Armonk, NY: Sharpe.

Vygotsky, L.S. (1981b). The genesis of higher mental functions. In J.V. Wertsch (ed.), *The concept of activity in Soviet psychology* (pp. 144–188). Armonk, NY: Sharpe.

Vygotsky, L.S. (1981c). The instrumental method in psychology. In J.V. Wertsch (ed.), *The concept of activity in Soviet psychology* (pp. 134–143). Armonk, NY: Sharpe.

Vygotsky, L.S. (1982a). *Sobranie sochinenii, Tom pervyi: Voprosy teorii i istorii psikhologii* [Collected works, Vol. 1: Problems in the theory and history of psychology]. Moscow Izdatel'stvo Pedagogika.

Vygotsky, L.S. (1982b). *Sobranie sochinenii, Tom Vtoroi, Problemy obshchei psikhologii* [Collected works, Vol. 2: Problems of general psychology]. Moscow: Izdatel'stvo Pedagogika.

Vygotsky, L.S. (1983a). Sobranie sochinenii, Tom tretii. Problemy razvitiya psikhiki [Collected works, Vol. 3: Problems in the development of mind]. Moscow: Izdatel'stvo Pedagogika.

Vygotsky, L.S. (1983b). *Sobranie sochinenii, Tom pyati: Osnovy defektologii* [Collected works, Vol. 5: Foundations of defectology]). Moscow: Izdatel'stvo Pedagogika.

Vygotsky, L.S. (1984a). *Sobranie sochinenii, Tom chetvertyi: Detskaya psikhilogii* [Collected works, Vol. 4: Child psychology]. Moscow: Izdatel'stvo Pedagogika.

Vygotsky, L.S. (1984b). *Sobranie sochinenii, Tom shestoi: Nauchnoe nasledstvo* [Collected works, Vol. 6: Scientific legacy]. Moscow: Izdatel'stvo Pedagogika.

Vygotsky, L.S. (1986). *Thought and language* (Abridged from 1934: A. Kozulin, trans.). Cambridge, MA: MIT Press.

Vygotsky, L.S. (1987). *Thinking and speech* (N. Minick, ed. and trans.). New York: Plenum (translation of Vygotsky, 1982b).

Vygotsky, L.S. (in press). *Foundations of defectology* (J. Knox, ed. and trans.). New York: Plenum (translation of Vygotsky, 1983b).

Vygotsky, L.S. and Luria, A.R. (1930). *Etyudy po istorii povedeniya: Obez'yana, primitiv, rebenok* [Essays on the history of behavior: Ape, primitive, child]. Moscow and Leningrad: Gosudarstvennoe Izdatel'stvo.

Wertsch, J.V. (1979a). From social interaction to higher psychological processes: A clarification and application of Vygotsky's theory. *Human Development*, *22*, 1–22.

Wertsch, J.V. (1979b). The regulation of human action and the given-new organization of private speech. In G. Zivin (ed.), *The development of self-regulation through private speech* (pp. 79–98). New York: Wiley.

Wertsch, J.V. (1980). The significance of dialogue in Vygotsky's account of social, egocentric, and inner speech. *Contemporary Educational Psychology*, 5, 150–162.

Wertsch, J.V. (ed.). (1985a). *Culture, communication, and cognition: Vygotskian perspectives*. New York: Cambridge University Press.

Wertsch, J.V. (1985b). *Vygotsky and the social formation of mind*. Cambridge, MA: Harvard University Press.

Wertsch, J.V. (1991). *Voices of the mind: A sociocultural approach to mediated action*. Cambridge, MA: Harvard University Press.

Wertsch, J.V., Tulviste, P. and Hagstrom, F. (in press) A sociocultural approach to agency. In E. Forman, N. Minick and C.A. Stone (eds), *Knowledge construction and social practice: Institutional and interpersonal contexts of human development*. New York: Oxford University Press.

Whorf, B.L. (1956). *Language, thought, and reality*. Cambridge, MA: MIT Press.

Yaroshevskii, M. (1989). *Lev Vygotsky*. Moscow: Progress.

Zinchenko, V.P. (1985). Vygotsky's ideas about units of analysis of mind. In J.V. Wertsch (ed.), *Culture, communication, and cognition: Vygotskian perspectives* (pp. 94–118). New York: Cambridge University Press.

3 On the social nature of human cognition: an analysis of the shared intellectual roots of George Herbert Mead and Lev Vygotsky

Jaan Valsiner and René van der Veer

Inner consciousness is socially organized by the importation of the social organization of the outer world.

(Mead, 1912a, p.406)

. . . All higher psychological functions are internalized relationships of the social kind, and constitute the social structure of personality. Their composition, genetic structure, ways of functioning, in one word, all their nature – is social. Even when they have become psychological processes, their nature remains quasi-social. The human being who is alone retains the function of interaction.

(Vygotsky, 1960, p.198)

Contemporary psychology seems to become aware of the 'crisis state' of its theoretical system and methodological knowhow. This awareness shows itself in different areas of psychology in different forms. Perhaps social psychologists have been the most explicit in their calls for re-organization of their discipline (e.g., Gergen, 1982; Gergen and Gergen, 1985; Gergen and Davis, 1985; McClintock, 1985; Thorngate, 1986). However, psychologists in other areas have been wrestling with similar issues (e.g., Brandt, 1973; Cronbach, 1975; Luria and Artemieva, 1970; Meehl, 1986; Toulmin and Leary, 1985; Valsiner, 1987; Vroon, 1986).

There seem to be two focal topics that underlie the crisis of contemporary psychology: the *intentional* nature of thinking and acting by human beings, and the *interdependence of individual consciousness with its social context* (Hales, 1986a, 1986b; Vollmer, 1986). Neither of these issues have been satisfactorily handled by psychology. The intentional nature of human conduct has been overlooked in traditional experimentation (Danziger, 1985; Toulmin, 1986), and personality has been usually conceptualized outside its relationships with its social surroundings (Valsiner and Benigni, 1986). At the same time, a research tradition has emerged at the intersection of cognitive and social psychology – predictably labelled 'social cognition' research.

The multitude of approaches that are united behind the label 'social cognition' is in need of a comprehensive theory. Such a theory has not emerged in recent decades, and thus its seekers often end up turning to theoretical systems of the past that are built around the idea that cognitive processes are a product of social life. Two major theorists who have become recognized as proponents of that view are frequently mentioned in the contemporary literature – the American George Herbert Mead (e.g., Harré, 1981a; Natsoulas, 1985), and the Russian Lev Vygotsky. Similarities between the ideas of Mead and Vygotsky have been pointed out (Bruner, 1962, Glock, 1986, Kozulin, 1986, Luckmann, 1977, Van der Veer, 1985; 1987, Wertsch & Stone, 1985), but the common origins of their ideas have largely remained hidden in the obscurity of the history of social sciences. The aim of this article is to analyze the historical connection between Vygotsky's and Mead's theoretical views. We will also show how contemporary theorizing in social and cognitive psychology could benefit from the core ideas shared by Mead, Vygotsky and their predecessors.

THE SOCIAL NATURE OF HUMAN COGNITION, AND ITS STUDY

The 'sociogenetic view' on human cognition can be described in general terms by a limited set of postulates. In fact, two are sufficient. First, the ontological postulate: *all human cognition is social in its nature*. By that is meant that adult human thinking processes are interdependent with the social discourse of the given society. Second, the developmental postulate: *the social nature of human cognition emerges in the process of internalization of external social experiences by individuals in the process of socialization*. How, then, have these general postulates emerged in the history of the sociogenetic perspective? What particular ideas have been devised by different thinkers to understand sociogenesis of human cognition and personality? And what are the historical ties that link Mead's and Vygotsky's theorizing?

It is historically correct to say that Vygotsky and Mead did not directly influence each other. Mead's name is never referred to in the whole corpus of currently available 6–volume *Collection of Works* by Vygotsky (1982a, 1982b, 1983, 1984a, 1984b, 1984c). Likewise, Vygotsky was neither referred to by Mead in his lectures (which were published after his death as his major books – Mead, 1932, 1934; Miller, 1982), nor in his posthumously published volume of papers (Mead, 1938). The lack of explicit connection between the two thinkers is not surprising, given the geographical distance (Chicago versus Moscow), disciplinary (philosophy versus psychology), linguistic barriers (Vygotsky's work in psychology was published mostly in Russian in Mead's lifetime), and differences between them in the ways in which their academic careers proceeded. In the latter respect, Vygotsky's work in psychology started only in 1924 (see Van der Veer, 1984), at the time when Mead had been teaching at the University of Chicago for almost three decades. Nevertheless, both Vygotsky and Mead developed along parallel lines. Careful reading of their original published work – Mead's articles from the turn of the century, and Vygotsky's various publications in Russian – make it possible to find out about the intellectual roots of their similarity. Both thinkers developed under the influence of other scholars who were associated with the sociogenetic viewpoint. Who, then, were those scholars, and how were Vygotsky and Mead indebted to them?

The common predecessors of Mead and Vygotsky were largely inhabitants of the New World: the American philosophers and psychologists James Mark Baldwin, Josiah Royce, William James, John Dewey, and Charles Cooley. All these scholars travelled to Europe for either purposes of education, or in search for convenient working environments. The European philosophical traditions of Kant, Hegel, Dilthey, Wundt, as well as other ideas widespread in European academic circles of the time, were close to the American originators of the sociogenetic viewpoint. Furthermore, it was the influence of French sociology, aside from German philosophy, that had a guiding influence on the originators of the idea that human cognition originates in the social life of its carriers (see Royce, 1894a; Tarde, 1884). Concerns about society's influences on the individuals, and its connection with clinical phenomenology of hypnotic suggestion, were popular in Europe during the last decades of the nineteenth century. The originators of the sociogenetic perspective were sensitive to these issues – hence their interest in social imitation.

BALDWIN'S VIEWS ON THE SOCIOGENESIS OF PERSONALITY

The life and work of James Mark Baldwin was remarkable in a multiplicity of ways (see Baldwin, 1930; Wozniak, 1982). One of his major scientific contributions was his introduction of a developmental perspective in psychology that took place through his conceptualization of imitation (Baldwin, 1894a). A number of themes from Baldwin's thinking constitute the cornerstone of the sociogenetic perspective.

Development of novelty through imitation

Baldwin's conceptualization of imitation did not emerge on an empty place, but was closely intertwined with the intellectual environment of science and philosophy of his time. The early clinical work of Pierre Janet, especially his *L'Automatisme psychologique* (Janet, 1889), was an important source of case descriptions of the abnormal side of human psyche. Baldwin's own efforts to develop evolutionary thinking further (e.g., Baldwin, 1896, 1897a, 1897b) framed his contributions to developmental psychology, and on the sociogenetic perspective to cognition at large.

For Baldwin, the ontogeny of imitation was embedded in the context of *suggestions* – an explicit link of Baldwin's thinking to that of early Janet, whose definition of suggestion ('a motor reaction brought about by language or perception' – see Baldwin, 1895, p.106–107) he accepted, Suggestion is of three types. First, the *pre-imitative suggestion* covers the whole range of infants' movement responses to external stimulation prior to the rise of imitation. The second type – *imitative suggestion* – was described as

> peculiar only because of its greater or lesser approximation of the "copy" imitated. Further, by reproducing the "copy" this reaction tends to restimulate itself without improvement. The child imitates a word, gets it wrong, and repeats its own mistake over and over.
>
> (Baldwin, 1892a, p.50)

In contrast, in the case of *persistent imitation* (Baldwin's third type), the child is characterized by a persistent effort to generate novel imitations of the 'model'. That takes the form of introducing novel ways of acting that are absent in the 'model', into the imitative process:

> In persistent imitation the first reaction is not repeated. Hence we must suppose the development, in a new centre, of a function of coordination by which the two regions excited respectively by the original suggestion and the reported reaction coalesce in a common more volumnious and intense stimulation of the motor centre. A movement is thus produced which, by reason of its greater mass and diffusion, includes more of the elements of the "copy". This is again reported by eye or ear, giving a "remote" excitement, which is again co-ordinated with the original stimulation and with the after effects of earlier imitations. The result is yet another motor stimulation, or effort, of still greater mass and diffusion, which includes yet more elements of the "copy".
>
> (Baldwin, 1892b, p.287)

Baldwin's description of the process of persistent imitation involves the use of the feedback principle, long before Norbert Wiener, in a process where successive motor imitations of the model are compared with their previous 'traces' in the nervous system. The concept of persistent imitation allows for explanation of how children's voluntary movements emerge. By way of persistent effort, children's muscular activities become more purposive, new combinations of motor elements can be assembled in novel situations, and in conjunction with novel goals (Baldwin, 1892a, p.54).

The sociogenesis of personality

Although worked out in a most detailed way in the context of motor development in infancy, Baldwin's concept of persistent imitation was subsequently taken by him to the domain of human cognition and personality.

The development of cognition can be seen as a process that involves persistent imitation as one of its major mechanisms. Human personality, according to Baldwin, develops with the help of 'personality-suggestion' – by the suggestive models of acting by the 'social others' (Baldwin, 1894b). These models provide the 'input material', from which the developing children learn to assemble their own, novel patterns of personality, still within the frame that is provided for them by the society:

> The growth of human personality has been found to be predominantly a matter of social suggestion. The material from which the child draws is found in the store of accomplished activities, forms, patterns, organizations, etc., which society already possesses. These serve as ready stimulating agencies, loadstones so to speak, to his dawning energies, to draw him ever on in his career of growth into the safe, sound, useful network of personal acquisitions and social relationships which the slow progress of the race has set in permanent form. All this he owes, at any rate in the first instance, to society. His business is to be teachable. He must have the plastic nervous substance known popularly as a brain; he must have organs of sense and sufficient organic equipment to enable him to profit by the methods of personal reaction necessary in the presence of his social fellows; he must be able to imitate, to attend, to invent.
>
> (Baldwin, 1902, p.75)

Baldwin's integration of the two seemingly opposite views on suggestion can be seen in this quote. One of those – following Tarde (1884) – emphasized the suggestive (we might call it 'socially hypnotic') role that the society is seen to play for the development of individual persons. Everything that would end up in individual persons' cognition as a result of their development within their society is therefore a result of the social suggestion process. On the other hand, the personal results of social suggestion were seen by Baldwin to go beyond the suggested models – along the lines of 'persistent imitation' that makes the person active agent in the internalization process.

Active internalization

Baldwin refused to adhere to the inherently passive view of the developing person who cannot escape the social suggestion and who accepts it. He emphasized the active role of the developing child in the development of his self, which in the context of society follows the logic of 'circular reaction' (persistent imitation). In both acting and speaking, the developing child constantly advances and tests 'inventive interpretations' of the world which he has made up through imitation. The social environment with all its 'suggestions' obviously constitutes the testing ground on which these 'innovative interpretations' are acted out. Feedback from the results of such testing leads to the modification of those interpretations, which are organized as a structure of knowledge. Gradually, the process of selection (both inside the child's mind – 'systematic determination', and by the environment) leads to the retainment of some form of structured knowledge. In the course of development of knowledge, the external (social) selection mechanisms become internal (personal):

> selection by a social criterion *becomes personal to the learner through his renewed action.* The selected functions, with their knowledge contents *are added to the organization within, so that the 'systematic determination' of the future is influenced by the assimilation of each new selected element.* Thus the inner attitude which the individual brings to his experience undergoes gradual determination by the continued action of the social environment. He himself comes more and more to reflect the social judgement in his own systematic determination of knowledge; and there arises within himself a criterion of a private sort which is in essential harmony with the social demand, because genetically considered it reflects it. The individual becomes a law unto himself, exercises his private judgement, fights his own battles for truth, shows the virtue of independence and the vice of obstinancy. But he has learned to do it by the selective control of his social environment, *and in his judgement he has just a sense of this social outcome.*
>
> (Baldwin, 1898, pp. 19–20)

The principle of internalization as the developmental-link between personality and its social context is clearly evident in this quote. Later, the same principle was expressed in a modified version by Janet, whom Vygotsky followed quite closely in formulating it in the context of his cultural-historical theory (see Van der Veer and Valsiner, 1987). The linking of actor-bound innovation with the concept of imitation made it possible for Baldwin to grasp the nature of socially guided development of individuals in realistic terms, making him one of the founders of the sociogenetic viewpoint on cognition. He was not alone, though. Baldwin's theorizing was anchored in evolutionary biology. In contrast, his contemporaries were more inclined to address issues of social ethics. In that direction, Baldwin's sociogenetic thinking was complemented by the sociogenetic ideas of Josiah Royce which stemmed from his moral philosophy.

JOSIAH ROYCE'S VERSION OF SOCIAL FORMATION OF PERSONALITY

The American idealist moral philosopher Josiah Royce (1855–1916) is better known in the circles of philosophers (Clendenning, 1985) than among psychologists. His work on psychological issues at Harvard in the 1890s was mostly theoretical, but on rare occasions moved into the realm of experimental psychology (with the help of Hugo Muensterberg – see Royce, 1895a), to the use of parents' everyday observations of their children's imitative tendencies (Royce, 1894a), analysis of clinical cases (Royce, 1895b) and psychohistory (Royce, 1894b). His analysis of social ontogeny borrowed substantially from Baldwin's work on imitation. Royce, however, extended it in a number of ways. His extension of the idea of imitation to the area of psychopathology (Royce, 1895b) was claimed to be original at his time. Royce's narrowing down of Baldwin's concept of imitation (see Royce, 1895a), and his emphasis on the 'internal dialogue' of the Ego and non-Ego makes his contribution to the sociogenetic perspective unique. The philosophical background for Royce's version of the sociogenetic view of human cognition was his adherence to absolute idealism, paired with Hegelian dialectics.

Royce's sociogenetic view of cognition stems directly from his philosophy – as human beings are social in their thinking, then the idea of the existence of objective (experienced) reality cannot be proved independently of the socially influenced minds (Royce, 1894c). His ontological treatment of human consciousness as a full-fledged result of social influences was intricately related to the developmental interest in the question of how the socially determined individual consciousness emerges. Royce's basis for the elaboration of the sociogenetic nature of consciousness involved a conviction that 'a child is taught to be self-conscious just as he is taught everything else, by the social order that brings him up' (Royce, 1895c, p.474). The details of that process, as well as those of the functioning of the self, are of interest.

Affectively flavoured dialogue between 'Ego' and 'non-Ego'

Similarly to Baldwin, Royce was interested in the internalization of external (social) experience that becomes transformed into the internal system of 'Ego' and 'non-Ego', the dialectical relationship of which leads to one or another act that the person performs. The emotions are intertwined with the dialogue of Ego and non-Ego, in fact they 'distribute' the roles of Ego and non-Ego in a particular situation:

> When social situations involving particular contrasts of Ego and non-Ego are remembered or imagined, we become self-conscious in memory, or idea. When emotions, associated by old habit with social situations, dimly or summarily suggest such situations, with their accompanying contrast of Ego and non-Ego, our self-consciousness gets colored accordingly. Finally, when the varied contents of our isolated consciousness involve in any way, as they pass, contrasts which either remind us of the social contrast between Ego and non-Ego, or excite us to acts involving social habits, such as questioning, or internal speech, we become reflectively self-conscious, even when quite alone with our own states.
>
> (Royce, 1895b, p.584)

Royce viewed the internalization process in the context of imitation. However, he considered Baldwin's way of using that term too wide in its universal applicability. In contrast, Royce narrowed down the term 'imitation', using it in ways that are similar to the semiotic emphasis that Vygotsky adhered to much later (see Wertsch, 1983, 1985):

> . . . imitation is definable, from the psychological side, as an act that interprets an uncontrollable perceptive series by setting over it a series of experiences that appear to be similar in content, but to be also in contrast with it by virtue of their controllableness . . . an imitation is an act that tends to the interpretation of what is beyond my power, or is independent of my movements, by contrasting it with what otherwise resembles it, but is in my power, and is a result of my movements.
>
> (Royce, 1895a, p.223)

The context in which Royce wrote about imitation was experimental, and borrowed largely from his empirical research endeavours (see Royce, 1895a).

Social opposition

Aside from the processes of imitation, processes labelled 'social opposition' were posited to be influential in social life and in the internalization of external experience by him. If Royce's view of imitation looks similar to Vygotsky's views decades later, then his emphasis on 'social opposition' parallels Mead's insistence on the role of comparison of 'self' with the 'generalized other' (Mead, 1934). For Royce, 'social opposition' entailed contrasting one's self with others (and opposing them) in behaviour, opinion, and power (Royce, 1903, p.277). The empirical material that gave Royce multiple insights into the process of social opposition came from his study of parental reports about their children's conduct (see Royce, 1894a).

Restless eagerness, and its social guidance

Both imitation and social opposition are made possible by the child's consistent 'restless eagerness' (Royce, 1903, pp. 322–323), which drives the child to approaching the same activity persistently in novel ways. That pertains equally to the 'try, try again' aspect of child's action (to use Baldwin's term here), to the construction of new images in the child's contrast of 'ego' and 'non-ego', and in child's interaction with others where social contrasting and opposition is used. For Royce, the 'restless eagerness' of children constituted the condition that makes it possible for the child to participate in his own development. However, the 'restless eagerness' is socially guided by people surrounding the child. Thus, the teacher of the child '. . . is to assist the child *to become eager to do something that is in itself of a rationally significant tendency*' (Royce, 1903, p.332). This emphasis on socially guided formation of motivation is remarkably similar to the emphasis that Vygotsky put on the children's learning within the 'zone of proximal development' (see Wertsch, 1984). Vygotsky's version of the socially guided learning was, however, wider. It went beyond the formation of children's motivation to the formation of all of their knowledge through learning within the 'zone of proximal development.'

To summarize, Royce constructed a view of human cognition that is explicitly social in its nature, and where the developmental process of internalization of social experience by imitation leads to the construction of the reality in terms that make it possible to doubt the existence of the world (beyond that of subjective construction) at all. In this, Royce's philosophical idealism and his psychological research were united in a rather non-contradictory way. As a by-product, Royce developed an elaborate theoretical system to explain the sociogenetic nature of cognition that served as a source for George Herbert Mead.

FROM BALDWIN AND ROYCE TO MEAD AND VYGOTSKY: DIVERGENCE OF SOCIOGENETIC IDEAS

Royce and Baldwin can be seen to occupy a central position in the history of the sociogenetic view of human cognition and personality. In Figure 3.1, we have tried to capture the major connections between Royce and Baldwin on the one hand, and Mead and Vygotsky on the other.

Royce had direct influence on Mead (see Mead, 1917) and Pierre Janet (1926, 1928, 1929, 1936), who in his turn was one of Vygotsky's major intellectual resources (Van der Veer and Valsiner, 1987). Baldwin's work was closely

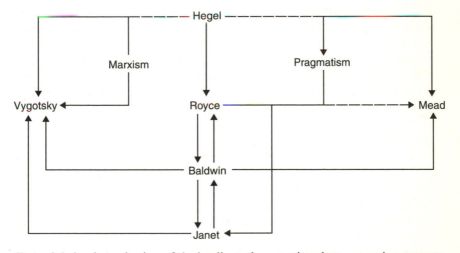

Figure 3.1 A schematic view of the intellectual connections between major representatives of the sociogenetic perspective and their intellectual background.

connected with Royce's – he acknowledged Royce's work, and although their emphases remained different both of them were careful to agree with each other on major similarity of their ideas, while carefully pointing to their dissimilarities. Both Baldwin and Royce (although the former more than the latter) influenced Janet's later work, who was a major source from which Vygotsky started to develop his theoretical system. Mead, likewise, is located in the web of the intellectual influences represented in Figure 3.1, as will be seen below.

GEORGE HERBERT MEAD'S CONTRIBUTIONS TO THE SOCIAL ORIGIN OF PERSONALITY

The fate of Mead's ideas in the social sciences is interesting. His major books (1932, 1934) were never written by him as such, but are only edited versions of his lecture notes. Mead has been labelled a 'social behaviorist', although that label is rather misleading (see Cook, 1977). Mead's earlier publications that appeared in his lifetime exclusively in the form of journal articles or book reviews have been rarely studied in depth (Joas, 1985). However, it is in these less known articles that we can trace the roots of Mead's thinking, and its development.

Development of Mead's views

Mead's earlier work includes short published articles, many of which are reviews of other authors' books (Mead, 1894a, 1894b, 1895a, 1905, 1909). In the context of reviewing others' work, Mead introduced his own ideas in the form of little diversions from the basic reviewing of the target books. These diversions address different local issues of philosophy, ethics, and psychology. Mead's work in the course of the two decades (from the beginning of 1890s to that of 1910s) led him to develop his version of the sociogenetic perspective, which can be seen as basically formulated by him by 1912 (see Mead, 1912b).

The particular ideas by which Mead enriched the sociogenetic perspective were by far more complicated, borrowing in complex ways from the work of his contemporary pragmatists (Dewey), other sociogenetic thinkers (Baldwin and Royce), as well as early contributors to social psychology (Cooley, Wundt, McDougall), Mead explicitly utilized different aspects of the work of his contemporaries: Baldwin's ideas on attention and imitation (Mead, 1894a, 1903, 1909, 1913), Royce's emphasis on the social nature of consciousness (Mead, 1909, 1910c, 1913), Dewey's philosophical (Mead, 1903) and educational views (Mead, 1910a), Cooley's and McDougall's social psychology (Mead, 1910b), Wundt's treatment of myth (Mead, 1906) and language (Mead, 1903, 1904). Mead accepted many of the ideas of his contemporaries, but none of them uncritically. He was critical of the concept of imitation as the ultimate basis of self (cf. Mead, 1909, pp. 405–406), claiming that the probable beginning of human communication was in cooperation rather than imitation. In that latter emphasis, he benefitted from Cooley's work (see Mead, 1930b), while his position is close to Janet's idea that cooperation is originally a social (divided) act.

Internalization of "I" – "Me" relations

It is in connection with Wilhelm Wundt's theory of gestures that Mead arrives at his idea of internalization of the external social experience (Mead, 1904). In his version, like Royce's, the idea of internalization relates closely to the emotional sphere of interpersonal phenomena (Mead, 1910b). However, differently from Vygotsky (and Baldwin before him), the developmental view of sociogenetic nature of the self was of peripheral relevance for Mead. Although he did at times describe the process by which children develop (Mead, 1925, 1934), what was explained by such description was the adult outcome (e.g., how taking of others' social roles in childhood play leads to the development of self – Mead, 1934, pp. 149–160). This is different from the focus of Baldwin and Royce, for whom the sociogenetic process in personality formation was as important as its outcome.

For Mead, however, the major interest in the person's internalization of the experience is the development of the self, which involved the functioning of the 'I' – 'me' system within the social personality. The beginning of the 'I' – 'me' personality structure were evident in Mead's early major work (Mead, 1903, p.104 and p.109). Baldwin's contribution to Mead's thinking about the sociogenesis of the self can be traced rather directly in that period (Mead, 1903, pp.104–105, 1905 pp.403–404). He seems to follow Baldwin and Royce in the ways in which the self-system of 'I' – 'me' is set up.

However, Mead was critical of Baldwin's efforts to 'exhaust subjectivity' through his imitation-based view on human development. In Mead's concept of self, similarity to Royce's thinking is evident. His separation of the 'I' (the agent self) from 'me' (the object self) seems to mirror Royce's ego vs. non-ego separation and relationships. Like Royce's respective distinction, Mead's 'I' – 'me' opposition is dynamic:

> I talk to myself, and I remember what I said and perhaps the emotional content that went with it. The "I" of this moment is present in the "me" of the next moment. There again I cannot turn around quick enough to catch myself. I become a "me" in so far as I remember what I said. The "I" can be given, however, this functional relationship. It is because of the "I" that we say that we are never fully aware of what we are, that we surprise ourselves by our own action. It is as we act that we are aware of ourselves. It is in memory that the "I" is constantly present in experience. We can go back directly a few moments in our experience, and then we are dependent upon memory images for the rest. So that the "I" in memory is there as the spokesman of the self of the second, or minute, or day

ago. As given, it is a "me", but it is a "me" which was the "I" at the earlier time.

(Mead, 1934, p.174)

The 'I' – 'me' relationships in Mead's thought serve as the mechanism by which the person relates to the society: the active 'I' is constantly in the process of taking social roles (thus becoming 'me', i.e., 'the organized set of attitudes of others which one himself assumes' – Mead, 1934, p.175). In that process, the 'I' of the given moment becomes stored in memory. The 'I' aspect of the self introduces personal innovation into the process of social role-taking ('me'), while the latter curbs the excesses of such innovation.

To summarize, Mead was not involved in research on developmental psychology, but contemplated self and society relationships mostly in the context of social (folk) psychology. From that perspective, the interaction between the self and its social roles was naturally more important for Mead, than the complex development of such interaction in ontogeny. Mead was closer in his thinking to Royce than to Baldwin. Vygotsky, being a developmental psychologist, was in his turn indebted to Baldwin, and not to Royce. This difference may perhaps explain how Mead and Vygotsky proceeded along parallel but clearly distinct routes in the advancement of their thinking, starting from the same roots.

LEV VYGOTSKY AND THE SOCIAL ONTOGENY OF COGNITION

Vygotsky's thinking emerged and developed within an intellectual context that was highly international, and interdisciplinary, in its nature. His intellectual ties with Piaget, the school of Gestalt psychology, and N. Ach are evident on the surface of his writings, and therefore clearly detectable. However, Vygotsky's deeper intellectual roots go back to the originators of the sociogenetic school, more specifically to the work of Baldwin. His intellectual connection with Baldwin was in its a greater part mediated by Pierre Janet's writings, which habitually reflected Baldwin's influence (see Van der Veer and Valsiner, 1987). However, somewhat less extensively, in ways that are more scattered around in Vygotsky's diverse writings, his direct indebtedness to Baldwin is evident.

Vygotsky's appreciation of Baldwin's 'self' – 'other' relationships

The most direct link of Vygotsky's thought with that of Baldwin can be seen in conjunction with the question of the nature of personality. Vygotsky emphasized the social nature of personality development along the lines of Baldwin's 'self' – 'other' dialectics:

The decisive moment in the development of child's personality at that stage [of first words] is the child's cognizing of his own 'I'. As is known, the child first calls himself by his name and masters the personal pronoun with some difficulty. J. Baldwin was right to note that the child's concept of 'I' develops out of the concept of others. The concept 'personality' is, thus, a social, reflective concept that is built on the basis of the child's use in relation to oneself, of those means of adaptation that he uses in relation to others. That is why it can be said that personality is the social in ourselves.

(Vygotsky, 1983, p.324)

In other places in Vygotsky's writings, his indebtedness to Baldwin's sociogenetic thinking surfaces along similar lines, at times without explicit reference to his work:

The mechanism of cognition of oneself (self-cognition) and of others is the same. We are conscious of ourselves because we cognize [Russian: *soznaem*] others, and in the same way which we use to cognize others – since we are the same in relation to us that others are in relation to us. We are aware of our self only to the extent that we are *the other* for our self, i.e. in so far as we can perceive our own reflexes again as stimuli.

(Vygotsky, 1982, p.52)

A similar statement about the primacy of the social experience in self-cognition occurs later in the same text by Vygotsky, in an interesting combination with Freud's thinking about personality organization (Vygotsky, 1982, p.96).

Vygotsky and the concept of 'circular reaction'

Vygotsky recognized the relevance of Baldwin's idea of 'circular reaction' (which he called 'chain reaction' – *tsepnaia reaktsia* in Russian), and noted Piaget's use of that concept, while writing about action development in infancy (Vygotsky, 1983, p.320). Aside from Janet, Vygotsky mentioned Baldwin (again in conjunction with Piaget) while describing the social origin of signs (Vygotsky, 1983, p.141). Again, Baldwin is mentioned in connection with the idea that collective disputes of children antedate their development of thinking (Vygotsky, 1983, p.141; 1984a, p.222; 1984b, p.203). Baldwin's developmental emphasis on the unity of evolution and involution was used by Vygotsky from time to time (Vygotsky, 1983, p.178; 1984a, p.21).

Internalization

Vygotsky's indebtedness to the sociogenetic school of thought became transformed into novel forms that went beyond his predecessors. The most relevant aspect of this development was his elaboration of the idea of internalization (see Wertsch & Stone, 1985, for an analysis). The concept of internalization in Vygotsky's thought is closely connected with Janet's similar concept (see Van der Veer & Valsiner, 1987). In the context of children's speech development, Vygotsky related the basic principle of sociogenesis with the actual developmental process:

> If, in the earliest stages of child's development, the egocentric speech does not yet include references to the means by which the [experimental] problem can be solved, then the latter is expressed in the speech directed towards the adult. The child, who could not reach the goal by direct means, turns to the adult and formulates the solution means that he cannot use himself, in words. The big change in the child's development takes place when the speech becomes socialized, when, instead of turning to the experimenter with a plan for a solution, the child turns to himself. In the latter case, the speech that takes part in the problem-solving process, turns from being in the category of the inter-psychical into that of an intra-psychical function. The child, organizing his own behaviour along the lines of the social type, applies to himself that means of behaviour that he previously applied to the other. Consequently, the source of the intellectual activity and control over one's own behaviour in the process of practical problem-solving lies not in the invention of a purely logical act, but in the application to one's self of a social relationship, in the transfer of a social form of behaviour into one's own psychic organization.
>
> (Vygotsky, 1984c, pp. 33–34)

Our treatment of Vygotsky's theoretical thinking necessarily remains fragmentary in the present context (see Van der Veer and Valsiner, 1987). However, we have demonstrated the particular point we set out to make: Vygotsky's thinking emerged along a direct historical line on the basis of his predecessors, Baldwin and Janet. Given Vygotsky's concentration on issues of ontogeny, he extended the basic ideas of the sociogenetic school of thought further in the directions that made it more closely applicable in child psychology. Mead, in contrast, was not working in that domain of psychology. The domain-specificities of the work of Vygotsky and Mead may be behind their differences in particular ways of developing the sociogenetic perspective in the social sciences in this century.

CONCLUSIONS: IMPLICATIONS FROM THE HISTORY OF THE SOCIOGENETIC PERSPECTIVE FOR CONTEMPORARY RESEARCH

Our historical overview of the sociogenetic perspective on personality reveals a fundamental issue that has not been studied directly in contemporary psychology. All the four sociogenetic theorists whose work we overviewed in this article emphasized the *dynamic*, dialectical nature of the emergence and functioning of the self in its social context. Furthermore, ontogenetically the self has been conceptualized as a result of the *process* of internalization. However, neither the dynamic functioning of the self, nor the process of internalization, are currently studied empirically in ways that would preserve the dynamic or developmental nature of the processes under study. There are rather simple reasons for the lack of such empirical endeavours – psychologists' uncritical acceptance of traditional methodology (see Hales, 1986a, p.268) has eliminated the dynamic side of the phenomena from research (Valsiner, 1987).

The lack of empirical methodology for the study of dynamics of the functioning of the self, and of its development, could be remedied by constructing novel ways of doing research. If the constructionist perspective on human psychology is used as a starting point for one's scientific endeavours (Gergen, 1982; Gergen and Gergen, 1984; Gergen and Davis, 1985, Harré, 1981a), then a step-by-step (time dependent) analysis of the ways in which subjects construct their selves, relationships, world views, prejudices, etc., can become of high priority for investigators. The new methodology must be adequate both to the nature of the phenomena and to the theoretical perspective of the investigators. For example, if Mead's theoretical perspective of "I" – "Me" relationships is taken seriously, the empirical method should specify the specifics of the "I" and "Me" *at every time interval* in the course of ongoing observations of the functioning of the Self. Subsequently, the transformation of the "I" – "Me" relationship, and the emergence of new aspects of the Self, can be traced from the empirical record that preserves the temporal structure of the phenomena under study.

The empirical study of internalization is likewise feasible, if the theoretical heritage of the sociogenetic theorists is advanced further in the more empirical direction. We suggest that the process of internalization can be studied through longitudinal investigation of the process of interaction between the person and others, in conjunction with the description of the unfolding of the person's 'internal dialogue'. In this respect, the empirical methodology involves parallel analyses of two 'dialogues' unfolding over time, one external (the interactive process), and the other internal (the intra-active process). In Mead's terms, the dynamics of the "I" and "Me" can be traced through prospective analysis of the interaction process. In parallel, the internal dialogues of the interactants ("Ego" – "Non-ego" relationships a la Royce) can be traced through interactants' self-analysis (the intra-active process). Both processes – the interactive and the intra-active – are coordinated with each other. However, that coordination does not take the form of 'mirror-image' reflection of interactive processes in the intra-active sphere of the self. Instead, the intra-active processes may 'persistently imitate' (instead of being cases of 'imitative suggestions' – to use Baldwin's terms) the interactive ones. In other terms – the internalized cognition goes beyond the external social experiences of the person in some ways. Hence, psychologists' efforts to find 'behavior – cognition' consistency are misguided on principal grounds. Active selves construct their understanding of the world not in ways that slavishly remain faithful to those experiences, but rather in ways that constantly go beyond them. Human beings consistently create novelty both by their actions and by their thinking, using their social environment as a resource for both. The originators of the sociogenetic perspective, as well as their heirs (Mead and Vygotsky) understood that very well. They, however, did not proceed very far in the empirical study of the self, as viewed from that perspective. Nevertheless, careful analysis of their thinking, and efforts to go beyond that and try to solve the fundamental problem that psychology has in constructing *adequate* empirical research techniques, is a challenging alley for innovation in our discipline.

ACKNOWLEDGEMENTS

We are grateful to all three editorial reviewers of the earlier version of this paper for encouragement to connect our historical analysis with the needs of psychology of our present time.

REFERENCES

Bakhurst, D.J. (1986). Thought, speech and the genesis of meaning: On the 50th anniversary of Vygotsky's *Myshenie i rech*. *Studies in Soviet Thought*, **31**, 103–129.

Baldwin, J.M. (1892a). Suggestion and will. *International Congress of Experimental Psychology. Second Session* (pp. 49–54). London: Williams & Norgate.

Baldwin, J.M. (1892b). Origin of volition in childhood. *Science*, **20**, No. 511, 286–287.

Baldwin, J.M. (1894a). Imitation: a chapter in the natural history of consciousness. *Mind, 3 (new series)*, 26–55.

Baldwin, J.M. (1894b). Personality-suggestion. *Psychological Review*, **1**, 274–279.

Baldwin, J.M. (1895). *Mental development in the child and the race*. New York: Macmillan.

Baldwin, J.M. (1896). Consciousness and evolution. *Psychological Review*, **3**, 300–309.

Baldwin, J.M. (1897a). Organic selection. *Nature*, **55** (No. 1433), 558.

Baldwin, J.M. (1897b). Determinate evolution. *Psychological Review*, **4**, 393–401.

Baldwin, J.M. (1898). On selective thinking. *Psychological Review*, **5**, 1–24.

Baldwin, J.M. (1902). *Social and ethical interpretations in mental development*, New York: Macmillan.

Baldwin, J.M. (1930). James Mark Baldwin. In C. Murchison (Ed.), *A history of psychology in autobiography* (pp. 1–30). New York: Russell & Russell.

Brandt, L.W. (1973). The physics of the physicist and the physics of the psychologist. *International Journal of Psychology*, **8**, 61–72.

Bruner, J. (1962). Introduction. In L. Vygotsky, *Thought and language* (pp.v–x). Cambridge, Mass: MIT Press.

Clendenning, J. (1985). *The life and thought of Josiah Royce*. Madison: University of Wisconsin Press.

Cook, G.A. (1977). G.H. Mead's social behaviourism. *Journal of the History of the Behavioral Sciences*, **13**, 307–316.

Cronbach, L.J. (1975). Beyond the two disciplines of scientific psychology. *American Psychologist*, **30**, 2, 116–127.

Danziger, K. (1985). The methodological imperative in psychology. *Philosophy of Social Sciences*, **15**, 1–13.

Gergen, K.J. (1982). *Toward transformation of social knowledge*. New York: Springer.

Gergen, K.J., and Gergen, M.M. (Eds.). (1984). *Historical social psychology*. Hillsdale, N.J.: Erlbaum.

Gergen, K.J., and Davis, K.E. (Eds.). (1985). *The social construction of the person*. New York: Springer.

Glock, H.-J. (1986). Vygotsky and Mead on the self, meaning and internalisation. *Studies in Soviet Thought*, **31**, 131–148.

Hales, S. (1986a). The inadvertent rediscovery of self in social psychology. *Journal for the Theory of Social Behaviour*, **15**, 3, 237–282.

Hales, S. (1986b). Rethinking the business of psychology. *Journal for the Theory of Social Behaviour*, **16**, 1, 57–76.

Harré, R. (1981a). The positivst-empiricist approach and its alternative. In P. Reason and J. Rowan (Eds.), *Human inquiry* (pp.3–17). Chichester: Wiley.

Harré, R. (1981b). Rituals, rhetoric and social cognition. In J.P. Forgas (Ed.), *Social cognition* (pp.211–224). London: Academic Press.

Janet, P. (1889). *L'Automatisme psychologique*, Paris: Alcan.

Janet, P. (1926). *De l'angoisse a l'extase*. Vol. 1. Paris: Felix Alcan.

Janet, P. (1928). *De l'angoisse a l'extase*. Vol. 2. Paris: Felix Alcan.

Janet, P. (1929). *L'evolution psychologique de la personnalite*. Paris: A. Chahine.

Janet, P. (1936). *L'intelligence avant le langage*. Paris: Flammarion.

Joas, H. (1985). *G.H. Mead: A contemporary re-examination of his thought*. Cambridge, Mass: MIT Press.

Kozulin, A. (1986). Vygotsky in context. In L.S. Vygotsky, *Thought and language*. Revised ed (pp. xi–lvi). Cambridge, Mass: MIT Press.

Luckmann, T.C. (1977). Einfuehrung. L.S. Wygotski, *Denken und Sprechen*. Frankfurt/Main: Fischer.

Luria, A.R., and Artemieva, E. Iu. (1970). On two ways of granting the validity of the psychological investigation. *Voprosy psikhologii*, No. 3., 105–112.

McClintock, C.G. (1985). The metatheoretical bases of social psychological theory. *Behavioral Science*, **30**, 155–173.

Mead, G.H. (1894a). Herr Lasswitz on energy and epistemology. *Psychological Review*, **1**, 172–175.

Mead, G.H. (1894b). *Die moderne Energetik in ihrer Bedeutung fur die Erkenntnisskritik* Kurt Lasswitz. *Psychological Review*, **1**, 210–213.

Mead, G.H. (1895a). *An introduction to comparative psychology* C.L. Morgan. *Psychological Review*, **2**, 399–402.

Mead, G.H. (1903). The definition of the psychical. *Decennial Publications of the University of Chicago*, Vol. 3 (first series), 77–112.

Mead, G.H. (1904). The relations of psychology and philology. *Psychological Bulletin*, **1**, 375–391.

Mead, G.H. (1905). *Du Role de l'Individu dans le Determinisme Social, Le Probleme du*

Determinisme Social, Determinisme biologigue et Determinisme social. D. Draghis-cesco. *Psychological Bulletin*, **2**, 399–405.

Mead, G.H. (1906). The imagination in Wundt's treatment of myth and religion. *Psychological Bulletin*, **3**, 393–399.

Mead, G.H. (1909). Social psychology as counterpart of physiological psychology, *Psychological Bulletin*, **6**, 401–408.

Mead, G.H. (1910a). The psychology of social consciousness implied in instruction. *Science*, **31**, No. 801, 688–693.

Mead, G.H. (1910b). What social objects must psychology presuppose? *Journal of Psychology*, **7**, 174–180.

Mead, G.H. (1910c). Social consciousness and the consciousness of meaning. *Psychological Bulletin*, **7**, 397–405.

Mead, G.H. (1912). The mechanism of social consciousness. *Journal of Philosophy*, **9**, 401–406.

Mead, G.H. (1913). The social self. *Journal of Philosophy*, **10**, 374–380.

Mead, G.H. (1917). Josiah Royce – a personal impression. *International Journal of Ethics*, **27**, 168–170.

Mead, G.H. (1925). The genesis of the self and social control. *International Journal of Ethics*, **35**, 251–277.

Mead, G.H. (1930a). The philosophies of Royce, James, and Dewey in their American setting. *International Journal of Ethics*, **40**, 211–231.

Mead, G.H. (1930b). Cooley's contribution to American social thought. *American Journal of Psychology*, **35**, 693–706.

Mead, G.H. (1932). *The philosophy of the present*. Chicago and London: Open Court.

Mead, G.H. (1934). *Mind, self and society*. Chicago: University of Chicago Press.

Mead, G.H. (1938). *The philosophy of the act*. Chicago: University of Chicago Press.

Meehl, P.E. (1986). What social scientists do not understand. In D.W. Fiske and R.A. Shweder (Eds), *Metatheory in social science* (pp.315–338). Chicago: University of Chicago Press.

Miller, D.L. (Ed.) (1982). *The individual and the social self: Unpublished work of George Herbert Mead*. Chicago: University of Chicago Press.

Natsoulas, T. (1985). George Herbert Mead's conception of consciousness. *Journal for the Theory of Social Behaviour*, **15**, 1, 60–75.

Royce, J. (1894a). The imitative functions, and their place in human nature. *Century Magazine*, **26** (new series), 137–145.

Royce, J. (1894b). The case of John Bunyan. *Psychological Review*, **1**, 22–33 (I), 134–151 (II), and 230–240 (III).

Royce, J. (1894c). The external world and the social consciousness. *Philosophical Review*, **3**, 513–545.

Royce, J. (1895a). Preliminary report on imitation. *Psychological Review*, **2**, 217–235.

Royce, J. (1895b). Some observations on the anomalies of self-consciousness. *Psychological Review*, **2**, 433–457 (I) and 574–584 (II).

Royce, J. (1895c). Self-consciousness, social consciousness and nature. *Philosophical Review*, **4**, 465–485 (I) and 577–602 (II).

Royce, J. (1903). *Outlines of psychology*. New York: Macmillan.

Sampson, E.E. (1986). What has been inadvertently rediscovered? *Journal for the Theory of Social Behaviour*, **16**, 1, 33–39.

Tarde, G. (1884). Qu'est ce qu'une societe? *Revue Philosophique*, **18**, 489–510.

Thorngate, W. (1986). The production, detection, and explanation of behavioral patterns. In J. Valsiner (Ed.), *The individual subject and scientific psychology* (pp.71–93). New York: Plenum.

Toulmin, S. (1986). The ambiguities of self-understanding. *Journal for the Theory of Social Behaviour*, **16**, 1, 41–55.

Toulmin, S. and Leary, D.E. (1985). The cult of empiricism in psychology, and beyond. In S. Koch and D.E. Leary (Eds.) *A century of psychology as science* (pp.594–616). New York: McGraw-Hill.

Valsiner, J. (1987). *Culture and the development of children's action*. Chichester: Wiley.

Valsiner, J., and Benigni, L. (1986). Naturalistic research and ecological thinking in the study of child development. *Developmental Review*, **6**, 203–223.

Van der Veer, R. (1984). *Cultuur en cognitie*. Groningen: Wolters-Noordhoff (in Dutch).

Van der Veer, R. (1985). Similarities between the theories of G.H. Mead and L.S. Vygotsky: An explanation? In S. Bem, H. Rappard, and W. van Hoorn (Eds.), *Studies in the history of psychology and the social sciences*, Vol. 3. (pp.1–11). Leiden: Psychologisch Instituut.

Van der Veer, R. (1987). The relation between Vygotsky and Mead reconsidered. A note on Glock. *Studies in Soviet Thought*, **34**, 91–93.

Van der Veer, R., and Valsiner, J. (1987). On the origin of Vygotsky's concept of sociogenesis. *Developmental Review* (in press).

Vollmer, F. (1986). Intentional explanation and its place in psychology. *Journal for the Theory of Social Behaviour*, **16**, 3, 285–298.

Vroon, P.A. (1986). Man-machine analogs and theoretical mainstreams in psychology. In M. Hyland, H. van Rappard, and A.W. Staats (Eds), *Advances in theoretical psychology* (pp. 1–22). Amsterdam: North-Holland.

Vygotsky, L.S. (1960). *Razvitie vysshikh psikhicheskikh funktsii* (Develoment of higher psychical functions). Moscow: Izd. Akademii Pedagogicheskikh Nauk (in Russian).

Vygotsky, L.S. (1982a). *Sobranie sochinenii*. Vol. 1. *Voprosy teorii i istorii psikhologii*. Moscow: Pedagogika (in Russian).

Vygotsky, L.S. (1982b). *Sobranie sochinenii*. Vol. 2. *Problemy obschei psikhologii*. Moscow: Pedagogika (in Russian).

Vygotsky, L.S. (1983). *Sobranie sochinenii*. Vol. 3. *Problemy razvitia psikhiki*. Moscow: Pedagogika (in Russian).

Vygotsky, L.S. (1984a). *Sobranie sochinenii*. Vol. 4. *Detskaia psikhologia*. Moscow: Pedagogika (in Russian).

Vygotsky, L.S. (1984b). *Sobranie sochinenii*. Vol. 5. *Osnovy defeklologii*. Moscow: Pedagogika (in Russian).

Vygotsky, L.S. (1984c). *Sobranie sochinenii*. Vol. 6. *Nauchnoe nasledie*. Moscow: Pedagogika (in Russian).

Vygotsky, L.S. (1986). *Thought and language* (revised edition). Cambridge, Mass.: MIT Press.

Wertsch, J. (1983). The role of semiosis in L.S. Vygotsky's theory of human cognition. In B. Bain (Ed.), *The sociogenesis of language and human conduct* (pp.17–31). New York: Plenum.

Wertsch, J. (1984). The zone of proximal development: some conceptual issues. *New Directions for Child Development*. **23**, 7–18.

Wertsch, J. (1985). *Vygotsky and the social formation of mind*. Cambridge, Mass.: Harvard University Press.

Wertsch, J., and Stone, C.A. (1985). The concept of internalization in Vygotsky's account of the genesis of higher mental functions. In J. Wertsch (Ed.), *Culture, communication, and cognition: Vygotskian perspectives* (pp.162–197). Cambridge: Cambridge University Press.

Wozniak, R. (1982). Metaphysics and science, reason and reality: The intellectual origins of genetic epistemology. In J.M. Broughton and D.J. Freeman-Moir (Eds.), *The cognitive-developmental psychology of James Mark Baldwin* (pp.13–45). Norwood, N.J.: Ablex.

4   The concept of activity in Soviet psychology

Vygotsky, his disciples and critics

Alex Kozulin

The concept of activity plays as important and ambiguous a role in Soviet psychology as did the concept of behavior in American studies circa 1920 to 1950 and the concept of consciousness in European psychology of the late nineteenth century. Activity has been the chief category of psychological research in contemporary Soviet psychology since the beginning; and exactly for that reason, the concept of activity has been extremely difficult for Soviet psychologists to define clearly. Since the time of its inception in the 1920s, this category has undergone a metamorphosis and has been the subject of so many disputes that it cannot be adequately comprehended out of the context of its history.

The goal of this chapter is to provide a historical–theoretical analysis of the evolution of the concept of activity in Soviet psychology. The origin of this concept can be found in the early writings of Lev Vygotsky (1896–1934), who suggested that socially meaningful activity (*Tätigkeit*) may serve as an explanatory principle in regard to, and be considered as a generator of, human consciousness. Further, I review the process of incorporating the concept of activity into Vygotsky's cultural–historical theory of higher mental functions and discuss its relevance for Vygotsky's studies in the development of language and concept formation. The most dramatic event in the history of the concept of activity occurred in the mid-1930s when a group of Vygotsky's disciples came up with a "revisionist" version of activity theory that put practical (material) actions at the forefront while simultaneously playing down the role of signs as mediators of human activity. This revisionist position was elaborated theoretically by Alexei Leontiev, who subsequently gained the status of official interpreter of Vygotsky's ideas. Thus the myth of succession between Vygotsky's and Leontiev's schools of psychology was born. Only in the late 1970s has this myth been subjected to a critical scrutiny, and Vygotsky's genuine views have attracted a renewed interest.

For a long period of time, the concept of activity has remained a local affair of Soviet psychology. In his classical book. *The New Man in Soviet Psychology*, Raymond Bauer (1952) neglected entirely the concept of activity. More recent studies, such as those of Ted Payne (1968), Levy Rahmani (1973), and Luciano Mecacci (1979), mentioned this problem but hardly made it a center of their work. The major breakthrough occurred when a volume of translations, *The Concept of Activity in Soviet Psychology*, edited by James Wertsch, appeared in 1981. Since then, there has been a growing interest among American psychologists in the problem of activity. To comprehend this problem properly, one should, however, be cognizant of its complex history and the current re-evaluation of it by the younger generation of Soviet psychologists.

ACTIVITY AS AN EXPLANATORY PRINCIPLE

The problem of activity emerges in Vygotsky's studies for the first time in his article, "Consciousness as a Problem of Psychology of Behavior" (Vygotsky, 1979). The task Vygotsky set for himself in this article was to restore the legitimacy of the concept of consciousness – which was aggressively challenged by behaviorists and adherents of Pavlovian and Bekhterevian reflexology – but not at the expense of the return of introspective mentalistic psychology. Vygotsky's major objection to the mentalistic tradition was that it confined itself to a vicious cycle of theorizing in which states of consciousness are explained through the concept of consciousness. Reflexology, in its turn, suggested an equally lopsided solution by banning consciousness altogether and attempting to reduce all psychological phenomena to reflex-like behavior.

In his discussion of the concept of consciousness, Vygotsky took a "methodological" – that is, a metapsychological, epistemologically orientated – position.[1] This position helped him discover a number of activities capable of serving as *generators* of consciousness. Vygotsky distinguished such specifically human aspects of individual experience as its historicity (indebtedness to the experience of previous generations), its social character (shared experiences of others), and its "double nature," by which Vygotsky meant the existence of mental images and schemas prior to actual action (Vygotsky, 1979, pp.13–14).

In the context of the future development of Vygotsky's ideas, one thesis of Vygotsky's article seems particularly important: building consciousness from outside through the relations with others. Vygotsky explained that

> the mechanism of social behavior and the mechanism of consciousness are the same. . . . We are aware of ourselves, for we are aware of others, and in the same way as we know others; and this is as it is because we in relation to ourselves are in the same [position] as others are to us.
>
> (Vygotsky, 1979, pp. 29–30)

The same thought rendered in terms less offensive to reflexologists reads, "I am aware of myself only to the extent that I am another for myself, i.e., only to the extent that I can perceive anew my own responses as new stimuli" (Vygotsky, 1979, p. 30).

There is a striking similarity between the just-mentioned statement of Vygotsky and the concept of significant symbol developed by George H. Mead:

> As we shall see, the same procedure which is responsible for the genesis and existence of mind or consciousness – namely, the taking of the attitude of the other toward one's self, or toward one's own behavior – also necessarily involves the genesis and existence at the same time of significant symbols, or significant gestures.
>
> (Mead, 1974, pp. 47–48)

It seems that Mead's revision of behaviorism and Vygotsky's struggle for consciousness had much in common: both authors pointed to the same phenomena and followed similar methodological paths.[2]

In the article, Vygotsky suggested a number of hypotheses concerning the generation of consciousness "from outside." Only a few of them survived in his later works. His major achievement, however – as recent interpretations have suggested (Davydov and Radzikhovskii, 1985; Yudin, 1976) – was in making a philosophical demarcation between the "subject of study" and the "explanatory principle." If consciousness is to become a *subject* of psychological study, some other layer of reality should be referred to in a course of explanation. Socially laden activity, then, may serve as such a layer and as an explanatory principle. Vygotsky thus broke the vicious circle of explanation of consciousness through consciousness, and of behavior through behavior, and established premises for the unified theory of behavior and mind.

THEORETICAL BACKGROUND

To understand the theoretical background against which activity emerged as an explanatory principle, we must look into the intricate circumstances that characterized Soviet psychology in the 1920s. To begin with, the surface appearance of Soviet psychology scholarship of that period is quite misleading. Soviet psychology seemed to be almost totally reflexological and to be permeated with random, and often quite meaningless quotations from Marx, Engels, and Lenin. This "surface structure" of Soviet psychology was, however, rather thin. Two deeper trends turned out in the long run to be much more powerful and creative.

One of them is the dependence of Russian psychology, both pre- and post-Revolutionary, on the European psychological tradition. Even though appearing to be completely captured by the slogans of reflexological behaviorism, Soviet psychology never experienced the "Age of Behaviorism" of the American type. Even when the Pavlovian doctrine became dominant in the late 1940s, this came through physiologization rather than behaviorization of psychology. Soviet psychologists of the 1920s were quite familiar with the major figures of European psychology. Wilhelm Wundt was known not only as an "introspectionist" but also as the author of *Völkerpsychologie* (Wundt, 1900–1920). The French psychological school of Pierre Janet, which emphasized the problem of activity and pointed out the role of "others" in the creation of the individual psyche, deeply influenced Vygotsky and his group. The holistic approach of the Gestaltists and Kurt Lewin found a receptive audience in Russia. As a result, Vygotsky had a solid psychological backing in his attempt to consider human activity as irreducible to the stimulus–response (S–R) schema elaborated in animal experiments. Vygotsky emphasized that the task of psychology is to investigate those mechanisms that distinguish human conduct from animal behavior rather than to look for those that might be similar.

The second trend that was instrumental in the development of the concept of activity in psychology was Marxist philosophy, whose position is essentially activistic. In order to appreciate the influence of Marxism, one must be able, however, to distinguish between the hodgepodge of Marxist quotations that became a trademark of the so-called "Marxist psychology" of Konstantin Kornilov and others and the use of Marxist and Hegelian philosophy by Vygotsky and his students. First of all, Vygotsky decisively rejected Marxism as a dogmatic ideological yardstick and ridiculed the attempts to create a "new" psychology by concocting a number of "dialectical" and "materialistic" passages. His critique was harsh and his verdict rigorous: Vygotsky considered that his opponents sought Marxist support "in the wrong places," that they assimilated "the wrong material," and that they used the texts available "in a wrong way" (Vygotsky, 1982a, p. 397).

What Vygotsky himself sought and found in Marx and Hegel was a social theory of human activity (Tätigkeit) set in opposition to naturalism and the passive receptivity of the empiricist tradition. From Hegel, Vygotsky also took a thoroughly historical view of the stages of development and the forms of realization of human consciousness. Marx attracted Vygotsky by his concept of human praxis, that is, concrete historical activity that is a generator behind the phenomena of consciousness (Vygotsky, 1978a, p. 54).

This historically concrete human praxis that accounts for the specificity – that is, the social and historical character – of human survival and development became a prototype for the concept of activity as an explanatory principle.

According to Vygotsky, human behavior and mind must be considered in terms of purposive and culturally meaningful actions rather than as biological, adaptive reactions. Objects of human experience – and therefore objects in psychological experiments – are socially and culturally meaningful things and not just abstract stimuli. Activity then takes the place of the dash in the formula S–R, turning it into a formula object ↔ activity ↔ subject, where both object and subject are historically and culturally specific.

CULTURAL–HISTORICAL THEORY OF HIGHER MENTAL FUNCTIONS

According to Vygotsky, the actualization of human activity requires such intermediaries as *psychological tools* and the means of interpersonal communication. The concept of psychological tool arose first by loose analogy with the material tool that serves as a mediator between human hand and the object of action. Like material tools, psychological tools are artificial formations. By their nature, both are social. Whereas material tools are aimed at the control of the processes in nature, psychological tools master the natural behavioral and cognitive processes of the individual. Among the best known psychological tools, Vygotsky named sign and language systems, mnemonic techniques, and decision-making procedures that use such "tools," for example, dice.

Unlike material tools, which serve as conductors of human influences on the objects of activity and which are, therefore, externally oriented psychological tools are internally oriented, transforming natural human abilities and skills into higher mental functions. For example, if an elementary, natural memorizing effort connects event A with event B through the natural ability of the human brain, then in mnemonics this relation is replaced by two others; A to X and X to B, where X is an artificial psychological tool, such as a knot in a handkerchief, a written note, or a mnemonic scheme (Vygotsky, 1981, p. 138).

Vygotsky thus made a principal distinction between "lower," natural mental functions such as elementary perception, memory, attention, and will, and the "higher" or cultural functions, which are specifically human and which appear gradually in a course of radical transformation of the lower functions. The lower functions do not disappear in a mature psyche but are structured and organized according to specifically human social goals and means of conduct. Vygotsky used the Hegelian term *superseded (aufgehoben)* to designate the transformation of natural functions into cultural ones.

If one decomposes a higher mental function into its constituent parts, one finds nothing but the natural, lower skills. This fact, argued Vygotsky, secures the scientific status of his method, which needs no speculative metaphysical categories to approach the higher forms of behavior. All the building blocks of higher behavior seem absolutely materialistic and can be apprehended by ordinary empirical methods. The latter assumption does not imply, however, that the higher function can be reduced to lower ones. Decomposition shows us only the material the higher functions are built with but says nothing about their construction.

The constructive principle of the higher functions lies outside the individual – in psychological tools and interpersonal relations. Referring to psychological tools as instruments for the construction of higher functions, Vygotsky wrote, "In the instrumental act, humans master themselves from the outside – through psychological tools" (Vygotsky, 1981, p. 141). Concerning the structural role of interpersonal relations, Vygotsky followed Janet's thesis that interpersonal processes are transformed into intrapersonal ones. "Every function in the child's cultural development appears twice: First, on the social level, and later, on the individual level; first, *between* people (*interpsychological*), and then inside the child (*intrapsychological*)" (Vygotsky, 1978a, p. 57).

Vygotsky devoted the years from 1926 through 1930 to experimental study of the mechanisms of the transformation of natural functions into the higher functions of memory, attention, will, arithmetic operations, and comprehension of language. Besides Alexander Luria and Alexei Leontiev, who joined Vygotsky as early as 1924, his group of collaborators included Lidia Bozhovich, Alexander Zaporozhets, Natalia Morozova, Rosa Levina, and Liya Slavina. Studies were developed along three avenues of research: instrumental, developmental, and cultural–historical.

The instrumental aspect centered on the use of external means, that is, psychological tools, to facilitate the higher forms of memory, attention, and decision making. Here the study by Leontiev on natural and instrumentally mediated memory and attention remains classical (Leontiev, 1932).

Calling his psychology "developmental" (*geneticheskii* – from genesis), Vygotsky meant much more than a mere analysis of the unfolding of behavior in ontogenesis. As a matter of fact, the very idea of development as unfolding and as maturation was alien to him. Vygotsky perceived psychological development as a dynamic process full of upheavals, sudden changes, and reversals. This process, however, ultimately leads to the formation of the cultural, higher mental functions. A study of the dynamics of this formation and its behavioral objectification become major goals of Vygotsky's developmental program. The first round of developmental studies was summarized by Vygotsky in his monograph *History of the Development of Higher Mental Functions*, which was finished in 1931 (in Vygotsky, 1960).

The cultural–historical dimensions of Vygotsky's theory aimed at the analysis of historical transformations of human psychological functions under the influence of changing psychological tools. It was assumed that the transition from natural functions to cultural ones takes place not only in ontogenesis, but also in human history. "Primitive mentality" should, therefore, correspond to a system of psychological tools essentially different from those of the modern mind, which is to a great extent a product of such mediating systems as written language and logicomathematical operations. This approach was formulated theoretically by Vygotsky and Luria (1930) in their *Essays in the History of Behavior*. In the early 1930s, Luria undertook a field study in Soviet Central Asia that yielded rich material confirming a hypothesis about decisive influences of symbolic mediating systems on the development of psychological functions. These materials were published, however, only in 1974 (for the English version, see Luria, 1976).

THOUGHT AND LANGUAGE

Although Vygotsky's theory embraced all higher mental functions, Vygotsky himself was primarily interested in the development of language in its relation to thought. Vygotsky's "psycholinguistics" covered a number of neighboring subjects, such as signs as psychological tools, stages in the child's concept formation, the development of word meanings and senses, and the problem of inner speech. This circle of studies was summarized in *Thought and Language* (Vygotsky, 1962).

The development of "instrumental" metaphors led Vygotsky to a hypothesis that the structural properties of language must leave their imprint on the entire activity of a child and that experience itself, so to speak, is structured as language. These ideas were most explicitly developed in "The Prehistory of Written Language" (Vygotsky, 1978b). Vygotsky brought together such seemingly disparate phenomena as gesture, symbolic play, and children's drawing and writing in an attempt to show that they all are but steps in the process of mastering symbolism and conventionalism, which are essential for the development of written language.

Following Wundt's analysis of gesture, Vygotsky drew parallels between gesture, primitive pictography, and children's early drawings. These drawings are the fixation of gesture rather than the reflection of visual properties of objects. Gesture provides a link connecting pictography with symbolic play.

> For children some objects can readily denote others, replacing them and becoming signs for them, and the degree of similarity between a plaything and the object it denotes is unimportant. What is most important is the utilization of the plaything and the possibility of executing a representational gesture with it. This is the key to the entire symbolic function of children's play. . . . From this point of view, therefore, children's symbolic play can be understood as a very complex system of "speech" through gestures that communicate and indicate the meaning of playthings.
>
> (Vygotsky, 1978b, p. 108)

In the course of play, the plaything absorbs the meaning of the signified object and already carries it without the assigning gesture. During the next developmental stage, children "discover" some differential features of playthings that fit their roles. "For example, when we put down a book with a dark cover and say that this will be a forest, a child will spontaneously add, 'Yes, it's a forest because it's black and dark' " (Vygotsky, 1978b, p. 109). Children thus come to the intuitive use of metonymy. Children's play, therefore, is a powerful source of mastering symbolism and the conventional character of the relation between signifier and signified, which is one of the cognitive bases of writing.

Symbolism and the conventionality of signs were perceived by Vygotsky as important characteristics of human activity that are imposed on an individual's behavior, shaping it and reconstructing it along the lines of the sociocultural matrix. The concept of activity thus was perceived as an actualization of culture in individual behavior, embodied in the symbolic function of gesture, play, and speech systems.

The other aspect of Vygotsky's inquiry into the problem of thought and language concerns the development of concept formation in children. This study started within the framework of the instrumental model but later went beyond the original schema. Vygotsky argued that it is not one particular function but rather the development of the whole interfunctional system, like that of verbal intelligence, that should be made a center of study. Neither language nor thought can be described adequately unless the history of the changing relationships between these two functions is revealed (Vygotsky, 1982b). Later this idea of functional systems became a theoretical basis of Luria's neuropsychological works (Luria, 1966).

But let us return to a study of concept formation. Using the method of "double stimulation," that is, marking each object in the sorting test by a coded triplet of letters, Vygotsky succeeded in setting up an experimental situation in which the instrumental process of sorting and classification revealed a corresponding stage in the development of a child's concepts. Vygotsky discovered a number of such stages, from that of unorganized congeries through that of scientific, logical concepts (Vygotsky, 1962).

In the work of his student, Zhozephina Shif, this study was extended into an educational setting (Shif, 1935). Different forms of children's experience were put into correspondence with appropriate stages in the development of concept formation. In this respect, Vygotsky's study closely resembled that of Heinz Werner in cognitive development (Werner, 1948). It is not surprising that Werner's disciples enthusiastically used Vygotsky's sorting test in their study of the preconceptual thinking of schizophrenics (Hanfmann and Kasanin, 1942). Vygotsky observed that preconceptual and even "mythological" thinking not only is characteristic of children but also forms the basis for everyday adult thinking. This latter perspective, like many others, has been neglected by Vygotsky's disciples, and the problem of everyday behavior has remained practically untouched in Soviet studies.

Vygotsky distinguished two forms of experience that give rise to two different, albeit interrelated, groups of concepts. The first group, which Vygotsky designated as "scientific," has its roots in specialized and operationalized educational instruction activity that imposes scientifically defined concepts upon a child. The second group, which comprises concepts emerging from the child's reflection upon everyday experience, was called "spontaneous."

Vygotsky argued that scientific concepts, far from being units assimilated by a child in a ready-made form, in reality undergo substantial development. This development essentially depends on the existing level of the child's ability to comprehend concepts. The level of comprehension, in its turn, is connected with the development of spontaneous concepts.

In working its slow way upward, an everyday concept clears a path for the scientific concept in its downward development. It creates a series of structures necessary for the evolution of a concept's more primitive, elementary aspects, which give it body and vitality. Scientific concepts in turn supply structures for the upward development of the child's spontaneous concepts toward consciousness and deliberate use.

(Vygotsky, 1962, p. 109)

Two special forms of activity were thus distinguished. One of them, a highly structured educational activity, later attracted the attention of all Soviet psychologists and has been thoroughly investigated in the works of Davydov (1972; Davydov and Markova, 1983) and Galperin (1969). The much less articulated "spontaneous" activity of the child was perceived rather as an obstacle on the road of concept formation, and its characteristic features were mostly neglected.

The last of the major problems discussed in *Thought and Language* (Vygotsky, 1962) was the phenomenon of inner speech. The problem of inner speech entered Vygotsky's discourse twice: the first time in the context of polemics with Piaget concerning child egocentrism, and the second time in connection with a problem of personal senses of words. Vygotsky challenged Piaget's thesis that the inherent autism of the child's thought manifests itself in egocentric speech. According to Piaget, autism is the original, earliest form of thought; logic and socialized speech, from his point of view, appear rather late, and egocentric thought is a genetic link between autism and logic. Vygotsky, who repeated some of Piaget's experiments, insisted, however, that the earliest speech of the child is already social. At a certain age, this original social speech becomes sharply divided into egocentric speech-for-oneself and communicative speech-for-others. Egocentric speech, splintered off from general social speech, gives rise to inner speech. Inner speech is therefore a rather late product of the transformation into individualized verbal thought of speech that earlier served the goals of communication.

Thus, in Piaget's vision, the uniqueness of speech-for-oneself, which is incomprehensible to others, is rooted in the original autism and egocentrism of a child and ultimately in the pleasure principle. In the course of the child's development, this individual speech dies out and gives way to socialized speech, which is easily understood by any interlocutor and which is ultimately connected with the reality principle.

Without denying the phenomenon of autism as such, Vygotsky suggested that egocentric speech is rather a transitory form situated between social, communicative speech and inner speech. For Vygotsky the major problem was not that of socialization but rather of individualization of the originally communicative speech-for-others. As mentioned earlier, Vygotsky believed that the outward, interpsychological relations become the inner, intrapsychological mental functions. In the context of this idea, the transition from egocentric to inner speech manifests the internalization of an originally communicative function that becomes the inner mental function of a given individual. The peculiar grammar and syntax that are characteristic of inner speech indicate this submergence of communication-for-others into one's reasoning-for-oneself. In inner speech, culturally prescribed forms of language and reasoning find their individualized realization. Culture-of-all is remodeled into the verbal thought of the individual. The principal steps toward this remodeling include the transition from overt dialogue to dialogue with oneself.

The problem of interpersonal versus intrapersonal communication (*obschenie*) thus was at the forefront of Vygotsky's theory. An objective development of his ideas now required that the typology of semiotic means of mediation be complemented by the typology of the overt and inner dialogues in which culture acquires its psychologically individualized form.

Unfortunately, Vygotsky had no time to develop this aspect of his study; he just outlined it, mentioning that the differences in the conditions of social interaction among children in different settings play a decisive role in the understanding of the coefficients of egocentric speech. Piaget's children, children observed by William Stern (Stern and Stern, 1928) in German kindergartens, and Vygotsky's subjects all had different social milieus and consequently different prevalent types of communication that shaped the development of their verbal thoughts (Vygotsky, 1962).

Vygotsky returned to the problem of inner speech in a study of generalization versus contextualization of word meaning. He made a distinction between word meaning (*znachenie*), which reflects a generalized concept, and word sense (*smysl*), which depends on the context of speech:

> The sense of word . . . is the sum of all the psychological events aroused in our consciousness by the word. It is a dynamic, complex, fluid whole, which has several zones of unequal stability. Meaning is only one of the zones of sense, the most stable and precise zone. A word acquires its sense from the context in which it appears; in different contexts, it changes its sense.
>
> (Vygotsky, 1934/1962, p. 146)

According to Vygotsky, in inner speech "the predominance of sense over meaning, of sentence over word, and of context over sentence is the rule" (Vygotsky, 1962, p. 147). Whereas meaning stands for "socialized" speech in Piaget's terminology sense represents a borderline between one's individual and thus incommunicable thinking and verbal thought.

> Inner speech is not the interior aspect of external speech – it is a function in itself. It still remains speech, i.e., thought connected with words. But while in external speech thought is embodied in words, in inner speech words die as they bring forth thought.
>
> (Vygotsky, 1962, p. 149)

In inner speech, two important processes are interwoven: the transition from external communication to inner dialogue and the translation of intimate thoughts into a linguistic and thus a communicative form. Inner speech thus becomes a psychological interface between culturally fixated symbolic systems that represent the general *Tätigkeit* and the individual "language" and imagery. The concretization of activity in this context appears as a psychological mechanism that creates new symbols and word senses that may eventually be incorporated into the stock of culture. Vygotsky here examined the enigmatic problem of creativity. The process of artistic or intellectual creation may be considered as an antipode of internalization. In such an action, the inner context-dependent sense gradually unfolds its meaning as symbol-for-others. Vygotsky mentioned that in a title like *Don Quixote* the whole sense of the work is contained in one name. Initially such a name makes sense only in the context of a plot conceived in the author's head. Through "exteriorization," that is, in the course of becoming a literary fact, Don Quixote ceases to be merely the name of a character. It acquires a meaning that is immediately recognized by any educated person and thus becomes a generalized concept.

Vygotsky here intrepidly trespassed the boundaries of purely psychological discussion, plunging into the much broader subject of human creativity and the production of culture. This is not strange, for Vygotsky, after all, started his career as a literary critic, and his first large work was *The Psychology of Art*, which was written in 1925 but was not published until 1965 (Vygotsky, 1971). For a number of years he considered psychology as a temporary diversion from his main subject of art theory. One might guess that Vygotsky hoped to sort out the psychological aspect and to return to his original task. As it turned out, he never went back, and the field of psychology occupied him for the rest of his life.

Vygotsky, however, remained an outsider in psychology, no matter how paradoxical it may sound. His approach was essentially "methodological," that is, focused on elaboration of the subject and construction of the method of psychological study. These tasks, however, belong to philosophy rather than to professional psychology, at least as the latter was perceived by Vygotsky's contemporaries. The features of an outsider may account both for the novelty of Vygotsky's approach and for the difficulty with which it has been absorbed by professional psychology. The Soviet philosopher of psychology Georgy Schedrovitsky suggested that this well may be so:

> The range of ideas introduced by Vygotsky, alien to traditional psychology, called for special means of discussion and analysis. And he drew many of these means from philology and linguistics. . . . It turned out, however, that in the process Vygotsky broke down the traditional object of psychology. His works were not psychological in the common meaning of the word.
>
> (Schedrovitsky, 1982, p. 62)

THE KHARKOV GROUP

The early 1930s were destined to become a critical period in the development of Soviet psychology. Stalin, who pronounced 1929 "the year of great break-through," was clearly tightening party control over the soft fringes of culture and science. Soviet psychologists, in their turn, could hardly show any group resistance, for they were engaged in a bitter struggle with each other. Each of the rival groups claimed to be the closest to the Marxist ideal of objective science. At the height of the polemics, ideological labels and political insinuations were used liberally. In this atmosphere of intolerance, psychology became easy prey to party apparatchiks. Soon all independent trends in psychology were suppressed. From then on, Soviet psychologists were expected to derive psychological categories directly from the works of Marx, Engels, and Lenin (see Kozulin, 1984).

This turn of events seriously undermined Vygotsky's research program, which relied on such "bourgeois" theories and methods as psychoanalysis, Gestalt psychology, and the cross-cultural analysis of consciousness. All of these trends were labeled anti-Marxist, and Vygotsky's work was pronounced "eclectic" and "erroneous." Luria's field study in cross-cultural development of thinking was severely criticized for its alleged bias against national minorities. Luria was also forced to renounce his interest in psychoanalysis. One might guess that these events had something to do with Luria's decision to change his field of study and to concentrate on clinical aspects of neuro-psychology (Luria, 1979).

Alexei Leontiev also obviously ran into some troubles. The exact circumstances remain obscure because the official Soviet biography of Leontiev simply states that "in 1930 the constellation of circumstances forced Alexei Nikolaevich [Leontiev] to resign from the Academy of Communist Education and to leave his [teaching] position at the State Institute of Cinematography" (Leontiev, A.A., 1983, p. 11).

Vygotsky, who was already gravely ill, continued working in Moscow until 1934, when an attack of tuberculosis led to his death. Even before the death of their leader, a group of Vygotsky's students, which included Leontiev, Zaporozhets, and Bozhovich, opted for leaving Moscow for the Ukrainian city of Kharkov, where they eventually established a program in developmental psychology.

Studies conducted by the Kharkov group between 1934 and 1940 centered on the problem of interiorization and the relation between the external activity of a child and mental operations correspondent to it. The Kharkovites developed an extensive experimental program comparing children's external sensory-motor activity with their mental actions and outlining the respective morphologies. As a general conclusion, the Kharkovites came to believe that the structure of cognitive processes more or less repeats the structure of external operations. From this circle of studies came some of the notions that much later, in the 1960s, were accepted as the basic premises of Soviet developmental psychology. Among them were the concept of *perception as the action* of Zaporozhets (Zaporozhets and Elkonin, 1971) and the concept of the *step-by-step formation of intellectual actions* of Galperin (1969).

The problem of the relationship between consciousness and activity had been resolved in the following way: "Development of the consciousness of a child occurs as a result of the development of the system of psychological operations; which in their turn, are determined by the actual relations between a child and reality" (Leontiev, 1980, p. 186). This insistence on the "actual relations with reality" became a major point of disagreement between the Kharkovites and Vygotsky. As Michael Cole accurately observed, "As even a superficial reading of this work indicates, Leontiev and the young researchers who worked with him established a good deal of distance between themselves and their teacher Vygotsky" (Cole, 1980, p. 5).

It is very tempting to attribute this distancing to extra scientific factors. In 1936 a special Decree of the Communist Party was issued condemning pedology (roughly, interdisciplinary educational psychology). Vygotsky then became a real heresy, because its author had collaborated with pedologists. Moreover, this thesis of "actual relations with reality" fitted the Soviet dialectical–materialistic credo circa the 1930s much better than the more complex cultural–historical model suggested by Vygotsky.

Nevertheless, there are solid grounds to believe that Leontiev's revisionism, apart from its ideological benefits, did have serious scientific underpinnings. That is to say, even if Vygotsky were not persona non grata, Leontiev and his group most probably still would have challenged some of his basic notions. Ideological caution, honest scientific disagreement, and also a misunderstanding of certain of Vygotsky's ideas all were intricately interwoven in the phenomenon that later became known as Leontiev's theory of activity.

As I have mentioned, the center of the dispute happened to be the problem of the relationships among consciousness, activity, and reality. The Kharkovites insisted that it is practical acquaintance with and the use of objects that leads the child toward the cognitive mastery of a situation. According to Asnin,

> Thus, even in children of early preschool age, practical activity assumes a new property, intelligibility or rationality; and practical activity is transformed into practical and intellectual activity. In other words, practical–operational, or practical thinking emerges. This form of thinking is obviously not an independent, completely formed, theoretical activity at this stage of development. It exists within practical activity as an element of that activity and as one of the properties of that activity is inseparable from it. Consequently, practical intellectual activity contains in its rudimentary aspects certain theoretical elements, elements of thought.
>
> (1980, p. 27)

As such, Asnin's statement hardly departs from Vygotsky's thesis "from action to thought," and yet the studies that stand behind it resemble those in generalization and transfer more than those on the effect of the involvement of psychological tools. The role of a sign as the chief mediator has been played down by the Kharkovites.

It was not a peripheral but a central notion of the cultural–historical theory that was attacked by the Kharkovites. As P. Zichenko stated,

> Indeed, one of the most basic of all problems, the conceptualization of the nature of mind, was incorrectly resolved. The central characteristic of the human mind was thought to be *mastery* of the natural or biological mind through the use of auxiliary psychological means. Vygotsky's fundamental error is contained in this thesis, in which he misconstrued the Marxist conception of the historical and social determination of the human mind. Vygotsky understood the Marxist perspective idealistically. The conditioning of all human mind by social and historical factors was reduced to the influence of human culture on the individual. The source of mental development was thought to be the interaction of the subject's mind with a cultural, ideal reality rather than his actual relationship to reality.
>
> (1984, pp. 66–67)

In a word, Zinchenko claimed that practical activity provides a mediation between the individual and reality, whereas Vygotsky insisted that such an activity, in order to fulfill its role as a psychological tool, must necessarily be of semiotic character.

Vygotsky's theory was attacked by Zinchenko in general, and in particular as a concept of the cultural–historical mastering of natural functions, and as an erroneous methodological base for a study of memory (the latter subject was the focus of Zinchenko's experimental work).

General, theoretical critique centered on Vygotsky's distinction between natural, biological, and higher culturally mediated psychological functions. Zinchenko (1984) argued that such an approach would ruin an attempt to understand the early stages of mental development as psychological rather than physiological: "This loss of the 'mental' in the biological stage of development produced a situation in which the human mind was contrasted with purely physiological phenomena" (p. 67).

Zinchenko suggested that the role of semiotic means of mediation was overinflated by Vygotsky:

> He began with the thesis that the mastery of the sign-means was the basic and unique feature of human memory processes. He considered the central feature of any activity of remembering to be the relationship of the means to the object of that activity. But in Vygotsky's thinking, the relationship of the means to the object was divorced from the subject's relationship to reality considered in its actual and complete content. In

the strict sense, the relationship between the means and object was a logical rather than psychological relationship. But the history of social development cannot be reduced to the history of the development of culture. Similarly, we cannot reduce the development of the human mind – the development of memory in particular – to the development of the relationship of "external" and "internal" means to the object of activity. The history of cultural development must be included in the history of society's social and economic development: it must be considered in the context of the particular social and economic relationships that determine the origin and development of culture. In precisely this sense, the development of "theoretical" or "ideal" mediation must be considered in the context of the subject's real, practical relations with reality, in the context of that which actually determines the origin, the development, and the content of mental activity.

(1984, p. 70)

Concerning memory studies, Zinchenko suggested approaching involuntary memory as a psychological rather than a physiological phenomenon and seeking its roots in the practical activity of a child. Zinchenko's experiments revealed that either pictures or numbers are remembered depending on which one of these two groups of stimuli plays an active role in the child's activity, which in both cases was an activity not of memorizing but of classification. Zinchenko emphasized that it is the stimuli's involvement in the child's activity of classification that ensures their involuntary memorizing. Involuntary memory thus appeared, on the one hand, as a psychological rather than a natural, biological function, and on the other, as a process intimately connected with the practical activity of a child rather than the means of semiotic mediation. In order to challenge Vygotsky's position, Zinchenko made his readers believe – incorrectly from my point of view – that Vygotsky saw no difference between natural, eidetic memory and involuntary memorizing. Zinchenko also chose to ignore Luria's cross-cultural study, which showed, in the framework of the psychological tools concept, a number of stages in the development of higher mental functions, one of them closely resembling the phenomena of practical thinking revealed in the experiments of the Kharkovites.

What Zinchenko failed to recognize was the existence of different levels of analysis and theory construction in Vygotsky's works. The distinction between higher (cultural) and lower (natural) functions and the idea that natural functions are mastered with the help of psychological tools belong to the foundation of Vygotsky's theory. Without such presuppositions, any theory of higher mental functions is either doomed to be naturalistic or will encounter serious difficulties in interpreting the elementary functions as "already psychological." These presuppositions, however, did not preclude further elaboration of the stages through which the elementary functions pass on their way to cultural maturity. Neither Vygotsky nor Zinchenko, however, had adequate experimental data concerning the earliest stages of mental development of the child, to which alone the term *natural* could be applied in the strict sense of the word.

The major theoretical disagreement between the Kharkovites' position and Vygotsky's was epitomized by Zinchenko's (1984) statement that "social development cannot be reduced to the history of the development of culture" (p. 70). Whereas in Vygotsky's theory activity as a general explanatory principle found its concretization in the specific, culturally bound types of semiotic mediation, in the Kharkovites' doctrine, activity assumed a double role – that of a general principle and that of a concrete mechanism of mediation. In order to be socially meaningful, however, the concrete actions had to be connected in some way with human social and economic relationships with reality. The task of elaborating this overall structure of activity was taken up by Leontiev.

LEONTIEV'S THEORY OF ACTIVITY

The first sketch of A.N. Leontiev's theory of psychological activity appeared in his *Essays in the Development of Mind* (1947), followed by the highly popular *Problems of the Development of Mind* (1981), and *Activity, Consciousness, and Personality* (1978). Leontiev suggested the following breakdown of activity: activity correspondent to a motive, action correspondent to a goal, and operation dependent on conditions.

> The main thing which distinguishes one activity from another, however, is the difference of their objects. It is exactly the object of an activity that gives it a determined direction. According to the terminology I have proposed, the object of an activity is its true motive.
>
> (1978, p. 62)

When entering human activity, an object loses its apparent naturalness and appears as an object of collective, social experience.

> Consequently, it is the activity of others that provides an objective basis for the specific structure of individual activity. Historically, i.e., in terms of its origin, the connection between motive and object of activity reflects objective social, rather than natural relations.
>
> (Leontiev, 1981, p. 281)

For example, food as a motive for human activity already presupposes a complex structure of the division of labor. Such a division provides a basis for a proliferation of activities and actions:

> The actions that realize activity are aroused by its motives but appear to

be directed toward a goal. . . . For satisfying the need for food [one] must carry out actions that are not aimed directly at getting food. For example, the purpose of a given individual may be preparing equipment for fishing.

(Leontiev, 1978, p. 63)

Motives thus belong to the socially structured reality of production and appropriation, whereas actions belong to the immediate reality of practical goals:

When a concrete process is taking place before us, external or internal, then from the point of its relation to motive, it appears as human activity, but when it is subordinated to purpose, then it appears as an action or accumulation of a chain of actions.

(Leontiev, 1978, p. 64)

Psychologically, activity has no constituent elements other than actions. "If the actions that constitute activity are mentally subtracted from it, then absolutely nothing will be left of activity" (Leontiev, 1978, p. 64). And yet activity is not an additive phenomenon: it is realized in actions, but its overall social meaning cannot be derived from the individual actions.

At this point, Leontiev's concept of activity ran into serious theoretical trouble, which did not escape the attention of his opponents, Sergei Rubinstein and his students. When discussing human activity (*Tätigkeit*) in general, Leontiev used such categories of Marxist social philosophy as production, appropriation, objectivation, and disobjectivation. The subject assumed in these categories is the social–historical subject rather than the psychological–individual. At the same time, "actual relationships with reality" were sought by Leontiev in the concrete practical actions and operations of the individual. The intermediate link between these two facets of activity – which Vygotsky identified as culture in general and the semiotic systems in particular – has been lost because of the rejection of Vygotsky's position. Rubinstein, who noticed this gap in Leontiev's theoretical schema, accused him of "illegitimate identification of the psychological problem of mastering operations with the social process of the disobjectivation of the social essence of Man" (Rubinstein, 1960, p. 7).

Rejecting semiotic mediation and insisting on the dominant role of practical actions, the Kharkovites obliged themselves to elaborate the connection between the philosophical categories of production and objectivation, and the psychological category of action. Leontiev, however, was reluctant to provide such an elaboration, substituting for it a standard "sermon" on the alienation of activity under capitalism versus the free development of personality in socialist society (Leontiev, 1981, pp. 318–349).

Moreover, when Leontiev made an attempt to outline the forms of human consciousness correspondent to activity, he chose to use the categories of meaning and sense rather than those of internalized operations. Thus, an interplay between personal sense and socially fixated meaning, rather than "actual relations with reality," was invoked by Leontiev when he encountered the problem of human consciousness. In this way, he unwittingly acknowledged the advantage of Vygotsky's approach. This theoretical inconsistency also was noticed by his critics, who claimed that

> although the concept of object-orientedness of the psyche aims at derivation of the specificity of psyche from the practical, and even the material, activity of society, actually it turns out that this *practical activity*. . . . Becomes identified as a system of *social meanings*. . . . One important point remained, however, unnoticed here, namely that although social modes of action do find their fixation in meanings, the latter represent the forms of *social consciousness*, and by no means the forms of *social practice*.
>
> (Abulkhanova, 1973, p. 157; emphasis in the original)

Unfortunately, Rubinstein's students made no distinction between Leontiev and Vygotsky, and so their critique remained mostly unheeded by those who chose to work in the framework of Vygotsky's tradition. Moreover, this critique was often perceived as an assault on the cultural–historical theory as such.

THE CONCEPT OF ACTIVITY RECONSIDERED

Beginning in the late 1950s, the relationship between Leontiev's concept of activity and Vygotsky's theoretical legacy took a new form. As were many others, Vygotsky's ideas were "rehabilitated" in the course of de-Stalinization. Some of his works were reprinted and some published for the first time (see Vygotsky, 1956, 1960). Once again it became fashionable to be considered his disciple.

At the same time, the former Kharkovites were solidly established in Moscow: Leontiev became Chair of the Division of Psychology at Moscow University; Zaporozhets founded and directed the new Institute for Preschool Education; and Galperin, Bozhovich, and Elkonin held senior professorial positions at Moscow University and the Moscow Institute of Psychology.

In 1963, Leontiev's *Problems of the Development of Mind* (1981) won the Lenin prize for scientific research and thus achieved the status of official Soviet psychological doctrine. It was not difficult for Leontiev, under those circumstances, to gain the status of official interpreter of Vygotsky, and his interpretation enjoyed a wider circulation than the original texts. Gradually Vygotsky came to be regarded as a mere predecessor to Leontiev, a predecessor who made some theoretical mistakes that were later rectified in Leontiev's theory. In his 1956 preface to Vygotsky's volume, Leontiev reasserted his own interpretation of activity, simultaneously suggesting that the emphasis on signs as the principal psychological tools was transitory for Vygotsky and that therefore Leontiev's theory accomplished the authentic development of Vygotsky's research program (Leontiev and Luria, 1956).

In the later 1970s, however, Leontiev's theory started to be scrutinized more critically. This criticism originated partly in the works of the younger psychologists, like Vasili Davydov and Vladimir Zinchenko, who, although brought up in the shadow of Leontiev's theory, managed to recognize its limits and disadvantages. An important role in this re-evaluation movement was played by the rediscovery of some of Vygotsky's works, which were then prepared for publication as the *Collected Papers* (Vygotsky, 1982–1984). Finally, some Soviet philosophers took a deep interest in the problem of activity, thus bringing new critical remarks into the already heavily charged atmosphere of psychological discussion.

Leontiev's theory of activity, being elevated to the level of an all-embracing psychological doctrine, ran precisely into the trouble against which Vygotsky had warned in his early article on consciousness (1979). The notion of activity was used at one and the same time as the explanatory principle and as a subject of concrete psychological study. The phenomena of activity were "explained" through the principle of activity. This returned it to the vicious circle of tautology, mentioned by Vygotsky in his critique of mentalism – consciousness explained through consciousness – and behaviorism – behavior explained through behavior.

In philosophically elaborated form, the distinction between activity as an explanatory principle and activity as a subject of scientific inquiry was made by Eric Yudin (1976), First of all, Yudin took pains to restore the connection between the notion of activity and its original meaning developed in the philosophy of Hegel and Marx. It must be taken into account that at the height of the polemics, psychologists often neglected the theoretical roots of the very concepts they defended or attacked. Yudin emphasized that it was Hegel who made activity the universal explanatory principle and thus reversed the individualistic model of human conduct suggested by empiricists. In Hegel's philosophical theory, the individual appears as an "organ" of activity. Activity, in its role of the ultimate explanatory principle, cannot be reduced to the manifestations of individual consciousness. On the contrary, these manifestations are referred to activity as their real source.

Yudin further pointed out that activity could also become a subject of concrete scientific study. But in this case – and this is a crucial point – the structural elements elaborated for activity as an explanatory principle will be irrelevant. Activity as a subject of psychological study should have its own system of structural elements and even its own explanatory principles. One and the same notion of activity cannot successfully carry out both functions simultaneously. But this is precisely what happened in Leontiev's theory. Structural elements of activity – activity–action–operation and motive–goal–condition – once suggested as the elaboration of the explanatory principle, were later used in the context of the subject of study.

It was the other philosopher of psychology, Georgy Schedrovitsky, who, addressing the Colloquium of Vygotsky in 1979, challenged the myth of succession and suggested that Leontiev's theory substantially deviated from Vygotsky's program. Schedrovitsky emphasized that the principle of semiotic mediation and the role of culture in Vygotsky's theory were by no means accidental or transient. Only with their help may the tautological explanation of activity through activity be avoided.

As I see it, the real opposition between Vygotsky's theory and Leontiev's thus appears as an opposition of the following two schemas: Vygotsky's theory views higher mental functions as a subject of study, semiotic systems as mediators, and activity as an explanatory principle. In Leontiev's theory, activity, now as activity, and now as action, plays all roles from subject to explanatory principle.

EPILOGUE

It would be premature to claim that the polemics surrounding the concept of activity have subsided. Currently all leading Soviet psychologists feel obliged to address this issue (Davydov, 1981; Lomov, 1982; Zinchenko, V., 1985).

The recent publication of Vygotsky's *Collected Papers* (1982–1984) and particularly the publication of his major historical–methodological work, *Historical Meaning of the Crisis of Psychology* (Vygotsky, 1982a; see also Kozulin, 1983), have helped bring recognition to him as an original thinker whose interests were not confined to professional psychology alone. Vygotsky actually succeeded in redefining the subject of psychology, precisely because he went beyond its borders.

Studies addressing the problem of semiotic mediation have started to appear in Soviet journals (Akhutina, 1984). Some attempts have been made to reintegrate Vygotsky's ideas concerning signs as mediators into Leontiev's theory (Leontiev, A.A., 1981, 1983). But what is probably more important, Soviet as well as Western psychologists have found Vygotsky's tradition capable of further development. A number of current studies show that linguistic and cultural differences are quite surmountable and that American psychologists can incorporate Vygotsky's methods and ideas in their work.

For example, studies in early infant development have shown that complex symbolic interactions occur between one-year-olds and their caretakers (see Lock, 1978). The controversial issue of natural versus higher mental functions, which was a focus of Zinchenko's critique of Vygotsky, thus has proved to be a real problem that has substantive rather than historical significance. As another example, Vygotsky's concept of the "zone of proximal development" of the child has become the framework for a series of experimental studies of educational activity (see Rogoff and Wertsch, 1983). Finally, a wide range of

Vygotsky's ideas has been reviewed and applied by James Wertsch (1981, 1985a, 1985b). A collection of articles, *Culture, Communication and Cognition: Vygotskian Perspectives* (1985a), edited by Wertsch, clearly shows that the period of acquaintance is over and that Vygotsky's ideas have succeeded in penetrating American psychological thinking. What quite recently seemed to be an obscure and dramatic feud within Soviet psychology now appears to be a new, inspiring source of ideas for psychology in general.

NOTES

1 The term *methodology* has a somewhat different meaning in Russian, referring to metatheological or philosophical study of the method used in a particular science. Descartes's *Method* is in this sense a paradigmatic example of methodological study as it is understood in Russia.
2 It goes without saying that Vygotsky is simply a Russian version of Mead. For a detailed discussion of similarities and differences between Vygotsky's and Mead's treatment of such problems as functionalism, social construction of self, and origins of meaning, see Glock (in press), "Vygotsky and Mead on Self, Meaning, and Internalization."

REFERENCES

Abulkhanova, K.A. (1973). *O sub'ekte psikhicheskoi deiatelnosti* [The subject of psychological activity]. Moscow: Nauka.

Akhutina, T.V. (1984). Teoriia rechevogo obscheniia v trudakh M.M. Bakhtina i L.S. Vygotskogo [The theory of verbal communication in works of M.M. Bakhtin and L.S. Vygotsky]. *Vestnik Moskovskogo Universiteta: Psikhologiia, 3*, 3–12.

Asnin, V. (1980). The development of visual-operational thinking in children. *Soviet Psychology, 18*(2), 23–26. (Original work published 1941)

Bauer, R. (1952). *The new man in Soviet psychology*. Cambridge, MA: Harvard University Press.

Cervantes, M. (1949). *Don Quixote* (S. Putnam, trans.). New York: Modern Library.

Cole, M. (1980). The Kharkov School of developmental psychology. *Soviet Psychology, 18*(2), 3–8.

Davydov, V. (1972). *Vidy obobscheniia v obuchenii* [The types of generalization in learning]. Moscow: Pedagogika.

Davydov, V. (1981). The category of activity and mental reflection in the theory of A.N. Leontiev, *Soviet Psychology, 19*, 3–29.

Davydov, V., and Markova, A. (1983). A concept of educational activity for school children. *Soviet Psychology, 21*, 50–76.

Davydov, V. and Radzikhovskii, L. (1985). Vygotsky's theory and the activity-orientated approach in psychology. In J. Wertsch (ed.), *Culture, communication and cognition: Vygotskian perspectives* (pp. 35–65). New York: Cambridge University Press.

Galperin. P. (1969). Stages in the development of mental acts. In M. Cole and I. Maltzman (eds.), *A handbook of contemporary Soviet psychology*. New York: Basic Books.

Glock, H.J. (in press). Vygotsky and Mead on self, meaning, and internalization. *Studies in Soviet Thought*.

Hanfmann, E. and Kasanin, J. (1942). *Conceptual thinking in schizophrenia*. New York: Nervous & Mental Disease Publishing Co.

Kozulin, A. (1983). Review of *Historical meaning of the crisis in psychology* by L.S. Vygotsky. *Studies in Soviet Thought, 26*, 249–256.

Kozulin, A. (1984). *Psychology in utopia: Toward a social history of Soviet psychology*. Cambridge, MA: MIT Press.

Leontiev, A.A. (1981). Sign and activity. In J. Wertsch (ed.), *The concept of activity in Soviet psychology* (pp. 241–255). New York: Sharpe.

Leontiev, A.A. (1983). Tvorcheskii put' A.N. Leontieva [The productive career of A.N. Leontiev]. In A.V. Zaporozhets, V.P. Zinchenko, O.V. Ovchinnikova and O.K. Tikhomirov (eds), *A.N. Leontiev i sovremennaia psikhologiia* [A.N. Leontiev and modern psychology] (pp. 6–39). Moscow State University.

Leontiev, A.N. (1932). Studies on the cultural development of the child. *Journal of Genetic Psychology, 40*, 52–83.

Leontiev, A.N. (1947). *Ocherk razvitiia psikhiki* [Essays in the development of mind]. Moscow.

Leontiev, A.N. (1978). *Activity, consciousness, and personality*. Englewood Cliffs, NJ: Prentice-Hall.

Leontiev, A.N. (1980). Ovladenie uchaschimisia nauchnymi poniatiiami kak problema pedagogicheskoi psikhologii [The acquisition of scientific concepts by schoolchildren as a problem of educational psychology]. In *Khrestomatiia po vozrastnoi i pedagogicheskoi psikhologii* (Vol. 1, pp. 173–186). Moscow: Moscow State University. (Original work published 1935)

Leontiev, A.N. (1981). *Problemy razvitiia psikhiki* [Problems of the development of mind]. Moscow: Moscow State University. (Original work published 1959).

Leontiev, A.N. and Luria, A. (1956). Psikhologicheskie vozzreniia Vygotskogo [Vygotsky's views on psychology]. In L. Vygotsky, *Izbrannye psikhologicheskie issledovaniia* [Selected psychological investigations]. Moscow: Academy of Pedagogical Sciences.

Lock, A. (ed.). (1978). *Action, gesture and symbol: The emergence of language*. New York: Academic Press.

Lomov, B. (1982). The problem of activity in psychology. *Soviet Psychology, 21*, 55–91.

Luria, A. (1966). *Higher cortical functions in man*. New York: Basic Books.

Luria, A. (1976). *Cognitive development*. Cambridge, MA: Harvard University Press.

Luria, A. (1979). *The making of mind*. Cambridge, MA: Harvard University Press.

Mead, G.H. (1974). *Mind, self and society*. Chicago: University of Chicago Press. (Original work published 1934)

Mecacci, L. (1979). *Brain and history*. New York: Brunner/Mazel.

Payne, T. (1968), *S.L. Rubinstein and the philosophical foundations of Soviet psychology*. Dordrecht, The Netherlands: Reidel.

Rahmani, L. (1973). *Soviet psychology: Philosophical, theoretical and experimental issues*. New York: International Universities Press.

Rogoff, B. and Wertsch, J. (eds). (1983). *Children's learning in the "zone of proximal development."* San Francisco: Jossey-Bass.

Rubinstein, S.L. (1960). Problema sposobnostei i voprosy psikhologicheskoi teorii [The problem of abilities and the questions of psychological theory]. *Voprosy Psikhologii, 3*.

Schedrovitsky, G.P. (1982). The Mozart of psychology: An imaginary exchange of views. In K. Levitin (ed.), *One is not born a personality* (pp. 59–63). Moscow: Progress.

Shif, Z. (1935). *Razvitie zhiteiskikh i nauchnykh poniatii* [The development of everyday and scientific concepts]. Moscow: Uchpedgiz.

Stern, C. and Stern, W. (1928). *Die Kindersprache*. Leipzig: Barth.

Vygotsky, L. (1956). *Izbrannye psikhologischeskie issledovaniia* [Selected psychological investigations]. Moscow: Academy of Pedagogical Sciences.

Vygotsky, L. (1960). *Razvitie vysshikh psikhicheskikh funkstii* [Development of higher mental functions]. Moscow: Academy of Pedagogical Sciences.

Vygotsky, L. (1962). *Thought and language*. Cambridge, MA: MIT Press. (Original work published 1934)

Vygotsky, L. (1971). *Psychology of art*. Cambridge: MIT Press (Original work published (1965)

Vygotsky, L. (1978a). *Mind in society: The development of higher psychological processes*. Cambridge, MA: Harvard University Press.

Vygotsky, L. (1978b). The prehistory of written language. In L. Vygotsky, *Mind in society*. Cambridge: Harvard University Press. (Original work published 1935)

Vygotsky, L. (1979). Consciousness as a problem of psychology of behavior. *Soviet Psychology*, *17*, 5–35. (Original work published 1925)

Vygotsky, L. (1981). The instrumental method in psychology. In J. Wertsch (ed.), *The concept of activity in Soviet psychology* (pp. 134–143). New York: Sharpe.

Vygotsky, L. (1982a). Istoricheskii smysl psikhologicheskogo krizisa [Historical meaning of the crisis in psychology]. In L. Vygotsky, *Sobranie sochinenii* [Collected papers] (Vol. 1, pp. 291–436). Moscow: Pedagogika. (Original work written in 1926)

Vygotsky, L. (1982b). O psikhologicheskikh sistemakh [On systems in psychology]. In L. Vygotsky, *Sobranie sochinenii* [Collected papers] (Vol. 1, pp. 109–131). Moscow: Pedagogika. (Original work written in 1930)

Vygotsky, L. (1982–1984). *Sobranie sochinenii* [Collected papers] (Vols. 1–6). Moscow: Pedagogika.

Vygotsky, L. and Luria, A. (1930). *Ocherk istorii povedeniia* [Essays in the history of behavior]. Moscow: Gosizdat.

Werner, H. (1948). *The comparative psychology of mental development*. New York: International Universities Press.

Wertsch, J. (ed.). (1981). *The concept of activity in Soviet psychology*. New York: Sharpe.

Wertsch, J. (ed.). (1985a). *Culture, communication and cognition: Vygotskian perspectives*. New York: Cambridge University Press.

Wertsch, J. (1985b). *Vygotsky and the social formation of mind*. Cambridge: Harvard University Press.

Wundt, W. (1900–1920). *Volkerpsychologie*. Leipzig: Engellmann.

Yudin, E. (1976). Deiatel'nost' kak ob'iasnitel'nyi printsyp i kak predmet nauchnogo issledovaniia [Activity as an explanatory principle and as a subject of scientific study]. *Voprosy Filosofii*, No. 5, 65–78.

Zaporozhets, A. and Elkonin, D. (1971). *The psychology of preschool children*. Cambridge, MA: MIT Press.

Zinchenko, P. (1984). The problem of involuntary memory. *Soviet Psychology*, *22*(2), 55–111. (Original work published 1939)

Zinchenko, V. (1985). Vygotsky's ideas about units for the analysis of mind. In J. Wertsch (ed.), *Culture, communication and cognition: Vygotskian perspectives* (pp. 94–118). New York: Cambridge University Press.

5 Dialogue, difference and voice in the zone of proximal development

J. Allan Cheyne and Donato Tarulli

BAKHTIN AND VYGOTSKY ON DIALOGUE

Both in the Russian (e.g. Bibler, 1984; Radzikhovskii, 1987, 1991) and North American (e.g. Kozulin, 1990; Sampson, 1993; Shotter, 1993; Tappan, 1997; Wertsch, 1991) psychological communities, the ideas of Bakhtin and Vygotsky have been compared, contrasted and integrated in an effort to construct a more radical cultural-historical model of human consciousness. Wertsch (1991), for example, draws upon such Bakhtinian notions as *voice, utterance, speech genres* and *dialogicality* to extend and elaborate foundations laid by Vygotsky. For, as Wertsch and others have noted, Vygotsky's project of a cultural-historical theory of the development of higher psychological processes was never fully realized. Vygotsky's available writings focus more on the immediate interactional precursors of intramental functioning than on the broader cultural, historical and institutional context of human experience. It is clearly the goal of many Vygotsky scholars to develop this latter aspect of his project.

We agree that a constructive integration of the views of Bakhtin and Vygotsky holds considerable promise for the advancement of the cultural-historical project in psychology. Accordingly, the following discussion was motivated by a number of questions originating in a general concern regarding the extent to which the writings of Bakhtin and Vygotsky may truly be said to converge in their elaboration of a common notion of dialogue.

Several scholars have argued that the writings of these two thinkers rather naturally converge in their commitment to articulating a dialogical consciousness. Yet, while Bakhtin's commitment to a dialogic rendering of mind is central in his writing and beyond contention, the ambiguity of Vygotsky's remarks regarding the dialogicality of thought, and inner speech more specifically, is reflected in the lack of interpretive consensus surrounding the matter among Vygotsky scholars. There are those, for example, who argue that Vygotsky promoted a view of human mental functioning as inherently dialogic, and who thereby argue that the writings of these two thinkers find common ground in their articulation of a dialogical consciousness:

Vygotskian ideas of the dialogical nature of human thought, together with those of his contemporary Mikhail Bakhtin, provide the foundation for a philosophical inquiry into the interaction of culturally diverse forms of thinking.

(Kozulin, 1990, p. 9)

For Vygotsky, dialogue was the concrete, psychological equivalent of the social nature of the mind, i.e., the totality of all social relations constituting the human essence. Thus, dialogue characterizes the human mind and consciousness.

(Radzikhovskii, 1991, p. 12)

On the other hand, there are those who, acknowledging Vygotsky's own rather ambiguous references to the dialogical quality of inner speech, show greater equivocation in ascribing this quality to inner speech. 'It is unclear', writes Tappan (1997), 'whether Vygotsky viewed *monologue* or *dialogue* as the fundamental characteristic of inner speech' (p. 86). With similar equivocation, Wertsch (1980) notes that:

> Vygotsky's explicit claims about dialogue seem to have been limited to external social speech. As we will see, there are compelling reasons for assuming that he also viewed egocentric and inner speech as being dialogic. However, given the absence of explicit statements by Vygotsky on this matter, we should note that what follows is an attempt to elucidate what he would have stated, had he addressed the issue.
>
> (p. 152)

More recently there has been a growing sensitivity to the differences between the dialogical views of Bakhtin and Vygotsky (e.g. Day & Tappan, 1996: Wertsch, 1991). It is in this spirit that we examine the respective positions of Bakhtin and Vygotsky on the dialogicality of speech, with a view to uncovering and explicating significant divergences on this subject. Further, we argue that there are implications of such differences for an extended notion of the Zone of Proximal Development. We will attempt to keep before us, however, an awareness that each was pursuing his own unique project and that both were remarkably generative thinkers producing an impressive array of genuinely novel insights, few of which were pursued in detail.

Vygotsky: inner speech as dialogue and monologue

How is the dialogical quality of speech represented in Vygotsky's writings? How, in particular, does dialogue figure in his understanding of inner speech? Wertsch (1980) offers the suggestion that a close analysis of Vygotsky's writings concerning egocentric and inner speech reveals 'that more appropriate terms for what he was studying would be "egocentric dialogue" and "inner dialogue" ' (p. 151). Wertsch argues that although 'Vygotsky never made claims that were as specific about the dialogic nature of inner speech as [Bakhtinian claims] . . . a detailed examination of some of his writings reveals that he was thinking along very similar lines' (p. 152).

When the notion of dialogue is invoked by Vygotsky, it is most often to describe face-to-face oral-aural speech and only rarely and ambiguously with reference to inner speech, writing and thinking. Significantly, many of Vygotsky's limited references to dialogue appear in his discussion of the syntactic characteristics, predication in particular, that define inner speech and differentiate it from other speech forms. On these differences Vygotsky (1987) was quite clear: 'Written speech and inner speech are monologic speech forms. Oral speech is generally *dialogic*' (p. 271). 'Inner speech', Vygotsky explains, 'is speech for oneself. External speech is speech for others' (p. 257). Moreover, we are told that adults' inner speech and pre-schoolers' egocentric speech 'are divorced from social speech which functions to inform, to link the individual with others' (pp. 71–72). For Vygotsky, egocentric and inner speech serve a radically different function from outer speech: namely, the individualized activity of self-mastery. Just as action becomes transformed into thought under internalization (Vygotsky & Luria, 1994), so too does language. Speech for oneself becomes isolated, functionally and structurally distinct from speech for others, such that it is difficult for inner speech to find expression in social speech. 'Speech for oneself is very different in its structure from speech for others. It simply cannot be expressed in the foreign structure of external speech' (Vygotsky, 1987, p. 261). This is entirely consistent with Vygotsky's (1981) more general genetic law of cultural development, on which he comments that 'it goes without saying that the internalization transforms the process itself and changes its structure and functions' (p. 163).

Hidden dialogicality and quasi-social inner speech

Notwithstanding Vygotsky's views on the transformations wrought by internalization, Wertsch (1991) has argued that aspects of Vygotsky's account of the genesis of higher mental functions may be recast in a Bakhtinian dialogism. In particular, he has argued that intrapsychological functioning bears an affinity to Bakhtin's notion of *hidden dialogicality*.

Imagine a dialogue of two persons in which the statements of the second speaker are omitted, but in such a way that the general sense is not at all violated. The second speaker is present invisibly, his words are not there, but deep traces left by these words have a determining influence on all the present and visible words of the first speaker. We sense that this is a conversation, although only one person is speaking, and it is a conversation of the most intense kind, for each present, uttered word responds and reacts with its every fiber to the invisible speaker, points to something outside itself, beyond its own limits, to the unspoken words of another person.

(Bakhtin, 1984b, p. 197)

That a dialogicality of this sort may be predicated of intramental functioning follows, according to Wertsch (1991), from Vygotsky's ideas concerning 'the ways in which the dialogic organization of speech on the intermental plane is mastered, thereby shaping the intramental plane of functioning' (p. 86). Wertsch and Stone (1985) argue that the dialogical structure of external transactions is retained in the realm of egocentric and inner speech, albeit implicitly, as the Bakhtinian term *hidden dialogicality* suggests. Although in such inner speech only one person is actually speaking, the effect of the invisible other's presence, of his or her unspoken words, can still be sensed in the speaker's utterances.

Wertsch (1991) offers an ethnographic analysis of a series of three interchanges between a two-and-a-half-year-old child and her mother during a puzzle-copying task to illustrate the hidden dialogicality of intramental functioning. Wertsch was interested in the degree to which, over the course of the problem-solving session, the child came to internalize her mother's directives and questions and, consequently, to perform the task in the absence of her mother's explicit regulative utterances. The first two episodes were characterized by the presence of overt, external mother–child dialogue in which the mother responded to the child's question about the proper placement of a puzzle piece by directing the child's attention to the model puzzle. By the third episode, however, the child was consulting the model independently of the mother's explicit directives. In the first two episodes, the child's consultation of the model represented a rejoinder first to the explicit and then to the implicit utterance of the mother. The self-guiding utterance of the child is taken to be a response to the 'invisible presence' of the mother's utterance. By the last episode in this series 'the child's egocentric and inner speech (intramental plane) guided this process' (Wertsch, 1991, p. 88). As Wertsch remarks, in the third episode

. . . the child did not produce a fully expanded question about where a piece should go . . . and more important, when she looked at the model puzzle . . . it was not in response to an adult's directive in overt social dialogue. She did not rely on the adult to provide a regulative utterance but pre-supposed the utterance that would have occurred on the intermental plane and responded in egocentric and inner dialogue.

(p. 89)

The microgenetic change of particular importance here is the increasing degree of hidden dialogicality embodied in the child's speech over the course of the mother–child interaction. By the final episode the mother's directive questions were partially presupposed in the child's egocentric speech and entirely presupposed, later on in the interaction, in inner speech. In other words, the question and answer structure that characterized the external social dialogue between mother and child, that is, their dialogue on the intermental plane, was now taken to be a feature of the child's intramental functioning.

That, for Vygotsky, intramental functioning has its origins in social interaction, in the realm of interpsychological functioning, is central and undeniable. On this point, he writes:

> It is necessary that everything internal in higher forms was external, i.e., for others it was what it now is for oneself. Any higher mental function necessarily goes through an external stage in its development because it is initially a social function. This is the center of the whole problem of internal and external behavior. . . . When we speak of a process, 'external' means 'social.' Any higher mental function was external because it was social at some point before becoming an internal, truly mental function . . . the composition, genetic structure, and means of action [of higher mental functions]—in a word, their whole nature—is social. Even when we turn to mental processes, their nature remains quasi-social. In their own private sphere, human beings retain the functions of social interaction.
>
> (Vygotsky, 1981, pp. 162–164)

Wertsch (1991) goes further and argues that the dialogicality explicitly informing Bakhtin's conception of the utterance is also at play in Vygotsky's account of intermental functioning. A full understanding of Vygotsky's construal of dialogue may be achieved, however, only through a consideration of the role and status of the other in dialogue.

Vygotsky (1987) also refers to inner speech as a unique mode of internal collaboration with oneself. Of course such speech for self might well be taken as monologue, for what else could monologue be but discourse with oneself? However, there is a fundamental reason why Vygotsky could take the self to be the recipient of inner speech and still hold a dialogical view of inner speech. This follows from a central and quite explicit assumption he makes about the relationship between interlocutors, between self and other, in dialogue. According to Vygotsky (1987), what enables dialogue is 'the commonality of the interlocutors' apperceptive mass' (p. 269) concerning the matter at hand. The notion that there is a need for common presuppositions among interlocutors is quite commonly accepted and has been discussed under various rubrics, such as the given–new (topic–comment) distinction (Steiner, 1982), mutual knowledge (N. V. Smith, 1982) and intersubjectivity (Trevarthen, 1979). 'When the thoughts and consciousness of the interlocutors are one,' Vygotsky (1987) argues, 'the role of speech in the achievement of flawless understanding is reduced to a minimum' (p. 269). Vygotsky draws on the following highly romantic exchange between Kitty and Levin in Tolstoy's *Anna Karenina* to illustrate this notion of shared apperception:

'Here,' he said and wrote the initial letters: 'W, Y, A, M, I, C, B, D, T, M, N, O, T.' These letters meant: 'When you answered me, "It cannot be," did that mean never or then?' It seemed impossible that she would understand this complex phrase. Blushing, she said, 'I understand.'

(cited in Vygotsky, 1987, p. 268)

Commenting on this rather far-fetched example, Vygotsky notes that: 'Here the shared orientation of consciousness is complete' (p. 275). The common apperceptive mass that guarantees the success of dialogue among interlocutors is, in the case of dialogue with oneself, amplified in that it refers to the self-certainty that comes with the identity embodied in a single consciousness. 'This shared apperception is complete and absolute in the social interaction with oneself that takes place in inner speech' (p. 274). The predicativity that characterizes inner speech in Vygotsky's analysis is a reflection of this self-same certainty. The common apperceptive mass is, for Vygotsky, a prior achievement that has reduced *difference* to a minimum. Why Vygotsky takes a very strong stand on this issue becomes clear when one considers his emphasis on development and on the notion of internalization, which is nothing less than the acquisition and interiorization of the culturally common apperceptive mass.

Vygotsky appropriated from linguistic studies the broad conceptual differentiation of speech into dialogic and monologic forms and applied it to an analysis of the more specific functional varieties of speech. He illustrates how abbreviated speech and simplified syntax may result either in mutual understanding, typically the case when the interlocutors' thoughts concerning the matter at hand are connected, or in failed and potentially 'comic misunderstandings'. These latter outcomes are most likely to occur when the interlocutors' respective views diverge or when a common focus is mistakenly assumed. Complete unity of the interlocutors' perspectives, on the one hand, and complete divergence of views, on the other, define

... two extremes ... between which the abbreviation of external speech moves. Where the thoughts of the interlocutors focus on a common subject, full understanding can be realized with maximal speech abbreviation and an extremely simplified syntax. Where they do not, understanding cannot be achieved even through expanded speech. Thus, two people who attribute different content to the same word or who have fundamentally different perspectives often fail to achieve understanding. As Tolstoy says, people who think in original ways and in isolation find it difficult to understand the thought of others. They also tend to be particularly attached to their own thought. In contrast, people who are in close contact can understand mere hints which Tolstoy called 'laconic and clear.' They can communicate and understand the most complex thoughts almost without using words.

(Vygotsky, 1987, p. 269)

For Vygotsky the ideal speech situation is one in which the shared 'given' is maximal and misunderstanding is minimized. This is a view of dialogue in which the task is a faithful replication by a listener of the information contained in the speech of the speaker. Each interlocutor is an 'insider' to the other's world. This requirement is premised on the assumption that dialogue is basically a cooperative enterprise overcoming miscommunication and the fallibility of language and that it is aimed at ever greater agreement. Such a view appears to be the current orthodox view of the 'social psychology of language' (Giles & Weimann, 1993). Implicit in this view is a commitment to what, following Bakhtin, we call *monologism*.

In its broadest philosophical connotations, monologism reflects a particular stance toward the other and, most generally, toward difference. Monologism is a feature of any form of thinking that values unity over diversity, sameness over difference. Monologism, in this broad sense, characterizes any effort, philosophical, linguistic, political or other, that strives for elimination of differences in, and, ultimately, a fusion of, voices, ideas, consciousnesses, and so forth. The formalization of this press to synthesis found its most obvious and self-conscious expression in Hegel's idealism. However, monologism may be seen to be a foundational assumption in: the defense of the Enlightenment of an abstract, disembodied 'consciousness in general' (Bakhtin, 1984b); Mead's (1934) ideal of a 'universal community' in which all social interests are shared and discourse reflects and achieves a perfect communion of minds; and, as intimated above, Vygotsky's requirement of a shared apperceptive mass as the ground or goal of dialogue. In each of these cases, otherness is conceived as a condition to be overcome and superseded by a more encompassing unity of mind.

Dialogism in the broad sense, on the other hand, valorizes difference and otherness. It is a way of thinking about ourselves and the world that always accepts non-coincidence of stance, understanding and consciousness. In dialogism, the subversion by difference of movements towards unity and the inevitable fracturing of univocality into multivoicedness represents the fundamental human condition. These qualities are, as we hope to demonstrate, inherent in Bakhtin's theory of the utterance, in his understanding of the otherness of the other, and in the forms of dialogue that follow from such understanding.

Bakhtin: the dialogical nature of the utterance

For Bakhtin, dialogue constitutes a key conceptual pivot in all his writings (e.g. Clark & Holquist, 1984), one that informs his epistemology, ontology and theory of language.

> The dialogic nature of consciousness, the dialogic nature of human life itself. The single adequate form for *verbally expressing* authentic human life is the *open-ended dialogue*. Life by its very nature is dialogic. To live

means to participate in dialogue: to ask questions, to heed, to respond, to agree, and so forth. In this dialogue a person participates wholly and throughout his whole life: with his eyes, lips, hands, soul, spirit, with his whole body and deeds. He invests his entire self in discourse, and this discourse enters into the dialogic fabric of human life, into the world symposium.

(Bakhtin, 1984b, p. 293)

For Bakhtin, the situated act of dialogic discourse, the *utterance*, is where the being of language resides. 'Language', writes Bakhtin (1984b), 'lives only in the dialogic interaction of those who make use of it. . . . The entire life of language, in any area of its use . . . is permeated with dialogic relationships' (p. 183). The utterance, in Bakhtin's view, is neither a unit of a system of language, on the one hand, as in the tradition of Saussure's *langue*, nor simply a matter of free individual instantiations of language (*parole*), on the other. Rather, the notion of utterance emphasizes the historical event of speaking. There are, moreover, a number of features associated with the utterance that reflect this historicity and serve to distinguish it from conventional linguistic units (such as word, proposition, sentence, etc.). Here we consider two closely related aspects that mark the fundamental sociality or dialogicality of the utterance for Bakhtin: (1) the relation of each utterance to preceding utterances; and (2) the *addressivity* of the utterance, that is, its orientation to the other, and, in particular, to the other's responsive understanding.

For Bakhtin, an utterance is constrained by a dialogical relation with other utterances handed down through a tradition of discourse. Each utterance, however monologic or univocal in its external presentation, is characterized by an 'internal dialogism' (Bakhtin, 1981), that is, inescapably responds to utterances that have come before it such that it 'refutes, affirms, supplements, and relies on the others, presupposes them to be known, and somehow takes them into account' (Bakhtin, 1986, p. 91). Our utterances are thereby inhabited by the voices of others. An utterance, however, not only reaches backwards to preceding utterances in the chain of speech communion, but also speaks to future possible utterances. This is because, 'from the very beginning, the utterance is constructed while taking into account possible responsive reactions, for whose sake, in essence, it is actually created' (Bakhtin, 1986, p. 94). Bakhtin is referring here to the utterance's 'quality of being directed to someone, its addressivity' (p. 95). We construct our utterance in anticipation of the other's active responsive understanding. The other constitutes not a passive listener, nor a receiver of a ready-made message and whose communicative task is one of decoding—as assumed in conventional communication models—but rather a co-participant simultaneously creating and created by the utterance in the event that is the utterance, and a factor in its content, structure and style. Moreover, this addressee will vary depending on the sphere of human activity in which the utterance is situated.

This addressee can be an immediate participant-interlocutor in an everyday dialogue, a differentiated collective of specialists in some particular area of cultural communication, a more or less differentiated public, ethnic group, contemporaries, like-minded people, opponents and enemies, a subordinate, a superior, someone who is lower, higher, familiar, foreign, and so forth. And it can also be an indefinite, unconcretized *other*.

(Bakhtin, 1986, p. 95)

Thus, the quality and productivity of dialogue depend upon many aspects of the other and of the relationship between the utterance and the other. On the face of it, much of the foregoing seems, by and large, not much at variance with a monological stance. Once again, however, a closer consideration of the nature and role of the other may prove to be quite revealing.

Bakhtin's other

Within the Bakhtinian framework, all speech, including inner speech, is structured dialogically in that it always presupposes an addressee. Indeed, as noted earlier, in Bakhtin's view the utterance is permeated with presuppositions. To this extent, Vygotsky and Bakhtin are in agreement. For Bakhtin, moreover, the utterances of inner speech are permeated also with the evaluations of actual and potential addressees (Voloshinov, 1981). On the other hand, a leitmotif running through Bakhtinian discussions of dialogue is the distinctiveness of the *other*. Indeed, it is the very *otherness* of the other, the fact that the other speaks from a different horizon, that constitutes the enabling condition for the productivity of dialogue. Here Bakhtin and Vygotsky may be seen to diverge considerably. Bakhtin (1990) asks:

> In what way would it enrich the event if I merged with the other, and instead of *two* there would be now only *one*? And what would I myself gain by the other's merging with me? If he did, he would see and know no more than what I see and know myself; he would merely repeat in himself that want of any issue out of itself which characterizes my own life. Let him rather remain outside of me, for in that position he can see and know what I myself do not see and do not know from my own place, and he can essentially enrich the event of my own life.
>
> (p. 87)

This passage constitutes an explicit rejection of the notion of a shared apperceptive mass as either ground or goal of communication. Similarly, the Bakhtinian dialogical mind does not itself constitute a common apperceptive mass, but rather a community of different and often conflicting voices that cannot be resolved into one comprehensive self. Dialogical thinking is each voice speaking in anticipation (often with misguided and misdirected presuppositions) of the answering voice of another. Thus, in our view, the fundamental difference between the Bakhtinian and Vygotskian notions of dialogue hinges on the status of the other and of the relationship between self and other. For Bakhtinian dialogism, the distance and difference of the other is not only always retained but deemed essential. It is from differences in understanding that dialogue and thought are productive; moreover, productivity is not necessarily measured by consensus. Vygotsky, on the other hand, emphasizes the need for interlocutors to occupy the same epistemological space and for communication to strive for congruence. This emphasis is entirely consistent with Vygotsky's seminal notion of the Zone of Proximal Development, a region of growth (of nearest or most proximal development) for the child to incorporate the knowledge structure of her culture so that she may occupy the same epistemological spaces as her compatriots.

For Bakhtin, self–other differences, rather than impeding communication, motivate and generate dialogue. There is, nonetheless, a recognition of a strong psychological need to achieve understanding and legitimization from others. One particularly important instantiation of the other, in this regard, is that of the *superaddressee*. In addition to the other who is the *second* person, that is, the interlocutor whom we are addressing in any particular instance, there is, Bakhtin (1986) suggests, a *third* person implicit in dialogue. The superaddressee stands above the particularity of dialogue as a kind of reference and authority 'whose absolutely just responsive understanding is presumed, either in some metaphysical distance or in distant historical time' (p. 126). This 'ideally true responsive understanding assume[s] various ideological expressions (God, absolute truth, the court of dispassionate human conscience, the people, the court of history, science, and so forth)' (p. 126). In subsequent sections, we argue that the notion of the 'third person', or 'third voice', of the superaddressee is an absolutely essential, though implicit, feature of Vygotsky's Zone of Proximal Development. This must be so because the goal of dialogue within this zone is not merely the creation of a common apperceptive mass for two interlocutors but something more broadly shared among members of communities.

DIALOGUES IN THE ZONE OF PROXIMAL DEVELOPMENT

It is in Vygotsky's emphasis on the social-interactional origins of individual mental functioning that the notion of dialogue figures most prominently for him. The Zone of Proximal Development (ZPD) has proven to be among the most useful, both theoretically and practically, of the many productive concepts he advanced. The ZPD serves as a connecting concept in Vygotsky's work, bringing together in a single construct the various strands of his thought pertaining to the sociogenesis of specifically cultural forms of thought (Bruner, 1986; Cole, 1985; Moll, 1994). The ZPD is defined as '*the distance between the actual developmental level as determined by independent problem solving and the level of potential development as determined through problem solving under adult guidance or in collaboration with more capable peers*' (Vygotsky, 1978, p. 86). The ZPD represents, in particular, a concrete and programmatic manifestation of Vygotsky's broader theoretical contention regarding the genetic relationship between interpsychological and intrapsychological functioning.

Practically, the construct was introduced also as a critical response, and alternative, to received approaches to instruction and psychological testing. With respect to the latter, Vygotsky polemicizes against the use of static, individual forms of assessment. He argues that, in their tendency to rely exclusively on the analysis of a child's independent intellectual activity in some task setting, traditional methods of psychological testing uncover only the presence in the child of those mental functions that have already matured, functions that constitute the 'fruits' or 'end products of development' (Vygotsky, 1978, p. 86). Competencies or mental functions that are still developing or that are yet to develop, emerging *in vivo* as it were, remain hopelessly beyond the methodological purview of this traditional, individualistic approach to psychological assessment. The notion of the ZPD, in contrast, was formulated precisely to reflect the presence of these competencies *in potentia*, the 'buds' or 'flowers' of development. This dynamic, emergent aspect of mental functioning is reflected more specifically in the child's assisted performance on a task, in the joint, collective activity of child and more competent other. Here we have the most significant role of the other within the Vygotskian framework, that of the tutor.

The emergence of specific cognitive processes is not an invariable or self-evident consequence simply of the opportunity to engage in joint problem solving with a more capable other. Joint activity with a more competent adult or peer, in other words, is not in and of itself a condition sufficient to create a ZPD or to promote independent task mastery. Accordingly, much research on the ZPD attempts to determine the nature and quality of the more competent other's assistance that is most conducive to the development of strategic, self-regulated thought and action (Díaz, Neal, & Amaya-Williams, 1990).

The metaphor of the *scaffold* has proven particularly useful in this effort. Scaffolding is described as a 'process that enables a child or novice to solve a problem, carry out a task or achieve a goal which would be beyond his unassisted efforts' (Wood, Bruner, & Ross, 1976, p. 90). In other words, the developmental *telos* of scaffolded instruction is independent task mastery or, in terms of the metaphor, functioning with the external instructional scaffold withdrawn. Scaffolded instruction within the ZPD is informed by the tutor's constant appraisal of, and sensitivity to, the learner's level of functioning. More specifically, the successful scaffolding of instruction requires that the teacher perform a number of functions, among which are the selection, organization and presentation of suitable tasks. These tasks must also allow for: the teaching of emerging skills; ongoing evaluation of the task's suitability to its purpose; the generation and maintenance of the learner's interest in the task; the use of modeling, questioning and explanation to clarify the goals of the task; and the presentation of approximations and appropriate approaches to the task (Palincsar, 1986; Wood et al., 1976). Sensitivity is important here because of the need to detect, and respond to, emerging capacities and critical absences. Both the detection of, and the response to, appropriate child characteristics depend upon the character, abilities and, above all, the agenda of the tutor. It is through this agenda that a third party enters into the socialization of the child. The tutor, by definition, must have an agenda, or curriculum, however implicit. That curriculum, to be effective, must have some force of authority that goes beyond the tutor. The tutor, teacher and even parent, ultimately, as it were, serve in *loco communis*.

The scaffolding literature suggests that a major feature of the ZPD is its broadly monological goals. Tutor and learner are engaged in an exchange that aims to create a consensus regarding, among other things, the goal-structure of the problem at hand and the actions most apposite to the problem's solution. Ideally, the teacher's utterances are aimed at ensuring the learner's maximal involvement in completing the task at hand, even in the absence of the latter's full understanding of the task situation. In this way, the teacher nudges the child 'from one level of competence to the next and eventually to independent application of the instructed skill' (Palincsar, 1986, p. 74). This requires an attentiveness to the child's performance, an attentiveness that will be reflected in the teacher's dialogical utterances. Indeed, Palincsar (1986) is most explicit in considering dialogue the very means by which directive support in the ZPD is provided and modified, the means, in other words, by which children are provided with scaffolded instruction. But more specifically, what we want here to argue is that this is a dialogue of a particular kind, one with clear monological goals.

In at least one discussion of internalization Vygotsky (1981) invokes the master–slave or supervisor–subordinate relationship. The social relationship that stands as a model for Vygotsky is markedly asymmetrical, hierarchical, and organized around the developmental goal of instrumental control. Moreover, the master–slave, supervisor–subordinate relationship is itself a social transformation of the worker–tool relation, and hence it is easy for Vygotsky to recover, through reciprocal transformation, the tool-like instrumentality of inner speech from such social relationships. Social relationships are based on the same labor–production instrumentality as action–tool relations. All of this is organized around the issue of control, which, through ontogenesis, becomes transformed from that of an external agent over a subordinate to one of an internal agent over self and ultimately to a principle over an instance. 'A major step in the evolution of labor is that the work of the supervisor and that of the slave are united in one person' (Vygotsky, 1981, p. 160). For Vygotsky, the leading edge of cultural-historical development is the progressive evolution and internalization of control and mastery of action and production. He focuses on the technical, principled, hierarchical and paradigmatic in the ontogenetic (and ontological) assimilation of the person into the cultural. The guiding interests for Vygotsky are clearly technical and epistemic. As we have noted, Vygotsky was particularly focusing on the development of scientific-technical thought. Vygotsky's metaphor also highlights another significant ingredient of such dialogue: power. Like Bourdieu (1984), Vygotsky, at least in his view of the ZPD, clearly portrays a knowledge differential as power differential. That differential brings into focus the role of the other in the ZPD.

The other enters into dialogue in many ways. We need to consider 'multiple others' just as we recognize that there are 'multiple selves'. Yet it just seems obvious that there are multiple others. Indeed, there is less of an illusion of unity in the other than in the self. There is a multiplicity in the other, however, that exceeds the mere plurality of the multiple persons and roles. Most often in speaking of the other, we are thinking of our interlocutors, concrete and implied, and these are legend. The notion of a third voice in dialogue raises what might be called the question of the *other* other of dialogue, not an interlocutor, but an implicit third presence: an authoritative voice.

Three dialogical genres for the ZPD

To pursue the respective implications of the different social perspectives of Vygotsky and Bakhtin, we will be drawing distinctions among several dialogical genres relevant to an extended view of the ZPD. We begin with a discussion of the *Magistral dialogue*, which we consider as the prototypical and 'official' dialogical genre of the ZPD. The functioning of the Magistral dialogue depends upon an asymmetry of interlocutors, based, in turn, on an asymmetry of cultural and technical knowledge, and, hence, of power. This asymmetry arises, as we have intimated, from a third factor, beyond self and other, from which knowledge and power flow: an authoritative *third voice* implicit in dialogue (Bakhtin, 1981, 1986; Jauss, 1989). Alternative forms of dialogue ultimately grow out of the ZPD, we will argue, as a progressive reaction to that asymmetry.

Magistral dialogue: the authoritative other

The structure of Vygotsky's ZPD bears a remarkable similarity to the theological tradition of the Magistral dialogue. A Magistral dialogue is characterized by a superiority of the *first* (Magistral) voice over the *second* (novitiate) voice: the parent over the child, the teacher over the student, the tutor over the apprentice. The maintenance of this asymmetry requires a *third* voice, an authoritative and institutional third party upon which the first voice may draw. The sacred text, the word of the prophet, the received view of science, the democratically constituted government, the school curriculum, 'what everybody knows' about child development, medical or 'Aesculapian' (Sarbin, 1995) authority, or even rationality itself, are all common enough exemplars of the third voice of Magistral dialogue. The Magistral discussion centers itself on a deficit or an absence (*quaestio*) on the part of the second voice (child/pupil/apprentice) that is responded to by the first voice (parent/teacher/ mentor/tutor) that interprets (*interpretatio*) the third voice in the given situation (Jauss, 1989). The third voice might be said to 'inhabit', or speak through, the first voice as an instance of ventriloquation (Bakhtin, 1981). This may be signaled by certain conventions in the discourse of the tutor, such as the use of indirect or reported speech to signal the remote source, and authority, of the utterance (Morson & Emerson, 1990; Parmentier, 1994). The tutor does not act as such in a vacuum but out of a cultural and historical context. 'In each epoch,' Bakhtin (1986) writes, 'there are always authoritative utterances that set the tone—artistic, scientific, and journalistic works on which one relies, to which one refers, which are cited, imitated, and followed' (p. 88).

In the Magistral dialogue the first and third voices authoritatively formulate meaning in reaction to the perceived deficit in the second voice. The second voice occasions the dialogue but the first and third voices guide the conversation to its proper end. There is thus a *telos* (developmental endpoint, educational goal, skill to be acquired, character to be formed, etc.) implicit in the Magistral dialogue that is given by the third voice. The productivity of the Magistral dialogue depends, as we have noted above, upon the appropriate sensitivity to the *quaestio*. Nonetheless, the openness of the Magistral dialogue is constrained by the authority of the third voice that serves as both a stabilizing and directing force. The first and third voices presume to know where the dialogue is heading. Deviations from the proper trajectory are noted and corrections initiated.

Magistral dialogue is thus a pedagogical technique for promoting the initiate's acquisition of institutionally constituted cognitive strategies. As such this dialogue affords the means by which scaffolded instruction takes place in the ZPD (Palincsar, 1986). Through dialogue, the helplessness of the *quaestio* is replaced by the self-mediated autonomy of the child's own *interpretatio*. In principle, the Magistral dialogue pays homage to what we have called monologism, a stance within which, according to Bakhtin (1984b), 'the genuine interaction of consciousnesses is impossible, and thus genuine dialogue is impossible as well' (p. 81). It is a dialogue in which a single form of interaction prevails: 'someone who knows and possesses the truth instructs someone who is ignorant of it and in error; that is, it is the interaction of a teacher and a pupil, which, it follows, can only be a pedagogical dialogue' (p. 81). The Magistral dialogue assumes the progressive and deterministic trajectory of a traditional growth curve homing in rheostatically on a set-goal. Significantly, the final phase of the Magistral dialogue is the *communio* in which the Magistral voice strives to draw the participants together consensually in the third voice that they now share, jointly striving to create, in essence, Vygotsky's goal of a shared apperceptive mass.

It should be noted that Bakhtin did not focus on nor provide a systematic view on the ontogeny of what he viewed as the dialogical imagination. In contrast, Vygotsky provides precisely this by placing the child in a concrete apprenticeship within the Magistral dialogue of the ZPD. One might even imagine the ZPD as Vygotsky's quite serious answer to Bakhtin's rhetorical question: 'And what would I myself gain by the other's merging with me?' The gain for the child is enculturation.

Socratic dialogue: the questioning other

Dialogue is always open-ended and may be turned at any moment against any participant, including the third voice. The power of dialogue, as Foucault (1978) has argued, does not simply flow from above but is distributed and heteronomous, potentially available to all who enter into the discursive practices of a culture. Although the Vygotskian tradition has focused on socialization and enculturation in the ZPD as internalization, contemporary interpretive scholars have attempted to treat socialization as a developing *participation* in social networks (e.g. Corsaro, 1992). The child not only gets something *out* of the ZPD but also gets *into* the dialogical context. For the apprentice there is an '*assimilation*—more or less creative—of others' words' (Bakhtin, 1986, p. 89). The apprentice may 'rework and re-accentuate' the words of the other. Eventually, the Magistral dialogue becomes transformed into a Socratic dialogue as the pupil takes a more active role in the educational process and children become more sensitive to ambiguity and more skilled at negotiating meaning (Bruner, 1986). If enculturation were simply a matter of internalization, presumably the dialogue would be enhanced and the productivity of the ZPD would grow with the developing child. Indeed, to a considerable extent that is what appears to happen, but the increasingly active and empowered second voice does entail some interesting complications.

Two important features of the Socratic dialogue are that, first, it is forever suspicious of consensus, and second, it often eludes the *telos* of the third voice. It resists the constraints of the scaffold. The *quaestio* of the second voice (now a Socratic questioning voice) is no longer so easily silenced by appeals of the first voice to the authority of the third voice. Under the increasingly informed voice of the apprentice, the tutor's voice may become confused, lose its way in the conversation, become rather meandering 'until it finally produces a meaning that is the result of a mutual inquiry, and that emerges out of a knowledge of one's lack of knowledge' (Jauss, 1989, p. 210). Yet this meandering may be more than a result of an individual lack of knowledge and rather reflect substantive differences in understanding and, in the limiting case, an exploration of the limits of received knowledge. Moreover, in the Socratic dialogue, there is no guarantee of resolution and consensus. Indeed, many of the original Socratic dialogues (e.g. *Lysis*) end in general disarray and confusion (C.P. Smith, 1980).

It should be noted that this account of the Socratic dialogue differs from many accounts of 'Socratic method' as proposed, for example, to characterize certain forms of psychotherapy (e.g. Friedberg & Fidaleo, 1992; Moss, 1992; Overholster, 1994). A close examination of the so-called 'Socratic method' as used in these contexts reveals that what is being promoted is a

Magistral dialogue in which clients are taught to ask the 'right' questions for self-discovery and certainly not to enter into social critique. In education, the work of Corsaro (1992), for example, reveals that teachers are often willing to allow children to take a leading role and to make adjustments just to the extent that the children's activities incorporate educational and developmental goals. This is a risky business, however. While these adjustments are typically made with a view to maintaining a Magistral dialogue, they may quickly develop into more purely Socratic dialogue.

The other in the Socratic dialogue is no longer conceived unambiguously as an expert or more competent other into whose more highly developed cognitive space the apprentice inevitably moves in the course of enculturation. The hierarchically structured relations of expert and novice in the Magistral version of the ZPD, with its attendant conceptions of the self-possessed tutor and the child-on-the-way-to-self-possession, give way to a looser relational structure that is characterized by a greater mutuality of question and answer. This new sphere is conceived not exclusively in terms of unidirectional influence in which the less able apprentice is pulled up into the intellectual world of the parent, teacher or tutor, but rather as an encounter of differences that carries the potential for *inter*illumination among the voices in dialogue. That the self-understanding of the tutor, no less than that of the apprentice, is subject to change is, of course, entirely consistent with the widely accepted truism of 'bi-directional effects' in developmental psychology. However, there are many levels at which this truism may be acknowledged and understood. In the context of the Magistral dialogue the 'child effects' are acknowledged as the necessary initiating and constraining forces of the *quaestio*. Power resides, nonetheless, with the second and third voices that motivate and direct development. In the Socratic dialogue control shifts to a more directive and active *quaestio* of the second voice, one that may require a modification of the stance of the first voice, indeed one whose response, as Bakhtin (1984b) puts it, 'could change everything in the world of my consciousness' (p. 293). Another way of putting this is to point out that the Magistral dialogue proceeds most clearly when 'child effects' are passive and thoroughly anticipated with responsive strategies ready to hand. To the extent that the child's voice asserts itself in unpredicted and challenging ways, the dialogue becomes Socratic and the opportunity arises for the role of the tutor to be modified. The tutor's stance toward the child may now require an openness not only to the limitations of the child but also to otherwise previously unquestioned prejudices guiding Magistral dialogue in the ZPD. Here the sensitivity is not simply to the limits of the second voice but also to the self-understanding of the first voice. The correctness of the tutor's understanding of the third voice may be questioned and the authoritativeness of the third voice itself may be challenged. Indeed, in our pluralistic culture with its loss of 'grand narratives' (Lyotard, 1984) legitimating traditional authorities, we are sometimes free to change our allegiance to any given third voice or to seek out new authorities. 'Unsuccessful' parents, for example, may seek 'counseling', and enter into another Magistral dialogue in which they take on the second voice in order better to learn to parent.

The ideal Socratic dialogue will be guided by an openness to the emerging truth of the given subject matter and not simply by the adult's prepossessed knowledge. Now this is never more than an ever-present possibility. Certainly, Socrates' interlocutors were not distinguished by their ready abandonment of their Magistral voice, and many adolescents do not appear to feel that parents are any more ready to accept challenges to their own authoritative voice (e.g. Collins, 1990). Hence, in a Socratic dialogue the conflict of voices may escalate.

Menippean dialogue: carnival, misbehaved children and other horrors

To the continuing technical and epistemic interests of the foregoing dialogues an emancipatory interest may be added. When the first voice resists the changing status of the second voice, conflict and a deterioration of relationships are ever-present dangers. Levinson (1978) and Handel (1990) have described the breakdown in mentoring relationships among adults resulting from a questioning by the apprentice either of the mentor's source of authority (i.e. the authority itself) or of the mentor's capacity to continue to interpret authority to the apprentice (i.e. the mentor's hypocrisy). Similarly, an adolescent's conflict with parents or adults in general may be of either of these two sorts. Either parents may be seen as hypocritical, not in fact living up to their own standards, or, on the other hand, as (mis)guided by false standards. Questioning of the second voice may be associated with, result from or lead to the rejection of the third voice. One common consequence or symptom of this rejection is one form or other of relativism in which all potential authorities are questioned, perhaps as a mark of an intellectual coming of age. The second voice now may turn from the skeptical but basically sincere questioning of the Socratic dialogue to the mocking and cynical questioning of what, after the Menippean satire that Bakhtin (1984a, 1984b) associated closely with his notion of carnival, we will call the Menippean dialogue.

The route from the Socratic to the Menippean dialogue is fairly direct. Indeed, in his writings on the Socratic dialogues, Bakhtin (1984b) emphasized the already satirical and unofficial aspects of Socrates. The Socratic dialogue introduces perplexity and so is on the way to becoming a 'war machine', and Socrates himself a 'nomad' (Deleuze & Guattari, 1986) or an 'undisciplined child' (Misgeld & Jardine, 1989). There is always more than a mere suggestion of suspicion of the third voice in Socrates' querulousness, and Bakhtin (1984b) very much stressed the hint of carnival in the Socratic dialogue. The Socratic dialogue is a kind of 'discursive game' (Lyotard, 1984) that escapes the relatively tidy systematization of the Magistral dialogue. For Bakhtin, the Socratic dialogue challenges the centripetal, unifying forces of the Magistral dialogue with its own centrifugal, dispersing forces. As the Socratic dialogue evolves into a Menippean dialogue, the linear, logistic development of the Magistral dialogue, merely disrupted by the Socratic dialogue, is thoroughly displaced by a discursive Borgesian 'garden of forking paths' (Weissert, 1991). Ultimately, the third voice may be mocked, authority turned on its head, flags burned, and leaders burned in effigy (at least). Voices multiply and become inverted, high and low change places in a full-fledged carnival. Both Bakhtin (1984a, 1984b) and Frye (1957) emphasize the comedic, carnivalistic features of the Menippean genre, but it is a hard humor with an ever-present threat of violence. 'The laughter of the carnival', as Kristeva (1980) notes, 'is not simply parodic; it is no more comic than tragic; it is both at once, one might say that it is *serious*' (p. 80). The unruly class, the disenfranchised mob and the raucous demonstration in which a politician's bad faith is parodied are all threatening enough to those speaking in the first voice.

The conflict of dialogues

In the Socratic dialogue the third voice is constantly put at risk of being plunged into the chaos of Menippean dialogue. Such moves away from Magistral dialogue are therefore justly viewed with suspicion, and the Menippean second voice is often stigmatized as immature, deviant, sick or subversive. Counter-moves against incipient Menippeanism may be initiated. Avatars of the third voice may, through various instruments of the state, attempt to re-educate, discipline, cure, shun, silence or banish the unruly second voice (Foucault, 1965, 1975). Authority continually strives to manage dialogue successively through stigmatization, suppression and, ultimately, incorporation into a stable Magistral dialogue. The tendency may be seen in such diverse contexts as Plato's latter dialogues (especially after the *Meno*), which become more didactic, or in the legitimization of the trade union movement, or in the domestication of experimental education in the form of government commissions and federal grants. If the parent is perceived to be an ineffective first voice and does not or cannot accept a second-voiced role in a sanctioned Magistral dialogue, then there are institutional and instrumental remedies to be invoked. In its enlightened tack, the liberalized modern state with its myriad first-voiced agencies ventriloquating the diminishingly authoritative third voice has generally preferred to pursue the educational option of dealing with the second voice, and remediation for the 'failing' child. Hence, the collapse of orderly civil dialogue may be attributed to failures in educational technique or to deficits in the second voice ('bad parenting', poor teacher training, etc.). Techniques are developed and implemented to overcome the developmental lags, deficits or incapacities revealed in developmental research. When the educational option falters, the state turns to other technical resources, typically medical or quasi-medical therapies, and ultimately legal options may be employed or, in extreme cases, terror. Modernist educational theory tends to proceed on two fronts with constant restructuring of the technical educational apparatus of the state and ever-renewed efforts at quasi-medical assessment and remediation of nomadic or deviant second voices and their treatment within a Magistral dialogue.

Disciplines and professions such as psychology are a growing part of this system. These are not merely theoretical systems but social institutions, and increasingly a third voice immanently present in countless Magistral dialogues.

Social discourse gives rise not merely to conflicts about subject matters but more fundamentally to conflicts over dialogical genres. The notion of internalization, as articulated by Vygotsky, itself presupposed a rather structuralist view of culture as a set of interconnected and relatively complete rules. Discourse is viewed as largely consisting of overcoming differences in understanding of the rules and of the appropriateness of local applications in particular circumstances. This monological view is most consistent with the Magistral dialogue and relatively 'weak' forms of the Socratic dialogue. A more post-structuralist view of culture, one that offers an alternative image of, at best, a loosely connected set of guides, ever open to reinterpretation and constantly under renegotiation, opens up more radical forms of Socratic dialogue and even the possibility of Menippean dialogue. The conflict of dialogues, or contentious dialogue among dialogues, provides a ground for social unrest and, ultimately, of construction and destruction forming a higher-order ZPD for, at least the possibility of, sociogenesis. In this context a ZPD is created that is relevant to a broader notion of cultural-historical psychology.

The three dialogical types discussed here are all, we submit, relevant to the notion of ZPD and, moreover, are offered as a potential typology to identify different phases of the ZPD. These dialogical genres reflect transformations in the ZPD as the voices, particularly the second voice, are transformed. As the dialogical genre of the ZPD changes, however, the potential for change extends to the other voices: first to the first voice and, finally, to the third voice. A central feature of all is the generative capacity of asymmetry induced by the third voice. There are asymmetries of knowledge, expertise, resources and, ultimately, power. All offer an opportunity for productive change, on the one hand, and for oppression or disorder, on the other. In the developmental literature the ZPD is almost invariably presented as a rather cozy, nurturant, extended 'womb', but, as we, and others, have argued, it also has the capacity to dominate, discourage and oppress (e.g. Goodnow, 1990). These latter tendencies may be mitigated by the possibility of the Socratic dialogue. Yet, just as Magistral dialogue may range from benevolent paternalism to oppressive authoritarianism, so the Socratic dialogue may range from a subtly modified Magistral dialogue, to creative emancipation, to the nauseating *mise en abîme* of Menippean deconstructive carnival. These are risks for all who enter into dialogue.

We are of the view that the meaning of the ZPD, like any meaning, emerges as part of an unfinalizable dialogue on the topic at hand. While we are not arguing for an abandonment of the ZPD notion as traditionally conceived, we do hope that by contrasting its inherent Magistral qualities to those of the Socratic and Menippean dialogue genres—by, as it were, bringing the Magistral genre into a dialogue with these other genres—we have made some of the assumptions on which it is premised more explicit, and thereby more amenable to critical questioning. In this connection, we are not too far from Bakhtin's (1984b) own views on the dialogizing of genres, according to which a genre's dialogic encounter with other, rival genres promotes a genre's greater self-consciousness. Commenting on the influence of new genres on old ones, Bakhtin (1984b) writes:

> . . . no new artistic genre ever nullifies or replaces old ones. But at the same time each fundamentally and significantly new genre, once it arrives, exerts influence on the entire circle of old genres: the new genre makes the old ones, so to speak, more conscious; it forces them to better perceive their own possibilities and boundaries, that is, to overcome their own *naiveté* . . . [and] promotes their renewal and enrichment.

(p. 271)

Dialogue has often been viewed, by more critically oriented psychologists, as inherently emancipatory and decentering or, in contrast, by many of those in the mainstream, as an essentially neutral field of communication within which may be discovered many differently valenced contents. We have argued that Bakhtin and Vygotsky promote rather different views of dialogue and consider that each illuminates different possibilities. This heterogeneity of dialogue must give us pause to reflect on the contemporary valorizations of 'dialogism' and ask in each case: 'What kind of dialogue is this?'

ACKNOWLEDGEMENTS

The authors gratefully acknowledge the thoughtfully critical comments and suggestions of the Editor and four anonymous reviewers.

REFERENCES

Bakhtin, M.M. (1981). *The dialogical imagination* (M. Holquist, Ed.; C. Emerson & M. Holquist, Trans.). Austin: University of Texas Press.

Bakhtin, M.M. (1984a). *Rabelais and his world* (H. Iswolsky, Trans.). Bloomington: Indiana University Press.

Bakhtin, M.M. (1984b). *Problems of Dostoevsky's poetics* (C. Emerson, Ed. & Trans.). Minneapolis: University of Minnesota Press.

Bakhtin, M.M. (1986). *Speech genres and other late essays* (C. Emerson & M. Holquist, Eds.; V.W. McGee, Trans.). Austin: University of Texas Press.

Bakhtin, M.M. (1990). *Art and answerability* (M. Holquist & V. Liapunov, Eds.; V. Liapunov, Trans.). Austin: University of Texas Press.

Bibler, V.S. (1984). Thinking as creation (Introduction to the logic of mental dialogue). *Soviet Psychology, 22*(2), 33–54.

Bourdieu, P. (1984). *Distinction: A social critique of the judgment of taste* (R. Nice, Trans.). Cambridge, MA: Harvard University Press.

Bruner, J. (1986). *Actual minds, possible worlds*. Cambridge, MA: Harvard University Press.

Clark, K., & Holquist, M. (1984). *Mikhail Bakhtin*. Cambridge, MA: Harvard University Press.

Cole, M. (1985). The zone of proximal development: Where culture and cognition create each other. In J.V. Wertsch (Ed.), *Culture, communication, and cognition: Vygotskian perspectives* (pp. 146–161). Cambridge: Cambridge University Press.

Collins, W.A. (1990). Parent–child relationships in transition to adolescence: Continuity and change in interaction, affect, and cognition. In R. Montemayor, G.R. Adams, & T.P. Gullotta (Eds.), *From childhood to adolescence: A transitional period?* (pp. 85–106) New York: Sage.

Corsaro, W.A. (1992). Interpretive reproduction in children's peer cultures. *Social Psychology Quarterly, 55*, 160–177.

Day, J.M., & Tappan, M.B. (1996). The narrative approach to moral development: From the epistemic subject to dialogical selves. *Human Development, 39*, 67–82.

Deleuze, G., & Guattari, F. (1986). *Nomadology: The war machine* (B. Massumi, Trans.). New York: Semiotext(e).

Díaz, R.M., Neal, C.J., & Amaya-Williams, M. (1990). The social origins of self-regulation. In L.C. Moll (Ed.), *Vygotsky and education: Instructional implications and applications of sociohistorical psychology* (pp. 127–154). Cambridge: Cambridge University Press.

Foucault, M. (1965). *Madness and civilization: A history of insanity in the age of reason* (R. Howard, Trans.). New York: Random House.

Foucault, M. (Ed.). (1975). *I, Pierre Rivière, ...* (F. Jellinek, Trans.). Lincoln: University of Nebraska Press.

Foucault, M. (1978). *The history of sexuality* (R. Hurley, Trans.). New York: Vintage.

Friedberg, R.D., & Fidaleo, R.A. (1992). Training inpatient staff in cognitive therapy. *Journal of Cognitive Psychotherapy, 6*, 105–112.

Frye, N. (1957). *Anatomy of criticism*. Princeton, NJ: Princeton University Press.

Giles, H., & Weiman, J.M. (1993). Social psychological studies of language: Current trends and prospects. *American Behavioral Scientist, 36*, 262–270.

Goodnow, J.J. (1990). Using sociology to extend psychological accounts of cognitive development. *Human Development, 33*, 81–107.

Handel, A. (1990). Formative encounters in early adulthood: Mentoring relationships in a writer's autobiographical reconstruction of his past self. *Human Development, 33*, 289–303.

Jauss, H.J. (1989). *Question and answer: Forms of dialogical understanding*. Minneapolis: University of Minnesota Press.

Kozulin, A. (1990). *Vygotsky's psychology: A biography of ideas*. Cambridge, MA: Harvard University Press.

Kristeva, J. (1980). *Desire in language: A semiotic approach to literature and art* (L.S. Roudiez, Ed.; T. Gora, A. Jardine, & L.S. Roudiez, Trans.). New York: Columbia University Press.

Levinson, D.J. (1978). *The seasons of a man's life*. New York: Knopf.

Lyotard, J.-F. (1984). *The postmodern condition: A report on knowledge* (G. Bennington & B. Massumi, Trans.). Minneapolis: University of Minnesota Press.

Mead, G.H. (1934). *Mind, self, and society: From the standpoint of a social behaviorist*. Chicago, IL: University of Chicago Press.

Misgeld, D., & Jardine, D.W. (1989). Hermeneutics as the undisciplined child:

Hermeneutics and technical images of education. In M.J. Packer & R.B. Addison (Eds.), *Entering the circle: Hermeneutic investigation in psychology* (pp. 259–273). Albany: State University of New York Press.

Moll, I. (1994). Reclaiming the natural line in Vygotsky's theory of cognitive development. *Human Development, 37*, 333–342.

Morson, G.S., & Emerson, C. (1990). *Mikhail Bakhtin: Creation of a prosaics.* Stanford, CA: Stanford University Press.

Moss, D.P. (1992). Cognitive therapy, phenomenology, and the struggle for meaning. *Journal of Phenomenological Psychology, 23*, 87–102.

Overholster, J.C. (1994). Elements of the Socratic method: III. Universal definitions. *Psychotherapy, 31*, 286–293.

Palincsar, A.S. (1986). The role of dialogue in providing scaffolded instruction. *Educational Psychologist, 26*, 73–98.

Parmentier, R.J. (1994). *Signs in society.* Bloomington: Indiana University Press.

Radzikhovskii, L.A. (1987). Activity: Structure, genesis, and unit of analysis. *Soviet Psychology, 25*(4), 82–98.

Radzikhovskii, L.A. (1991). Dialogue as a unit of analysis of consciousness. *Soviet Psychology, 29*(3), 8–21.

Sampson, E.E. (1993). *Celebrating the other: A dialogical account of human nature.* San Francisco, CA: Westview Press.

Sarbin, T.R. (1995). A narrative approach to repressed memories. *Journal of Narrative and Life History, 5*, 51–66.

Shotter, J. (1993). *Cultural politics of everyday life: Social constructionism, rhetoric and knowing of the third kind.* Toronto: University of Toronto Press.

Smith, C.P. (1980). Translator's introduction. In H.-G. Gadamer, *Dialogue and dialectic: Eight hermeneutical studies on Plato* (P.C. Smith, Trans.), (pp. ix–xv) New Haven. CT: Yale University Press.

Smith, N.V. (Ed.). (1982). *Mutual knowledge.* London: Academic Press.

Steiner, P. (Ed.). (1982). *The Prague School: Selected writings 1929–1946.* Austin: University of Texas Press.

Tappan, M.B. (1997). Language, culture, and moral development: A Vygotskian perspective. *Developmental Review, 17*, 78–100.

Trevarthen, C. (1979). Instincts for human understanding and for cultural cooperation: Their development in infancy. In M. von Cranach, K. Foppa, W. Lepenies, & D. Ploog (Eds.), *Human ethology: Claims and limits of a new discipline* (pp. 530–571). Cambridge: Cambridge University Press.

Voloshinov, V.N. (1981). La structure de l'énoncé. In T. Todorov (Ed.), *Mikhail Bakhtine: Le principe dialogique* (pp. 287–316). Paris: Éditions du Seuil.

Vygotsky, L.S. (1978). *Mind in society: The development of higher psychological processes* (M. Cole, V. John-Steiner, S. Scribner, & E. Souberman, Eds.). Cambridge, MA: Harvard University Press.

Vygotsky, L.S. (1981). The genesis of higher mental functions. In J.V. Wersch (Ed. & Trans.), *The concept of activity in soviet psychology* (pp. 144–188) Armonk, NY: M.E. Sharpe.

Vygotsky, L.S. (1987). Thinking and speech. In R.W. Reiber & A.S. Carton (Eds.), *The collected works of L.S. Vygotsky: Vol. 1. Problems of general psychology* (N. Minick, Trans.) (pp. 39–285) New York: Plenum.

Vygotsky, L.S., & Luria, A. (1994). Tool and symbol in child development. In R. van der Veer & J. Valsiner (Eds.), *The Vygotsky reader* (pp. 99–174). Oxford: Blackwell.

Weissert, T.P. (1991). Representation and bifurcation: Borges's garden of chaos dynamies. In N.K. Hayles (Ed.), *Chaos and disorder: Complex dynamics in literature and science* (pp. 223–243) Chicago, IL: University of Chicago Press.

Wertsch, J.V. (1980). The significance of dialogue in Vygotsky's account of social, egocentric, and inner speech. *Contemporary Educational Psychology, 5*, 150–162.

Wertsch, J.V. (1991). *Voices of the mind: A sociocultural approach to mediated action.* Cambridge, MA: Harvard University Press.

Wertsch, J.V., & Stone, C.A. (1985). The concept of internalization in Vygotsky's account of the genesis of higher mental functions. In J.V. Wertsch (Ed.), *Culture, communication, and cognition: Vygotskian perspectives* (pp. 162–179). Cambridge: Cambridge University Press.

Wood, D., Bruner, J.S., & Ross, G. (1976). The role of tutoring in problem solving. *Journal of Child Psychology and Psychiatry, 17*, 89–100.

6 Practice, person, social world[1]

Jean Lave and Etienne Wenger

All theories of learning are based on fundamental assumptions about the person, the world, and their relations, and we have argued that this monograph formulates a theory of learning as a dimension of social practice. Indeed, the concept of legitimate peripheral participation provides a framework for bringing together theories of situated activity and theories about the production and reproduction of the social order. These have usually been treated separately, and within distinct theoretical traditions. But there is common ground for exploring their integral, constitutive relations, their entailments, and effects in a framework of social practice theory, in which the production, transformation, and change in the identities of person, knowledgeable skill in practice, and communities of practice are realized in the lived-in world of engagement in everyday activity.

INTERNALIZATION OF THE CULTURAL GIVEN

Conventional explanations view learning as a process by which a learner internalizes knowledge, whether "discovered," "transmitted" from others, or "experienced in interaction" with others. This focus on internalization does not just leave the nature of the learner, of the world, and of their relations unexplored; it can only reflect far-reaching assumptions concerning these issues. It establishes a sharp dichotomy between inside and outside, suggests that knowledge is largely cerebral, and takes the individual as the nonproblematic unit of analysis. Furthermore, learning as internalization is too easily construed as an unproblematic process of absorbing the given, as a matter of transmission and assimilation.

Internalization is even central to some work on learning explicitly concerned with its social character, for instance in the work of Vygotsky. We are aware that Vygotsky's concept of the zone of proximal development has received vastly differing interpretations, under which the concept of internalization plays different roles. These interpretations can be roughly classified into three categories. First, the zone of proximal development is often characterized as the distance between problem-solving abilities exhibited by a learner working alone and that learner's problem-solving abilities when assisted by or collaborating with more experienced people. This "scaffolding" interpretation has inspired pedagogical approaches that explicitly provide support for the initial performance of tasks to be later performed without assistance (Greenfield 1984; Wood, Bruner, and Ross 1976; for critiques of this position, see Engeström 1987, and Griffin and Cole 1984). Second, a "cultural" interpretation construes the zone of proximal development as the distance between the cultural knowledge provided by the sociohistorical context – usually made accessible through instruction – and the everyday experience of individuals (Davydov and Markova 1983). Hedegaard (1988) calls this the distance between understood knowledge, as provided by instruction, and active knowledge, as owned by individuals. This interpretation is based on Vygotsky's distinction between scientific and everyday concepts, and on his argument that a mature concept is achieved when the scientific and everyday versions have merged. In these two classes of interpretation of the concept of the zone of proximal development, the social character of learning mostly consists in a small "aura" of socialness that provides input for the process of internalization viewed as individualistic acquisition of the cultural given. There is no account of the place of learning in the board of context of the structure of the social world (Fajans and Turner in preparation).

Contemporary developments in the traditions of Soviet psychology, in which Vygotsky's work figures prominently, include activity theory (Bakhurst 1988; Engeström 1987; Wertsch 1981, 1985) and critical psychology (Holzkamp 1983, 1987; Dreier in press; see also Garner 1986). In the context of these recent developments, a third type of interpretation of the zone of proximal developments takes a "collectivist," or "societal" perspective. Engeström defines the zone of proximal development as the "distance between the everyday actions of individuals and the historically new form of the societal activity that can be collectively generated as a solution to the double bind potentially embedded in . . . everyday actions" (Engeström 1987: 174). Under such societal interpretations of the concept of the zone of proximal development researchers tend to concentrate on processes of social transformation. They share our interest in extending the study of learning beyond the context of pedagogical structuring, including the structure of the social world in the analysis, and taking into account in a central way the conflictual nature of social practice. We place more emphasis on connecting issues of sociocultural transformation with the changing relations between newcomers and old-timers in the context of a changing shared practice.

PARTICIPATION IN SOCIAL PRACTICE

Participation focuses attention on ways in which it is an evolving, continuously renewed set of relations; this is, of course, consistent with a relational view, of persons, their actions, and the world, typical of a theory of social practice.

Theorizing about social practice praxis activity, and the development of human knowing through participation in an ongoing social world is part of a long Marxist tradition in the social sciences. It influences us most immediately through contemporary anthropological theorizing about practice. The critique of structural and phenomenological theory early in Bourdieu's *Outline of a Theory of Practice*, with its vision of a conductorless orchestras, and regulation without rules, embodied practices and cultural dispositions concerted in class habitus, suggest the possibility of (crucially important) break with the dualisms that have kept persons reduced to their minds, mental processes to instrumental rationalism, and learning to the acquisition of knowledge (the discourse of dualism effectively segregates even these reductions from the everyday world of engaged participation). Insistence on the historical nature of motivation, desire, and the very relations by which social and culturally mediated experience is available to persons in practice is one key to the goals to be met in developing a theory of practice. Theorizing in terms of practice, or praxis, also requires a broad view of human agency (e.g., Giddens 1979), emphasizing the integration in practice of agent, world, and activity (Bourdieu 1977; Ortner 1984; Bauman 1973).

Briefly, a theory of social practice emphasizes the relational interdependency of agent and world, activity, meaning, cognition, learning, and knowing. It emphasizes the inherently socially negotiated character of meaning and the interested, concerned character of the thought and actions of persons-in-activity. This view also claims that learning, thinking and knowing are relations among people in activity in, with, and arising from the socially and culturally structured world. This world is socially constituted; objective forms and systems of activity, on the one hand, and agents' subjective and intersubjective understandings of them, on the other, mutually constitute both the world and its experienced forms. Knowledge of the socially constituted world is socially mediated and open ended. Its meaning to given actors, its furnishings, and the relations of humans with/in it, are produced, reproduced, and changed in the course of activity (which includes speech and thought, but cannot be reduced to one or the other). In a theory of practice, cognition and communication in, and with, the social world are situated in the historical development of on-going activity. It is, thus, a critical theory; the social scientist's practice must be analyzed in the same historical, situated terms as any other practice under investigation. One way to think of learning is as the historical production, transformation, and change of persons. Or to put it the other way around, in a thoroughly historical theory of social practice, and historicizing of the production of persons should lead to a focus on processes of learning.

Let us return to the question of internalization from such a relational perspective. First, the historicizing of processes of learning gives the lie to ahistorical views of "internalization" as a universal process. Further, given a relational understanding of person, world, and activity, participation, at the core of our theory of learning, can be neither fully internalized as knowledge structures nor fully externalized as instrumental artifacts or overarching activity structures. Participation is always based on situated negotiations and renegotiation of meaning in the world. This implies that understanding and experience are in constant interaction – indeed, are mutually constitutive. The notion of participation thus dissolves dichotomies between cerebral and embodied activity, between contemplation and involvement, between abstraction and experience: persons, actions, and the world are implicated in all thought, speech, knowing, and learning.

THE PERSON AND IDENTITY IN LEARNING

Our claim, that focusing on the structure of social practice and on participation therein implies an explicit focus on the person, may appear paradoxical at first. The individualistic aspects of the cognitive focus characteristic of most theories of learning thus only seem to concentrate on the person. Painting a picture of the person as a primarily "cognitive" entity tends to promote a nonpersonal view of knowledge, skills, tasks, activities, and learning. As a consequence, both theoretical analysis and instructional prescriptions tend to be driven by reference to reified "knowledge domains," and by constraints imposed by the general requirements of universal learning mechanisms understood in terms of acquisition and assimilation. In contrast, to insist on starting with social practice, on taking participation to be the crucial process, and on including the social world at the core of the analysis only seems to eclipse the person. In reality, however, participation in social practice – subjective as well as objective – suggests a very explicit focus on the person, but as person-in-the-world, as members of a sociocultural community. This focus in turn promotes a view of knowing as activity by specific people in specific circumstances.

As an aspect of social practice, learning involves the whole person; it implies not only a relation to specific activities, but a relation to social communities – it implies becoming a full participant, a member, a kind of person. In this view, learning only partly – and often incidentally – implies becoming able to be involved in new activities, to perform new tasks and functions, to master new understandings. Activities, tasks, functions, and understandings do not exist in isolation; they are part of broader systems of relations in which they have meaning. These systems of relations arise out of and are reproduced and developed within social communities, which are in part systems of relations among persons. The person is defined by as well as defines these relations. To ignore this aspect of learning is to overlook the fact that learning involves the construction of identities.

Viewing learning as legitimate peripheral participation means that learning is not merely a condition for membership, but is itself an evolving form of membership. We conceive of identities as long-term, living relations between persons and their place and participation in communities of practice. Thus identity, knowing, and social membership. We conceive of identities as long-term, living relations between persons and their place and participation in communities of practice. Thus identity, knowing, and social membership entail one another.

There may seem to be a contradiction between efforts to "decenter" the definition of the person and efforts to arrive at a rich notion of agency in terms of "whole persons." We think that the two tendencies are not only compatible but that they imply one another, if one adopts as we have a relational view of the person and of learning: it is by the theoretical process of decentering in relational terms that one can construct a robust notion of "whole person" which does justice to the multiple relations through which persons define themselves in practice. Giddens (1979) argues for a view of decentering that avoids the pitfalls of "structural determination" by considering intentionality as an ongoing flow of reflective moments of monitoring in the context of engagement in a tacit practice. We argue further that this flow of reflective moments is organized around trajectories of participation. This implies that changing membership in communities of practice, like participation, can be neither fully internalized nor fully externalized.

THE SOCIAL WORLD

If participation in social practice is the fundamental form of learning, we require a more fully worked-out view of the social world. Typically, theories, when they are concerned with the situated nature of learning at all, address its sociocultural character by considering only its immediate context. For instance, the activity of children learning is often presented as located in instructional environments and as occurring in the context of pedagogical intentions whose context goes unanalyzed. But there are several difficulties here, some of which will be discussed later when we address the traditional connection of learning to instruction.

Of concern here is an absence of theorizing about the social world as it is implicated in processes of learning. We think it is important to consider how shared cultural systems of meaning and political–economic structuring are interrelated, in general and as they help to coconstitute learning in communities of practice. "Locating" learning in classroom interaction is not an adequate substitute for a theory about what schooling as an activity system has to do with learning. Nor is a theory of the sociohistorical structuring of schooling (or simple extrapolations from it) adequate to account for other kinds of communities and the forms of legitimate peripheral participation therein. Another difficulty is that the classroom, or the school, or schooling (the context of learning activity cannot be unambiguously identified with one of these while excluding the other two) does not exist alone, but conventional theories of learning do not offer a means for grasping their interrelations. In effect, they are more concerned with furnishing the immediate social environment of the target action/interaction than with theorizing about the broader forces shaping and being shaped by those more immediate relations.

To furnish a more adequate account of the social world of learning in practice, we need to specify the analytic units and questions that would guide such a project. Legitimate peripheral participation refers both to the development of knowledgeably skilled identities in practice and to the reproduction and transformation of communities of practice. It concerns the latter insofar as communities of practice consist of and depend on a member-ship, including its characteristic biographies/trajectories, relationships, and practices.

Legitimate peripheral participation is intended as a conceptual bridge – as a claim about the common processes inherent in the production of changing persons and changing communities of practice. This pivotal emphasis, via legitimate peripheral participation, on relations between the production of knowledgeable identities and the production of communities of practice, makes it possible to think of sustained learning as embodying, albeit in trans-formed ways, the structural characteristics of communities of practice. This in turn raises questions about the sociocultural organization of space into places of activity and the circulation of knowledgeable skill; about the structures of access of learners to ongoing activity and the transparency of technology, social relations, and forms of activity; about the segmentation, distribution, and coordination of participation and the legitimacy of partial, increasing, changing participation within a community; about its character-istic conflicts, interests, common meanings, and intersecting interpretations and the motivation of all participants vis-à-vis their changing participation and identities – issues, in short, about the structure of communities of practice and their production and reproduction.

In any given concrete community of practice the process of community reproduction – a historically constructed, ongoing, conflicting, synergistic structuring of activity and relations among practitioners – must be deciphered in order to understand specific forms of legitimate peripheral participation through time. This requires a broader conception of individual and collective biographies than the single segment encompassed in studies of "learners." Thus we have begun to analyze the changing forms of participa-tion and identity of persons who engage in sustained participation in a community of practice: from entrance as a newcomer, through becoming an old-timer with respect to newcomers, to a point when those newcomers themselves become old-timers. Rather than a teacher/learner dyad, this points to a richly diverse field of essential actors and, with it, other forms of relationships of participation.

For example, in situations where learning-in-practice takes the form of apprenticeship, succeeding generations of participants give rise to what in its simplest form is a triadic set of relations. The community of practice encompasses apprentices, young masters with apprentices, and masters some of whose apprentices have themselves become masters. But there are other inflection points as well, where journeyfolk, not yet masters, are *relative* old-timers with respect to newcomers. The diversified field of relations among old-timers and newcomers within and across the various cycles, and the importance of near-peers in the circulation of knowledgeable skill, both recommended against assimilating relations of learning to the dyadic form characteristic of conventional learning studies.

Among the insights that can be gained from a social perspective on learning is the problematic character of processes of learning and cycles of social reproduction, as well as the relations between the two. These cycles emerge in the contradictions and struggles inherent in social practice and formation of identities. There is a fundamental contradiction in the meaning to newcomers and old-timers of increasing participation by the former; for the centripetal development of full participants, and with it the successful production of a community of practice, also implies the *replacement* of old-timers. This contradiction is inherent in learning viewed as legitimate peripheral participation, albeit in various forms, since competitive relations, in the organization of production or in the formation of identities, clearly intensify these tensions.

One implication of the inherently problematic character of the social reproduction of communities of practice is that the sustained participation of newcomers, becoming old-timers, must involve conflict between the forces that support processes of learning and those that work against them. Another related implication is that learning is never simply a process of transfer or assimilation: learning, transformation, and change are always implicated in one another, and the status quo needs as much explanation as change. Indeed, we must not forget that communities of practice are engaged in the generative process of producing their own future. Because of the contradictory nature of collective social practice and because learning processes are part of the working out of these contradictions in practice, social reproduction implies the renewed construction of resolutions to underlying conflicts. In this regard, it is important to note that reproduction cycles are productive as well. They leave a historical trace of artifacts – physical, linguistic, and symbolic – and of social structures, which constitute and reconstitute the practice over time.

NOTE

1 The authors request that it is made explicitly clear that the material reproduced is a chapter of a book and was not originally intended to stand on its own.

REFERENCES

Bakhurst, D. (1988). Activity, consciousness, and communication. Philosophy Department Report. Oxford: Oxford University.

Bauman, Z. (1973) *Culture as praxis*. London: Routledge and Kegan Paul.

Bourdieu, P. (1977) *Outline of a theory of practice*. Cambridge: Cambridge University Press.

Davydov, V. and Markova (1983). A concept of educational activity for school children. *Soviet Psychology, 11*(2), 50–76.

Dreier, O. (In press). Re-searching psychotherapeutic practice. In S. Chaiklin and J. Lave (eds), *Understanding practice*. New York: Cambridge University Press.

Engeström, Y. (1987). *Learning by expanding*. Helsinki: Orienta-Konsultit Oy.

Fajans, J. and T. Turner (In preparation) Where the action is: an anthropological perspective on "active theory", with ethnographic applications. Paper presented at the Annual Meeting of the American Anthropolitical Association, 1988.

Garner, J. (1986). *The political dimension of critical psychology*. Berlin: Psychology Institute, Free University of Berlin.

Giddens, A. (1979). *Central problems in social theory: action, structure, and contradiction in social analysis*. Berkeley: University of California Press.

Greenfield, P. (1984). A theory of the teacher in the learning activities of everyday life. In B. Rogoff and J. Lave (eds), *Everyday cognition: its development in social context*. Cambridge, MA: Harvard University Press.

Griffin, P. and M. Cole (1984). Current activity for the future: The ZOPED. In B. Rogoff and J. Wertsch (eds), *Children's learning in the zone of proximal development*. San Francisco: Jossey Bass.

Hedegaard, M. (1988). *The zone of proximal development as a basis for instruction*. Aarhus, Denmark: Institute of Psychology.

Holzkamp, K. (1983). *Grundelgung der Psychologie*. Frankfurt/Main: Campus.

Holzkamp, K. (1987). Critical psychology and overcoming of scientific indeterminacy in psychological theorizing (L. Zusne, trans.). In R. Hogan and W.H. Jones (eds), *Perspectives in personality*. Greenwich, CT: JAI Press.

Ortner, S.B. (1984). Theory in anthropology since the sixties. *Comparative Studies in Society and History*. 26(1): 126–66.

Wertsch, J. (ed.) (1981). *The concept of activity in Soviet psychology*. Armonk, NY: Sharpe.

Wertsch, J. (ed.) (1985) *Culture, communication, and cognition: Vygotskian perspectives*. New York: Cambridge University Press.

Wood, D., J. Bruner and G. Ross (1976). The role of tutoring in problem solving. *Journal of Child Psychology and Psychiatry, 17*: 89–100.

7 *Non scolae sed vitae discimus*

Toward overcoming the encapsulation of school learning

Yrjö Engeström

INTRODUCTION

In her 1987 American Educational Research Association Presidential Address, Lauren Resnick took up the issue of discontinuity between learning in school and cognition outside school.

> The process of schooling seems to encourage the idea that the "game of school" is to learn symbolic rules of various kinds, that there is not supposed to be much continuity between what one knows outside school and what one learns in school. There is growing evidence, then, that not only may schooling not contribute in a direct and obvious way to performance outside school, but also that knowledge acquired outside school is not always used to support in-school learning. Schooling is coming to look increasingly isolated from the rest of what we do.
>
> (Resnick, 1987, p. 15)

Brown, Collins, and Duguid (1989) subsequently initiated a discussion in *Educational Researcher* on new approaches aimed at overcoming this encapsulation of school learning. These authors suggested an educational strategy centered around the notions of "situated learning" and "cognitive apprenticeship" (see also Collins, Brown, and Newman, 1989). Their approach evoked critical commentaries (Palincsar, 1989; Wineburg, 1989), as well as presentations of related approaches like the "anchored instruction" of Bransford and his collaborators (The Cognition and Technology Group at Vanderbilt, 1990). Others, notably Gardner (1990), pursued the analysis elsewhere.

In this chapter, I will continue and expand this discussion. I will analyze three contemporary approaches, each attempting to break the encapsulation of school learning in a different way. The first of these approaches is the instructional theory of "ascending from the abstract to the concrete," developed in the Soviet Union over a period of three decades by the research group led by V.V. Davydov. The second approach is that of "legitimate peripheral participation," recently formulated by Jean Lave and Etienne

Wenger. The third approach, "learning by expanding," has been developed in my own research groups in Finland and in the United States.

While these three approaches are strikingly different, they also share some key ideas. The most important of such shared ideas is that of *joint activity* or *practice* as the unit of analysis. All three approaches draw in varying degrees upon the concept of activity developed by the cultural–historical school of psychology (Leont'ev, 1978; Wertsch, 1981). And all three put a heavy emphasis on the role of mediating artifacts in human cognition and learning.

My discussion of the three approaches is necessarily biased in that I myself work within the framework of the third approach. However, I also find myself in substantial agreement with several basic propositions of the two other approaches. What follows is not a comparison aimed at ranking the approaches according to their merits and weaknesses. Instead, I will try to do two things. On the one hand, I want to present the approaches as alternative and mutually complementary theories, each adding a unique and useful angle to our understanding of the issues at hand. On the other hand, I want to weave together some of their ideas in order to identify promising vistas for future research and theorizing.

In my analysis, I will use an empirical example drawn from my own research on the problems of school learning. The example is that of students' misconceptions of the phases of the moon. I will examine how each of the three approaches might propose to overcome the encapsulation of school learning in this particular content area.

FINDING OUT ABOUT THINGS IN EVERYDAY LIFE

Imagine that you become interested in a simple natural phenomenon. Why does the moon change its shape? In other words, what causes the phases of the moon?

If you took the action of finding out an explanation, you would probably turn to other people for help as well as to books containing graphic models that purport to explain the phenomenon. You might also observe the phenomenon more or less systematically, perhaps using a notepad and a pen to record and analyze your observations. This action of "finding out about it" is schematically depicted in Figure 7.1. Such an action may be embedded in a more enduring activity, such as astronomic hobby or child rearing, for example. But the action may arguably also emerge out of sheer curiosity, as a discrete short-term entity without an anchoring in a broader, more enduring activity system.

The structure depicted in Figure 7.1 is not necessarily an "ideal" model for learning. It takes discrete, situationally occurring problems, phenomena and procedures as "natural" units of learning. The need for and possibility of understanding broader contexts that may produce and explain the discrete

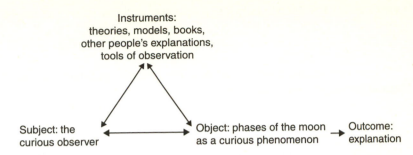

Figure 7.1 The everyday action of finding out about the phases of the moon

problems are not addressed by this kind of everyday learning. Resnick (1987, pp. 15–16) points out that such everyday learning tends to result in "highly situated skills" which – especially if routinized in repeated practice – are difficult to modify, abandon and replace with novel procedures when the task and the context change. As we will soon see, the model of everyday learning is in this respect surprisingly similar to the model of traditional school learning.

THE SEPARATION OF SCHOOL LEARNING FROM THE REST OF EXPERIENCE: THE PHASES OF THE MOON MISCONCEIVED

Several years ago, I published a paper titled "Students' Conceptions and Textbook Presentations of the Movement of the Moon: A Study in the Manufacture of Misconceptions" (Engeström, 1984). The study was based on the following simple question presented to a number of Finnish school students between ages 14 and 17.

> What is the reason for the fact that at times only a part of the moon is visible or it is not visible at all, even though the sky is cloudless? In other words: What causes the different phases of the moon? Clarify your answer with the help of a drawing.

The most common answer among both the younger and older students was that the moon is regularly covered by the shadow of the earth, which causes the new moon.

> "The earth casts its own shadow in front of the moon. That's why the moon is not always wholly visible, sometimes not visible at all."
>
> (Girl, grade 11)

"If the moon is not visible, it is behind the earth. If the moon is wholly visible, then it is directly in front of the earth and the sun shines straight on it."

(Girl, grade 11)

"The shadow of the earth is cast over the moon in different sizes as the moon revolves around the earth."

(Boy, grade 11)

"The earth comes in between the sun and the moon. Thus, the shadow of the earth is reflected upon the moon. That is why only part of the moon can be seen."

(Boy, grade 8)

A large number of subjects illustrated this explanation with drawings. The standard drawing looked as shown in Figure 7.2.

This, in fact, is a fairly accurate description of a relatively uncommon event, the lunar eclipse – and a completely incorrect explanation to the regular phenomenon of new moon.

As the next step of that research, I presented the same question to another group of Finnish secondary school students, aged 17. Again 50 percent of the subjects gave the answer "moon is covered by the shadow of the earth." This time, after the completion of the answer, each student was given the following further question.

Once in a while lunar eclipses takes place, too. Why do they take place? Clarify your answer with the help of a drawing.

While answering this second question, the students were allowed to keep the sheets containing their answers to the first question.

Obviously the same mechanism of "the shadow of the earth" cannot account for both the lunar eclipse and the new moon. By forcing the students to reflect upon the lunar eclipse, I wanted to check the effect of a conceptual conflict on their conceptions. Interestingly enough, almost all (81 percent) of the students who had produced the dominant misconception as their answer to the first question produced the same answer again to the second question.

Now what do these findings tell us? I got the initial idea for my study from a well known German educator Martin Wagenschein, who reported an informal inquiry he had conducted among the visitors of an observatory,

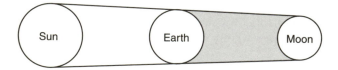

Figure 7.2 Depiction of the dominant misconception produced by students

using essentially the same question. The visitors were asked how it came about that the shape of the moon changes from full moon to half moon, to quarter moon, and to new moon.

> The result at the end was very interesting. About 80% of those who were asked knew no correct answer, regardless from which social stratum they came. (. . .) I can add to this finding from my own experience: among university students, about every fourth gives the same quick but absurd answer: it is the shadow of our earth that makes the moon time and time again into a crescent.
>
> The lack of knowledge as such is not bewildering. Honest ignorance about difficult things belongs to education. But here the truth is easy to see; and it is even easier to notice that it would be impossible for the shadow of the earth to cover the moon. For the crescent is never far away from the sun in the sky and never opposite to it (which would have to be the case, if our shadow were to be cast over it). The modern man has here often outright mislearned what the natural science could have taught him: to observe the thing. What is even more problematic, instead of knowing what he could see, if he had learned to look, he has empty sentences readily at hand. And these he has taken from another much more uncommon phenomenon which he also has left unobserved and not understood, namely the lunar eclipse. He has mislearned through so called learning.
>
> (Wagenschein, 1977, pp. 42–43)

Wagenschein calls this phenomenon "synthetic stupidity." He contends that the moon and the sun of the classroom have for the students nothing to do with the moon and the sun they can daily see in the sky.

> Thus, in astronomy, it is especially easy to realize how natural scientific knowledge can, quite unnecessarily, become alienated from reality and fragmented. It then fragments us, too. What fragments has nothing to do with education.
>
> (Wagenschein, 1977, p. 45)

Wagenschein does not go into the concrete mechanisms behind the "synthetic stupidity." However, his basic argument is provocative. It contains an account of the nature of the students' misconceptions fundamentally different from that given by most researchers in the field of "everyday conceptions" or "naive conceptions." The misconceptions are not indications of immature thinking. They are culturally produced artifacts which often persist regardless of maturation.

The phases of the moon and the lunar and solar eclipse are taught in grade 4 in the Finnish comprehensive school. I analyzed the textbooks officially approved for use in this subject and grade level in the comprehensive school.

The differences between the books were minimal. All textbooks build their explanation of the phases of the moon on a basic diagram, an example is shown in Figure 7.3.

The diagram looks perfectly reasonable. It is clear and graphical. One wonders what can cause the student's difficulties in assimilating this simple model. An analysis of the textbooks and adjunct materials reveals two rather evident problems concerning the treatment of the phases of the moon.

First, the relationship between the phases of the moon (especially the new moon) and the lunar eclipse is not problematized in any of the textbooks. The lunar eclipse is presented with the help of an equally simple and graphic diagram as the one used in connection with the phases of the moon. But it is presented as the next topic, neatly separated from the discussion of the phases of the moon. This is a prime example of the "discrete tasks" Levy (1976) named as the basic form of compartmentalization. The connection is never worked out. Obviously there is no automatic guarantee that such connections are realized in everyday learning outside school either.

Secondly, the basic diagram of the phases of the moon is not constructed and applied by the students as an instrument for the analysis of reality. It is given as such, in a finished form. The adjunct materials contain tasks that demand the identification, naming and classification of the different phases or shapes of the moon. The dynamic model behind the diagram is never constructed and tested by students.

These two problems are rather evident. They do not tell much about the specific cognitive mechanisms involved in the confusion between the new moon and the lunar eclipse. One step further in the analysis of the textbooks provides some indication of the nature of these mechanisms.

As you look at the basic diagram presented above, you may notice how conveniently close the earth and the moon are to each other and how little difference there is in their sizes. This is a fundamental, recurrent feature in all the textbooks and students' drawings I analyzed. In reality, if the sun were symbolized with a ball with a radius of little over 50 cm, the earth would be

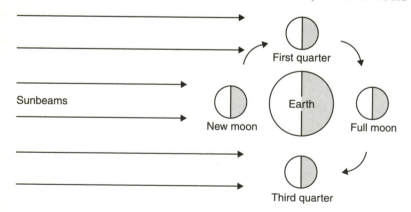

Figure 7.3 The standard textbook diagram of the phases of the moon

symbolized with a ball with a radius of just a little over 0.5 cm and located 150 m from the sun. The moon would then be symbolized with a ball whose radius would be 1.75 mm and which would be located nearly 40 cm from the earth. These distances and sizes are almost unthinkable on the basis of the neat textbook diagrams. Something very essential is destroyed with the loss of distance and sizes. The students cannot very easily grasp how small the likelihood is that the shadow of the earth hits exactly on the moon and makes it invisible. Actually this destruction of sizes and distances may lead children to give artificially "naive" answers to researchers who are using such distorted pictures as "props" (see e.g., Nussbaum, 1979, p. 86).

Even more fundamental than the loss of distances is the loss of the third dimension. The basic diagram is unable to show the depth of the space. In fact, the textbooks analyzed do not even mention it in this connection. As the image of space becomes flat and two-dimensional, it is nearly impossible to avoid the notion that the shadow of the earth must indeed necessarily hit the moon every time the moon revolves around the earth – especially since the moon in the diagram seems to be quite close to the earth.

The world of texts is very much a world of two-dimensional linearity. The relatively closed world of textbooks is certainly no exception. Traditionally, teachers have used simple mechanical telluriums to illustrate three-dimensionally the relations between the sun, the earth and the moon. Nowadays, these devices are commonly considered old-fashioned and clumsy, and the colorful books and workbooks are considered sufficient for purposes of illustration.

Expanding on the model used in Figure 7.1, we may now summarize the findings of this study as an example of the encapsulation of school learning (Figure 7.4).

Figure 7.4 differs from Figure 7.1 in important ways. It depicts the school text as the object of activity instead of being an instrument for understanding the world. When the text becomes the object, the instrumental resources of

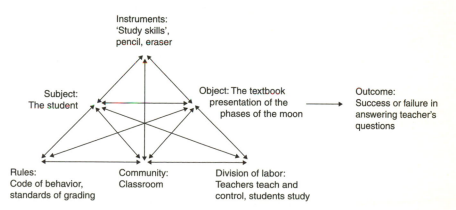

Figure 7.4 A traditional school learning model for studying the phases of the moon

the activity are impoverished – students are left "to their own devices". Resnick (1987, p. 13) points out that in school the greatest premium is placed upon "pure thought" activities – "what individuals can do without the external support of books and notes, calculators, or other complex instruments." This instrumental impoverishment produces what Resnick (1987, p. 18) calls "the symbol-detached-from-referent thinking."

School learning is obviously a collective and relatively enduring activity system. Therefore, I have added the components of community, division of labor, and rules to the rather self-explanatory triad of Figure 7.1. Community refers to those who share the same object of activity. In traditional school learning, it is typically a classroom. Division of labor refers to the division of functions and tasks among the members of the community. In traditional school learning the main division is between the teacher and the students while there is little division of labor between students. Rules refer to the norms and standards that regulate the activity. In traditional school learning, the most important rules are those that sanction behavior and regulate grading.

THE FORMATION OF THEORETICAL CONCEPTS BY ASCENDING FROM THE ABSTRACT TO THE CONCRETE IN INSTRUCTION

Among the various modern approaches to instruction and learning, V.V. Davydov's theory stands out both because of an exceptionally elaborate epistemological and conceptual framework (see Davydov, 1977, 1988a, 1988b) and because of the large body of experimental research accumulated on the basis of the theory both in the Soviet Union and elsewhere (see e.g., Aidarova, 1982; Davydov, Lompscher and Markova, 1982; Hedegaard, Hakkarainen and Engeström, 1984; Lompscher *et al.*, 1989; Markova, 1979; Steffe, 1975). In the present context, I will only briefly summarize some general tenets of the theory and then focus on its implications for the problem of encapsulation of school learning.

The core of Davydov's theory is the method of ascending from abstract to the concrete. This is a general epistemological approach, used by Karl Marx in *Capital* to derive a comprehensive, concrete theory of capitalism from the abstract and simple "germ cell" or "kernel" of commodity as a contradictory unity of use value and exchange value (see Ilyenkov, 1982). Davydov (1977, 1988b) demonstrates how this method can be turned into a powerful strategy of learning and teaching.

> When moving towards the mastery of any academic subject, schoolchildren, with the teacher's help, analyze the content of the curricular material and identify the primary general relationship in it, at the same time making the discovery that this relationship is manifest in many

other particular relationships found in the given material. By registering in some referential form the primary general relationship that has been identified, schoolchildren thereby construct a substantive abstraction of the subject under study. Continuing their analysis of the curricular material, they disclose the rule-governed link between this primary relationship and its diverse manifestations, and thereby obtain a substantive generalization of the subject under study.

The children utilize substantive abstraction and generalization consistently to deduce (again with the teacher's help) other, more particular abstractions and to unite them in an integral (concrete) academic subject. When schoolchildren begin to make use of the primary abstraction and the primary generalization as a way of deducing and unifying other abstractions, they turn the primary mental formation into a concept that registers the "kernel" of the academic subject. This "kernel" subsequently serves the schoolchildren as a general principle whereby they can orient themselves in the entire multiplicity of factual curricular material which they are to assimilate in conceptual form via an ascent from the abstract to the concrete.

(Davydov, 1988b, Part 2, pp. 22–23)

Davydov points out that the strategy of ascending from the abstract to the concrete leads to a new type of theoretical concepts, theoretical thinking, and theoretical consciousness. Theory is here understood not as a set of fixed propositions but as "an instrumentality for the deduction of more particular relationships" from a general underlying relationship (Davydov, 1988b, Part 2, p. 23). Theoretical concepts entail high-level metacognitive functions, such as reflection, analysis and planning.

The strategy of ascending from the abstract to the concrete has two characteristic traits. First, it moves from the general to the particular in that students initially seek out and register the primary general "kernel", then deduce manifold particular features of the subject matter using that "kernel" as their mainstay. Secondly, this strategy is essentially genetic, aimed at discovering and reproducing the conditions of origination of the concepts to be acquired. It requires that "schoolchildren reproduce the actual process whereby people have created concepts, images, values, and norms" (Davydov, 1988b, Part 2, pp. 21–22).

Davydov distinguishes six learning actions constitutive of learning activity that follows the logic of ascending from the abstract to the concrete.

(1) transforming the conditions of the task in order to reveal the universal relationship of the object under study;
(2) modeling the unidentified relationship in an item-specific, graphic, or literal form;
(3) transforming the model of the relationship in order to study its properties in their "pure guise";

(4) constructing a system of particular tasks that are resolved by a general mode;

(5) monitoring the performance of the preceding actions;

(6) evaluating the assimilation of the general mode that results from resolving the given learning task.

(Davydov, 1988b, Part 2, p. 30)

In recent years, Davydov's collaborators have paid special attention to mechanisms of group collaboration in learning activities ascending from the abstract to the concrete (see Jantos, 1989; Rubtsov, 1981; Rubtsov and Guzman, 1984–85).

Now what has this approach to offer toward breaking the encapsulation of school learning? In particular, how would it proceed to teach the phases of the moon?

In general terms, Davydov's theory suggests that the encapsulation of school learning is due to an empiricist, descriptive and classificatory bias in traditional teaching and curriculum design. Knowledge acquired in the school is usually of such quality that it fails to become a living instrumentality for making sense of the bewildering multitude of natural and social phenomena encountered by students outside school. In other words, school knowledge becomes and remains *inert* (Whitehead, 1929) because it is not taught genetically, because its "kernels" are never discovered by students, and consequently because students do not get a chance to use those "kernels" to deduce, explain, predict, and master practically concrete phenomena and problems in their environment. Thus, the encapsulation can be broken by organizing a learning process that leads to a type of concept radically different from those produced in prevalent forms of schooling.

In the particular framework of my example, the Davydovian approach would teach the solar system – and the entire conceptual system of astronomy – by first discovering and modeling the simple initial abstraction of astronomy. What that initial abstraction might be is a question to be solved by intensive analysis conducted jointly by subject-matter specialists, psychologists and educators. The movements of specific heavenly bodies, including the curious phases of the moon, would be problematized, observed and explained concretely with the help of the "kernel" formulated on the basis of the initial abstraction. Such experiments involving design and implementation of totally new curricula and teaching materials have produced impressive learning and transfer results in a variety of subject-matter areas during the past three decades (for a partial summary of the Soviet work, see Davydov, 1988b, Chap. 6; for a summary of the work conducted in the GDR, see Lompscher, 1989).

This solution is depicted in Figure 7.5. Notice that the school text is no more the object of the activity. Instead of a closed text, there is an open "context of discovery" to be reconstructed through practical actions by the students.

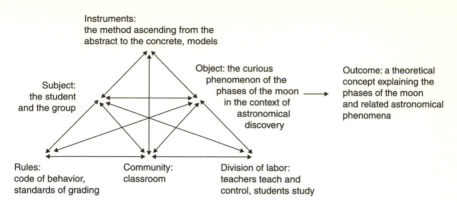

Figure 7.5 A Davydonian model for acquiring an understanding of the phases of the moon

While the upper sub-triangle of the model has changed rather dramatically, the bottom part remains curiously similar to the model depicting traditional school learning (see Figure 7.4). Davydov's theory does not predicate qualitative changes in the rules, community and division of labor existing in traditional school learning.

In summary, Davydov's solution to the encapsulation of school learning is *to push school knowledge out into the world* by making it dynamic and theoretically powerful in facing practical problems. In some sense, this looks like a narrowly cognitive and scientistic strategy. The social basis of school learning doesn't seem to be altered by this strategy, which makes one wonder whether there will be motivation among the students to carry out the strategy.

On the other hand, the strategy differs fundamentally from most cognitivist approaches to instruction in that it is not satisfied with improving the quality of learning texts. By making the practical historical *context of discovery* of theoretical knowledge the object of learning this approach opens up a whole new dynamic of contents. It does not pretend to eliminate the power of the teacher, but by putting students into dialog with the discoverers of the past, the strategy may well empower the students.

LEGITIMATE PEERIPHERAL PARTICIPATION AND COMMUNITIES OF PRACTICE

Jean Lave and Etienne Wenger are not satisfied with the yield of the Davydovian approach.

the social character of learning mostly consists of a small 'aura' of socialness that provides input for the process of internalization viewed as individualistic acquisition of the cultural given. There is no account of the place of learning in the broader context of the structure of the social world.

(Lave and Wenger, in press)

Lave and Wenger propose an alternative approach based on the notion of learning as gradually increasing participation in a "community of practice." The authors argue that "social practice is the primary, generative phenomenon, and learning is one of its characteristics" (Lave and Wenger). Thus, learning should be analyzed as an integral part of the social practice in which it is occurring. To change or improve learning, one should reorganize the social practice.

This point of departure leads the authors to an analysis of different forms of apprenticeship – ranging from Mexican Yucatec midwives to American meatcutters and anonymous alcoholics – as examples of legitimate peripheral participation. Lave and Wenger point out that in all their examples there is very little observable teaching but a lot of well-motivated and effective learning. Learning commonly proceeds from less important, simple tasks toward crucial and complete "core" tasks. At the same time, an overall picture of the activity gradually unfolds as the learner moves from one partial task to another.

There are strong goals for learning because learners, as peripheral participants, can develop in view of what the whole enterprise is about, and what there is to be learned. Learning itself is an improvised practice: a learning curriculum unfolds in opportunities for engagement in practice.

(Lave and Wenger, in press)

Lave and Wenger suggest that learning as participation in communities of practice is particularly effective (a) when participants have broad access to different parts of the activity and eventually proceed to full participation in core tasks, (b) when there is abundant horizontal interaction between participants, mediated especially by stories of problematic situations and their solutions, and (c) when the technologies and structures of the community of practice are transparent, that is, their inner workings can become available for the learner's inspection.

Although Lave and Wenger themselves decline to elaborate on the implications of their approach to school learning, their approach raises important questions. Obviously schooling as a social practice itself should be analyzed from the viewpoint of legitimate peripheral participation. In fact, this has been a preoccupation of many insightful students of the "hidden curriculum" in the past (e.g., Henry, 1963; Holt, 1964). Such analyses show that schooling produces a variety of learning experiences and results which are unintended, if not altogether objectionable, from the viewpoint of the official curricula. The question is, what can the approach formulated by Lave and Wenger offer in terms of an alternative?

The logical solution would be to create good communities of practice within schools. In other words, the social organization of the school should be changed so that it would allow for communities of practical activity demonstrating the three criteria listed above. Recent papers by Collins, Brown and Newman (1989) and Schoenfeld (in press) attempt to sketch properties and preconditions of such communities of practice within school.

How would this approach reorganize the teaching of the phases of the moon? To identify a relevant community of practice, one would simulate what astronomers, or those who apply astronomical knowledge, do in their daily activity. Such practices might involve astronomical observations, calendar making, or similar tasks where the phases of the moon would become a practically relevant question within the framework of a broader activity. Moreover, technologies for making astronomical phenomena transparent – perhaps computer simulations and videodisc applications – would be employed. These tools might provide for high-fidelity virtual worlds, simulated practices of gathering, representing and applying astronomical knowledge. The structure of this solution is depicted in Figure 7.6.

The object of the activity is now the *context of practical application*, in other words, of meaningful contemporary social use and formation of knowledge about the phenomena to be mastered. This is clearly different from the context of discovery suggested by the Davydovian model. Innovations are not precluded from the context of application, but the genetic origination of the key ideas of the discipline is not systematically sought and replicated.

The viability of this approach seems to be dependent on the successful identification of a meaningful social practice that can be transferred into school and still retain some degree of authenticity. Lave and Wenger admit that they are vague in their analysis of social practices. Their approach could easily be turned into just another theoretical legitimization for building technology-intensive microworlds in schools without serious consideration of

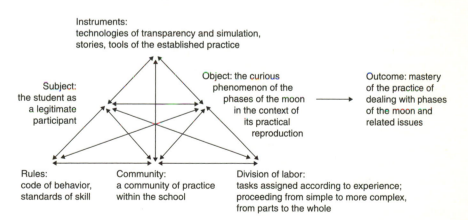

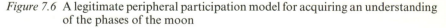

Figure 7.6 A legitimate peripheral participation model for acquiring an understanding of the phases of the moon

the meaning of those worlds in the lives and social circumstances of the participants.

In summary, the legitimate peripheral participation approach seems to propose to solve the problem of encapsulation of school learning by *pushing communities of practice from the outside world into the school*. This transition is not easy, however, as Wineburg (1989, p. 9) pointed out in his commentary.

> But to survive in the marketplace of ideas, a theory of learning has to be situated in a *theory of schooling*. Otherwise, it may leave its mark on archival journals, but leave the world of classrooms virtually untouched.

LEARNING BY EXPANDING

In the conclusion of my original paper on the misconceptions of the phases of the moon, I wrote:

> If it is true that textbooks create closed and often illusory compartments in the minds of the students, should it not be desirable that the students learn to treat the textbooks as historical artifacts, as attempts to fix and crystallize certain generally accepted conceptions of the epoch? This would imply that (...) the students are led to (...) analyze and use textbooks as limited sources, often in need of thorough criticism.
>
> (Engeström, 1984, p. 61)

This brief passage contains an important seed of the theory of expansive learning. Since school is a historically formed practice, perhaps the initial step toward breaking its encapsulation is that students are invited to look at its contents and procedures critically, in the light of their history. Why not let the students themselves find out how their misconceptions are manufactured in school?

Such a search will lead to questions like "Why is this being taught and studied in the first place?" Gregory Bateson points out that such questions are explosive. They open up a wider context into which the current problematic situation is put. Bateson calls such an expansion of context "Level III learning." He notes that "even the attempt at Level III can be dangerous and some fall by the wayside" (Bateson, 1972, pp. 305–306).

To turn expansive learning, or "Level III learning," into a nonpathological course, the learners must first of all have an opportunity to analyze critically and systematically their current activity and its inner contradictions. This I will call *the context of criticism*.

In a school setting, the critical analysis of current practice could well start with a hard look at textbooks and curricula in particular content areas. The "hidden curriculum" of tacit classroom practices could well be analyzed by students, for instance by using videotaped lessons as material. Students could analyze their own test and examination questions and answers, as well as outcomes of their own learning in terms of duration, understanding and transfer. These are substantive metacognitive procedures, quite different from the formal metacognitive skills commonly listed in literature.

But the context of criticism should be extended even further. Students do not come to school as empty vessels. They are exposed to a constant bombardment of information from multiple sources, particularly from mass mediated popular culture. In this sense, they live in a multilayered world of texts in which textbooks are only a visible tip of an iceberg. The relationship between the school knowledge offered by textbooks and the fantasies nurtured by media and artifacts of popular culture are of particular interest in the context of criticism (see Engeström, 1985).

Secondly, the learners must have an opportunity to design and implement in practice a way out, a new model for their activity. This means that the learners work out a new way of doing school work. In other words, students must learn something that is not yet there; they acquire their future activity while creating it (see Engeström, 1987).

This second component also proceeds through particular contents. It seems possible that the three approaches discussed above – Davydov's ascending from the abstract to the concrete, Lave and Wenger's legitimate peripheral participation, and critical analysis of the current practice of learning and instruction – could be employed as complementary modes of inquiry by students and teachers in particular content areas. This would make the *relationships between the context of criticism, the context of discovery, and the context of practical social application* the new, expanded object of learning.

Envision a school where students proceed through (1) a critical analysis of the traditional way of presenting and misconceiving astronomical material, as well as of images and fantasies created in encounters with mass mediated popular culture, (2) a Davydovian process of finding, modeling and using a "kernel" abstraction to make sense of the entire subject matter of astronomy, and (3) an involvement in using and reproducing astronomical concepts in a relevant social practice inside or outside school, whatever that practice might be. These three steps don't necessarily have to be successive. They can also be parallel, even performed by different collaborating groups of students and teachers, providing for multivoiced exchanges.

This idea is in line with the recent emphasis on the multiplicity of "ways of knowing" (Eisner, 1985; Gardner, 1983) and on the distributed, multivoiced nature of human cognition (Cole and Engeström, in press; Wertsch, 1991). Each of the suggested three complementary modes of knowing and learning has distinct cognitive, motivational and social strengths. The context of criticism highlights the powers of resisting, questioning, contradicting, and debating. The context of discovery highlights the powers of experimenting, modeling, symbolizing, and generalizing. The context of application highlights the powers of social relevance and embeddedness of knowledge, community involvement and guided practice. Moving between these contexts provides for intertextuality in the sense discussed by Carpay and Van Oers (1990).

This kind of an expansion in the object implies a qualitative transformation in the entire activity of school learning. Miettinen (1990) characterizes this as formation of networks of learning that transcend the institutional boundaries of the school. He describes an advanced network of learning as follows.

> It includes educational researchers, researchers of certain fields of science, practitioners, teachers, parents, and pupils. There are several examples of this kind of collaboration. A project called *Art and Built Environment* was carried out in England between 1976 and 1982. In this project, the network consisted of architects, community planners, teachers, and pupils. The idea of the project was to study the surroundings of the school and give pupils models and instruments to influence their surroundings.
>
> (Miettinen, 1990, p. 24)

Moll and Greenberg (1990) provide a recent example of such a network in the making. They are working with parents, teachers and students in a Hispanic community of Tucson, Arizona, looking for new ways of literacy instruction that draw upon knowledge and skills found in local households.

> We build on the idea that every household is, in a very real sense, an educational setting in which the major function is to transmit knowledge that enhances the survival of its dependents. (. . .) In order to examine the instructional potential of these household activities, we have created an after-school "lab" within which researchers, teachers, and students meet to experiment with the teaching of literacy. We think of the lab setting, following Vygotsky, as a "mediating" structure that facilitates strategic connections, multiple paths, between classrooms and households.
>
> (Moll and Greenberg, 1990, p. 320; for further examples,
> see Sutter and Grensjö, 1988; Cole, 1990)

Eventually the school institution has to be turned into a collective instrument for teams of students, teachers, and people living in the community. Figure 7.7 depicts the transition from traditional school learning to expansive learning with the help of vertical arrows placed in the different components of the model.

The crucial difference between Figure 7.7 and the preceding models is that in expansive learning the context of learning itself is altered. School learning reflectively reorganizes itself as an activity system. This kind of collective and reflective self-organization is becoming a necessity in practically any kind of social practice. Resnick (1987, p. 18) notes that people must become "good *adaptive learners*, so that they can perform effectively when situations are unpredictable and tasks demand change." I would rephrase the idea:

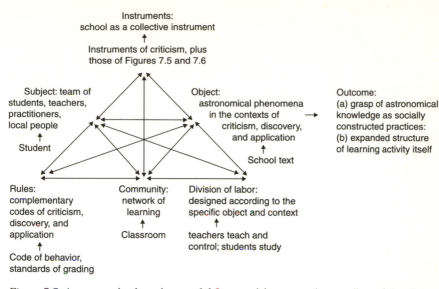

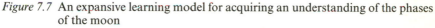

Figure 7.7 An expansive learning model for acquiring an understanding of the phases of the moon

collectives of people must become good expansive learners, so that they can design and implement their own futures as their prevalent practices show symptoms of crisis. The notions of "progressive problem solving" and "working at the edge of one's competence," recently put forward by Bereiter and Scardamalia (in preparation), are in line with the concept of expansive learning.

In summary, expansive learning proposes to break the encapsulation of school learning by expanding the object of learning to include the relationships between traditional school text, the context of discovery and the context of practical application, thus *transforming the activity of school learning itself from within*. This transformation is carried out through particular curriculum contents. It is a long, distributed process, not a once and for all transformation dictated from above.

How likely is such a scenario in real life? There is one point that makes this approach perhaps more realistic than either the Davydovian approach or the legitimate peripheral participation approach would be alone. The expansive learning approach exploits the actually existing conflicts and dissatisfactions among teachers, students, parents and others involved in or affected by schooling, inviting them to join in a concrete transformation of the current practice. In other words, this approach is not built on benevolent reform from above. It is built on facing the current contradictions and draws strength from their joint analysis.

CONCLUSION

The Davydov solution to the encapsulation of school learning is to create such powerful intellectual tools in instruction that students can take them into the outside world and grasp its complexities with the help of those tools. While there is sample evidence of the relative power of the Davydovian approach in particular areas of subject matter, we know little of its overall effects on the lives of students and on the activity system of the school. It is not clear how one would motivate schools to adopt the demanding instructional strategy of ascending from the abstract to the concrete.

The legitimate peripheral participation approach would break the encapsulation the other way around, by creating genuine communities of practice within schools or perhaps by partially replacing school learning with participation in such communities of practice outside school. It is not known to what extent and under what preconditions such a transformation might be possible and what would be the specific qualities of desirable communities of practice. Again, it is an open question whether schools could be motivated to engage in such a transformation.

The expansive learning approach would break the encapsulation of school learning by a stepwise widening of the object and context of learning. The expanded object of learning consists of the context of criticism, the context of discovery, and the context of application of the specific curricular contents under scrutiny. This kind of expansive transition is itself a process of learning through self-organization from below. The self-organization manifests itself in the creation of networks of learning that transcend the institutional boundaries of the school and turn the school into a collective instrument.

REFERENCES

Aidarova, L. (1982). *Child development and education*. Moscow: Progress.

Bateson, G. (1972). *Steps to an ecology of mind*. New York: Ballantine Books.

Bereiter, C. and Scardamalia, M. (In preparation). *Expertise as process*.

Brown, J.S., Collins, A. and Duguid, P. (1989). Situated cognition and the culture of learning. *Educational Researcher*, **18**, 32–42.

Carpay, J. and Van Oers, B. (1990). *Didactic models and the problem of intertextuality and polyphony*. Paper presented at the Second International Congress for Research on Activity Theory, Lahti, Finland.

The Cognition and Technology Group at Vanderbilt (1990). Anchored instruction and its relationship to situated cognition. *Educational Researcher*, **19**(6), 2–10.

Cole, M. (1990, May). *Cultural psychology: Some general principles and a concrete example*. Paper presented at the Second International Congress for Research on Activity Theory, Lahti, Finland.

Cole, M. and Engeström, Y. (in press). A cultural–historical interpretation of distributed cognition. In G. Salomon (ed.), *Distributed cognition*. Cambridge: Cambridge University Press.

Collins, A., Brown, J.S. and Newman, S.E. (1989). Cognitive apprenticeship: Teaching and crafts of reading, writing and mathematics. In L.B. Resnick (ed.), *Knowing, learning, and instruction: Essays in honor of Robert Glaser* (pp. 453–494). Hillsdale, NJ: Erlbaum.

Davydov, V.V. [Dawydow, W.W.] (1977). *Arten der Verallgemeinerung im Unterricht: Logisch psychologische Probleme des Aufbaus von Unterrichtsfächern*. Berlin: Volk und Wissen.

Davydov, V.V. (1988a). Learning activity: The main problems needing further research. *Multidisciplinary Newsletter for Activity Theory*, **1**(1–2), 29–36.

Davydov, V.V. (1988b). Problems of developmental teaching: The experience of theoretical and experimental psychological research. Parts 1–3 *Soviet Education*, **30**, (8–10).

Davydov, V.V. [Dawydow, W.W.], Lompscher, J. and Markova, A.K. [Markowa, A.K.] (eds) (1982). *Ausbildung der Lerntätigkeit bei Schülern*. Berlin: Volk und Wissen.

Eisner, E. (ed.) (1985). *Learning and teaching the ways of knowing*. Eighty-fourth yearbook of the National Society for the Study of Education. Part II. Chicago: NSSE.

Engeström, Y. (1984). Students' conceptions and textbook presentations of the movement of the moon: A study in the manufacture of misconceptions. In H. Nielsen and P.V. Thompsen (eds), *Fysik i skolen: Problemer og perspektiver* (pp. 40–62). Aarhus: Aarhus Universitet, Det Fysiske Institut.

Engeström, Y. (1985). Multiple levels of nuclear reality in the cognition, fantasy and activity of school age children. In T. Solantaus, E. Chivian and M. Vartanyan (eds), *Impact of the threat of nuclear war on children and adolescents* (pp. 39–52). Boston: IPPNW.

Engeström, Y. (1987). *Learning by expanding: An activity-theoretical approach to developmental research*. Helsinki: Orienta-Konsultit.

Gardner, H. (1983). *Frames of mind: The theory of multiple intelligences*. New York: Basic Books.

Gardner, H. (1990). The difficulties of school: Probable causes, possible cures. *Daedalus*, **119**(2), 85–113.

Hedegaard, M., Hakkarainen, P. and Engeström, Y. (eds) (1984). *Learning and teaching on a scientific basis: Methodological and epistemologial aspects of the activity theory of learning and teaching*. Aarhus: Aarhus Universitet, Psykologisk institut.

Henry, J. (1963). *Culture against man*. New York: Vintage Books.

Holt, J. (1964). *How children fail*. New York: Pitman.

Ilyenkov, E.V. (1982). *The dialectics of the abstract and the concrete in Marx's Capital*. Moscow: Progress.

Jantos, W. (1989). Kooperation und Kommunikation in der Lerntätigkeit. In J. Lompscher (ed.), *Psychologische Analysen der Lerntätigkeit* (pp. 91–136). Berlin: Volk und Wissen.

Lave, J. and Wenger, E. (in press). *Situated learning: Legitimate peripheral participation*. Cambridge: Cambridge University Press.

Leont'ev, A.N. (1978). *Activity, consciousness, and personality*. Englewood Cliffs: Prentice-Hall.

Levy, R.I. (1976). A conjunctive pattern in middle class informal and formal education. In T. Schwartz (ed.), *Socialization as cultural communication* (pp. 177–188). Berkeley: University of California Press.

Lompscher, J. (ed.) (1989). *Psychologische Analysen der Lerntätigkeit*. Berlin: Volk und Wissen.

Markova, A.K. (1979). *The teaching and mastery of language*. White Plains, NY: Sharpe.

Miettinen, R. (1990, May). *Transcending the traditional school learning: Teachers' work and the networks of learning*. Paper presented at the Second International Congress for Research on Activity Theory, Lahti, Finland.

Moll, L.C. and Greenberg, J.B. (1990). Creating zones of possibilities: Combining social contexts for instruction. In L.C. Moll (ed.), *Vygotsky and education: Instructional implications and applications of sociohistorical psychology* (pp. 319–348). Cambridge: Cambridge University Press.

Nussbaum, J. (1979). Children's conceptions of the earth as a cosmic body: A cross-age study. *Science Education*, **63**, 83–93.

Palincsar, A.S. (1989). Less charted waters. *Educational Researcher*, **18**(4), 5–7.

Resnick, L.B. (1987). Learning in school and out. *Educational Researcher*, **16**(9), 13–20.

Rubtsov, V.V. (1981). The role of cooperation in the development of intelligence. *Soviet Psychology*, **29**(4), 41–62.

Rubtsov, V.V. and Guzman, R.I. (1984–85). Psychological characteristics of the methods pupils use to organize joint activity in dealing with a school task. *Soviet Psychology*, **23**(2), 65–84.

Schoenfeld, A.H. (in press). Ideas in the air: Speculations on small group learning, environmental and cultural influences on cognition, and epistemology. *International Journal of Educational Research*.

Steffe, L.P. (ed.) (1975). *Children's capacity for learning mathematics. Soviet studies in the psychology of learning and teaching mathematics* (vol. 7). Chicago: School Mathematics Study Group.

Sutter, B. and Grensjö, B. (1988). Explorative learning in the school? Experiences of local historical research by pupils. *The Quarterly Newsletter of the Laboratory of Comparative Human Cognition*, **10**(2), 39–54.

Wagenschein, M. (1977). *Verstehen Lehren. Genetisch – Sokratisch – Exemplarisch*. Weinheim: Beltz.

Wertsch, J.V. (ed.) (1981). *The concept of activity in Soviet psychology*. Armonk, NY: M.E. Sharpe.

Wertsch, J.V. (1991). *Voices of the mind*. Cambridge: Harvard University Press.

Whitehead, A.N. (1929). *The aims of education*. New York: Macmillan.

Wineburg, S.S. (1989). Remembrance of theories past. *Educational Researcher*, **18**(4), 7–10.

8   Social memory in Soviet thought

David Bakhurst

REMEMBERING SOVIET CONCEPTIONS OF MEMORY

The recent literature on collective or social memory contains two principal themes. The first emphasizes the significance of "group remembering", of those social practices by which the members of a community preserve a conception of their past. Such practices, it is argued, must be brought from the periphery to the centre of social theory, for within them a community's very identity is sustained and the continuity of social life made possible. The second theme is the social constitution of individual memory. Here we find a radical challenge to the orthodox view that memory is located solely within the head, a challenge which suggests that the nature of individual memory cannot be analysed without essential reference to notions such as "society", "community" and "history".

This chapter is devoted primarily to the second of these themes. Any argument that memory is an essentially social phenomenon flies in the face of the individualist conceptions of mind dominant in Western philosophy and psychology and provokes a range of predictable, yet worrisome, objections. Thus, for example, it will be argued that memories are undeniably states of the brain, or at least of "the mind", and to admit this is surely to locate memories in the individual head. Moreover, since "remembering" is just an operation on memories, it is natural to hold that it too goes on in the head. Of course, the objection continues, we are certainly often caused to (mis)remember events by "social interaction", but that is no more grounds to believe that memory is essentially social than my Siamese cat's reminding me of days spent in Toronto is grounds to believe that memory is essentially feline!

I propose to examine whether such objections can be met by arguments in the writings of certain Soviet thinkers, in particular the psychologist Vygotsky (1896–1934). Vygotsky is well known to have advanced a theory of the social genesis of the mental, and work on memory was central to the development of his position. Vygotsky's legacy is thus an obvious place to look for an argument that memory, at least in its "higher", human manifestations, is a capacity of social origin. Furthermore, other like-minded Soviet thinkers seem to offer ways to strengthen and develop Vygotsky's position. In the work of his contemporary, V.N. Voloshinov (1895–1936), for example, we find the suggestion that since remembering involves giving a *reading* of the past, our memories are the product of interpretative skills that are social in both nature and origin. In addition, the philosopher Evald Ilyenkov (1924–79) offers a vision of how human social activity serves to preserve the past in the present, thereby constituting a form of memory irreducible to happenings in any individual mind. The Soviet tradition, then, seems rich in resources for defending a strong reading of the social foundation of individual memory, and one which represents a marked departure from the prevailing orthodoxy in the West.

However, as we contruct the argument we shall find ourselves drawn inexorably into a discussion of the first of the two themes, into cultural issues of collective remembering and forgetting. The writings of these Soviet thinkers are often complex and inaccessible; to use them as a resource requires much interpretative work. In this, the socio-political context in which they were produced is inescapable. It determines both the agenda and the mode of expression of these thinkers' contributions. Especially significant is that social and political circumstances have greatly determined how this Soviet work has been remembered, commemorated and (in some cases) forgotten by subsequent generations. The way in which it is read today is the outcome of a long and sometimes mysterious process of collective remembering.

Consider Vygotsky, a thinker with an explicit political commitment to founding a "Marxist psychology", whose views took shape in the lively intellectual milieu of the Soviet Union in the 1920s. He was immediately recognized as a leading figure within Soviet psychology, a discipline charged with making a significant contribution to the success of the new regime. Accordingly, Vygotsky often addressed the questions with immediate consequences for Soviet educational, clinical and academic political commitments. This role must have called for considerable sensitivity to the political situation, and as the climate darkened with the rise of Stalinism, he and his group moved the base of their activities from Moscow to the Ukraine. Nonetheless, soon after his premature death in 1934 his works were banned and erased from the history of Soviet psychology. For twenty years his thought was preserved by his former collaborators, largely within an oral culture which itself was influenced greatly by changing social and political circumstances. Since Vygotsky's rehabilitation in 1956, his works have been gradually republished in the USSR, where he is celebrated (in some circles) as the founder of Soviet psychology, though the issues to which his views are read as contributions have changed since the time he was writing. Vygotsky's brilliance has also been recognized in the West, though many who cite him know only a small number of translations, some highly edited.

This history makes clear that the path leading from Vygotsky's contribution to our present ways of representing it is an extremely tortuous one. It is therefore significant that the political context of his work is virtually ignored by modern scholars concerned to recover it. Vygotsky is portrayed not so much as a Marxist theorist who negotiated a tense political environment and whose work was a victim of Stalin's purges, but as a thinker whose genius "transcend[s] historical, social and cultural barriers" (Wertsch, 1985: 231; also Levitin, 1982: ch. 1; and Luria, 1979: ch. 3). It is easy to understand why this is so. The very political climate that has so influenced how Vygotsky has been remembered has also served to inhibit discussion of its influence. There is therefore no tradition in the USSR of scholars writing serious histories of their disciplines. The situation has been scarcely easier for the few Western scholars in the area, for those who have mastered the Soviet tradition have done so by entering the oral culture which sustains it, and have found themselves subject to the constraints and responsibilities such participation entails.[1]

Vygotsky has been our example, though similar stories could be told about Voloshinov and Ilyenkov (see Bakhurst, in press). It is clear that anyone who would seek to draw on their insights must be aware that their work has been preserved in a collective memory under extraordinary constraints and pressures, paramount among which is that the nature of this process of remembering must never be explicit in the memories it yields. The memory of their tradition suffers from amnesia about its own history. This cannot be irrelevant to the interpretation of the substance of their theories.

Thus, issue from both the themes identified will be interwoven in what follows. We shall explore how a strong reading of the social nature of memory can be defended by appeal to these Soviet thinkers, but we shall do so in a way which reveals the collective memory of their contributions to be an exceedingly relevant factor in the construction of that defence.

VYGOTSKY'S CONCEPTION OF MIND AND MEMORY

I begin with an exposition of Vygotsky's basic theoretical stance – faithful, I hope, to the way it is usually remembered. I shall then present Vygotsky's account of memory.[2]

Vygotsky made his entrance on the Soviet psychological stage in 1924, when he presented his "Methods of reflexological and psychological investigation" to the 2nd All-Russian Psychoneurological Congress in Leningrad. In this and other early works, his main concern was to identify what he called the "crisis in contemporary psychology". Vygotsky argued that, like most young disciplines, psychology was a battleground of warring schools. Gestalt psychology, psychoanalysis, behaviourism and Stern's personalism, for example, all seemed to offer insightful suggestions for a theory of mind. Yet since each school employed an explanatory framework incommensurable with the others, it was impossible to integrate their separate findings. It therefore seemed that psychology would become a unified science only if one of the competing schools defeated its rivals. But, Vygotsky argued, none of the existing frameworks had sufficient explanatory power to ground a science embracing all psychological phenomena. Each offered insights in its own limited domain but threatened to become vacuous when its principles were applied more widely.

The weakness of the prevailing schools was clearest in their failure to make good sense of *consciousness*, the phenomenon Vygotsky saw as the principal subject of psychological enquiry. Psychologists, he argued, adopted either one of two strategies to its analysis: either (a) a subjectivism which treated consciousness as a sui generis, non-physical phenomenon occurring in a self-contained, "inner" world of thought and accessible to the investigator only through "non-scientific" modes of enquiry (for example, through the intro-spective reports of the subject or phenomenological analysis); or (b) an objectivism which held that consciousness is reducible to a set of objectively observable physical happenings governed by a specifiable set of physical laws (of which laws relating "stimuli" to "responses" seemed the most likely candidates).[3]

For Vygotsky, the debate between these positions was structured by two widely held beliefs: first, that the two strategies exhausted the possible alter-natives for a theory of consciousness; and secondly, that psychology could be scientific only by adopting a reductionist approach. Neither belief could be true, Vygotsky argued, since both subjectivism and objectivism were unten-able. While the former transformed the mind into an occult entity beyond the reach of scientific investigation, the latter brought the mental into the ambit of science only by doing violence to the higher forms of human psychological functioning. Thus, if the Soviets were to establish a scientific psychology, their task was to carve a path between subjectivism and objectivism.

Vygotsky's proposal for this project invoked a sharp distinction (drawn from Marx and German classical philosophy) between "elementary" and "higher" mental functions. The elementary functions are said to be character-istic of purely animal, in contrast to human, psychological functioning. They include non-verbal thought (single problem-solving activity), involuntary memory and primitive forms of attention, perception and desire. Vygotsky held that an organism possesses such elementary functions purely in virtue of its physical organization, and that they develop and mature as the organism develops physically. The character of a creature's elementary mental func-tioning is thus determined exclusively by natural or biological considerations, and *can* therefore be explained in reductionist terms.

In the case of the human child, however, psychological development is not limited to the natural evolution of the elementary mental functions with which it is endowed by nature. On the contrary, the child comes to develop "higher" mental functions which are distinctively human in kind. These include verbal thought, intellectual speech, voluntary or "logical" memory and attention, and rational volition. The higher mental functions form a system or totality of psychological capacities said to be "interfunctionally" related; that is, the character of each is determined by the developing rela-tions it bears to the others. On a Vygotskian perspective, consciousness is portrayed not as one among other higher mental functions, but as the system of interrelated functions itself. As the child develops this system, so its innate, elementary functions are totally restructured or cease to exist altogether.

Crucial to Vygotsky's position is the claim that higher mental functions are qualitatively distinct from, and hence irreducible to, their primitive antecedents. This is so, he argues, because higher mental functions represent *mediated* forms of psychological activity.

Vygotsky's elusive notion of mediation underwent significant development as his work progressed. It first emerged as a response to stimulus–response (S–R) theory. Vygotsky held that in analysing psychological states in terms of behavioural responses caused by specific stimuli, the S–R model was unduly unidirectional. It concerned itself with the effect of the world on the psychological subject without considering the subject's effect on the world. Vygotsky demanded that psychology be concerned with the consequences of human action as well as its causes, arguing that the distinguishing feature of human behaviour is that human beings actively change their environment so as to create new stimuli. We fashion special artefacts, tools, solely for the purpose of manipulating the world and, thereby, the behaviour the world elicits from us. And we create signs, a class of artificial stimuli that act as means to control behaviour (by tying a knot in a handkerchief we create the cause of our own later rememberings). Hence the relation between world and subject is never simply unidirectional, but is constantly mediated by tool and sign. The linear connection between stimulus and response is replaced by a triangular interrelation between stimulus, response and "mediational means".

From the outset, Vygotsky stressed how the creation of the sign vastly broadens the horizons of the human mind. Just as the tool helps us master nature, so the sign enables us to master our own psychological functioning (hence Vygotsky calls signs "psychological tools"). We employ signs to draw attention, to aid recall, to represent problems in a way that facilitates their solution and so on. Hence, Vygotsky concluded, the key to the nature of higher psychological functioning lies in the mediating role of the sign.

As Vygotsky explored this role, so he became fascinated with the notion of *meaning* and, with this, his account of mediation underwent an important change. While earlier he had portrayed signs as a class of special artificial stimuli, operating alongside other "natural" stimuli, he now came to focus on our ability to create elaborate symbolic systems, such as natural language and mathematics, which mediate our relation to the world through the power of representation. For the later Vygotsky, the introduction of such semiotic systems of mediation completely transforms our psychological relation with reality. We now stand in relation not just to a brute, physical world, but to an *interpreted* environment, an environment conceived as being *of a certain kind*. This being so, our behaviour can never be simply "called forth" by the world in itself. Rather, we act in the light of some reading of reality, a reading that renders our behaviour an appropriate response to the perceived situation. On this view, our actions are more like conclusions to arguments than effects of physical causes. Such a position places the semiotic at the very heart of the relation between psychological subject and reality; the world is an environment endowed with significance, and the trajectory of the subject's behaviour is determined by the meaning he or she takes from the world.

While Vygotsky's early account of mediation may seem a variation on the stimulus–response theme, the later "semiotic" approach represents a radical departure from the framework. The attraction of the S–R model derived from its promise to establish law-like relations between stimuli and responses described in purely physical terms. However, on this Vygotskian position, the subject's acts, and the situation in which they are undertaken, are described not in a purely physical vocabulary, but in words which render those actions meaningful in the light of the subject's interpretation of the situation. Moreover, the project of establishing laws which relate world and action described in such meaning-laden terms is hopeless. Thus, when Vygotsky recognized semiotic analysis to be "the only adequate method for analysing human consciousness" (quoted in Wertsch, 1985: 79), he strengthened his conviction that a scientific psychology cannot be achieved by treating human mental capacities on the model of physical phenomena governed by natural laws.

Thus, for Vygotsky, for psychology to be scientific it must employ, not a reductionist method, but one adequate to the specific character of semiotic mediation. To this end, he urged that psychology become a "socio-historical" discipline. The systems of mediation which form the fundamental basis of human mental functioning are, he argued, cultural creations. They are products of social history and are preserved in human activity, in what might be called the "interpretative practices" of the community. The development of the child's higher mental functions must therefore be seen, not as the outcome of some process of natural evolution, but as the consequence of the child's appropriation, or "internalization", of such interpretative practices, in particular, natural language. Psychology must therefore make systematic sense of the child's assimilation into its culture and of the qualitative transformations in mental functioning that this precipitates. These transformations will be captured, Vygotsky believe, only by a "genetic" account which reveals the history of the developing system.

The Vygotskian model, then, is this. The human child enters the world endowed by nature with only elementary mental capacities. The higher mental functions constitutive of human consciousness are, however, embodied in the social practices of the child's community. Just as the child's physical functions are at first maintained only through connection with an autonomous system beyond the child, so his or her psychological life is created only through inauguration into a set of external practices. Only as the child internalizes or masters those practices is he or she transformed into a conscious subject of thought and experience.

The distinction between "elementary" and "higher" mental functioning is central to Vygotsky's research on memory. Vygotsky describes "natural" memory as "mechanistic" or "instinctive". This is purely involuntary recall, evoked spontaneously by some state of affairs in the world. The infant may be caused to remember his or her last meal by the smell of the next, or that it is bath time by the sound of water running, but these are cases of remembering over which he or she exercises no control. In contrast, the higher mental function of memory permits us to search at will for an image or an account of the past. In such voluntary or "logical" memory, it is not that the mind is just prompted to "go and get" an image by some encounter in the present; rather, the past is deliberately recalled for a determinate reason. Vygotsky argues that logical memory is made possible by the mediating power of signs. By using signs as aids to memory human beings are able deliberately to control the conditions of their future remembering. He writes:

> The very essence of human memory is that human beings actively remember with the help of signs. It is a general truth that the special character of human behaviour is that human beings actively manipulate their relation to the environment, and through the environment they change their own behaviour, subjugating, it to their control. As one psychologist has said [Dewey], the very essence of civilization consists in the fact that we deliberately build monuments so as not to forget. In the knotted handkerchief and the monument we see the most profound, most characteristic and most important feature which distinguishes human from animal memory.
>
> (Vygotsky, 1931a: 86; 1978: 51)

In the late 1920s and early 1930s, Vygotsky and his colleagues designed a series of experiments to explore the influence of mediational means on children's remembering. These experiments used cases of simple memorization and recall. Children were asked to remember lists of words, the members of which bore no special relation to another. Vygotsky compared the children's performance in cases (a) where they were required to recall the list "by heart" and (b) where they were offered symbolic devices in conjunction with the list as an aid to recall. (From the various accounts of these experiments, it seems that these symbolic aids were usually schematic representations, pictographs, or objects which, when suitably interpreted, could be linked with the word to be recalled; thus a picture of a jug of milk might be employed to help remember "cat", and so on.) Vygotsky found that, after the age of 4, children were able actively to employ the pictographs as memory aids and that their performance was significantly improved as a result. Conducting similar experience with adolescents and adults, however, revealed that for these groups the availability of symbolic aids caused a less significant improvement in their ability to remember, and sometimes even inhibited their performance. Vygotsky concluded that the adolescents and adults were indeed employing symbolic devices as aids to memory, only now their techniques had become *internalized*; they worked with various mnemonic systems which they had silently invented in thought, and which could easily be disrupted if they were forced to use external aids.

Vygotsky consistently maintained that these findings confirmed his general theory of the mind. His interpretation of their significance, however, altered in a way which reflects the shift in his understanding of mediation. At first, Vygotsky argued that the use of signs as memory aids can be understood on the stimulus–response framework: signs figure as artificial stimuli which we consciously employ to cause ourselves to respond in the desired way. Thus in 1929 he wrote that mediated memory can "be divided without remainder into the same conditional reflexes as natural memorizing" (1929: 420). However, as he began to consider exactly how signs facilitate remembering, Vygotsky came to recognize that the character of semiotic mediation could not be explained by extending the S–R model.

In some versions of the experiment, the children had been allowed to choose which pictures to use as memory aids. The experimenters noticed some unexpected choices and asked the children to explain how these signs had helped them remember. Thus, for example, one child who had chosen a sketch of a camel to remember the word "death" explained that the camel was in a desert where its rider was dying of thirst. Another, who had taken a picture of a crab on the beach to remind him of the world "theatre", replied that the crab spends all day looking at a beautiful stone (also represented in the picture) as if it were at the theatre (Vygotsky, 1931a: 242). Faced with such accounts, Vygotsky moved to the position that the sign could not be represented as simply an extra, artificial link in a causal chain. Rather, it seemed that the sign facilitated remembering as part of an argument in which the word to be recalled figured as the conclusion. It was as if the child used the picture to construct a story which led to the required word as its punchline. This suggests that the structure of mediated memory must be seen as *narrative*, delivering its results in virtue of the meaning of the employed mediational means, and not as straightforwardly causal. We remember by constructing narratives which require the recall of past events for their intelligible completion.

I believe that as Vygotsky came to appreciate this insight, he began to regret that the memory research he and his collaborators had so far conducted had not explored in more depth the semiotic dimension of mediation. In 1932, he wrote that while their research had successfully set the debate on memory into motion, it had not produced definitive conclusions. "Moreover", he continued, "I am inclined to think that it represents a colossal oversimplification, even though at first it was often criticised as unduly complex [because of its rejection of a linear S–R model]" (Vygotsky, 1932: 392; the passage is mistranslated in Vygotsky, 1987; see also Leontiev and Luria, 1968: 345). Sadly, Vygotsky's life was cut short before he could take this work further.

What, then, does this work contribute to our understanding of the claim that individual memory is a social phenomenon? Vygotsky, it appears, would endorse a very strong reading of that claim. Throughout his career he held that the distinctive character of human memory is that it is mediated by symbolic means which are cultural phenomena; the human child thus only acquires the higher mental function of memory in so far as he or she is led to appropriate those cultural means by adult members of the community. Moreover, towards the end of his life Vygotsky began to develop a distinctive view of symbolic mediation which introduced a yet richer conception of the social basis of memory. On this view, to possess "logical memory" involves more than a sensitivity to the instrumental use of cultural artefacts; it requires the ability to engage in the specific practice, social in origin, of the production and interpretation of narrative forms constructed in the most powerful of socially forged symbol systems, natural language. Furthermore, Vygotsky holds that the genesis of logical memory entails the complete reorganization of the elementary forms of memory the child is given by nature. Thus, it seems that, for Vygotsky, no form of adult memory can be rendered intelligible without essential reference to the concepts of "society", "community" and "culture".

Yet, however attractive Vygotsky's conclusion may be, his writings fail to provide arguments which would make them truly compelling. The experimental research, though often novel and ingenious, remains underdeveloped, relying heavily on Vygotsky's theoretical framework for its interpretation. In turn, while I have argued elsewhere that Vygotsky's theoretical vision can be developed and defended (for example, Bakhurst, 1986), it remains that much of it consists of pregnant insights in need of further elaboration. This is particularly true of his later ideas about semiotic mediation, the development of which would appear so central to the defence of his mature position.

Thus, if Vygotsky's legacy is to provide the basis for a theory of social memory we must find ways to strengthen and develop his insights. A natural place to look is the work of his students and followers, Soviet and Western, who see themselves as members of a "socio-historical" school of psychology with its roots in Vygotsky's thought. Such a project, however, draws us inevitably into a discussion of how Vygotsky's thought has been preserved in the complex collective memory of the Soviet psychological tradition.

VYGOTSKY REMEMBERED

Two crucial elements of Vygotsky's insights about memory which need further clarification are, first, his conception of the relation of "the cultural" and "the natural" which lies behind his distinction between "higher" and "elementary" mental functions; and secondly, his understanding of the nature of semiotic mediation. I want to argue now that the way these features of Vygotsky's thought are presently remembered has been significantly influenced by events largely forgotten in accounts of his contribution – namely, the suppression of his writings in the 1930s. This will prove relevant to how Vygotsky's position should be defended and strengthened.

The Soviet intellectual climate at the beginning of the 1930s was dominated by the "Great Break", a period of massive cultural revolution in which groups of young Party activists in several fields called for the "bolshevization" of their disciplines and accused the first generation of Soviet scholars of a multitude of sins. These included "formalism", a failure to produce theories responding to the practical needs of the Soviet state, inadequate "party spirit" and a betrayal of the "Leninist stage" in Soviet thought. Although these criticisms were mostly without substance, they were forcefully endorsed by the Party leadership and precipitated a wave of persecution throughout the Soviet academic world.

Little has been written about the bolshevization of Soviet psychology in 1931 (see Joravsky, 1978; Kozulin, 1984: 20–3; Valsiner, 1988: 95–8). It seems, however, to have drawn inspiration from the assault on philosophy of the previous year (see, for example, Bakhurst, 1985; and in press: ch. 2; Joravsky, 1961; Valsiner, 1988: 89–95). In this, Abram Deborin's school of Hegelian Marxism, which had dominated Soviet philosophy for several years, was accused of "menshevizing idealism", an epithet apparently coined by Stalin himself. The same heresy was soon detected among psychologists, including Konstantin Kornilov, the influential "reactologist" who directed the institute where Vygotsky and his collaborators pursued their research. Menshevizing idealism in psychology, it was asserted, was "rotten at its roots [and] contributed nothing to the practice of socialism, but rather slowed down socialist development with the help of its objectively reactionary, pessimistic theories" (Zalkind, 1931: 19). The currency of such dangerous nonsense in the capital must, at least in part, explain the Vygotsky group's decision to move the base of their activities from Moscow to Kharkov in 1931. As the mythology around menshevizing idealism grew, to remain under Kornilov's patronage was to risk not only the preservation of the group's research, but the very lives of its members. Several philosophers perished in the prison camps, and there was no reason to believe that psychologists guilty of "ideological deviation" would not suffer a similar fate.

Although the move to the Ukraine secured the survival of the group's research, Vygotsky's legacy remained under threat. After his death in 1934, his work suffered a barrage of criticisms. First, he was attacked for "cosmopolitanism"; that is, for showing respect for the work of "bourgeois" authors. Secondly, despite his well-known critique of conventional intelligence tests, his interest in psychological testing was dismissed as reactionary. Such testing, it was argued, always serves to preserve the status quo, representing the less educated as the intellectually inferior. Finally, a third criticism zeroed in on just those elements of his work we have found central to his views on memory. He was argued to have emphasized semiotic and cultural phenomena at the expense of practical activity in his account of the development of consciousness, thereby implying that the mind is formed not in "material production" (that is, in the process of object-orientated activity with material objects), but through interpersonal relations (that is, participation in communicative and representational practices). He was thus held to have misrepresented the relation between the "natural" and "cultural" forces in development, overemphasizing the significance of enculturation, while ignoring the (purportedly) natural process of the child's material interaction with the physical environment.

The second of these criticisms is usually cited as most significant. When the Central Committee's 1936 decree outlawed "paedology", a form of child psychology which emphasized testing, his work was withdrawn from public consumption for the remainder of the Stalin era. However, the effect of the third criticism's assault on Vygotsky's semiotic and cultural emphasis should not be underestimated. With Vygotsky's writings banned, his legacy could only be preserved in an oral culture sustained by his followers. I shall argue that this third criticism significantly shaped how his disciples came to represent and remember his contribution.

Despite its more scholarly tone, the third criticism is no less ideologically motivated than the others. In this period, Soviet polemicists would typically seek to discredit their opponents by associating their work with some form of philosophical idealism. This is precisely the criticism's implication: Vygotsky's recognition of the fundamental explanatory importance of "ideal" phenomena such as meaning and communication is perceived as an idealist departure from the orthodox dialectical materialism of the founders of Marxism, with its emphasis on human beings' material transformation of nature. In the Stalin period, no one would have made such a critique without realizing its implications; the third criticism is certainly a charge of ideological heresy in academic guise. It is therefore interesting that those who raised this criticism included members of the Kharkov group itself, such as Alexei Leontiev, and Peter Zinchenko, who explicitly attacked Vygotsky's account of memory.

To be fair, the Kharkovites may initially have made this criticism in self-defence. With Vygotsky in disgrace, they surely had little choice but to distance themselves from his views. Since they could not avoid an ideological pronouncement, it would have made sense to produce a critique with some theoretical content, for this at least required them to give voice to Vygotsky's position in the course of "refuting" it. Nonetheless, whatever the Kharkovites' intentions the criticism quickly became a habitual feature of their presentation of Vygotsky's work. Indeed, they began to define their research programmes in response to these supposed weaknesses of their teacher's contribution. A good illustration is Leontiev's "activity theory" (see Leontiev, 1975), an approach which has proved very influential in the USSR and the West. The initial rationale for this theory, which identifies object-orientated activity (*predmetnaya deyatel'nost'*) as the developmental root of human consciousness, was precisely to replace Vygotsky's cultural–semiotic orientation with an account on which psychological operations "are determined by the actual [that is, physical, material] relations between child and reality" (Leontiev, 1935: 14). Thus, it seems that the scholars responsible for keeping

Vygotsky's thought alive through the Stalin period internalized an image of his work which, paradoxically, had its origins in the Stalinist attempts to suppress it.

This image endured long after Vygotsky's rehabilitation. In 1968, for example, in an article introducing Vygotsky's work to a Western audience, Leontiev and Luria still maintain that his "cultural–historical" theory of the mind "has serious shortcomings related to an insufficient regard for the formative role of man's practical activity in the evolution of his own consciousness. Thus it counterposed too sharply the various forms of conscious activity of social origin with 'naturally formed' mental processes" (1968: 342). These remarks reproduce almost exactly the case Peter Zinchenko made against Vygotsky some thirty years earlier (P.I. Zinchenko, 1936; see Kozulin, 1986: xlv-lii).

Since the Kharkov school was the guardian of theoretical culture which preserved Vygotsky's memory, it is natural that its representation of his contribution should have enormous influence on how it is presently interpreted and assessed. An excellent example of this influence is found in James Wertsch's exposition of Vygotsky's view in his recent *Vygotsky and the Social Formation of Mind* (1985). Wertsch's text is the finest book-length treatment of its subject, Western or Soviet. One of the reasons for its excellence is its author's ability to speak with the authority of a participant in the debate; Wertsch absorbed himself in the Soviet tradition and arrived at his interpretation through discussions with many of Vygotsky's former collaborators (Wertsch, 1985, xiii). A consequence of this, however, is that Wertsch's presentation reproduces the Kharkovites' critique. Despite his admiration for many of Vygotsky's ideas on meaning, Wertsch argues that Vygotsky was wrong to take a semiotic category, "word meaning", as the basic unit of analysis of consciousness in his classic *Thought and Language*. Wertsch proposes the notion of "tool-mediated action" as an alternative unit, which he draws from the work of Vladimir Zinchenko (Peter Zinchenko's son) (V.P. Zinchenko, 1985; see Wertsch, 1985: 196–7, 205–8). Moreover, like the Kharkovites, Wertsch maintains that Vygotsky's work is flawed for its opposition of the natural and cultural, which, he suggests, is so radical that it precludes a proper explanation of their interaction (1985: 197–8). Again like the Kharkovites, Wertsch argues that this weakness is "directly tied" to Vygotsky's account of meaning (1985: 197). Thus we find that our contemporary reading of Vygotsky bears the mark of a critique forged in the political machinations of the Stalin era.

At the opening of this section, two elements of Vygotsky's thought were identified that need further elaboration if his suggestions about the social essence of memory are to be developed into theory: namely, his conception of semiotic mediation and his view of the relation between the natural and the cultural. We now know it is unlikely we shall find the inspiration for this project in the work of those psychologists to whom we owe the preservation of Vygotsky's legacy. On the contrary, since the Stalinist attempt to suppress

Vygotsky, the collective memory of his thought has consistently marginalized its semiotic orientation and sought to reshape his view of the natural and cultural.

We have no choice, then, but to look beyond the mainstream of Soviet psychology. We turn first to a theorist of language also working in the 1920s, V.N. Voloshinov, whose ideas have been argued to complement Vygotsky's (Emerson, 1983; Wertsch, 1985: 224–6). In Voloshinov, I believe, we find the means to develop the semiotic dimension of Vygotsky's stance. As expected, the result is a radical view of the cultural constitution of mind in general, and memory in particular.

VOLOSHINOV AND THE TEXTUALITY OF THE MENTAL

Our present understanding of Voloshinov's work is a legacy of collective remembering every bit as intriguing as the processes which have preserved Vygotsky's thought. Little is known of Voloshinov's life. He was born in 1895 or 1896 in St. Petersburg, where he began studying law some twenty years later. By 1918 he had moved to the provincial town of Nevel where he became a member of the circle of thinkers surrounding the now famous scholar Mikhail Bakhtin. He followed Bakhtin to Vitebsk and eventually back to Leningrad in 1924, where he re-enrolled at the University. His interests included not only philosophy of language and psychology, but also music-ology and composition. He died in 1936 from tuberculosis. During his life, he published two books, a critique of Freud, *Freudism* (1927), and his seminal work on language, *Marxism and the Philosophy of Language* (1929). He also produced several scholarly articles.

The controversy around Voloshinov's legacy began when, at the com-memoration of Bakhtin's 75th birthday in 1970, the Soviet linguist Vyacheslav Ivanov declared that Bakhtin was the author of the major works published under Voloshinov's name. Invanov's claim was neither confirmed nor denied by Bakhtin himself and, as the evidence remains inconclusive, scholars have taken contrasting views of its authenticity. In the West, Bakhtin's biographers, Katerina Clark and Michael Holquist, are adamant that he is the true creator of these works, while Voloshinov's translator, I.R. Titunik, maintains that Voloshinov should be regarded as their sole author. Still others, such as Tzventan Todorov, treat Voloshinov's writings as one voice among many in the Bakhtinian discourse and call their author "Voloshinov/Bakhtin" (Todorov, 1984: 11).

This puzzle is significant because the different solutions invite different readings of the Voloshinov texts. Those who treat Bakhtin as their author must somehow account for the Marxist idiom, conspicuously absent in Bakhtin's other writings. Clark and Holquist, for example, suggest that refer-ences to Marxism were added to the already completed texts to get them past the censor (see for example, 1984: 159). from such a perspective, the Voloshinov texts are read primarily as stages in the development of Bakhtin's theory of language, "ventriloquated" through the persona of an orthodox Marxist (Holquist, 1983: 6).

However, once Voloshinov is restored as author, it becomes possible to treat the professed Marxism of these writings as central to their concerns. We can read Voloshinov as setting out, like Vygotsky, to re-establish his discipline on a Marxist foundation. Indeed, there are many interesting parallels between the way in which Voloshinov and Vygotsky conceived their respective objects. For example, Voloshinov shares Vygotsky's conviction that a Marxist approach must carve a path between subjectivism and objectivism. Hence, in the philosophy of language, Voloshinov seeks an account which neither treats the individual mind as the sole source of meaning, nor construes meaning as a property of language conceived as a purely formal system (see 1929: II, ch. 1). Moreover, also like Vygotsky, Voloshinov argues that an alternative to subjectivism and objectivism is possible only by recognizing the essentially social nature of the phenomenon under study. For Voloshinov, the linguistic act (the utterances) "is born, lives, and dies in the process of social interaction. . . . Its form and meaning are determined basically by the form and character of this interaction" (1926: 105). Finally, despite his emphatic appeal to the social, Voloshinov is as anxious as Vygotsky to avoid a crude social reductionism. He denies the claim of some Soviet Marxists that the content and character of a discourse is exhaustively explained merely by citing the socio-economic situation of its participants. Rather, he advances a more subtle position where the voices we may choose to speak in, and the ways in which we shall be understood, can be rendered intelligible only in light of the specific character of the communicative practices of our culture, which, in turn, cannot be explained without essential reference to socio-economic factors.

On this reading, Voloshinov's texts appears as part of a developing Soviet Marxism, rather than as a contribution to another intellectual tradition dressed up in Marxist attire. I find such an interpretation more plausible than that of Clark and Holquist. The parallels with Vygotsky – whose professions of Marxism are now generally regarded as sincere – are only one example of how Voloshinov's work is indeed characteristic of (good) Soviet Marxist writing in the 1920s. Although Bakhtin was certainly clever enough to write in this idiom, had he done so he would in fact have been making a contribution to Soviet Marxism. Thus, in so far as the argument for Bakhtin's authorship of the Voloshinov text falsely implies that their Marxism is a deceit (or alternatively that Bakhtin was a Marxist), we should continue to consider Voloshinov to be their author.

Voloshinov offers an argument to strengthen Vygotsky's account of the social nature of memory. The first step is Voloshinov's claim that conscious psychological states are essentially semiotic phenomena. They are all forms of *utterance* (or "verbal reaction"). This is true, he argues, not only of those mental states which are clearly propositional in content (such as beliefs, desires, intentions and so on), but also of the human subject's conscious experiences. "Experience exists", he writes, "even for the person undergoing it only in the material signs" (1929: 28). Hence, for Voloshinov, there is no pure experience of reality to which we later give words; rather, the world we confront is one already organized by our modes of representation. There is no access to reality which is not an interpretation or reading, and hence the world our minds encounter is always a read or interpreted world (1929: 26). Hence, he concludes, "*consciousness itself can arise and become viable only in the material embodiment of signs*" (1929: 11; his emphasis); if we deprive consciousness of its semiotic content, there would be "absolutely nothing left" (1929: 13).

It follows that the content of our mental states is determined by the meaning of the signs which comprise them. However, Voloshinov maintains that signs do not possess meaning in virtue of their intrinsic properties, but take on meaning only in the context of communicative practices in which they are interpreted. And as we have seen, Voloshinov argues that these practices are essentially social in nature. Thus, just as the author's intentions do not fix the meaning of his or her work, so the individual subject does not occupy a logically privileged position in the interpretation of their own thoughts. He writes:

> *The verbal component of behaviour is determined in all fundamentals and essentials of its content by objective-social factors*. The social environment is what has given a person words and what has joined words with specific meanings and value judgements; the same environment continues ceaselessly to determine and control a person's verbal reactions throughout his entire life.
>
> Therefore, nothing verbal in human behaviour (inner and outward equally) can under any circumstances be reckoned to the account of the individual subject in isolation; the verbal is not his property but the property of his *social group*.
>
> (Voloshinov, 1927: 86; his emphasis)

Thus, if "the reality of the inner psyche is the same reality as that of the sign", and the sign derives its meaning from the interpretative practices of the speech community rather than the fiat of the individual (Voloshinov, 1926: 105; 1927: 79; 1929: 86), then psychological states are, in a very strong sense, socially constituted phenomena. "The logic of consciousness", it transpires, "is the logic of ideological communication, of the semiotic interaction of the social group" (1929: 13).

What, then, of memory? For Voloshinov, the social essence of individual memory follows simply from the social constitution of all mental states. On this position, to remember is always to give a reading of the past, a reading which requires linguistic skills derived from the traditions of explanation and story-telling within a culture, and which issues in a narrative that owes its meaning ultimately to the interpretative practices of a community of speakers. This is true even when what is remembered is one's own past experience (Voloshinov, 1927: 87). For Voloshinov, memory can never be understood as an immediate relation between the thinking subject and some private mental image of the past. The image, he argues, becomes a phenomenon of consciousness only when clothed with words, and these owe their meaning to social practices of communication.

Voloshinov's argument greatly strengthens Vygotsky's position. First, while Vygotsky's studies focus narrowly on a specific species of remembering (recall of lists mediated by the use of mnemonic devices), Voloshinov's conclusions are quite general in kind, stressing the social constitution of all forms of individual memory. Secondly, Voloshinov's account is consonant with Vygotsky's account of higher mental functioning in general and the role of semiotic mediation in particular. Moreover, Voloshinov's writings contain material that suggests how a Vygotskian theory of semiotic mediation might be developed; they are a rich resource for any theory which represents consciousness as a developmental achievement precipitated by the internalization of communicative practices broadly understood.

Significantly, if we enrich Vygotsky's account of semiotic mediation by appeal to Voloshinov, we find further support for the former's radical opposition of the "cultural" and the "natural". Like Vygotsky, Voloshinov insists that the human mind cannot be treated as a natural phenomenon intelligible by appeal to natural laws. Mind is "a socio-ideological fact and, as such, beyond the scope of physiological methods or the methods of any other of the natural sciences" (Voloshinov, 1929: 25). We are not born conscious persons, but *become* them after "a second birth, a *social* birth" when we "enter into history" (Voloshinov, 1927: 15; his emphasis). Such Vygotskian thoughts abound in Voloshinov's writings. However, Voloshinov's position suggests a way to defend them not articulated by Vygotsky himself. For Voloshinov the relation between the contents of consciousness and the physical states of the thinking subject's body or brain is analogous to the relation between the meaning of a text and the physical form in which it is inscribed, or (to use a more dynamic model) between the content of a drama and the physical states of the medium (for example, television) in which it is presented. Just as it would be hopeless to look for law-like relations between the physical states of television and the semantic content of the programmes it transmits, so the search for laws relating the states of mind and brain is, for Voloshinov, equally in vain.

As the Kharkovites would have predicted, taking the notion of semiotic mediation seriously leads to a very radical opposition between "the natural" and "the cultural", and to the view that human psychological phenomena are essentially cultural, and hence non-natural, phenomena. Such a view was too radical for many of the Kharkov group, and may be too much for Vygotsky's Western followers. If Vygotsky's thought is developed in this way, there seems little prospect of reconstructing him as an "emergent interactionist" (Wertsch,

1985: 43–7), where the mental development is traced as the outcome of an interplay between biological and cultural forces. For while Vygotsky and Voloshinov hold that mind emerges in the transformation of the child's biological being through the appropriation of culture, they both invoke quite different principles of explanation for the natural and cultural realms. It thus seems unclear how there could be a systematic *theory* of their interaction.

ILYENKOV, IDEALITY AND MEMORY

Now that we have used Voloshinov's writings to strengthen Vygotsky's position we should briefly return to the Kharkovites' critique of it. We observed that, since the 1930s, the mainstream of Soviet psychology has tended to marginalize the semiotic dimension of Vygotsky's legacy. The theories of his best-known followers (Leontiev, Luria, Zaporozhets, Galperin, Mescheryakov, V. Zinchenko and Davydov) have all taken "object-orientated activity, rather than a semiotic category, as the basis of the genesis of consciousness. It would seem that there are two conflicting trends within Soviet Marxist philosophy of mind; one, seen in the contributions of Vygotsky and Voloshinov, which treats semiotic mediation as the foundation of consciousness, and another, dominant since the 1930s, which adopts the "activity approach".

It would be wrong, however, to take the conflict between the two camps at face value. The judgement that there is a genuine theoretical incompatibility between them, itself a product of the 1930s, may owe more to the political shadow-boxing of orthodoxy and heresy than to genuine argument.

This can be seen, I think, if we consider the work of Evald Ilyenkov, one of the most interesting Soviet philosophers of the modern period. In his work of the early 1960s Ilyenkov sought to revitalize Soviet philosophy after the stagnant years of Stalinism. Though he never referred to the thinkers of the 1920s, he reintroduced many issues and ideas which had been prominent in their debates. It is interesting, therefore, that despite his constant emphasis on activity as the foundation of the mental (which endeared him to Leontiev), Ilyenkov seems to share Vygotsky's and Voloshinov's presupposition that there need be no grand opposition between the practical and the semiotic in a Marxist theory of the mind.

Consider, for example, Ilyenkov's theory of "the ideal" (see Ilyenkov, 1962; 1977; a fuller exposition is given in Bakhurst, 1988; and in press: ch. 6). This theory is an attempt to explain the nature and possibility of ideal (that is, non-material) phenomena (for example, values, reasons, psychological processes and states) in the material world. Ilyenkov turns to the concept of activity for his explanation. A Marxist form of materialism, he argues, must hold that ideal phenomena are genuine constituents of objective reality that ultimately have their source in human activity. On this view, the natural world comes to embody non-material properties as objectified forms of social activity. Ilyenkov's argument presupposes, however, that the act of transforming nature is itself a semiotic act: by acting on the world, human beings endow their natural environment with meaning, with the significance which is its "ideal form". This is illustrated by appeal to a concept important to Vygotsky: the tool. An inanimate lump of matter is elevated into a tool through the significance with which it is invested by activity. It stands as an embodiment of human purpose in virtue of the way it is fashioned and employed by human agents. And the artefact created through the manipulation of matter by tools is, Ilyenkov argues, more than merely material because of the meaning it derives from incorporation into human practice.

Ilyenkov takes his theory of the idealization of the natural world very seriously, arguing that his account of the ideality of the tool and artefact may be generalized into a wholesale theory of the relation of culture and mind. For Ilyenkov, "humanity's spiritual culture", the total structure of normative demands objectively confronting each individual member of the community (including the demands of logic, language and morality), must be conceived not as a realm of super-material phenomena, but as patterns of meaning embodied in the form of our material environment through the influence of our activity. In turn, Ilyenkov argues that the capacity to think is just the ability to inhabit such a meaning-laden environment. For him, the higher mental functions must be seen primarily as capacities to engage in a certain species of activity: the negotiation of ideal properties and relations.

Like Vygotsky and Voloshinov, Ilyenkov argues that the human child does not possess the capacity to inhabit an idealized environment from birth, but is inaugurated into the relevant species of activity by adult members of the community. As the child masters or "internalizes" these activities, so he or she becomes a thinking subject. Ilyenkov, again like Vygotsky, conceives of internalization as the appropriation of patterns of social meaning, as the assimilation of a culture, and he would accord language learning a special place in this process. But Ilyenkov would certainly not claim that the internalization of these patterns of meaning should be contrasted with engaging in "real practical activity", since, for him, to assimilate a culture is to appropriate the forms of social activity which sustain it. To learn a language, for example, is to learn to manipulate a special class of artefacts, words.

Thus, for Ilyenkov, activity is the root of consciousness. It is so, however, only because in activity the natural world is invested with enduring patterns of meaning, the negotiation of which constitutes thought. In Ilyenkov's work, the practical and semiotic orientations in Soviet theory live in harmony.

Ilyenkov's contribution, however, offers more to the present discussion than the suggestion that there need not be a theoretical impasse between those trends of Soviet thought which take semiotic mediation as the unit of analysis of consciousness and those which adopt an "activity approach". His theory of the ideal offers another dimension to our account of social memory. Ilyenkov holds that the socially significant practices of the community represent thought made objective. Each human child enters the world to find the forms of activity which constitute thinking embodied in the community's activities and expressed in the shape impressed upon the physical environment by human labour. Just as our status as conscious subjects requires that we master these activities, so the continuity of our mental lives over time depends on the preservation of the world of shared significance the activities sustain. Thus, this idealized world of "humanity's spiritual culture" can itself be seen as a form of memory, and one which is essentially collective in kind.

CONCLUSION

I have argued that a distinctive theory of the social nature of memory may be drawn from the work of three distinguished Soviet thinkers, Vygotsky, Voloshinov and Ilyenkov. This theory holds, first, that memory is a psychological function which is essentially social in origin; secondly, that memories are socially constituted states; and thirdly, that certain forms of collective activity represent a form of social memory, irreducible to the happenings in any individual mind, yet essential to the continuity of the mental life of each individual.

Our discussion revealed that the contributions on which we sought to draw have themselves been preserved by complex processes of collective remembering that have influenced how they are interpreted and commemorated today. In particular, we found that two ideas central to Vygotsky's conceptions of social memory have been marginalized in the Soviet tradition since the Stalin era – namely, the notion of semiotic mediation and the specific distinction between "the cultural" and "the natural" which follows from it. I have tried to tell a story which restores these ideas to the centre of discussion. Such a strategy does not, I believe, compromise the integrity of the Soviet Marxist tradition, despite the way it has perceived itself since the 1930s. It does, however, have some radical consequences. The account of social memory we have constructed is no self-contained theory but follows from a general conception of the social constitution of the thinking individual. This idea, which will seem wild and unscientific from the perspective of contemporary cognitive science, remains enigmatic and underdeveloped. It is to be hoped that a greater understanding of this idea's Soviet past will lead to its fruitful elaboration in the future.[4]

NOTES

1 It is notable that the scholars who offer the most detailed picture of the political setting of Vygotsky's work are the émigrés Alex Kozulin (1984; 1986) and Jaan Valsiner (1988).
2 For accounts of Vygotsky's theory see Bakhurst, 1986; Kozulin, 1986; Leontiev and Luria, 1968; Minnik, 1987; Valsiner, 1988; and Wertsch, 1985. My treatment in this section draws on Vygotsky, 1924; 1925; 1927; and 1934, and those writing which deal explicitly with memory (Vygotsky, 1929; 1931a; 1931b; 1932; and 1978).

3 Both strategies were represented in Russian psychology at the beginning of the century, the first by Chelpanov and other advocates of "subjective psychology" who formed the psychological orthodoxy prior to 1917, the second of Pavlov, Kornilov, Bekhterev and the "reflexologists" who sought an account of all psychological phenomena in stimulus–response terms. The latter approach won institutional supremacy immediately after the Revolution as most consonant with the Bolsheviks' call for a Marxist psychology built on scientific materialistic foundations.

4 I am grateful to the British Council, the British Academy and the Committee on Research at the University of California, San Diego, for funding research which made this chapter possible. Thanks are also due to Christine Sypnowich and David Middleton for their insightful comments and suggestions on the manuscript.

REFERENCES

Bakhurst, David (1985) "Debornism versus mechanism: a clash of two logics in early Soviet philosophy", *Slavonic and East European Review*, June.

Bakhurst, David (1986) "Thought, speech and the genesis of meaning: on the 50th anniversary of Vygotsky's *Myshlenie I rech*" *Studies in Soviet Thought*, 31 (January).

Bakhurst, David (1988) "Activity, consciousness and communication", *Quarterly Newsletter of the Laboratory of Comparative Human Cognition*, 10 (2).

Bakhurst, David, (in press) *Consciousness and Revolution in Soviet Philosophy*. Cambridge: Cambridge University Press.

Clark, Katerina and Holquist, Michael (1984) *Mikhail Bakhtin*. Cambridge, MA: Harvard University Press.

Emerson, Caryl (1983) "Bakhtin and Vygotsky on the internalisation of language", *Quarterly Newsletter of the Laboratory of Comparative Human Cognition*, 5 (1).

Holquist, Michael (1983) "The politics of representation", *Quarterly Newsletter of the Laboratory of Comparative Human Cognition*, (5)1.

Ilyenkov, E.V. (1962) "Ideal'noe" ["The ideal"], in *Filosofskaya entsikolopediya, tom. 2 [Philosophical Encyclopaedia, volume 2]*. Moscow: Sovetskaya entsiklopediya.

Ilyenkov, E.V. (1977) "The concept of the ideal", in *Philosophy in the USSR: Problems of Dialectical Materialism*, tr. by Robert Daglish. Moscow: Progress.

Joravsky, David (1961) *Soviet Marxism and Natural Science*. London: Routledge & Kegan Paul.

Joravsky, David (1978) "The construction of the Stalinist psyche", in Sheila Fitzpatrick (ed.), *Cultural Revolution in Russia, 1928–1931*. Bloomington: Indiana University Press.

Kozulin, Alex (1984) *Psychology in Utopia*. Cambridge, MA: MIT Press.

Kozulin, Alex (1986) "Vygotsky in context" in L.S. Vygotsky, *Thought and Language*, tr., rev. and ed. by Alex Kozulin. Cambridge, MA: MIT Press.

Leontiev, A.N. (1931) "The development of the higher forms of memory", in his *Problems of the Development of Mind*. Moscow: Progress, 1981.

Leontiev, A.N. (1935) "Ovladenie uchashchimisya nauchnymi ponyatiyami kak problema pedagogicheskoi psikhologii" ["The acquisition of scientific concepts by school pupils is a problem of pedagogical psychology"], in *Khrestomatiya po vozrastnoi i pedagogicheskoi psikhologii [Handbook of Developmental and Pedagogical Psychology]*, vol. 1. Moscow: MGU, 1980.

Leontiev, A.N. (1975) *Activity, Consciousness, and Personality*. Englewood Cliffs, NJ: Prentice Hall, translation, 1978.

Leontiev, A.N. and Luria, A.R. (1968) "The psychological ideas of L.S. Vygotsky", in Benjamin B. Wolman (ed.), *Historical Roots of Contemporary Psychology*. New York: Harper & Row.

Levitin, Karl (1982) *One is not Born a Personality*. Moscow: Progress.

Luria, A.R. (1979) *The Making of Mind*. Cambridge, MA: Harvard University Press.

Minnik, Norris (1987) "The development of Vygotsky's thought: an introduction", in Vygotsky (1987).

Todorov, Tzvetan (1984) *Mikhail Bakhtin: the Dialogical Principle*, tr. by Wlad Godzich. Manchester: Manchester University Press.

Valsiner, Jaan (1988) *Developmental Psychology in the Soviet Union*. Bloomington: Indiana University Press.

Voloshinov, V.N. (1926) "Discourse in life and discourse in art", in Voloshinov (1927).

Voloshinov, V.N. (1927) *Freudism: a Critical Sketch*, tr. by I.R. Titunik and ed. in collab. with Neal H. Bruss. Bloomington: Indiana University Press, 1987.

Voloshinov, V.N. (1929) *Marxism and the Philosophy of Language*, tr. by Ladislav Matejka and I.R. Titunik. Cambridge, MA: Harvard University Press, 1986.

Vygotsky, L.S. (1924) "Metodologiya refleksologicheskogo i psikhicheskogo issledovanie" ["The methodology of reflexological and psychological research"], in Vygotsky (1982a).

Vygotsky, L.S. (1925) "Soznanie kak problema sikhologii povedeniya" ["Consciousness as a problem in the psychology of behaviour"], in Vygotsky (1982a).

Vygotsky, L.S. (1927) "Istoricheskii smysl psikhologicheskogo krizisa" ["The historical meaning of the crisis in psychology"], in Vygotsky (1982a).

Vygotsky, L.S. (1929) "The problem of the cultural development of the child", *Journal of Genetic Psychology*, 36.

Vygotsky, L.S. (1931a) *Istoriya razvitiya vysshschyk psikhicheskikh funktsii [The history of the development of the higher mental functions]*, in Vygotsky (1983).

Vygotsky, L.S. (1931b) "Predislovie k knige A.N. Leont'ieva *Razvvitie pamyati*" ["Preface to A.N. Leontiev's *The Development of Memory*"], in Vygotsky (1982a).

Vygotsky, L.S. (1932) "Lektsii po psikhologii" ["Lectures on Psychology"], in Vygotsky (1987).

Vygotsky, L.S. (1934) *Myshlenie I rech' [Thinking and Speech]*, in Vygotsky (1982b); tr. in Vygotsky (1987).

Vygotsky, L.S. (1978) *Mind in Society*, ed. by Michael Cole, Vera John-Steiner, Sylvia Scribner and Elen Souberman. Cambridge, MA: Harvard University Press.

Vygotsky, L.S. (1982a) *Sobranie sochinenii, tom 1: Voprosy teorii I istorii psikhologii [Collected Works, Vol. 1: Questions of the theory and history of psychology]*. Moscow: Pedagogika.

Vygotsky, L.S. (1982b) *Sobranie sochinenii, tom 2: Problemy obshchei psikhologii [Collected Works, Vol. 2: Problems of General Psychology]*. Moscow: Pedagogika; tr. as Vygotsky (1987).

Vygotsky, L.S. (1983) *Sobranie sochinenii, tom 3: Problemy pazvitiya psikhiki [Collected Works, Vol. 3: Problems of the Development of Mind]*. Moscow: Pedagogika.

Vygotsky, L.S. (1987) *The Collected Works of L.S. Vygotsky, Vol. 1: Problems of General Psychology*, tr. by Norris Minnik. New York: Plenum.

Wertsch, James V. (1985) *Vygotsky and the Social Formation of Mind*. Cambridge, MA: Harvard University Press.

Zalkind, Aron (1931) "Psikhonevrologicheskii front i psikhologichyskaya diskussiya" ["The psychoneurological front and psychological discussion"] *Psikhologiya*, 4(1).

Zinchenko, P.I. (1936) "Problema neproizvol'nogo zapominaniya" ["The problem of involuntary memory"], in *Nauchnye zapiski khar'khovskogo gosudar-stvennogo pedagogicheskogo institut inostrannykh yazykov [The scientific record of the Khar'kov State Pedagogical Institute of Foreign Languages]*, vol. 1; tr. in *Soviet Psychology*, 22 (2) (1983–84).

Zinchenko, V.P. (1985) "Vygotsky's ideas about units for the analysis of mind", in James V. Wertsch, *Culture, Communication and Cognitive: Vygotskian Perspectives.* Cambridge: University Press.

9   Putting culture in the middle

Michael Cole

In this chapter I begin the process of reconstructing the cultural-historical approach to development by elaborating on the notion of tool mediation, and by retaining some features of the Russian approach while changing others. I initially found the Russian cultural-historical psychologists' ideas about culture attractive because they seemed to offer a natural way to build up a theory of culture in mind that begins from the organization of mediated actions in everyday practice. This was the same point to which our cross-cultural research had brought my colleagues and me, so it was an obvious point of convergence. But our cross-cultural experience had also induced a profound skepticism about concluding, on the basis of interactional procedures treated as if they were free of their own cultural history, that nonliterate, "nonmodern" people think at a lower level than their modern, literate counterparts. In their belief in historical and mental progress, the Russians were led into many of the same methodological traps we had fallen into in our own cross-cultural work (Cole, 1976).

In light of these considerations, I shall begin my attempt to create a conception of culture adequate to the theories and practices of a second, cultural psychology with the phenomenon of mediation. Rather than start with the concept of a tool, as did the Russians, I shall treat the concept of a tool as a subcategory of the more general conception of an artifact.

ARTIFACTS

Ordinarily one thinks of an artifact as a material object—something manufactured by a human being. In anthropology, the study of artifacts is sometimes considered part of the study of material culture, which is somehow distinct from the study of human behavior and knowledge. According to this "artifact as object" interpretation, it is easy to assimilate the concept of artifact into the category of tool—but from this nothing much is to be gained.

According to the view presented here, which bears a close affinity to the ideas of John Dewey and also traces its genealogy back to Hegel and Marx, an artifact is an aspect of the material world that has been modified over the history of its incorporation into goal-directed human action. By virtue of the changes wrought in the process of their creation and use, artifacts are simultaneously *ideal* (conceptual) and *material*. They are ideal in that their material form has been shaped by their participation in the interactions of which they were previously a part and which they mediate in the present.

Defined in this manner, the properties of artifacts apply with equal force whether one is considering language or the more usually noted forms of artifacts such as tables and knives which constitute material culture.[1] What differentiates the word "table" from an actual table is the relative prominence of their material and ideal aspects and the kinds of coordinations they afford. No word exists apart from its material instantiation (as a configuration of sound waves, hand movements, writing, or neuronal activity), whereas every table embodies an order imposed by thinking human beings.[2]

The dual material-conceptual nature of artifacts was discussed by the Russian philosopher Evald Ilyenkov (1977, 1979), who based his approach on that of Marx and Hegel. In Ilyenkov's system, ideality results from "the transforming, form-creating, activity of social beings, their aim-mediated, sensuously objective activity" (quoted in Bakhurst, 1990, p. 182). From this perspective, the form of an artifact is more than a purely physical form. "Rather, in being created as an embodiment of purpose and incorporated into life activity in a certain way—being manufactured for a *reason* and put into *use*—the natural object acquires a significance. This significance is the 'ideal form' of the object, a form that includes not a single atom of the tangible physical substance that possesses it" (Bakhurst, 1990, p. 182).

Note that in this way of thinking mediation through artifacts applies equally to objects and people. What differs in the two cases is the ways in which ideality and materiality are fused among members of these two categories of being, and the kinds of interactivity into which they can enter.

This view also asserts the primal unity of the material and the symbolic in human cognition. This starting point is important because it provides a way of dealing with the longstanding debate in anthropology and allied disciplines: Should culture be located external to the individual, as the products of prior human activity, or should it be located internally, as a pool of knowledge and beliefs? Both views have a long history in anthropology (D'Andrade, 1995; Harkness, 1992). However, over the past twenty years or so, coincident with the cognitive revolution in psychology and the advent of Chomskian linguistics, the study of culture as patterns of behavior and material products appears to have given way to the tradition that considers culture to be composed entirely of learned symbols and shared systems of meaning—the ideal aspect of culture—that are located in the head.

The concept of artifacts as products of human history that are simultaneously ideal and material offers a way out of this debate. At the same time, as I hope to demonstrate, it provides a useful point of contact between cultural-historical psychology and contemporary anthropological conceptions of culture in mind.[3]

THE SPECIAL STRUCTURE OF
ARTIFACT-MEDIATED ACTION

The Russian cultural-historical psychologists used a triangle to picture the structural relation of the individual to environment that arises *pari parsu* with artifact mediation (see Figure 9.1). Simplifying their view for purposes of explication, the functions termed "natural" (or "unmediated") are those along the base of the triangle; the "cultural" ("mediated") functions are those where the relation between subject and environment (subject and object, response and stimulus, and so on) are linked through the vertex of the triangle (artifacts).

There is some temptation when viewing this triangle to think that when cognition is mediated, thought follows a path through the top line of the triangle that "runs through" the mediator. However, the emergence of mediated action does mean that the mediated path replaces the natural one, just as the appearance of culture in phylogeny does not mean that culture replaces phylogeny. One does not cease to stand on the ground and look at the tree when one picks up an axe to chop the tree down; rather, the incorporation of tools into the activity creates a new structural relation in which the cultural (mediated) and natural (unmediated) routes operate synergistically; through active attempts to appropriate their surroundings to their own goals, people incorporate auxiliary means (including, very significantly, other people) into their actions, giving rise to the distinctive, triadic relationship of subject-medium-object.

In this and later chapters I will expand upon this basic structural diagram to develop an appropriately complex approach to the cultural mediation of

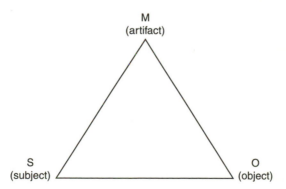

Figure 9.1 The basic mediational triangle in which subject and object are seen not only as "directly" connected but simultaneously as "indirectly" connected through a medium constituted of artifacts (culture).

thought. But even this basic notion that human thought is the emergent consequence of intermingling of "direct, natural, phylogenetic" and "indirect, cultural" aspects of experience is sufficient to bring to the fore the special quality of human thought referred to as the duality of human consciousness. Many expressions of this idea can be found in both the Russian and the Western European/American traditions (Durkheim, 1912). For example, the American anthropologist Leslie White wrote: "An axe has a subjective component; it would be meaningless without a concept and an attitude. On the other hand, a concept or attitude would be meaningless without overt expression, in behavior or speech (which is a form of behavior). Every cultural element, every cultural trait, therefore, has a subjective and an objective aspect" (1959, p. 236).[4]

True to the spirit of cultural-historical approaches, White emphasized the temporal aspect of cultural mediation and its psychological implications: "With words man creates a new world, a world of ideas and philosophies. In this world man lives just as truly as in the physical world of his senses . . . This world comes to have a continuity and a permanence that the external world of the senses can never have. It is not made up of present only but of a past and a future as well. Temporally, it is not a succession of disconnected episodes, but a continuum extending to infinity in both directions, from eternity to eternity" (White, 1942, p. 372).

Luria described this double world in the following way:

> The enormous advantage is that their world doubles. In the absence of words, human beings would have to deal only with those things which they could perceive and manipulate directly. With the help of language, they can deal with things that they have not perceived even indirectly and with things which were part of the experience of earlier generations. Thus, the word adds another dimension to the world of humans . . . Animals have only one world, the world of objects and situations. Humans have a double world.
>
> (1981, p. 35)

A great deal more can and will be said about this basic mediational conception and the peculiar form of consciousness to which it gives rise. Artifacts and artifact-mediated individual human action are only a starting point for developing the needed conceptual tools. Neither artifacts nor actions exist in isolation. Rather, they are interwoven with each other and with the social worlds of the human beings they mediate to form vast networks of interconnections (Latour, 1994). Some way is needed to talk about structure in the resulting cultural medium.

The minimal mediational structure given in Figure 9.1 cannot stand alone as a representation of mediated action in its social context. In order to elaborate a cultural-historical psychology to guide our research in complex, everyday settings, we need to be able to talk about aggregations of artifacts appropriate to the events they mediate and to include the mediation of inter-personal relationships along with mediation of action on the nonhuman world.

Three levels of artifacts

One useful suggestion for how to elaborate on the notion of artifact was made by Marx Wartofsky, who proposed a three-level hierarchy. Wartofsky described artifacts (including tools and language) as "objectifications of human needs and intentions *already* invested with cognitive and affective content" (1973, p. 204).

The first level of Wartofsky's framework consists of *primary artifacts*, those directly used in production. As examples, he gives "axes, clubs, needles, bowls"; my examples will include words, writing instruments, telecommunications networks, and mythical cultural personages. Primary artifacts correspond closely to the concept of artifact as matter transformed by prior human activity that I provided earlier, although I do not distinguish for current purposes between production of material goods and production of social life in general.

Secondary artifacts consist of representations of primary artifacts and of modes of action using primary artifacts. Secondary artifacts play a central role in preserving and transmitting modes of action and belief. They include recipes, traditional beliefs, norms, constitutions, and the like.

The third level is a class of artifacts "which can come to constitute a relatively autonomous 'world,' in which the rules, conventions and outcomes no longer appear directly practical, or which, indeed, seem to constitute an arena of non-practical, or 'free' play or game activity" (p. 208). Wartofsky calls these imagined worlds *tertiary artifacts*. Such imaginative artifacts, he suggests, can come to color the way we see the "actual" world, providing a tool for changing current praxis. In modern psychological jargon, modes of behavior acquired when interacting with tertiary artifacts can transfer beyond the immediate contexts of their use. Wartofsky applies his conception of tertiary artifacts to works of art and processes, of perception; I want to generalize his conception by linking the notion of artifact on the one hand to notions of schemas and scripts and on the other hand to notions of context, mediation, and activity found in contemporary cognitive psychology, anthropology, and allied parts of the cognitive sciences.

If one accepts this characterization of artifacts as the linchpin of cultural mediation along the lines suggested by Wartofsky, one next step is to look at ways in which artifacts of the three different kinds are woven together in the process of joint human activity. How patterned are the artifacts constituting human culture?

The cohesion and coherence of culture

Contemporary anthropologists are divided with respect to the closely linked issues of how different parts of culture are interconnected and how coherent culture is across situations. In a wide-ranging discussion of this issue a few years ago, Paul Kay suggested "semi-seriously" that the supposed coherence of culture is a coherence imposed on the anthropologist by the need to publish a coherent story. It is an illusion: "if I go out and study the 'whoevers,' I've got to come back and tell a consistent and entertaining story about what the 'whoevers' are like—and everything they do better fit into this one story" (in Shweder and LeVine, 1984, p. 17).

Kay was immediately challenged by Clifford Geertz, whose work was almost certainly one of the sources of Kay's provocative remark. Geertz is justly famous for developing the notion that different parts of culture cohere such that, for example, one could use a Balinese cockfight or puppet theater (tertiary artifacts in Wartofsky's scheme of things) as an organizing metaphor for all of Balinese society (Geertz, 1973). In the early 1970s Geertz cited with approval Max Weber's image of humankind as "an animal suspended in webs of significance he himself has spun," and declared: "I take culture to be those webs" (1973, p. 5). Later in the same work, Geertz suggested that culture should be conceived of by analogy with a recipe or a computer program, which he referred to as "control mechanisms."

Geertz's work is pivotal in my efforts to reconcile the ideas of the Russian cultural-historical psychologists with those of contemporary cultural anthropologists. Geertz is often read as an anthropologist who adopts the conception of culture as inside-the-head knowledge. While this is certainly an aspect of his thinking that has become more dominant over time (Geertz, 1983), I find it significant that he explicitly rejects the strictly idealist notion of culture in favor of a view that links up neatly with the notion of artifact mediation:

> The "control mechanism" view of culture begins with the assumption that human thought is basically both social and public—that its natural habitat is the house yard, the marketplace, and the town square. Thinking consists not of "happenings in the head" (though happenings there and elsewhere are necessary for it to occur) but of traffic in what have been called, by G. H. Mead and others, significant symbols—words for the most part but also gestures, drawings, musical sounds, mechanical devices like clocks.
>
> (1973, p. 45)

I hope it is clear that there is a close affinity between this notion of culture as control mechanism and the mediation of action through artifacts.

Geertz's use of Weber's metaphor of "webs of significance" evokes images of the beautiful patterning of a spider's web, while the recipe metaphor suggests that the patterning is quite local and specific to particular ingredients, the rules for combining them, and the circumstances in which they are cooked. Diversity and uniformity, no less than the internal versus external interpretations of culture, were warring in Geertz's definition.

When responding to Kay's suggestion that the coherence of culture may be entirely in the eye of the outside observer, Geertz sought a new metaphor to describe his sense that human beings' cultural medium is neither made up of unconnected bits and pieces nor a perfect configuration: "the elements of culture are not like a pile of sand and not like a spider's web. It's more like an octopus, a rather badly integrated creature—what passes for a brain keeps it together, more or less, in one ungainly whole" (quoted in Schweder, 1984, p. 19).

The Geertz-Kay discussion suggests two extremes to be avoided in anthropologists' efforts to characterize the overall degree of cultural cohesion: (1) human life would be impossible if every event was experienced *sui generis*, as an isolated instance, and (2) it is no more helpful to believe that a single, uniform configuration of cultural constraints is constitutive of all events within a culture. Rather, it is essential to take into account the fact that human activity involves elaborate and shifting divisions of labor and experience within cultures, so that no two members of a cultural group can be expected to have internalized the same parts of whatever "whole" might be said to exist (D'Andrade, 1989; Schwartz, 1978, 1990).

As a consequence of these difficulties, it is not possible to say, in general, how much cultural coherence and integration exists between the two extremes of uniqueness and chaos; in order to say anything useful, it is necessary to specify sources of coherence and patterning as a part of the ongoing activities that the inquirer wants to analyze. In fact, when one considers simultaneously the heterogeneous sources of structure in the cultural medium and the necessarily partial knowledge of the people who use it, the wonder is that human beings are capable of coordinating with one another at all (a point made many decades ago by Durkheim, 1912).

The "internal" and "external" approaches to culture, applied to how to locate structure in the cultural medium, veer in predictably different directions. As external sources of coordination one can point to the many material manifestations of human action, the intricate "webs of significance" in its outer aspect. These are clearly visible as embodied symbols, routines, and rituals for coordinating artifacts. The opposite, internal line of explanation posits internal psychological structures or cultural knowledge as the sources of intersubjectivity and coordinated action and seeks to understand the processes of interpretation.

The version of a cultural-historical approach that I am proposing identifies the point of articulation of these two sides of culture in the dual nature of artifacts. The challenge is to show that this formulation supersedes the "inner" and "outer" approaches to culture and mind that dominate contemporary discourse.

Cultural models, schemas, and scripts

It was my good fortune that when I began formulating the ideas described in this chapter I was a member of an informal interdisciplinary discussion group associated with the Center for Human Information Processing at the University of California at San Diego. Our topic was our differing approaches to human thought processes, and possible ways to bridge the differences between them.[5]

Several members of this group had pioneered the idea that human experience is mediated by cognitive schemas which channel individual thinking by structuring the selection, retention, and use of information. In psychology *schema* is a term used to refer to knowledge structures in which the parts relate to one another and the whole in a patterned fashion (Mandler, 1985). According to David Rumelhart, "a schema contains, as part of its specification, the network of interrelations that is believed normally to hold among constituents that are instances of the schema" (1978, p. 3). There are schemas representing our knowledge of objects, situations, events, sequences of events, actions, and sequences of action (Rumelhart and Norman, 1980).

Schemas are selection mechanisms. They specify how certain essential elements relate to one another while leaving other, less essential elements to be filled in as needed according to the circumstances. Some elements, so-called default values, may not be specified at all. For example, if I hear my cat mewing outside the door, the elements, "breathes," and "warm blooded" are plausible default values. I know they are true without having to think about them. Under some circumstances, such as when I see the cat lying under the car and it is not clear if it is dead or alive, those elements of the schema may be crucial to my reasoning.

One appealing characteristic of the kind of schema theory my colleagues were developing is that it implies the context-specificity of thinking. Rumelhart made this point with respect to adult reasoning, arguing that while schemas play a central role in reasoning, "most of the reasoning we do apparently *does not* involve the application of general-purpose reasoning skills. Rather it seems that most of our reasoning ability is tied to particular schemata related to particular bodies of knowledge" (1978, p. 39). Jean Mandler pointed out an implication of this view that seemed to describe both the cultural differences in thinking and the difficulties engendered by the use of standardized psychological testing in cross-cultural research when she remarked that behavior will differ in familiar and unfamiliar situations because "familiar situations are those for which schemata have already been formed and in which top-down processes play a larger role" (1980, p. 27).

Roy D'Andrade (1984, 1990, 1995) has generalized the notion of schemas for objects and events in order to link these concepts from psychology with the concepts and phenomena of psychological anthropology. He introduced the idea of *cultural* schemas, patterns of elementary schemas that make up the meaning system characteristic of any cultural group. In D'Andrade's terms, "Typically such schemas portray simplified worlds, making the appropriateness of the terms that are based on them dependent on the degree to which these schemas fit the actual worlds of the objects being categorized. Such schemas portray not only the world of physical objects and events, but also more abstract worlds of social interaction, discourse, and even word meaning" (1990, p. 93).

D'Andrade (1990, p. 108) refers to intersubjectively shared cultural schemas as *cultural models*. Cultural models function to interpret experience and to guide action in a wide variety of domains, "including events, institutions, and physical and mental objects." A monograph edited by Naomi Quinn and Dorothy Holland (1987) contains studies which illustrate how adults use cultural models to reason about objects (such as cats), social institutions (such as marriage), and general properties of human beings (such as how the mind works).

An especially important kind of schema for purposes of grounding a cultural-psychological theory in people's everyday activities is event schemas, often referred to as *scripts* (Schank and Ableson, 1977). A script is an event schema that specifies the people who appropriately participate in an event, the social roles they play, the objects they use, and the sequence of actions and causal relations that applies.

Both Jerome Bruner (1990) and Katherine Nelson (1981, 1986) base their analysis of cognitive development on such event representations. Nelson refers to scripts as "generalized event schemas." Scripts, she writes, provide "a basic level of knowledge representation in a hierarchy of relations that reaches upward through plans to goals and themes" (1981, p. 101). Nelson illustrates the development of script-mediated thinking using the following examples, the first from a three-year-old, the second from a child a little under five, responding to a request to "tell me about going to a restaurant." Here is the three-year-old:

Well, you eat and then go somewhere.

The five-year-old has more to say:

Okay. Now first we go to restaurants at night-time and we, um, we and we go and wait for a while, and then the waiter comes and gives us the little stuff with the dinners on it, and then we wait for a little bit, a half and hours or a few minutes or something, and um, then our pizza comes or anything, and um [interruption] . . . [The adult says, "So then the food comes . . ."] Then we eat it, and um, then when we're finished eating the salad that we order we got to eat our pizza when its done, because we get the salad before the pizza's ready. So then when we're finished with all the pizza and all our salad, we just leave.

(Nelson, 1981, p. 103)

Several points about these children's formulations stand out. First, they are indeed generalized, although grounded in particulars; the children are talking about a habitual event ("You eat," "We go"). Second, the descriptions are dominated by the temporal sequencing of actions. Third, the causal logic of the event inheres in the temporal ordering of actions (pizza is eaten after salad because it takes longer to prepare). Finally, there is a good deal left unsaid, in part because it is taken for granted—we open the door and enter the restaurant, we pick up our forks and use them to eat the salad, and so on—and in part because the child is not involved and most likely does not understand (for example, that one pays for the food and leaves a tip).

In her work on children's acquisition of event representations, Nelson highlights other important properties of scripts that mark their nature as mediators. First, she suggests that scripts, like the cultural schemas discussed by D'Andrade, serve as guides to action. When people participate in a novel event, they must seek out an answer to the question, "What's going on here?" Once a person has even a crude idea of the appropriate actions associated with going to a restaurant, he or she can enter the flow of the particular event with partial knowledge, which gets enriched in the course of the event itself, facilitating later coordination. "Without shared scripts," Nelson writes, "every social act would need to be negotiated afresh" (p. 109).

Nelson also points out that children grow up within contexts controlled by adults and hence within adult scripts. By and large, adults direct the children's action and set the goals, rather than engage in direct teaching. In effect, they use their notion of the appropriate script to provide constraints on the child's actions and allow the child to fill in the expected role activity. In this sense, "the acquisition of scripts is central to the acquisition of culture" (p. 110).

According to Bruner (1990), scripts are best considered elements of a narrative, which play a role in his theorizing similar to that of cultural models in D'Andrade's approach. For Bruner, it is narrative, the linking of events over time, that lies at the heart of human thought. The representation of experience in narratives provides a frame ("folk psychology") which enables humans to interpret their experiences and one another. If it were not for such narrativized framing, "we would be lost in a murk of chaotic experience and probably would not have survived as a species in any case" (p. 56).

Schemas and artifacts

Since schema theory started to gain wide acceptance among cognitive psychologists and anthropologists somewhat over a decade ago, schemas have generally been interpreted as mental structures inside the head. Interpreted in this way, schemas and scripts fit comfortably with the internal notion of culture as meanings, which come unmoored from their material instantiation. Interpreted in this light, the notion of schema is incompatible with the notion of artifact-mediation I have been seeking to develop. The solution, of course, is to say that scripts are not uniquely inside-the-head phenomena but, like all artifacts, participate on both sides of the "skin line."

Interestingly, F.C. Bartlett, whose ideas have inspired several modern schema theorists, provided an alternative interpretation of schema when the term came into psychology in the 1920s (Bartlett, 1932). Bartlett wrote about schemas as conventions, social practices which were both inside and outside the head; they are both materialized practices and mental structures (Edwards and Middleton, 1986). This notion of schema obviously coincides nicely with the notion of artifact mediation I am proposing.

Recent developments indicate that something akin to Bartlett's approach is finding favor in cognitive anthropology. For example, D'Andrade (1995), who once adhered to the "inside" view of culture, has recently argued for a definition of culture that harks all the way back to E. B. Tylor: culture as the entire content of a group's heritage, including both its cultural schemas and models and its material artifacts and cultural practices. Still, the two sides of culture remain separate in D'Andrade's approach. He posits two kinds of cognitive structures, schemas and symbols. *Schemas* are the ideal side of artifacts as conceived of here; they are abstract mental objects. *Symbols* are physical things: words, phrases, pictures, and other material representations. The meaning of the symbol is taken to be the schema which the symbol signifies.

D'Andrade summarizes the relationship of symbols, schemas, and the world as follows: "The schema which represents the sound of a word and the schema which represents the thing in the world referred to by that word are entirely different, although tightly connected in that the schema which represents the sound of a word signifies (has as its meaning) the schema which represents the thing in the world" (1995, p. 179). While differences remain, it is clear that there is agreement of a tight connection between symbol/schema and artifacts.

Edwin Hutchins (1995), another anthropologist who has sought to integrate the internal and external conceptions of culture, proposes a different way to think of the intimate three-way connection of culture, cognition, and the world. Culture, according to Hutchins, should be thought of as a process, not as "any collection of things, whether tangible or abstract." Culture "is a process and the 'things' that appear on list-like definitions of culture are residua of the process. Culture is an adaptive process that accumulates the partial solutions to frequently encountered problems . . . Culture is a human cognitive process that takes place both inside and outside the minds of people. It is the process in which our everyday cultural practices are enacted" (p. 354).

In more recent work, Bruner (1996) and Nelson (1986) also treat scripts as dual entities, one side of which is a mental representation, the other side of which is embodied in talk and action. For example, Bruner writes that "learning and thinking are always *situated* in a cultural setting and always dependent upon the utilization of cultural resources" (1996, p. 4).

Whether one draws on D'Andrade, Hutchins, or other like-minded anthropologists (see the volumes edited by D'Andrade and Strauss, 1992, and Holland and Quinn, 1987) or on Nelson and Bruner, I find encouraging the compatibility of their ideas with the notion of schemas as conventions (in Bartlett's terms) or artifacts (in mine). Nor am I alone in making this connection.[6]

THE NEED FOR MORE INCLUSIVE ANALYSIS

Secondary artifacts such as cultural schemas and scripts are essential components of the "cultural took kit." They partake of both the ideal and the material; they are materialized and idealized (reified) in the artifacts that mediate peoples' joint activities. By that very fact of reification they are present as resources both for the idiosyncratic interpretation that each person will have of their joint activity and for the constant reproduction of the coordination necessary to reproduce that activity.

However, it requires little reflection to realize that even when conceived of as secondary artifacts, scripts and schemas are insufficient to account for thought and action. Even under the most generous assumptions about mechanisms that link object schemas together into hierarchies or event schemas into sequentially ordered sets, such knowledge structures drastically underdetermine what one should think or how one should behave on any given occasion *even assuming that one has acquired the cultural model or script in question.*[7]

Every schema "leaves out an enormous amount and is a great simplification of the potential visual, acoustic, sensory, and propositional information that could be experienced" (D'Andrade, 1990, p. 98). Consequently, while culture is a source of tools for action, the individual must still engage in a good deal of interpretation in figuring out which schemas apply in what circumstances and how to implement them effectively. For example, a large, orange, striped, furry leg with a cat-like paw dangling from the shelf in our child's closet is likely to evoke a different schema, different emotions, and different actions from those evoked by a similar object glimpsed under our hammock in a lean-to in the middle of a Brazilian rain forest. Such considerations lead to the unavoidable conclusion that in order to give an account of culturally mediated thinking it is necessary to specify not only the artifacts through which behavior is mediated but also the circumstances in which the thinking occurs.

These considerations lead us back to the essential point that all human behavior must be understood relationally, in relation to "its context" as the expression goes. But implementation of this insight has been a source of continuing disagreement and confusion. These difficulties are indexed by the varied vocabulary used to speak about the "something more" that must be added to artifact mediation if one is to give an account of the relationship between culture and mind. In the previous paragraph I used the term *circumstances* as a commonsense gloss on what that something more might be. When we turn to technical discussions of this issue, the relevant terms include *environment, situation, context, practice, activity*, and many more. At issue here is a problem very similar to the one we encountered in thinking about the relation of the material and the ideal in artifacts. In that case argument swirled around which comes first in shaping artifacts, materiality or ideality. In this case the argument turns on which comes first in human thought, the object (text) or its surround (context).

As Kenneth Burke remarked several decades ago, considerations of action and context create inescapable ambiguity because the very notion of a *substance* (sub stance) must include a reference to the thing's context "since that which supports or underlies a thing would be a part of the thing's context. And a thing's context, being outside or beyond the thing, would be something the thing is *not*" (1945, p. 22). Faced with these complexities that have defeated so many others, I will not aspire to a definitive treatment of context in this book. But I will aspire to distinguishing between two principal conceptions of context that divide social scientists and to accumulating some necessary conceptual tools to act as heuristics in guiding research on culture and development.

Situations and contexts

Many years ago John Dewey (1938) proposed a relational theory of cognition in which he used the term *situation* in a manner that leads naturally into a discussion of context: "What is designated by the word 'situation' is *not* a single object or event or set of objects and events. For we never experience nor form judgments about objects and events in isolation, but only in connection with a contextual whole. This latter is what is called a 'situation' " (p. 66). Dewey goes on to comment that psychologists are likely to treat situations in a reductive fashion: "by the very nature of the case the psychological treatment [of experience] takes a *singular* object or event for the subject-matter of its analysis" (p. 67). But: "In actual experience, there is never any such isolated singular object or event; *an* object or event is always a special part, phase, or aspect, of an environing experienced world—a situation" (p. 67).

Isolating what is cognized from life circumstances is often fatally obstructive to understanding cognition. It is such isolation (typical of experimental procedures in psychological studies of cognition), Dewey argued, that gives rise to the illusion that our knowledge of any object, be it "an orange, a rock, piece of gold, or whatever," is knowledge of the object in isolation from the situation in which it is encountered.

Dewey's equation of situation with a contextual whole provides a proper relational orientation for the concept of *context*, perhaps the most prevalent term used to index the circumstances of behavior. Despite Dewey's prescient comments half a century ago, psychological analysis of context has all too often fallen into the difficulties about which he warned us.

Context as that which surrounds

When we retreat to Webster's dictionary as a starting point for examining the concept of context, we find crucial ambiguities that serve to obscure the errors to which Dewey pointed. Context is defined as "the whole situation, background, or environment relevant to a particular event," and "environment" is defined as "something that surrounds." "The whole situation" and "that which surrounds" are mixed together in the same definition.

The notion of context as "that which surrounds" is often represented as a set of concentric circles representing different "levels of context" (see Figure 9.2). The psychologist's focus is ordinarily on the unit "in the middle," which may be referred to as a task or activity engaged in by individuals. When using the "surrounds" interpretation of context, the psychologist seeks to understand how this task is shaped by the broader levels of context.

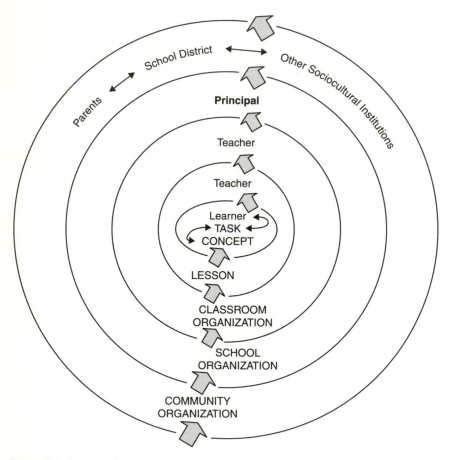

Figure 9.2 Concentric circles representing the notion of context as "that which surrounds," with a child at its center. The context here is the one surrounding children's performance in a classroom lesson.

This image is probably best known in connection with Urie Bronfenbrenner's (1979) book on the ecology of human development. He describes embedded systems, starting with the microsystem at the core and proceeding outward through mesosystems and exosystems, to the macrosystem. In applying the notion of context to issues of education, Peg Griffin and I took as the "unit in the middle" a teacher-pupil exchange that was part of a lesson that was part of a classroom that was part of a school that was part of a community (Cole, Griffin, and LCHC, 1987).

The study of language is an important domain in which the promise and problems of the idea of "layers of context" has been usefully applied (Bateson, 1972; Jakobson and Halle, 1956). A fundamental property of language is that its levels of organization are mutually constituted; a phoneme exists as such only in combination with other phonemes which make up a word. The word is the context of the phoneme. But the word exists as such—"has meaning"—only in the larger context of the utterance, which again "has meaning" only in a relationship to a large unit of discourse. Gregory Bateson summarized this way of thinking: "This hierarchy of contexts within contexts is universal for the communicational . . . aspect of phenomena and drives the scientist always to seek explanation in the ever larger units" (1972, p. 402).

Note that in this description there is no simple, temporal ordering. "That which surrounds" occurs before, after, and simultaneously with the "act/event." We cannot say sentences before we say words, nor words before we synthesize phonemes in an appropriate way; rather, there is a complex temporal interdependence among levels of context which motivates the notion that levels of context constitute one another. To take our example of the teacher-child exchange, it is easy to see such events as "caused" by higher levels of context: a teacher gives a lesson, which is shaped by the classroom it is a part of, which in turn is shaped by the kind of school it is in, which in turn is shaped by the community, and so on.

While more inclusive levels of context may constrain lower levels, they do not cause them in a unilinear fashion. For the event "a lesson" to occur, the participants must actively engage in a consensual process of "lesson making." Teachers often vary considerably in the way they interpret the conventions of the school, and school communities participate in the selection of the board of education. Without forgetting for a moment that the power relations among participants "at different levels of context" are often unequal, it is no less important when using the nested-contexts approach to take into account the fact that context creation is an actively achieved, two-sided process. (See Duranti and Goodwin, 1992; Lave, 1993; and McDermott, 1993, for trenchant criticisms of context treated as the container of objects and behaviors.)

Context as that which weaves together

In seeking uses of the term *context* which avoid the pitfalls of context as that which surrounds, I have found it useful to return to the Latin root of the term, *contexere*, which means "to weave together." A similar sense is given by the *Oxford English Dictionary*, which refers to context as "the connected whole that gives coherence to its parts."

The frequency with which metaphors of weaving, threads, ropes, and the like appear in conjunction with contextual approaches to human thinking is quite striking. For example, the microsociologist Ray Birdwhistell described context this way:

> I'll tell you what I like to think about: sometimes I like to think of a rope. The fibers that make up the rope are discontinuous; when you twist them together, you don't make them continuous, you make the thread continuous . . . even though it may look in a thread as though each of those particles are going all through it, that isn't the case. That's essentially the descriptive model . . . Obviously, I am not talking about the environment. I am not talking about inside and outside. I am talking about the conditions of the system.
>
> (quoted in McDermott, 1980, pp. 14–15)

When context is thought of in this way, it cannot be reduced to that which surrounds. It is, rather, a qualitative relation between a minimum of two analytical entities (threads), which are two moments in a single process. The boundaries between "task and its context" are not clear-cut and static but ambiguous and dynamic. As a general rule, that which is taken as object and that which is taken as that-which-surrounds-the-object are constituted by the very act of naming them.[8]

In light of my goal of studying artifacts and situations/context in terms of people's concrete activities, I was gratified to discover that there is an intimate connection between context, interpreted as a process of weaving together, and the notion of an event. This connection is provided by Stephen Pepper in his analysis of contextualism as a world view (what might currently be called a scientific paradigm).

Pepper (1942) suggests that the root metaphor underlying a contextualist world view is the "historic event." By this, he says,

> the contextualist does not mean primarily a past event, one that is, so to speak, dead and has to be exhumed. He means the event alive in its present. What we ordinarily mean by history, he says, is an attempt to *re-present* events, to make them in some way alive again . . . We may call [the event] an "act," if we like, and if we take care of our use of the term. But

it is not an act conceived as alone or cut off that we mean; it is an act in and with its setting, an act in its context.

(p. 232)

An "act in its context" understood in terms of the weaving metaphor requires a *relational* interpretation of mind; objects and contexts arise together as part of a single bio-social-cultural process of development.

Bateson (1972), in a way very reminiscent of Pepper's writing, discusses mind as constituted through human activity involving cycles of transformations between "inside" and "outside." "Obviously," he writes, "there are lots of message pathways outside the skin, and these and the messages which they carry must be included as a part of the mental system *whenever they are relevant*" (p. 458, emphasis added). He then proposes a thought experiment: "Suppose I am a blind man, and I use a stick. I go tap, tap, tap. Where do I start? Is my mental system bounded at the handle of the stick? Is it bounded by my skin? Does it start halfway up the stick? Does it start at the tip of the stick?" (p. 459).

Bateson argues that such questions are nonsensical unless one is committed to including in one's analysis not only the man and his stick but his purposes and the environment in which he finds himself. When the man sits down to eat his lunch, "the context changes," and with it the stick's relation to mind is changed. Now it is forks and knives that become relevant. In short, because what we call mind works through artifacts, it cannot be unconditionally bounded by the head or even by the body, but must be seen as distributed in the artifacts which are *woven together* and which weave together individual human actions in concert with and as a part of the permeable, changing, events of life.

The relevant order of context will depend crucially upon the tools through which one interacts with the world, and these in turn depend upon one's goals and other constraints on action. Similarly, relevant interpretation of context for the analyst of behavior will depend upon the goals of the analysis. According to this view of context, the combination of goals, tools, and setting (including other people and what Lave, 1988, terms "arena") constitutes simultaneously the context of behavior and ways in which cognition can be said to be related to that context.[9]

Activity and practice

While *context* and *situation* continue to appear in discussions of culture in mind, in recent years there has been increasing use of the terms *activity* and *practice* in their place. In part this shift has resulted from dissatisfaction with the concept of context in the reduced form of an environment or cause (Lave, 1988; Zuckerman, 1993). In part it has been brought about by the infusion of ideas from social and cultural theory which trace their roots back to Karl Marx and to post-Marxist debates about human agency and social determination.

In contemporary discussions, the terms activity and practice are sometimes taken as synonyms and sometimes treated as if they index different kinds of social structuration. This terminological confusion can be traced back to the formulations of Marx. In the first of his *Theses on Feuerbach* (1845), Marx wrote: "The chief defect of all materialism . . . is that the thing, reality, sensuousness, is conceived only in the form of the *object* or of *contemplation*, but not as *sensuous human activity, practice*, not subjectively."

This passage leads us to understand that Marx meant to rearrange the ontological separation among humans and artifacts as a way of superseding the dichotomy between the material and the ideal. His formulation of the interpenetration of activity and practice and materiality/ideality is based on the assumption that "The object or product produced is *not* something 'merely' external to and indifferent to the nature of the producer. It is his activity in an objectified or congealed form" (Bernstein, 1971, p. 44). It is this duality that gives activity "the power to endow the material world with a new class of properties that, though they owe their origin to us, acquire an enduring presence in objective reality, coming to exist independently of human individuals" (Bakhurst, 1991, pp. 179–180).

Activity/practice emerges in this account as medium, outcome, and precondition for human thinking. It is in the territory of activity/practice that artifacts are created and used.

Following the thread of practice

A great many contemporary scholars in anthropology, sociology, and cultural studies currently invoke the notion of practice in their discussions of human thought. Central to all of these accounts, despite differences among them, is the attempt to achieve something akin to a combination of the notion of context as that-which-surrounds and the weaving conception of context.

Charles Taylor (1987) suggests that humans' baseline, taken-for-granted social reality is composed of social practices, which provide the intersubjective medium of mind. The ensemble of a society's practices provides the foundation for community and discourse. Meanings and norms (secondary artifacts in my scheme of things) are "not just in the minds of the actors but are out there in the practices themselves; practices which cannot be conceived as a set of individual actions, but which are essentially modes of social relations" (p. 53).

Anthony Giddens (1979) adopts the unit of practices in order to create a theory of socialization which assumes neither that the subject is determined by the environment ("nurture") nor by its "inherent characteristics" ("nature"). The first view, he writes, "reduces subjectivity to the determined outcome of social forces, while the second assumes that the subjective is not open to any kind of social analysis" (p. 120).

According to Giddens, practices (rather than roles, for example) are the basic constituents of the social system. They are also a unit of analysis that overcomes such dualisms as "individual versus social," which re-create one-sided accounts of development. The resolution of such dualisms, he claims (following Marx) is to be found at the level of practices: "In place of each of these dualisms, as a single conceptual move, the theory of structuration sub-stitutes the central notion of *duality of structure*. By the duality of structure, I mean the essential recursiveness of social life, as constituted in social prac-tices: structure is both medium and outcome of the reproduction of practices, and 'exists' in the generating moments of this constitution" (1979, p. 5).

The French anthropologist-sociologist Pierre Bourdieu (1977) also seeks to block simplified notions of context as cause and to overcome dualistic theo-ries of cognition and social life. Bourdieu warns against theories that "treat practice as a mechanical reaction, directly determined by the antecedent con-ditions" (p. 73). At the same time, he warns against "bestowing free will and agency on practices."

Central to Bourdieu's strategy for balancing these two unacceptable extremes is the notion of *habitus*, "a system of lasting, transposable disposi-tions which, integrating past experiences, functions at every moment as a *matrix of perceptions, appreciations, and actions* and makes possible the achievement of infinitely diversified tasks" (pp. 82–83). In Bourdieu's approach, *habitus* is the product of the material conditions of existence and the set of principles for generating and structuring practices. Habitus, as its name implies, is assumed to take shape as an implicit aspect of habitual life experiences. It constitutes the (usually) unexamined, background set of assumptions about the world. It is, Bourdieu remarks, "history made nature" (p. 78). "The habitus is the universalizing mediation which causes an indi-vidual agent's practices, without either explicit reason or signifying intent, to be none the less 'sensible' and 'reasonable' " (p. 79).

Following the thread of activity

Activity theory is anything but a monolithic enterprise. Within Russia there are at least two schools of thought about how best to formulate Marx's ideas in psychological terms (Brushlinskii, 1968; Zinchenko, 1995). There is a long German tradition of research on activity theory (Raeithel, 1994), a Scandi-navian/Nordic tradition (Hydén, 1984; Engeström, 1993), and now, perhaps, an American tradition (Goodwin, 1994; Nardi, 1994; Scribner, 1984). A good statement of general tenets of this approach is provided by Engeström, who writes that an activity system

> integrates the subject, the object, and the instruments (material tools as well as signs and symbols) into a unified whole.
> An activity system incorporates both the object-oriented productive aspect and the person-oriented communicative aspect of human con-duct. Production and communication are inseparable (Rossi-Landi,

1983). Actually a human activity system always contains the subsystems of production, distribution, exchange, and consumption.

(p. 67)

The attractiveness of this formulation in light of the discussion of artifact mediation at the beginning of this chapter should be apparent: Engeström's formulation promises a way to incorporate ideas about the duality of artifacts but does not privilege production over social cohesion.

Engeström represents his conception of activity in a manner that both includes and enlarges upon the early cultural-historical psychologists' notions of mediation as individual action. Once again we see a triangle, but now it is a set of interconnected triangles (Figure 9.3). At the top of the figure is the basic subject-mediator-object relationship depicted in Figure 9.1. This is the level of mediated action through which the subject transforms the object in the process of acting upon it. But action exists "as such" only in relation to the components at the bottom of the triangle. The *community* refers to those who share the same general object; the *rules* refer to explicit norms and conventions that constrain actions within the activity system; the *division of labor* refers to the division of object-oriented actions among members of the community. The various components of an activity system do not exist in isolation from one another; rather, they are constantly being constructed, renewed, and transformed as outcome and cause of human life.

In activity theory, as summarized in Figure 9.3, contexts are activity systems. The subsystem associated with the subject-mediator-object relationships exists as such only in relationship to the other elements of the system. This is a thoroughly relational view of context.

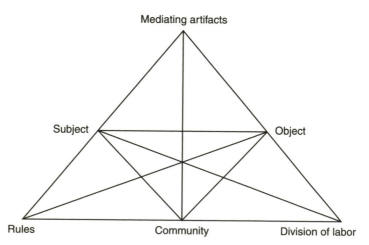

Figure 9.3 The basic mediational triangle expanded (after Engeström, 1987) to include other people (community), social rules (rules), and the division of labor between the subject and others.

Jean Lave (1993) provides a succinct summary of several themes uniting scholars interested in activity and practice theory:

1. An emphasis on the dialectical character of the fundamental relations constituting human experience (in Lave's terms, human agency is "partially determined, partially determining").
2. A focus on experience in the world that rejects the structure and dynamics of psychological test procedures as a universally appropriate template.
3. A shift in the boundaries of cognition and the environment such that, in Lave's phrasing, cognition "is stretched across mind, body, activity and setting" (a perspective sometimes referred to as "distributed cognition": Hutchins, 1995; Norman, 1991; Salomon, 1993).

Context/practice/activity and ecological world views

There are important affinities between the various views about a supra-individual unit of analysis associated with the notions of context, practice, activity, and so on, and the views of those who identify themselves as ecological psychologists (Altman and Rogoff, 1987). These affinities grow out of a common starting point, the ecology of everyday human activities, and are evident in the proclivity of researchers of both views to conduct their research in naturally occurring social settings rather than experimental laboratories.

These affinities can also be seen in the appearance of the metaphor of weaving in the writings of both groups. The following example is taken from the work of the pioneer ecological-developmental psychologists Roger Barker and Herbert Wright, who were attempting to characterize the relation of ecological setting to psychological processes. On the basis of their detailed records of children's activities, Barker and Wright were impressed that children's behavior appeared to be very strongly controlled by the settings they inhabited. They also noted the wide range of different behavioral settings children participated in daily:

> The number of things a child did in a day, according to our criteria of episodes, varied approximately from 500 to 1,300 . . . Most of the episodes did not occur in isolation. Behavior was more often like the interwoven strands of a cord than like a row of blocks in that the molar units often overlapped . . . The behavior continuum was cord-like, too, in the sense that overlapping episodes often did not terminate at the same time but formed an interwoven merging continuum.
>
> (1951, p. 464)

This metaphorical invocation of threads and cords echoes Birdwhistell's description of context in interpersonal interaction, although the contents of

their descriptions are markedly different. What makes such metaphorical cor-
respondences possible across levels of behavioral analysis is their grounding
in a unit of analysis corresponding to events and activities.

Although their vocabularies are somewhat different, I believe the same
points of agreement can be attributed to Dewey in his discussions of situation and to those context theorists, such as Bateson, who held firmly to the
conviction that it is essential to see an "action as *part* of the ecological subsystem called context and not as the product or effect of what remains of the
context after the piece which we want to explain has been cut out from it"
(1972, p. 338).

William Wentworth (1980) brings several threads of this discussion together.
Context, he writes, is the "unifying link between the analytic categories of
macrosociological and microsociological events": "The context is the world
as realized through interaction and the most immediate frame of reference
for mutually engaged actors. *The context may be thought of as a situation and
time bounded arena for human activity. It is a unit of culture*" (p. 92).

This notion of context recognizes the power of social institutions relative
to individuals and the potential of individuals to change the environments
that condition their lives. On the one hand, aspects of the "macro" level serve
as constraints/resources in constituting context (and hence local activity
tends to reproduce the relations in society). On the other hand, each situation
is idiosyncratic in the mix of resources/constraints brought to bear and hence
there is no strict determination of the consequences of action that result.[10]

Culture as helping things grow

The discussion thus far has characterized culture as a system of artifacts and
mind as the process of mediating behavior through artifacts in relation to a
supra-individual "envelope" with respect to which object/environment, text/
context are defined. This approach allows me to make use of the notion of
culture as medium and of context as both that which surrounds and that
which weaves together. It also provides me with a basic unit of analysis that
has natural linkages to the macro pole of society and its institutions and the
micro level of individual human thoughts and actions.

The final set of comments I invoke here for thinking about culture brings
many of the conceptual tools discussed thus far together in a manner that
I see as especially useful for developmentally oriented research on culture and
cognition. "Culture," wrote Raymond Williams, "in all of its early uses, was a
noun of process: the tending *of* something, basically crops or animals" (1973,
p. 87). From earliest times, the notion of culture has included a general theory
for how to promote development: create an artificial environment where
young organisms could be provided with optimal conditions for growth. Such
tending required tools, perfected over generations and designed for the special tasks to which they were put. So close were the concepts of growing
things and tools that the word for culture once referred to ploughshares.

In common parlance, we speak of an artificial environment for growing crops as a "garden," a conception encoded in the idea of a kindergarten (children's garden) where children are protected from the harsher aspects of their environment. A garden constitutes the linkages between the "microworld" of the individual plant and the "macroworld" of the external environment. A garden, in this sense, brings together the notion of culture and that of context, providing a concrete model for thinking about culture and human development.

In addition, the garden metaphor naturally links us to ecological thinking by reminding us that we must be concerned not only with the system of interactions within a particular setting, but also with the way the internal system is related to the "next higher level of context." While it is possible, given sufficient knowledge and resources, to induce a radish to grow in Antarctica or outer space, it is not nearly so easy to sustain the conditions that enable that growth. For the work of developmental psychologists to be widely applicable, they must be concerned not only with a theory of how to create the conditions for development *in vitro* (in artifically constructed environments such as a kindergarten) but with a theory of how to create conditions for development which will survive when the child moves out of the children's garden into the world at large *in vivo*.

We can summarize the view of culture given here in the following terms:

1　Artifacts are the fundamental constituents of culture.
2　Artifacts are simultaneously ideal and material. They coordinate human beings with the world and one another in a way that combines the properties of tools and symbols.
3　Artifacts do not exist in isolation as elements of culture. Rather, they can be conceived of in terms of a heterarchy of levels that include cultural models and specially constructed "alternative worlds."
4　There are close affinities between the conception of artifacts developed here and the notions of cultural models, scripts, and the like. Exploitation of these affinities requires conceiving of schemas and scripts as having a double reality in the process of mediation.
5　Artifacts and systems of artifacts exist as such only in relation to "something else" variously referred to as a situation, context, activity, and so on.
6　Mediated activity has multidirectional consequences; it simultaneously modifies the subject in relation to others and the subject/other nexus in relation to the situation as a whole, as well as the medium in which self and other interact.
7　Cultural mediation implies a mode of developmental change in which the activities of prior generations are cumulated in the present as the specifically human part of the environment. This form of development, in turn, implies the special importance of the social world in human

development, since only other human beings can create the special conditions needed for that development to occur.

A number of methodological prescriptions follow from this shift in culture's status vis-à-vis mind and behavior. Central is the need to study culturally mediated behavior developmentally to reveal the dynamic interactions uniting different parts of the overall life system. Equally important is the need to conduct research at several developmental/historical (genetic) levels in order to analyze the ways in which they intertwine and fuse in human life over time.

NOTES

1 For a discussion of language as a system of artifacts and the homology between words and what we usually think of as material artifacts, see Rossi-Landi (1983, pp. 120ff).
2 In my experience it is difficult at first to grasp the notion that language is artifactual, perhaps because the materiality of language seems transparent. A simple demonstration makes the point clearly. When you hear a language that you do not understand, you are experiencing only its material manifestations. The meaning of the words, their "ideal" aspect, is missing because you lack a past history of interactions using those artifacts as mediational means.
3 Here again I need to note the affinity of this approach to artifact mediation and Dewey's notions. As Larry Hickman points out in his analysis of Dewey's "pragmatic technology," Dewey believed that "the tools and artifacts we call technological may be found on either side of what he argued was an extremely malleable and permeable membrane that separates the 'internal' from the 'external' with respect to the organism only in the loosest and most tentative senses" (Hickman, 1990, p. 12).
4 Richard Barrett (1989) provides an interesting discussion of White's symbolic/mediational views in relation to his better-known ideas concerning materialist social evolutionism.
5 Members of this seminar included Aaron Cicourel, Roy D'Andrade, Jean Mandler, George Mandler, Jay McClelland, Bud Mehan, and Donald Norman.
6 Dorothy Holland and Jaan Valsiner (1988) point out that the anthropological notion of "cultural models" is very similar to the cultural-historical notion of a mediator. Holland and Valsiner use the term "mediational device" and find it useful to limit mediational devices to "circumscribed, tangible activities or objects of sensory dimensions." I prefer to think of cultural models as systems of artifacts in order to emphasize the dual materiality/ideality of both cultural models and artifacts with more obvious sensory dimensions.
7 This limitation of scripts as mediators underpins Milan Kundera's remark: "We leave childhood without knowing what youth is, we marry without knowing what it is to be married, and even when we enter old age, we don't know what it is we're heading for: the old are innocent children of their old age. In that sense, man's world is a planet of inexperience" (1988, pp. 132–133).
8 Ray McDermott (1993) provides a striking illustration of the shifting boundaries between object and context that provides phenomenalistic access to a process that seems semi-mystical in abstract discussions such as this one. He uses a visual illusion that is created by slightly shifting the frame of a pattern of intertwining

lines. Although we know that nothing has changed in the pattern, the pattern we see is no longer perceptually the same.

9 Bateson, who can be considered an expert on the topic, commented on the difficulty of thinking relationally about context: "Let me say that I don't know how to think that way. Intellectually I can stand here and give you a reasoned exposition of this matter; but if I am cutting down a tree, I still think, 'Gregory Bateson is cutting down the tree. *I* am cutting down the tree.' 'Myself' is to me still an excessively concrete object, different from the rest of what I have been calling 'mind.' The step to realizing—to making habitual—the other way of thinking, so that one naturally thinks that way when one reaches for a glass of water or cuts down a tree—that step is not an easy one" (1972, p. 462).

10 Readers familiar with contemporary sociological theories of action will readily recognize here a close affinity between the views about mediation derived from the writings of the cultural-historical school and those of Anthony Giddens (1984). For example, Giddens writes, "According to the notion of the duality of structure, the structural properties of social systems are both medium and outcome of the practices they recursively organize ... Structure is not to be equated with constraint but is always both constraining and enabling" (p. 25).

REFERENCES

Altman, I., and Rogoff, B. 1987. World views in psychology: Trait, interactional, organismic, and transactional perspectives. In D. Stokols and I. Altman, eds., *Handbook of Environment Psychology*, vol. 1. New York: Wiley.

Bakhurst, D. 1991. *Consciousness and Revolution in Soviet Philosophy: From the Bolsheviks to Evald Ilyenkov*. Cambridge: Cambridge University Press.

Barker, R. G., and Wright, H. E. 1951. *One Boy's Day: A Specimen Record of Behaviour*. New York: Harper.

Barrett, R. A. 1989. The paradoxical anthropology of Leslie White. *American Anthropologist*, 91, 986–999.

Bartlett, F. C. 1932. *Remembering*. Cambridge: Cambridge University Press.

Bateson, G. 1972. *Steps to an Ecology of Mind*. New York: Ballentine.

Bernstein, R. 1971. *Praxis and Action: Contemporary Philosophies of Human Activity*. Philadelphia: University of Pennsylvania Press.

Bourdieu, P. 1977. *Outline of a Theory of Practice*. New York: Cambridge University Press.

Bronfenbrenner, U. 1979. *The Ecology of Human Development*. Cambridge, Mass.: Harvard University Press.

Bruner, J. S. 1990. *Acts of Meaning*. Cambridge, Mass.: Harvard University Press.

—— 1996. *The Culture of Education*. Cambridge, Mass.: Harvard University Press.

Brushlinskii, A. V. 1968. *The Cultural-Historical Theory of Thinking* (in Russian). Moscow: Vysshyaya Shkola.

Burke, K. 1945. *A Grammar of Motives*. New York: Prentice-Hall.

Cole, M. 1976. Introduction. In A. R. Luria, *Cognitive Development*. Cambridge, Mass.: Harvard University Press.

Cole, M., Griffin, P., and The Laboratory of Comparative Human Cognition. 1987. *Contextual Factors in Education*. Madison: Wisconson Center for Education Research.

D'Andrade, R. 1984. Cultural meaning systems. In R. A. Shweder and R. A. Le Vine, eds., *Culture Theory: Essays on Mind, Self and Emotion.* New York: Cambridge University Press.

—— 1989. Cultural sharing and diversity. In R. Bolton, ed., *The Content of Culture: Constants and Variants: Essays in Honor of John M. Roberts.* New Haven: HRAF Press.

—— 1990. Some propositions about the relationship between culture and human cognition. In J. W. Stigler, R. A. Shweder, and G. Herdt, eds., *Culture Psychology: Essays on Comparative Human Development.* New York: Cambridge University Press.

—— 1995. *The Development of Cognitive Anthropology.* New York: Cambridge University Press.

D'Andrade, R., and Strauss, C. 1992. *Human Motives and Cultural Models.* New York: Cambridge University Press.

Dewey, J. 1938/1963. *Experience and Education.* New York: Macmillan.

Duranti, A., and Goodwin, C., eds. 1992. *Rethinking Context: Language as an Interactive Phenomenon.* New York: Cambridge University Press.

Durkheim, E. 1912/1947. *The Elementary Forms of Religious Experience.* Glencoe, Ill.: Free Press.

Edwards, D., and Middleton, D. 1986. Conversation with Bartlett. *Quarterly Newsletter of the Laboratory of Comparative Human Cognition, 8,* 79–89.

Engeström. Y. 1987. *Learning by Expanding.* Helsinki: Orienta-Konsultit Oy.

—— 1993. Developmental studies on work as a testbench of activity theory. In Chaiklin and Lave, eds., 1993.

Geertz, C. 1973. *The Interpretation of Cultures.* New York: Basic Books.

—— 1983. *Local Knowledge: Further Essays in Interpretive Anthropology.* New York: Basic Books.

Giddens, A. 1979. *Central Problems in Social Theory: Action, Structure, and Contradiction in Social Analysis.* Berkeley: University of California Press.

—— 1984. *The Constitution of Society.* Berkeley: University of California Press.

Goodwin, C. 1994. Professional vision. *American Anthropologist, 96,* 606–633

Harkness, S. 1992. Human development in psychological anthropology. In T. Schwartz, G. M. White, and C. A. Lutz, eds., *New Directions in Psychological Anthropology.* New York: Cambridge University Press.

Hickman, L. A. 1990. *John Dewey's Pragmatic Technology.* Bloomington: Indiana University Press.

Holland, D., and Quinn, N., eds. 1987. *Cultural Models in Language and Thought.* New York: Cambridge University Press.

Holland, D., and Valsiner, J. 1988. Cognition, symbols, and Vygotsky's developmental psychology. *Ethos, 16,* 247–272.

Hutchins, E. 1995. *Cognition in the Wild.* Cambridge, Mass.: MIT Press.

Hydén, L.-C. 1984. Three interpretations of the activity concept: Leontiev, Rubinshtein and critical psychology. In M. Hedegaard, P. Hakkarainen, and Y. E. Engeström eds., *Learning and Teaching on a Scientific Basis.* Arhus: Psykologisk Institut.

Ilyenkov, E. V. 1977. The problem of the ideal. In *Philosophy in the USSR: Problems of Dialectical Materialism.* Moscow: Progress.

—— 1979. Problema ideal'nogo (The problem of the ideal). In two parts. *Voprosy filosofii (Questions of Philosophy), 6,* 145–158 and 7, 128–140.

Jakobson, R., and Halle, M. 1956. *Fundamentals of Language.* The Hague: Mouton.

Kundera, M. 1988. *The Art of the Novel.* New York: Grove Press.

Latour, B. 1994. On technical mediation: Philosophy, sociology, genealogy. *Common Knowledge*, *3*, 29–64.

Lave, J. 1988. *Cognition in Practice*. Cambridge: Cambridge University Press.

—— 1993. The practice of learning. In Chaiklin and Lave, eds., 1993.

Luria, A. R. 1981. *Language and Cognition*. Washington: V. H. Winston: New York: J. Wiley.

Mandler, G. 1985. *Cognitive Psychology: An Essay in Cognitive Science*. Hillsdale, N.J.: Erlbaum.

Mandler, J. 1980. *Structural Invariants in Development*. University of California, San Diego: Center for Human Information Processing, no. 96, September.

Marx, K. 1845/1967. Theses on Feurbach. In L. D. Easton and K. H. Guddat, eds., *Writings of the Young Marx on Philosophy and Society*. Garden City, N.Y.: Doubleday, Anchor Books.

McDermott, R. P. 1980. Profile: Ray L. Birdwhistell. *Kenesis Reports*, *2*, 1–4, 14–16.

—— 1993. The acquisition of a child by a learning disability. In C. Chaiklin and J. Lave, eds., *Understanding Practice: Perspectives on Activity and Context*. New York: Cambridge University Press.

Nardi, B., 1996. *Context and Consciousness: Activity Theory and Human-Computer Interactions*. Cambridge, Mass.: MIT Press.

Nelson, K. 1981. Cognition in a script framework. In J. H. Flavell and L. Ross, eds., *Social Cognitive Development*. Cambridge: Cambridge University Press.

—— 1986. *Event Knowledge: Structure and Function in Development*. Hillsdale, N.J.: Erlbaum.

Norman, D. A. 1991. Aproaches to the study of intelligence. *Artificial Intelligence*, *46*, 327–346.

Pepper, S. 1942. *World Hypotheses*. Berkeley: University of California Press.

Quinn, N., and Holland, D. 1987. Culture and cognition. In D. Holland and N. Quinn, eds., *Cultural Models in Language and Thought*. New York: Cambridge University Press.

Raeithel, A. 1994. Symbolic production of social coherence. *Mind, Culture, and Activity*, *1*, 69–88.

Rossi-Landi, F. 1983. *Language as Work and Trade: A Semiotic Homology for Linguistics and Economics*. South Hadley, Mass.: Bergin and Garvey.

Rumelhart, D. 1978. Schemata: The building blocks of cognition. In R. Spiro, B. Bruce, and W. Brewer, eds., *Theoretical Issues in Reading Comprehension*. Hillsdale, N.J.: Erlbaum.

Rumelhart, D. E., and Norman, D. A. 1980. *Analogical Processes in Learning*. University of California, San Diego, Center for Human Information Processing, 97.

Salomon, G., ed., 1993. *Distributed Cognitions: Psychological and Educational Considerations*. Cambridge: Cambridge University Press.

Schank, R. C., and Ableson, R. P. 1977. *Scripts, Plans, Goals, and Understanding: An Inquiry into Human Knowledge Structures*. Hillsdale, N.J.: Erlbaum.

Schwartz, T. 1978. The size and shape of culture. In F. Barth, ed., *Scale and Social Organization*. Oslo: Universitetsforlaget.

—— 1990. The structure of national cultures. In P. Funke, ed., *Understanding the USA*. Tubingen: Gunter Narr Verlag.

Scribner, S. 1984. Cognitive studies of work. *Quarterly Newsletter of the Laboratory of Comparative Human Cognition*, *6*, nos. 1 and 2.

Shweder, R. A. 1984. Preview: A colloquy of culture theorists. In R. A. Shweder and

R. A. LeVine, eds., *Culture Theory: Essays on Mind, Self, and Emotion*. New York: Cambridge University Press.

Shweder, R. A. and LeVine, R. A., eds., 1984. *Culture Theory: Essays on Mind, Self and Emotion*. New York: Cambridge University Press.

Taylor, C. 1987. Interpretation and the sciences of man. In P. Rabinow and W. M. Sullivan, eds., *Interpretive Social Sciences: A Second Look*. Berkeley: University of California Press.

Wartofsky, M. 1973. *Models*. Dordrecht: D. Reidel.

Wentworth, W. 1980. *Context and Understanding: An Inquiry into Socialization Theory*. New York: Elsevier.

White, L. 1942. On the use of tools by primates. *Journal of Comparative Psychology*, *34*, 369–374.

—— 1959. The concept of culture. *American Anthropologist*, *61*, 227–251.

Williams, R. 1973. *Keywords*. Oxford: Oxford University Press.

Zinchenko, V. P. 1995. Cultural-historical psychology and the psychological theory of activity: Retrospect and prospect. In Wertsch, Del Rio, and Alvarez, eds., 1995.

Zuckerman, M. 1993. History and developmental psychology: A dangerous liaison: A historian's perspective. In G. H. Elder, Jr., J. Modell, and R. D. Parke, eds., *Children in Time and Place: Developmental and Historical Insights*. New York: Cambridge University Press.

10 The zone of proximal development as basis for instruction

Mariane Hedegaard

This chapter describes a teaching experiment combining psychological theory development with school teaching. The project took place in a Danish elementary school and followed the same class from third to fifth grade. Here I will report only on activities of the first year of our experiment, which was carried out in cooperation between researcher and teacher in a social science subject (biology, history and geography).

The aim of the project was to formulate a theory of children's personality development that considers development from a comprehensive point of view in a cultural and societal context and to formulate a related theory of instruction. We based our work on the methodology of the cultural-historical school, as formulated for Vygotsky (1985–1987) and developed by Leontiev (1978, 1981), Elkonin (1971, 1980), Davydov (1977, 1982), and Lompscher (1980, 1982, 1984, 1985).

In this chapter, I will focus on those aspects of the project that illustrate the importance of Vygotsky's concept of the zone of proximal development. I will show that, as an analytic tool for evaluation of school children's development in connection with schooling, this concept is of great value.

THE THEORETICAL BASIS

Vygotsky's zone of proximal development connects a general psychological perspective on child development with a pedagogical perspective on instruction. The underlying assumption behind the concept is that psychological development and instruction are socially embedded; to understand them one must analyze the surrounding society and its social relations. Vygotsky explained the zone of proximal development as follows:

> The child is able to copy a series of actions which surpass his or her own capacities, but only within limits. By means of copying, the child is able to perform much better when together with and guided by adults than when left alone, and can do so with understanding and independently. The difference between the level of solved tasks that can be performed

with adult guidance and help and the level of independently solved tasks
is the zone of proximal development.

(1982, p. 117)

Vygotsky wrote that we have to define both levels in the child's development
if we wish to know the relation between the child's process of development
and the possibilities of instruction. He pointed out that the main characteristic of instruction is that it creates the zone of proximal development, stimu-
lating a series of inner developmental processes. Thus the zone of proximal
development is an analytic tool necessary to plan instruction and to explain
its results.

> From this point of view, instruction cannot be identified as development,
> but properly organized instruction will result in the child's intellectual
> development, will bring into being an entire series of such developmental
> processes, which were not at all possible without instruction. Thus
> instruction is a necessary and general factor in the child's process of
> development – not of the natural but of the historical traits of man.
>
> (1982, p. 121)

The zone of proximal development includes the normative aspects of development. The direction of development is guided by instruction in scientific
concepts considered important by curriculum planners and the teacher.
Through instruction, the scientific concepts relate to and become the child's
everyday concepts. Leontiev describes the relation between scientific and
everyday concepts as follows:

> The degree to which the child masters everyday concepts shows his actual
> level of development, and the degree to which he has acquired scientific
> concepts shows the zone of proximal development.
>
> (1985, pp. 47–48)

At the same time, this relation describes the connection between learning and
development; the everyday concepts are spontaneously developed in a dialectical relation to the scientific concepts, which are mediated through the
instruction. However, if the scientific concepts are not included, the child's
entire development will be affected. Leontiev quotes Vygotsky to point out
this relation:

> But when scientific concepts result in development of a developmental
> stage through which the child has not yet passed . . . we will understand
> that the mediation of scientific concepts may play an important role in
> the child's psychic development. The only good instruction received in
> childhood is the one that precedes and guides development.
>
> (1985, p. 48)

Vygotsky's methodological basis

Vygotsky's theory integrates several approaches to form a comprehensive agenda for research of the genesis, development, function, and structure of the human psyche. These approaches include (1) an activity approach, (2) a historical societal approach, (3) a mediating instrumental approach, and (4) an interhuman genetic approach.

1   Vygotsky's successors have posited practical activity as a unit of analysis that allows for a comprehensive approach to the description of the development of the human pysche. This unit comprises all aspects of the genesis of the human psyche: social, cognitive, motivational, and emotional (Davydov and Radzikhovskii, 1985; Leontiev, 1985).
2   Vygotsky's methodology is based on the application of the Marxist historical societal approach. In psychology this approach emphasizes the concept of work activity: the relation between human beings and the world as mediated through tools (Leontiev, 1985, p. 33).
3   According to Vygotsky, the development of psychic tools determines humans' relations with their environment and with themselves. Psychic tools are analogous to industrial tools and are also characterized by being produced through social activity, rather than arising organically (Vygotsky, 1985–1987, p. 309). Psychic tools may be very complex systems; as examples, Vygotsky mentioned spoken language, systems of notation, works of art, written language, schemata, diagrams, maps and drawings.
4   The interprocessual aspect of the human psyche first appeared as practical activity between human beings. Shared and collective tool use is part of this interhuman practical activity. The interpersonal procedures for tool use gradually became acquired intrapsychic procedures. Through the procedures for tool use, humans are bearers of societal historical traditions; consequently, the interhuman activity, as it forms the child's inner activity, is always societal, historical, and cultural. Therefore, in order to understand the human psyche it is necessary to analyze it genetically as a societal and historical phenomenon (Hedegaard, 1987; Markova, 1982; Wertsch, 1985).

Development, teaching

According to Vygotsky, human development is characterized by the ability to acquire psychic tools. Vygotsky does not deny biological development (cf. Scribner, 1985); however, human biological development is shaped and concretized through societal and historical development. In specific culture, it may be historically characterized as the development of traditions through human activity. The development of traditions has its parallel in ontogenetic development (cf. Elkonin, 1971), although the ontogenetic development can be characterized by stages of activity determined by the child's biological capacity as well as by the historical traditions in which the culture involves the child.

According to Elkonin, the child's development is characterized by three periods, each including a motivational and a cognitive stage of development. The first period, the infant and early play period, includes the development of motives for emotional contact, methods for socializing, and situational mastery. The second period includes the age of role play and early school age. This period is dominated by the development of motives for mastery of the adult world and acquisition of analytic methods and related goals and means. The late school and youth period is characterized by the development of motives for social and societal involvement and methods for mastery of personal relations as well as work and societal requirements (see Figure 10.1).

At every stage, the child's development is related to one of the societally determined activities and traditions. During the first stage, the tradition for childcare, the building of emotional bonds, especially with the mother, is the determining activity for development. The next stage is characterized by traditions for creating supportive surroundings for the child's explorative and imaginary play activity. Kindergarten and school are the institutionalized traditions for determining the dominant activities for the following two stages: development of motives and development of skill and knowledge for relating theoretically and reflectively to the world. The fifth stage is characterized by traditions for peer activities institutionalized in different forms of after-school activities. Work activity is the determining activity for the last stage described by Elkonin. By analyzing the tradition we can critically evaluate whether the stages are relevant descriptions of child development today in Western society. For instance, one could argue that the period between late school age and work in today's society has become institutionalized as education for work. This evaluation of the stages underlines Leontiev's

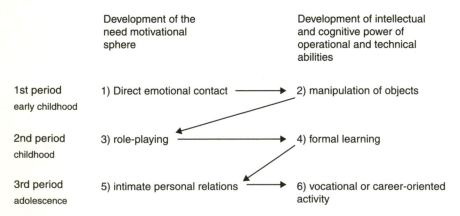

Development of the need motivational sphere

Development of intellectual and cognitive power of operational and technical abilities

1st period
early childhood
1) Direct emotional contact ⟶ 2) manipulation of objects

2nd period
childhood
3) role-playing ⟶ 4) formal learning

3rd period
adolescence
5) intimate personal relations ⟶ 6) vocational or career-oriented activity

Figure 10.1 The stages that, according to Elkonin's theory (1971), characterize the dominant forms of child development in Western society

description of stages in child development as societally and historically determined.

The zone of proximal development can be related to Elkonin's developmental stages (Griffin and Cole, 1984). As stated, the qualitatively new structures that arise in the course of a child's development are related to the changing demands made on children by social institutions.

When children enter school, the teacher confronts them with the zone of proximal development through the tasks of school activity, in order to guide their progress toward the stage of formal learning. These tasks help children acquire motives and methods for mastery of the adult world, as mediated by the teacher.

The zone of proximal development can also be viewed from the aspect of action within a certain activity. To the school child, action is related to the learning/teaching activity (cf. Engeström, 1986; Rogoff and Wertsch, 1984; Schneider, Hyland and Gallimore, 1985; Wertsch, 1985). The teacher's role is to direct action within school activity in a manner appropriate to the child's present level of development, the cultural and social context, and the teacher's theories of what the central subject matter is. For instance, the teacher's theory of what language and reading are – and what characterizes the logic of language and reading – will influence the teaching and learning actions of mother-tongue instruction.

Empirical knowledge, theoretical knowledge

The child is born into a society in which knowledge is available as the standard procedure for dealing with persons and things. It is important to distinguish between knowledge that exists independently of the child and the child's acquisition and development of this knowledge.

In a specific society, the standard procedures for solving societal problems can be seen as the culturally developed skills acquired and developed by each generation. Knowledge is accessible through different media, for example, language and pictures, and is the result of culturally and societally developed procedures for solving societal problems. The development of medicine is a typical example. According to Juul Jensen (1986), societal practices exist prior to societal knowledge, leading to a rejection of the assumption that knowledge is the essence of environmental phenomena and things existing independently of human societal practice. Societally developed skills are thus the basis for societally developed knowledge. Davydov has separated this societal knowledge into two forms of knowledge – empirical knowledge and theoretical knowledge – each with its associated epistemological procedures.

Empirical knowledge deals with differences and similarities among phenomena; has arisen via observation and comparison of phenomena; can be ordered hierarchically on the basis of formal characteristics; and the word or a limited term is the medium whereby it is communicated. Through empirical epistemological procedure, the individual object is grasped by isolating it from its spatial and chronological connections so that it can be observed, compared, categorized, and remembered. Imagery and language are the media used to this end. In the empirical exposure the individual object functions as an independent reality.

In contrast, theoretical knowledge deals with a connected system of phenomena and not the separate, individual phenomenon; arises through the development of methods for the solution of the contradictions in a societally central problem area; develops understandings of the origins, relations, and dynamics of phenomena; and models are the medium whereby this knowledge is communicated. Through the theoretical epistemological procedure, the object is observed as it transforms. By recreating the object in its relation to other objects, these relations are revealed. This reproduction has the character of experimental exploration of relations and changes, through both concretely changing the world and mentally imagining changes. Theoretical knowledge cannot be acquired via its verbal or literary form alone, even though it does appear primarily in verbal and literary forms at the scientific level.

Societal knowledge and skills are inseparably bound together. In the same way, the child's concept acquisition is tied to the acquisition of cognitive procedures. In teaching, if one wants children to acquire theoretical knowledge in the form of fundamental relations in a subject or a problem area, then the cognitive method in instruction must also characterize theoretical knowledge. If, on the other hand, one applies the epistemological method that characterizes empirical knowledge – that is, observation, comparison, categorization, and memory – together with a subject area's fundamental concepts, then knowledge acquisition will remain on the empirical level. School children have already learned the empirical epistemological procedure in their practical everyday activities; they have yet to acquire the theoretical epistemological procedures.

Theoretical knowledge must be acquired through exploratory activity. In school, this activity is controlled activity, consisting of the exploration of problems that contain the fundamental conflicts of the phenomenon. A prerequisite for theoretical knowledge acquisition is teaching activity built on tasks that illuminate the contrasts found in a phenomenon's fundamental relations. Through this exploration it becomes possible to gain insight into the development of the phenomenon.

As an example, I will discuss the problem area on which our teaching experiment is based: "the evolution of species." Darwin's theory of species and its elaboration in the more modern synthetic theory of evolution (Gould, 1977; Mayr, 1976, 1980; Simpson, 1962) demonstrate how knowledge has developed through problems that, for science, have been urgent.

The phenomenon of the evolution of species contains a fundamental conflict which has stimulated scientific development: How can an animal population adapt to changes in its habitat while many individual animals cannot manage this adaptation and die? This conflict has been of central importance to a theory of the evolution of animal species and is therefore useful as the basis for instruction in the evolution of species. However, such a conflict cannot be presented abstractly to pupils; rather, it must be presented via analyses of concrete animal species. For example, pupils can analyze how the polar bear adapts to its Arctic surroundings to survive as an individual, how it breeds and ensures the survival of its young. Students can analyze limits to this adaptation as well. The teacher must set tasks for pupils so that they become aware of the adaptations of the polar bear as well as the different ways in which other animals in the Arctic survive, breed, or die. Through the resulting insights children can arrive at the formulation of general laws about the survival and change of an animal species.

Theoretical knowledge as psychic tool

The tool character of theoretical knowledge becomes especially evident when formulated in a model. The model may become the tool that guides the teacher's instruction activity. This type of model is characterized as a germ-cell model (Davydov, 1982; Engeström and Hedegaard, 1986), which implies that every time the model becomes complicated by new relations it not only adds to the concepts already modeled but influences and changes their meaning, because the concepts are defined through their relations. The basic concepts in a germ-cell model are complementary in their explanatory value for the problem area being modeled. This means that the relation between the basic concepts in a germ-cell model is contradictory, and through explicating this contradiction related concepts are developed. This can be illustrated by the growth of the germ-cell model in the teaching experiment. The problem area to be modeled and explained was the evolution of animals. The basic concept relation in the modeling of this problem area was the relation animal – nature (see Figure 10.2).

The pupils may first acquire an external, auxiliary model that gives a general impression of the area taught. The auxiliary model then functions as a basic of information for the pupils' further work with the subject and for the development of their models of understanding, which in turn will become psychic tools for the pupils. Through experiencing the contradiction of their modeling of the problem area in their concrete problem solving, the pupils' concepts of their models become richer and new conceptual relations are included.

The school's task is generally considered to be the passing on of knowledge and skills, but the children do not necessarily develop a theoretical orientation toward reality. Their orientation may remain on an empirical level. The difference between theoretical and empirical orientation is connected with Vygotsky's differentiation between everyday concepts and scientific concepts (see Figure 10.3). These pairs of concepts are not identical because scientific concepts can also be empirical; for example, the periodic system in chemistry can be empirically presented.

Stage I: The relation between nature and animal life, and animals' adaptation to a given/specific/particular nature

Stage II: The adaptation of different animal species to the specific nature which is characteristic of a particular biotope (the relation between genetic and functional inheritance)

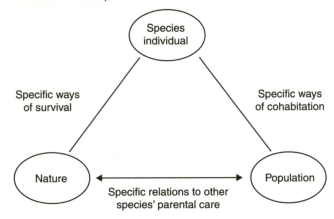

Stage III: The development of a species is determined by changes in the nature and by changes in the estate of the offspring

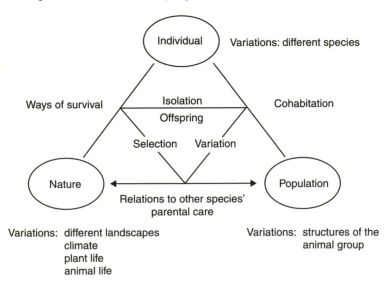

Figure 10.2 The three stages of the development of the germ-cell model (these stages are also present in the teaching process)

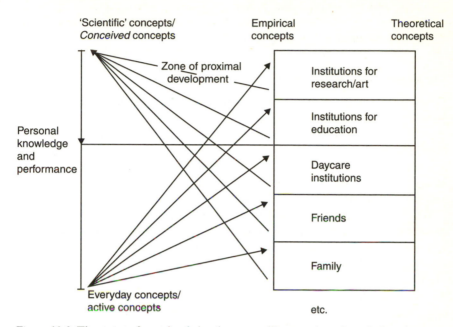

Figure 10.3 The zone of proximal development, illustrated as the relations between empirical and theoretical knowledge, according to Davydov's and Vygotsky's theories of everyday and scientific concepts

Theoretical knowledge that has become everyday knowledge can be found, for example, among young people who have both the electronic skill and the knowledge to build their own music equipment, or the mechanical skills and knowledge needed to repair their motorcycles, or the knowledge of both the composition and the history of their preferred type of music. Unfortunately, it is very difficult to find school knowledge that has become everyday theoretical knowledge and can be used as a tool for reflection and skilled activities. Most school knowledge is empirical knowledge, which means knowledge in the form of facts or text knowledge, and as such it never becomes very useful in the pupils' everyday life, either during their school years or later.

The school's task should be to teach children scientific concepts in a theoretical way by applying a theoretical epistemological procedure. Children's everyday concepts are thereby extended to include scientific theoretical concepts. If scientific concepts are learned as empirical concepts, children will have difficult in relating what they learn at school to the surrounding environment. Only by learning concepts theoretically can this development take place. As mentioned earlier, teaching should create zones of proximal development through involving children in new kinds of activity. By relating scientific concepts to everyday concepts, teaching provides children with new skills and possibilities for action.

The concept of the zone of proximal development can be used to guide children from the learned and understood scientific concepts to the spontaneously applied everyday concepts through a method of teaching I have called a *double move*.

The double move in teaching

Development of a theoretical basis requires that teachers, when planning instruction, have a profound knowledge of the concepts and general laws of the subject. This knowledge guides planning of the different steps of instruction. The teacher's planning must advance from the general laws to the surrounding reality in all its complexity. In order to explain these laws the teacher must choose concrete examples that demonstrate the general concepts and laws in the most transparent form.

Whereas the teacher's planning must advance from the general to the concrete, the children's learning must develop from preconceived actions to symbolization of the knowledge they obtain through their research, finally resulting in a linguistic formulation of relations. Initial activities must be oriented toward concrete exploration. In our teaching experiment such activities include exploratory analysis of objects, museum visits, and films. In the next step, the children must be able to symbolize the relations they perceive through their research activity. In our experiment, drawings and modeling of the initial findings were used to this end. Finally, the children must be able to formulate the relations they have perceived.

Thus there is a double move in instruction: The teacher must guide instruction on the basis of general laws, whereas the children must occupy themselves with these general laws in the clearest possible form through the investigation of their manifestations. This is why practical research activities with objects, films, and museum visits are such an important part of instruction, especially during the early periods.

The basis for instruction is the division of the learning activity into three different types of actions: (1) delineation of the problem; (2) problem solution and problem construction, which implies acquisition of capacities; and (3) evaluation and control. Davydov (1982) has described six steps in the learning activity, which can be seen as differentiating the phases in learning activity based on the use of models as learning tools. These steps are produced through the different structures of the instructional tasks. The steps are: (1) change or production of a problem so that the general relations are clearly seen; (2) modeling of these relations; (3) transformation of the model relations so that the connection is clear; (4) creation of new problems and tasks from model; (5) control of one's own learning action; and (6) evaluation of the model's sphere of application. As will be shown, these steps have influenced the planning of instruction in our experiments.

Children's learning activities may be characterized as guided investigations. Through working with the central conceptual relations and procedures that characterize a subject area, the children acquire the scientific concepts of the subject. The children acquire the concepts as active concepts when they have completed all six instructional steps, that is, when they are able to relate themselves to their own learning activity as well as the sphere of application of the concepts, allowing the children to orient themselves theoretically to the surrounding world.

THE TEACHING EXPERIMENT

The following teaching experiment is based on the idea of using germ-cell models as tools in instruction and the idea of the double move instruction, which implies that the instruction goes from specific concrete examples and the children's daily-life conceptions to general conceptualizing and modeling of the phenomena studied. The model should then become a research tool for the children, which can be used for analyzing and explaining the concrete world's phenomena in all their variation and complexity; in other words, the modeled concept relation should be a tool for the child in his or her daily life and thereby become usable and changeable as daily-life concepts.

As the content of teaching we chose social science subjects taught from third to fifth grade in the Danish elementary schools. The subjects include biology, history, and geography. As problem areas we chose "the evolution of species," "the origin of man," and "the historical change of societies" to integrate and relate the three subjects and emphasize their developmental aspect and the relations between the development of nature and society. The results of the teaching experiment presented here deal only with the first year of teaching the evolution of species. The next phase of the teaching experiment is still in progress.

The concepts forming the basis for instruction are demonstrated in the germ-cell model shown in Figure 10.2. The content of instruction included the following subthemes:

Accounts of creation
Prehistoric nature, animal life
Research method: the use of fossils and analogies
Visit to the Department of Denmark's Prehistory at the Natural History Museum
Evolution of species
Arctic nature, animal life
Desert nature, animal life
Desert hare, polar hare
Moving the polar hare to the Faroe Islands
Moving chimpanzees to Estonia

Arctic nature, animal life
Project work: Africa's animals
Wolves: summer and winter living conditions
Evolution from wolf to dog
Evolution of the horse
The catastrophe: the extinction of the saurians

The procedure for attaining theoretical concepts

One approach was based on the "scientific works" procedure described in Aidarova (1982) and also found in Kurt Lewin's work (1946) (see Figure 10.4).

The children were told to work exploratively like scientists. A goal-result board was used to record the steps attained in this exploration. Each teaching period started with a summary of the exploration related to the general problem area of research: the evolution of animals and the origin of humans. Furthermore, the teaching was built around the children's analysis of the concrete themes according to the questions in the scientific work procedure. For instance, in exploring the life of the polar bear, we wanted to address the following issues: What do we know and what do we not know about the polar bear's survival in Greenland? How can we model what we know, and how are we going to explore what we do not know? We developed specific questions based on the relations depicted in the germ-cell model at the start of this theme and by studying books and films about polar bear life. Through class discussions, we evaluated the germ-cell model and considered how it fitted with our knowledge: we also analyzed what our knowledge so far about the polar bear could tell us about why some animals survive, why some animals die, and why some change into new species.

Research method

The teaching experiment is a concretization of Vygotsky's statement that the formative genetic method is a necessary research method for investigating the formulation and development of the conscious aspects of humans' relation to the world. The experiment included the total planning of instruction in the social science subjects during a 3-year period.

The teaching experiment was characterized by the following procedures:

1   Developing a general plan for the entire school year.
2   Continuous and detailed planning in each lesson (3 hours), based upon the observation protocol for the previous lesson. This planning was formulated as a written sequence worked out in cooperation between the teacher and the researcher. It contained:

  (a) the goal of instruction
  (b) the concept in the instruction

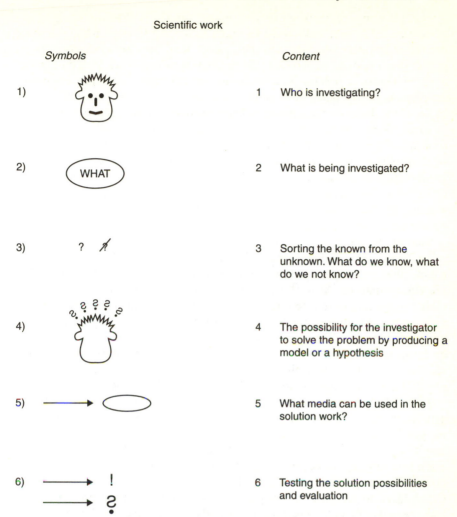

Figure 10.4 The procedure of "scientific work" which we, in different ways, adapted to (1) keep track on the goal-result board of the steps in exploring the main problem, "evolution of animals", and (2) analyze subproblems, which were steps in exploring the main problem

   (c) teaching materials used
   (d) plans for teacher activities
   (e) plans for pupil activities

The teaching of the theme "the evolution of species" required 32 periods of planned instruction over a 9-month period. The teaching process was documented through participant observations (cf. Hedegaard, 1987) and through the collection of pupils' written tasks.

The planning of instruction was based on the following six primary principles. First, each child must be taken into consideration when planning for the class as a collective. On the face of it, it appears contradictory to ensure the development of individual pupils as well as to work with the class as a whole. However, it is my impression that no contradiction exists; children's development takes place through their relation to the class and to the groups in the class. Thus we used group solving processes to develop the children's intellectual processes, instead of isolating each child to work on tasks in a trial-and error fashion. We attempted several times to produce a division of work in which the children would work on a number of different tasks in a group with a shared motive for the entire activity. This activity, in principle, is intended to develop a zone of proximal development for the class as a whole, where each child acquires personal knowledge through the activities shared between the teacher and the children and among the children themselves.

Second, the general content of the teaching must be related to the children's experiences. Class dialogue and children's drawings were the media through which children's experiences with the different subthemes were expressed in the class situation. Also, through the activity associated with these media their experiences were extended. The teaching was planned so that the children were active in investigating themes of instruction. It was not intended, however, that the children's investigations would result in blind trial and error or in an activity they had already mastered. We must emphasize that the teacher planned and gave direction to the activities to a certain extent but did not determine the concrete form of the activity or the results.

Third, the content of instruction must be clearly related as a whole to the general themes "the evolution of species" and "the origin of humans." The integration of the subjects into a whole was achieved through consistent emphasis on the themes that guided the teaching through the 3-year period. Each teaching period began with a class dialogue focused on the goal-result board. This goal-result board provided a permanent instrument for helping the children to record their progress in researching the evolution of species and the origin of man. The board was revised and expanded by the teacher when necessary through class dialogue and the use of the model.

Fourth, motivation and interest in the content of teaching must be developed in the children. In order to motivate their interest in the subjects, we utilized three main techniques. We took advantage of their interest in the big questions of life. Where do we come from? Where does the universe stop? Have the animals always looked like they do today? Have there always been human beings? How were humans created? We tried to maintain their interest through activities involving them in the procedure or researching the problems. Finally, in order to develop the children's motivation, we explored the following contrasts, problems, and conflicts:

1   The conflicting explanations for the descriptions of the origin and development of animals and humans.

2   The contrast between the animals in the Kalahari Desert (Africa) and the animals in Greenland, and the problems that would arise if the animals' habitats were exchanged.

3   The contrast between animal life in Denmark and animal life in Greenland and the Kalahari Desert.

4   The problem of survival that arose when the polar hare was moved to the Faroe Islands.

5   The problems that would occur if reptiles were moved from the desert to Greenland.

6   The problems that occurred when a group of chimpanzees were moved to an island in Estonia.

7   The contrast in the wolf's living conditions between winter and summer and the problems that would occur if either season disappeared.

Fifth, the children's capacities for modeling knowledge must be developed so that the models can become tools for analyzing the diversity of problems encountered in the world they live in. The tasks given to the children were intended to guide them through the central concepts of the subjects. These concepts were integrated in a germ-cell model, which was to function, first, as an external tool for the children's analyses of the relations between animal and nature and, second, as a psychic tool for the children's understanding of these relations in all their complexity. The model becomes a psychic tool when a child can use it for analyzing, solving and creating new problems (when Steps 3 and 4 in the structure of learning activity are acquired).

Sixth, knowledge must be integrated with performance in the children's acquisition of the subjects biology, history, and geography. The integration of knowledge and performance was made possible through the children's modeling of their knowledge and, later, their use of this model for analyzing and producing questions. This integration was based on the six steps in learning activity described earlier. These steps move from actions connected to the general aspects of reality to actions connected to the concrete complexity of reality. At the same time, an opposite movement occurs in the children's learning, from exploration based on action activities to symbolizing and, finally, describing the concept relation explored (see Figure 10.5).

ANALYSIS AND RESULTS

Our qualitative analysis is based on the observation protocols and on the children's task solutions throughout the year. The focus of the analysis of the teaching activity will be the problems encountered in the teaching process. In the learning activity, the focus will be on the concept learning of the children and the solution of motivational problems.

Content	Learning activities
Animals' historic development (the origin of man)	Formulation of the aim via conflict
Parallelization to the researcher's work. Exploration as a method	Method formulation
Development – historical time The time concept The nature concept	} Analyses of texts, pictures, films, museum visits

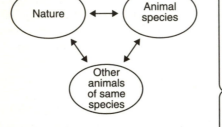

Nature ⟷ Animal life   Formulation of what we know

Why some animal species died out   Formulation of what we don't know

} Model formulation and application of the model

Different forms of adaptation:
survival via food
seeking, animal relations,
parental care, defence against
enemies

The mutual relations among   } Hypothesis-formulation
food seeking, cohabitation,
parental care, defence against   Transformation of the model
enemies

Limits of functional adaptation

Variation among members of a species   } Question formulation via
Selection   application of the model

The evolution of new species   Control of explanation in relation
to the initial problem

Figure 10.5 Plan for integrating the two aspects of knowledge and performance in the whole-teaching experiment

Problems in the teaching activity

Two different types of problems were identified in our analysis. The first is connected to the content of the teaching and concerns the children's problems with understanding the concepts introduced in the teaching process. These problems emerged as important because they lead to insights into the nature of obstacles encountered by children in the learning activity and the strategies utilized for overcoming them. The teacher who seeks to deal with this type of problem develops teaching which, in our opinion, reaches into the zone of proximal development.

An example is the problem some children had in understanding the time dimension and in separating animals' adaptations from animals' development. There were also problems with categories in the model connected to the introduction and proper placement of new dimensions; for instance, when the categories *food seeking, parental care, cohabitation* were introduced the children did not quite know how to use them, and when the concept of desert was introduced they did not know what desert conditions were. The children had no problems, however, in accepting modeling or in modeling their knowledge. The problems concerning time and evolution are, then, the central problems related to the children's acquisition of content. Very few of the problems were related to using the model.

The second type of problem is connected with the planning and realization of the teaching and concerns the problems that arise when instruction is not at an appropriate level. Some examples are the problems we had in achieving a balance between providing an overview of the general problem during each period and becoming too repetitious. In addition, we had to choose between sticking to the goals of the class and following up on the children's comments. Most importantly, we found that it was extremely difficult to capitalize on the children's knowledge of heredity. They were not able to relate what they know about heredity in their family relations with their investigation of heredity of animals.

The problems have shown us that we must reject the common assumption that concretization will facilitate children's understanding of problems. On the contrary, the result is often confusion for the children. Features such as self-centeredness and concretization are commonly used to explain children's performance because it is generally assumed that the children's thoughts are concrete and self-centered. Our results indicate that the children's dialogues and use of models and task solutions contradict this widely held assumption. Moreover, children did have problems understanding when they were allowed to be self-centered and were asked to use themselves and their families as examples in the lessons on heredity.

Analysis of children's learning

We can obtain knowledge about the children's concept learning through analyses of the observation protocols. Furthermore, the children's learning can be checked by analyzing their written task solutions.

One type of analysis focused on the children's learning actions as they acquired the conceptual relations of the germ-cell model. For example, we identified 12 types of learning actions during students' work with the evolution-of-animals theme. These actions are grouped under three headings: delineation of the problem, acquisition of capacities, and evaluation. They occurred in the following order:

Delineation of the problem

1 The children's comments are relevant to the themes of teaching.
2 The children precede the process of teaching in their comments.
3 The children keep each other and the teacher to the topic.
4 The children pose questions regarding the *why* of a phenomenon.

Acquisition of capacities in model use

5 The children look for relations instead of categorical solutions.
6 The children work with modeling of their knowledge.
7 The children want reasons for the relations in the model.
8 The children accept that the model changes and that they contribute to the changes.
9 The children's imagination and fantasy production increase.
10 The children produce tasks themselves.

Evaluation

11 The children become critical and evaluative of their own performances and capacities.
12 The children become critical and evaluate the content of teaching.

When the children's task solutions are analyzed and evaluated, it is important to remember that these tasks have been assigned not as part of the research procedure or as tests but as educational devices in the teaching process. The two most informative series of tasks were given in the middle of the teaching period just before and immediately after Christmas (December 12 and January 9). The tasks in these two series included the following:

First series

What do we know about the evolution of animals?
What do we not know?
What is important for the survival of a species?
What do we mean when we speak of nature?
What do we know about the origin of man?
Draw a model for the polar hare.
Draw a model for the desert hare.

Second series

Draw a model for the polar bear.
Draw a model that is valid for all animals.
Draw a model for the sperm whale.
When we write 'nature' in the model, what does that mean?
What does the model show as important for the survival of species?
Why can't a single member of a species survive without other members
of the same species?

A conclusion from our observation is that the children did not solve the tasks
connected to the procedure (the questions about what they know and do
not know) as well as the tasks connected to the model. All the children could
draw the models for the animals, and they could also draw the general model.
Of 16 children, 10 could draw a model of the sperm whale, which had not
been addressed in the teaching. From the tasks given immediately prior to
the completion of the theme, it was quite clear that the children understood
that changes in nature mean change for the reproduction and survival of a
species and that changes in species are always reflected in their offspring (see
Figure 10.6).

Development of motivation

The results from the first year of the teaching experiment demonstrate a
development in the ways in which the children related to the theme and
sub-themes in the evolution of species. A qualitative change occurred in
their interest in the content of the teaching. These changes in interest can be
characterized sequentially as follows:

1   Interest in the problem formulation and the research methods.
2   Interest in the relationship between nature and animals in relation to the
    specific living conditions of the animals introduced in the teaching.
3   Loss of interest in specific animals when they became too familiar.
4   Interest in formulating general models for the adaptation of animals to
    their living conditions.

5   Interest in sticking to the general problem formulation in their research.
6   Interest in influencing the process and content of instruction as related to problem formulation.
7   Critical evaluation of the content of teaching.
8   Desire to finish the evolution-of-animals theme and to start something new.

These changes in interest can be seen as a developmental shift in the children's motivation, moving from interest in concrete material to interest in developing principles that can be applied to new concrete material. The development of motivation has its parallel in the development of concepts, delineation of the problem, model formulation/model use, and evaluation. And both the structure in concept development and development of motivation can be seen as derived from the steps of instruction (cf. Figure 10.5).

   This result supports the conceptions in activity theory (Hedegaard, 1989; Leontiev, 1978) that motives and concepts are dialectically related. The concepts are the content and specify the object of the motives at the same time that the motives create the images and the objectives of concept learning.

CONCLUSION

The double move in teaching

Teaching that promotes children's theoretical concept learning must occur on a basis of profound teacher knowledge of the central concepts of the subject area. Knowledge of the general laws can guide the planning of the steps through which instruction must proceed. The teacher must guide the learning from the student involvement with general laws in the clearest possible form. Clearly, practical activities are an important part of teaching; however, these activities must, as mentioned, contain the general laws in their most transparent form. The conclusion from the teaching experiment based on this principle of the double move in teaching can be summarized as follows:

1   Teaching can be based on the central concepts of evolution whereby it integrates the different sub-themes into an exploration of the general problem the *evolution of animals*.
2   Furthermore, the children learn to integrate their knowledge into a general model, a germ-cell model, and to use this model on new and unknown animals. We found that the children had very few problems in modeling their knowledge; it was much more troublesome for the teacher and the researcher to do this.
3   The teaching resulted in qualitative changes in the children's capacities and interest in solving problems connected to the theme of the evolution of animals.

The zone of proximal development

To work with the zone of proximal development in classroom teaching implies that the teacher is aware of the developmental stages of the children and is able to plan for qualitative changes in the teaching toward a certain goal. Although each child is unique, children obviously share common traits with other children. Being of the same tradition, children in the same class have a lot of knowledge and skills in common. Instruction can build upon these common features if it takes into account that the children vary in their speed and form of learning. In this way, we have worked with the zone of proximal development as a relation between the planned instructional steps and the steps of the children's learning/acquisition process.

Elkonin (1971) pointed out that the stages in children's development are determined by the societal historical development. The conception of childhood as differentiated into separate life periods and as a quite large part of human life is only a couple of hundred years old. Before that children were taught to behave like adults; Ariès (1982) describes how, in the eighteenth century, children behaved like adults at the age of 4.

The fact that children have common traditions, prior to school and at school, in the form of shared knowledge and procedures for activities enables them to communicate and interact in shared concrete activities. The content and form of this interaction and communication should then be developed further in school.

A child is unique and individual, but children's individualities have common features. If these features are not developed, we tend to regard the child as deviant and offer special instruction to each child in a class. Instead, instruction must be based on development of common knowledge and skills.

Consequently, the zone of proximal development must be used as a tool for class instruction. In our teaching experiment, we saw that it is actually possible to make a class function actively as a whole through class dialogue, group work, and task solutions. The teaching experiment differed from traditional instruction in that the children were constantly and deliberately forced to act. The children's research activity was central in these guided actions, which gradually led the children to critical evaluations of the concepts. We can conclude, therefore, that we have succeeded in building a common basis for the children in the class from which future teaching can be developed.

We are quite certain that the teaching has built a common foundation in the children; however, we also recognize that some children achieve a more differentiated content in their concepts than other children. For the fast learners, our teaching experiment neither destroyed their interest nor inhibited their development of motivation. For the slow learners, our instruction has encouraged insight into and capacities for understanding the theme related to the evolution of animals.

A

B

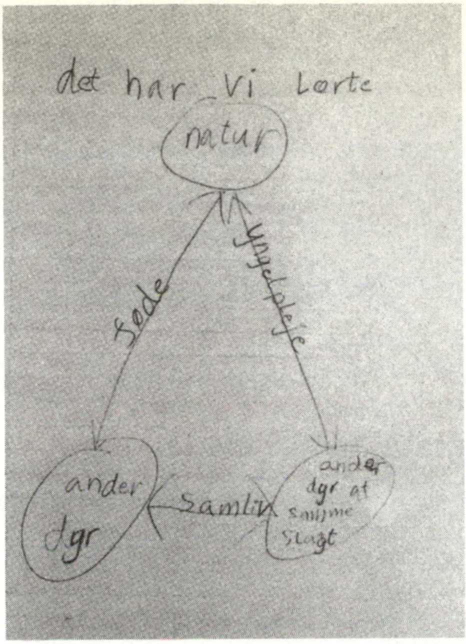

C

Figure 10.6 (Opposite and above) Examples of the children's models: *A* is a pupil's generalization in symbol form of the relation between nature and animal species. In *B*, the generalization is differentiated and the relation of an animal to other animals of the same species is represented; the model symbolizes the relations for the horse. *C* is a pupil's representation of the relations in general form for animal species

REFERENCES

Aidarova, L. (1982). *Child development and education.* Moscow: Progress.

Ariès, P. (1982). *Barndommens historie* [The history of childhood]. Copenhagen: Nyt Nordisk Forlag.

Davydov, V.V. (1977). *Arten der Verallgemeinerung im Unterricht* [The art of generalizing instruction]. Berlin: Volk & Wissen.

Davydov, V.V. (1982). Ausbildung der Lerntätigekeit [Development of learning activity]. In V.V. Davydov, J. Lompscher and A.K. Markova (eds), *Ausbildung der Lerntätigkeit bei Schülern* (pp. 14–27). Berlin: Volk & Wissen.

Davydov, V.V. and Radzikhovskii, L.A. (1985). Intellectual origins of Vygotsky's semiotic analysis. In J.W. Wertsch (ed.), *Culture, communication, and cognition* (pp. 35–65). Cambridge: Cambridge University Press.

Elkonin, D.B. (1971). Toward the problem of stages in the mental development of the child. *Soviet Psychology, 10*, 538–653.

Elkonin, D.B. (1980). *Psychologie des Spiels* [The psychology of play]. Berlin: Volk & Wissen.

Engeström, Y. (1986). The zone of proximal development as the basic category of educational psychology. *Quarterly Newsletter of the Laboratory of Comparative Human Cognition, 8*, 23–42.

Engeström, Y. and Hedegaard, M. (1986). Teaching theoretical thinking in elementary school. In E. Bol, J.P.P. Haenen and M.A. Wolters (eds), *Education for cognitive development* (pp. 170–193). Proceedings of the Third International Symposium on Activity Theory. Den Haag: SVO/SOO.

Gould, S. (1977). *Ever since Darwin*. London: Penguin.

Griffin, P. and Cole, M. (1984). Current activity for the future: The Zo-ped. In B. Rogoff and J.V. Wertsch (eds), *Children's learning in the "zone of proximal development"* (pp. 45–63). New Directions for Child Development, No. 23. San Francisco: Jossey-Bass.

Hedegaard, M. (1987). *Methodology in evaluative research on teaching and learning*. In F.J. Zuuren, F.J. Wertsch and B. Mook (eds), *Advances in qualitative psychology* (pp. 53–78). Sweetz North America Inc/Berwyn.

Hedegaard, M. (1989). Motivational development in schoolchildren. *Multidisciplinary Newsletter for Activity Theory, 1*, 30–38.

Juul Jensen, U. (1986). *Practice and progress: A theory for the modern healthcare systems*. Oxford: Blackwell Scientific Publications.

Leontiev, A.N. (1978). *Activity, consciousness, and personality*. Englewood Cliffs, NJ: Prentice-Hall.

Leontiev, A.N. (1981). *Problems in development of mind*. Moscow: Progress.

Leontiev, A.N. (1985). Einleitung: Der Schaffensweg Wygotskis [Introduction: Vygotsky's Works]. In L.S. Vygotsky, *Ausgewählte Schriften I* [Selected writings, Vol. 1]. Cologne: Pahl-Rugenstein.

Lewin, K. (1946). Behavior and development as a function of the total situation. In L. Carmichael (ed.), *Manual of child psychology* (pp. 918–983). New York: Wiley.

Lompscher, J. (1980). Ausbildung der Lerntätigkeit durch Aufsteigen vom Abstrakten zum Konkreten [Development of learning activity through advancing from the abstract to the concrete]. In A. Kossakowski (ed.), *Psychologie im Sozialismus* [Psychology in socialism]. Berlin: VEB Deutscher Verlag der Wissenschaften.

Lompscher, J. (1982). Analyse und Gestaltung von Lernanforderungen [Analysis and form of learning requirements]. In V.V. Davydov, J. Lompscher and A. Markova (eds), *Ausbildung der Lerntätigkeit bei Schülern* [Development of learning activity in school children] (pp. 36–50). Berlin: Volk & Wissen.

Lompscher, J. (1984). Problems and results of experimental research on the formation of theoretical thinking through instruction. In M. Hedegaard, P. Hakkarainen and Y. Engeström (eds), *Learning and teaching on a scientific basis* (pp. 293–357). Aarhus: Aarhus University.

Lompscher, J. (1985). *Persönlichkeitsentwicklung in der Lerntätigkeit* [Personality development through learning activity]. Berlin: Volk & Wissen.

Markova, A.K. (1982). Der ausbildende Experiment in der psychologischen Erforschung der Lerntätigkeit [The developmental experiment in psychological research of learning activity]. In V.V. Davydov, J. Lompscher and A. Markova (eds), *Ausbildung der Lerntätigkeit bei Schülern* [Development of learning activity in school children] (pp. 28–35). Berlin: Volk & Wissen.

Mayr, E. (1976). *Evolution and the diversity of life*. Cambridge, MA: Harvard University Press.

Mayr, E. (1980). Some thoughts on the history of the evolutionary synthesis. In E. Mayr and W.B. Provine, *The evolutionary synthesis* (pp. 1–48). Cambridge, MA: Harvard University Press.

Rogoff, B. and Wertsch, J.V. (eds) (1984). *Children's learning in the "zone of proximal development"*. New Directions for Child Development, No. 23. San Francisco: Jossey-Bass.

Schneider, P., Hyland, J. and Gallimore, R. (1985). The zone of proximal development in eighth grade social studies. *Quartely Newsletter of the Laboratory of Comparative Human Cognition, 7*, 113–119.

Scribner, S. (1985). Vygotsky's use of history. In J.V. Wertsch (ed.), *Culture, communication, and cognition* (pp. 119–145). Cambridge: Cambridge University Press.

Simpson, G.G. (1962). *The major features of evolution*. New York: Columbia University Press.

Vygotsky, L.S. (1978) *Mind in society*. Cambridge, MA: Harvard University Press.

Vygotsky, L.S. (1982). *Om barnets psykiske udvikling* [On the child's psychic development]. Copenhagen: Nyt Nordisk.

Vygotsky, L.S. (1985–1987). *Ausgewählte Schriften, I & II* [Selected writings, Vols. 1 & 2]. Cologne: Pahl-Rugenstein.

Wertsch, J.W. (1984). The zone of proximal development. In B. Rogoff and J.V. Wertsch (eds), *Children's learning in the "zone of proximal development."* New Directions for Child Development, No. 23. San Francisco: Jossey-Bass.

Wertsch, J.W. (1985). *The social formation of mind: A Vygotskian approach* (pp. 7–18). Cambridge, MA: Harvard University Press.

11 Signifying in the zone of proximal development

Carol D. Lee

In "Oral and Literate Traditions Among Black Americans Living in Poverty," Heath (1989) states:

> The school has seemed unable to recognize and take up the potentially positive interactive and adaptive verbal and interpretive habits learned by Black American children (as well as other nonmainstream groups), rural and urban, within their families and on the streets. These uses of language – spoken and written – are wide ranging, and many represent skills that would benefit all youngsters: keen listening and observational skills, quick recognition of nuanced roles, rapid-fire dialogue, hard-driving argumentation, succinct recapitulation of an event, striking metaphors, and comparative analyses based on unexpected analogies.
>
> (p. 370)

The uses of language described by Heath are epitomized in the form of talk known traditionally in the African American community as *signifying*. In this chapter I use a Vygotskian conceptual framework to argue that signifying as a form of social discourse in the African American community has the potential to serve as an effective scaffolding device for teaching complex skills in the interpretation of literature. I will argue that signifying as a construct bridges what Vygotsky called *spontaneous* and *scientific* concepts. I will further demonstrate the cultural dynamics of the process of semiotic mediation through which underachieving African American high school students were apprenticed into a community of literate problem solving by drawing on their knowledge of signifying.

A VYGOTSKIAN PERSPECTIVE ON LANGUAGE AND PROBLEM SOLVING

Lev Vygotsky (1986) saw language as a primary mediator of knowledge for humans. He saw language acquisition as evolving through a series of spiraling stages, each with a particular function in terms of shaping the problem-solving skills of humans. For Vygotsky, language at its core was a communicative tool that evolved within a specific sociohistorical context. He defined language acquisition as a mechanism for communicating to others. However, with the evolution of egocentric speech – the child talking to the self – language in addition becomes a tool for problem solving. In Vygotsky's studies, children use egocentric speech initially to accompany problem-solving strategies but later to direct problem-solving strategies. With the evolution of inner speech – using attenuated and often silent language – the learner uses language to direct problem-solving strategies. Egocentric speech and inner speech may be distinguished by the qualities of orality and elaborateness. These uses of egocentric and inner speech are examples of language being used to mediate the acquisition of knowledge. Both provide relational, causal, and temporal frameworks through which the learner internally conceptualizes the outside environment. Thus, in the Vygotskian framework, language serves as a conceptual organizer, a primary medium through which thinking occurs.

The use of language as both a socially communicative act and a medium for the internal organization of experience requires give-and-take, a dialectical interaction among interlocutors. Wertsch (1984) calls this dialectical dialogue *semiotic mediation* (Vygotsky, 1986). In many respects, the speech act for Vygotsky represented the quintessential unit for semiotic mediation. Through an ongoing process of semiotic mediation occurring in specific cultural, social, and historical contexts, the young learn the skills, values, and knowledge funds of the community of which they are a part. Through social and language interactions, older and more experienced members of a community teach younger and less experienced members the skills, values, and knowledge needed to be productive members of that community.

According to Vygotsky, learning is a product of the ongoing interaction between ontogenetic development (of which language acquisition is one key variable) and instruction. Vygotsky acknowledged that instruction may occur both within practical experiences and within formal school settings. Within the Vygotskian framework, however, there are fundamental differences in the qualities of concepts developed within the two settings. The concepts that develop within practical community experience he termed *spontaneous concepts*. The concepts that develop within formal school settings he termed *scientific concepts*. Although I question the limitation of scientific concepts to school settings and spontaneous concepts to practical community experience, it is important to point out that Vygotsky did acknowledge the fundamental interconnection between the two categories of concepts. Vygotsky characterized spontaneous concepts as situational, empirical, and practical. He characterized scientific concepts as systematic, as existing within a hierarchical network of related concepts, relative, generalizable, detached from the concrete, and used consciously and intentionally by people. The mental qualities that he believed were necessary to the acquisition of scientific concepts are deliberate attention, logical memory, abstraction, and the ability to compare and differentiate. He said that scientific concepts serve as the "propaedeutic guide" (Vygotsky, 1986) to the development of spontaneous concepts. That is, scientific concepts fine-tune and raise spontaneous concepts to a level of conscious, strategic use, whereas spontaneous concepts are the framework on which scientific concepts are built.

SIGNIFYING WITHIN A ZPD

Signifying is an oral genre of communication within the African American Vernacular English (AAVE) speech community. In a strict Vygotskian sense, signifying shares many of the characteristics attributed to spontaneous concepts. As a speech event, signifying occurs in specific social contexts (situational) and achieves specific goals for both the initiator and the receiver of the signifying act (practical). As these social contexts and goals may be both diverse and complex, I will save the specific examples until later when a full explication of signifying is offered.

Vygotsky (1986) says, "the absence of a system is the cardinal psychological difference distinguishing spontaneous from scientific concepts" (p. 205). In defining signifying, I will argue, however, that it is systematic, exists within a hierarchical network of related concepts, is used consciously and intentionally, and is both relative and generalizable. It is relative and generalizable because it is a rhetorical stance that must be generalized by its users to a multiplicity of specific situations that are potentially vast in number. In this sense, signifying shares attributes of scientific concepts as defined by Vygotsky. The difference, however, is that adolescents, in particular, who signify are not conscious of the rules of interpretation that operate within that discourse system, rules of interpretation that they know intuitively but not scientifically.

Vygotsky's (1978) analysis suggests that school learning may occur optimally when the novice has sufficiently developed spontaneous concepts learned in practical/community contexts that are related to scientific concepts learned in formal school contexts. The novice who has demonstrated an independent level of problem solving within the realm of a spontaneous concept is then placed in a social context with a more expert teacher who, through prodding, modeling, and questioning, guides the novice closer to a more adult-like, scientific representation of the task at hand. The learning context is considered social in that the learner does not acquire scientific concepts in isolation. Vygotsky called this condition the *zone of proximal development* (ZPD) and defined it as "the distance between the actual developmental level as determined by independent problem solving and the level of potential development as determined through problem solving under adult guidance or in collaboration with more capable peers" (p. 86).

Wertsch (1984) acknowledges that Vygotsky did not adequately and explicitly define "what constitutes problem solving under adult guidance or in collaboration with more capable peers" (p. 8). Inferring from the breadth of Vygotsky's writings, Wertsch states that there are three minimal constraints that define a ZPD. The first constraint is *situation definition*. Initially the student and the teacher may have different representations of the task to be completed. As the learning interaction progresses, the student's representation of the task should evolve to a representation closer to that of the teacher. The second constraint is *intersubjectivity*, which Wertsch defines as the extent to which the student and the teacher agree on what the task is. According to Wertsch, intersubjectivity may exist on a minimal level. For example, student and teacher may initially agree only on the tools to be used to complete the task. Through the process of *semiotic mediation* – the third constraint on any ZPD – the teacher may temporarily give up his or her representation of the task to accommodate the level of understanding of the student, while the student comes progressively closer to the representation of the task that the teacher/expert holds. Wertsch points out that the difference in the initial representation by the novice in the zone is not necessarily quantitatively different later on; rather, it is qualitatively different. Through the process of semiotic mediation, then, the level on which intersubjectivity exists spirals in complexity.

In this chapter, I propose that signifying as a form of social discourse within the speech community of speakers of AAVE demonstrates a useful example of semiotic mediation. Signifying is a linguistic tool that directs behavior and organizes the user's cognitive representation of the external environment.

THINKING IN SCHOOL AND COMMUNITY CONTEXTS

The enterprise of studying similarities in thinking between the contexts of school and community or work is a delicate matter. Scribner (1984) outlines two critical issues in such an enterprise. She resolves that cognition should be studied within the framework of practice:

> [1] This view attaches one definite, if not exhaustive, meaning to the ambiguous concept of experience. It particularizes experience as the active engagement of an individual in some pursuit involving socially organized domains of knowledge and technologies, including symbol systems. It conceives of functionality in the instrumental sense of supporting accomplishment of some goal-directed action. . . .
>
> (p. 14)

> [2] The general construct of practice offers a possibility for integrating social-cultural and psychological levels of analysis and achieving

explanatory accounts of how basic mental processes and structures become specialized and diversified through experience.

(p. 13)

Scribner raises the question of how "one locate[s] cognitive phenomena that can be classified as similar in kind and that are sufficiently bounded to be amenable to analysis" (p. 14). Scribner concludes that "practice and task" are such units of analysis. These units of analysis parallel the activity unit, as defined by Vygotskian psychologist Leont'ev (1981; Wertsch, Minick, & Arns, 1984). Scribner (1984), Lave (1977), Rogoff (1990), and others have investigated what Vygotsky calls the *higher mental functions* in socially routinized activity or practice. This approach is consistent with Vygotsky's general law of cultural development, in which higher psychological functioning first appears on the social plane, between people as "interpsychological," and then on the psychological plane, within the individual child, as "intrapsychological" (Vygotsky, 1978).

In this society (as in many others), the language practices of disenfranchised groups are not only devalued by schools (a condition of diglossia, as defined by Saville-Troike, 1989), but in fact have the effect of negatively impacting learning (Cazden, 1988; Cook-Gumperz, 1986; Delpit, 1990; Michaels, 1986; Philips, 1985). Under these circumstances, the act of analyzing the higher mental functions in socially routinized activity among poor and ethnically diverse student populations is a radical move. Up to this point, the bulk of such research has focused either on higher mental thinking in blue-collar workplaces or on the incorporation of nonmainstream verbal interaction patterns into classroom discourse in order to increase student participation in instructional talk. The major body of research that has investigated similarities in problem-solving strategies in practical/ community social contexts among poor and disenfranchised groups and problem solving in schools has been in the area of mathematics (La Rocha, 1985; Nunes, Schliemann, & Carraher, 1993; Reed & Lave, 1981; Saxe, 1988). Despite a popular focus on Vygotsky in literacy research, few studies have investigated the interactions between spontaneous and scientific concepts in language minority communities. Similarly, within the situated cognition framework, clearly influenced by Vygotsky, little attention has been given to the study of formal literacy as social practice outside school. In addition, this line of research has had little observable and lasting influence on schooling. The research that extends the framework offered in this chapter attempts to speak both to the need to locate shared spaces between home and school knowledge in a way that academically empowers under-achieving student populations and to offer practical alternatives that schools can use.

I shall attempt here to analyze signifying within a Vygotskian framework and to argue its use in a ZPD as a spontaneous concept – with the restrictions I've already addressed concerning the dubious distinctions defining spontaneous concepts. As a spontaneous concept in the Vygotskian sense, signifying has aspects that parallel literary "scientific" concepts such as irony, metaphor, symbolism, and the various rhetorical tropes through which double entendre and inferred meanings may be expressed in literary texts. Because of these shared characteristics, signifying is ripe for exploitation within a Vygotskian ZPD. Within the framework proposed in this chapter, African American students naive about the formal definitions and applications of these rhetorical tropes in literature are seen as novices within the ZPD, and the literature teacher, skilled in both signifying and literary analysis, is the expert. In such a ZPD the literature teacher scaffolds the spontaneous concept already understood – albeit intuitively – by the novice in order to bring the novice closer to the "expert" or "literary" understanding of these tropes. Signifying may be further defined, through the levels of analysis of activities put forward by Leont'ev (1981), as a series of actions motivated by specific goals and operationalized within a specific cultural context.

PROPERTIES OF SIGNIFYING

Signifying has been formally defined by many scholars, writers, and activists (Abrahams, 1970; Andrews & Owens, 1973; Brown, 1969; Cooke, 1984; Gates, 1984, 1988; Hurston, 1935; Kochman, 1972; Major, 1970; Mitchell-Kernan, 1981; Smitherman, 1977). Some define its characteristics in structural terms as a speech act with delineated functions (Abrahams, 1970; Kochman, 1972). Others define it as a rhetorical stance, an attitude toward language, and a means of cultural self definition (Cooke, 1984; Gates, 1984, 1988; Mitchell-Kernan, 1981; Smitherman, 1977). I do not see these categories as being mutually exclusive. In fact, both are necessary to the argument of this chapter. An understanding of signifying as a rhetorical stance, an attitude toward language, and a means of cultural self-definition is important in assessing the value given to signifying as an art form within the African American community. It is precisely because it is so highly valued and so widely practiced that signifying has the potential to serve as a bridge to literacy skills within a school environment.

Goodlad (1984) has commented on the boredom of American classrooms. If large numbers of African American students are not achieving academically, as measured by rates of high school graduation and standardized measures of literacy, then it is reasonable to assume that these students are often not engaged in the process of literacy instruction. Learning to interpret formal properties of literature is one critical aspect of literacy instruction. Irony, symbolism, and uses of metaphor and point of view are examples of such formal properties. An understanding of the structural properties and functions of signifying is what allows one to conceptualize its potential linkages with these formal literary concepts.

Both Gates (1984, 1988) and Mitchell-Kernan (1981) point to the specialized meanings attributed to the word *signify* within the African American community. Both of these authors contrast the European American dictionary-based definition of signification with the Afro-centric definition. To signify within the African American community means to speak with innuendo and double meanings, to play rhetorically on the meaning and sounds of words, and to be quick and often witty in one's response. There is no parallel usage of the terms *signify* or *signification* within other ethnic, English-speaking communities, although other speech communities have routine forms of language play. Gates punctuates the difference in the use of the term in the two communities by capitalizing the first letter to identify Signifying as a specialized concept of language use within the Black community. In many social settings within the African American community, the adolescent, in particular, who cannot signify has no status and no style, is a kind of outsider who is incapable of participating in social conversation. Although Signifying is a common language phenomenon across Black communities, Mitchell-Kernan (1981) observes:

> While the terminological use of signifying to refer to a particular kind of language specialization defines the Black community as a speech community in contrast to non-Black communities, it should be emphasized that further intra-community terminological specialization reflects social structural divisions within the community and related activity specializations.

> (p. 313)

Thus signifying and its many components may be called by different names in different communities or during different historical periods, and certain skills may be more dominant within one gender. Also, certain individuals may assume more specialized roles than other members of the general community, such as the role of contemporary rappers.

Gates (1984, 1988) and Cooke (1984) argue that signifying is a historical phenomenon within the African American community. Gates (1988) places the origin of signifying in 19th-century spirituals and slave narratives. He quotes from an ex-slave, Wash Wilson, who says, "When de niggers go round singin' 'Steal Away to Jesus,' dat mean dere gwine be a 'ligious meetin' dat night. Dat de sig'fication of a meetin' " (p. 68). Like Cooke, Gates identifies "Signifying as the slave's trope," an indirect way of reversing the relations of slave and master.

Signifying may be called or classified by many names. According to Gates (1984), "The Black rhetorical tropes subsumed under signifying would include 'marking,' 'loud-talking,' 'specifying,' 'testifying,' 'calling out' (of one's name), 'sounding,' 'rapping' and 'playing the dozens' " (p. 286). Other terms include *shucking* (as in "shucking and jiving") and *talking shit*.

Signifying in any given speech event or stretch of talk may fulfill one or many of the following functions:

1. Challenge and maintain a friendly but intense verbal duel.
2. Persuade – to direct through indirection, to use Abrahams's (1970) reference, to drive home a message "without preaching or lecturing" (Smitherman, 1977).
3. Criticize or insult through either carping or innuendo.
4. Praise – Rap Brown (1969) said, "Signifying allowed you a choice – you could either make a cat feel good or bad. If you had just destroyed someone or if they were just down already, signifying could help them over."
5. Reverse a relationship.
6. "Show off," to use Hurston's (1935) term or use it as a "way of expressing your own feelings," to use Rap Brown's (1969) words.

Mitchell-Kernan (1981), Ellison (1964), and Smitherman (1977) describe the formal properties of signifying. Mitchell-Kernan describes signifying as "a way of encoding messages or meanings which involves, in most cases, an element of indirection" (p. 311). She emphasizes that dictionary meanings of words in an act of signifying are not sufficient for constructing meaning. One must recognize the "implicit content or function, which is potentially obscured by the surface content or function" (p. 314). Ellison (1964) talks about "ironic signifying – 'signifying' here meaning, in the unwritten dictionary of American Negro usage, 'rhetorical understatements' " (pp. 249–250). Smitherman summarizes the formal properties of signifying as follows:

> indirection, circumlocution; metaphorical-imagistic (but images rooted in the everyday, real world); humorous, ironic; rhythmic fluency and sound; teachy but not preachy; directed at person or persons usually present in the situational context (siggers do not talk behind yo back); punning, play on words; introduction of the semantically or logically unexpected.
>
> (p. 121)

A NETWORK OF RELATED TROPES IN LITERATURE

The purpose of defining signifying in this chapter is to show its parallels to various formal literary tropes and also to highlight its formal characteristics that have much in common with the attributes that Vygotsky (1986) says characterize scientific concepts. The literary tropes of interest include irony, metaphor, symbolism, and use of unreliable narrators. What these tropes have in common is that where an author employs them, possible intended meanings must be inferred and strictly literal interpretations must be rejected. Use of any of these devices signals to an expert reader that some encoded meaning, some double entendre, is intended. In this sense, all of these literary devices share an attribute with signifying: "encoding messages or meanings which involve in most cases an element of indirection" (Mitchell-Kernan 1981, p. 311).

Once a reader has determined that the surface-level meaning is not sufficient, the reader must decide how to construct the encoded meaning or meanings. According to Winner (1988), if a passage is ironic, readers (or listeners in the case of oral communication) reconstruct an intended meaning in opposition to the literal one; if metaphoric, in addition to the literal one. Symbolism may be thought of as an extension of metaphor in that the image, character, object, event, or action has a potential meaning or set of meanings that are in addition to the literal meaning but also represent a generalizable proposition. Point of view, as represented by the use of unreliable narrators, may be thought of as an extension of irony. In response to the specialized question "Who is talking?" when we encounter unreliable narrators, we reject the surface meaning of what they communicate because we do not deem what they say trustworthy. In this sense, these four literary devices are systematically related. Rabinowitz (1987) calls those strategies readers use to recognize that something other than the literal meaning is intended *rules of notice*. The strategies and prior knowledge we draw on to impose meaning Rabinowitz calls *rules of signification*. The system of related literary tropes and devices is accessed by rules of notice and interpreted through rules of signification. Because these tropes and literary devices are systematically related, strategies used to detect irony are also applicable to detecting metaphor, symbolism, and manipulation of point of view through the use of an unreliable narrator. The nexus of related literary devices is represented in Figure 11.1.

In order to demonstrate the links between the spontaneous concept of signifying and formal literary devices, I will construct a case around irony. Because I have argued that irony stands within a nexus of interrelated literary tropes, a cognitive analysis of the act of interpreting irony within the

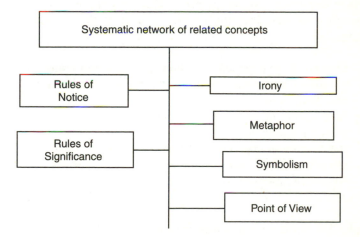

Figure 11.1 Systematic network of related literary concepts.

framework of activity theory (Leont'ev, 1981) is theoretically extended to the other related tropes.

In what follows, I will first discuss formal properties of irony in literature and strategies a reader may use in both identifying and reconstructing the meaning of ironic passages. Then, by analyzing several signifying dialogues, I will attempt to demonstrate the systematicity of the cognitive strategies one must use, whether implicitly or explicitly, in order to interpret the motives and goals and the shifts in meaning as the dialogue progresses.

I shall not attempt here to offer any authoritative definition of irony, for as Booth (1974) says, "There is no agreement among critics about what irony is" (p. ix). Yet, irony, like signifying, provides a well-used bridge between Vygotsky's scientific and spontaneous concepts. Booth accurately observes that irony "can be found on almost every page of many great writers, but you will also find it sprinkling the conversation of the rail-road workers in Utah and – I am told – the street sweepers in Bombay" (p. 30). A major thesis of this chapter is that the cognitive representations involved in recognizing and reconstructing meaning in acts of signifying are systematic, complex, and akin to similar representations in recognizing and reconstructing the meaning of an ironic, metaphoric, or symbolic passage in literature. Accordingly, Wittgenstein has said, "The tacit conventions on which the understanding of everyday language depends are enormously complicated" (cited in Booth, 1974).

Booth (1974) emphasizes the importance of context in interpreting irony: "The 'context,' then, is not just the words but the words as they relate to our total view of the subject, to our range of inferences about what the author would most probably mean by each stroke, and to our range of possible genres" (p. 99). Booth indicates that his purpose is to describe "the way irony works," and he points out that knowledge of the genre and the author influences how irony functions in particular works. Booth says that in order for the author and reader to engage each other in a shared understanding of the irony of a passage, they must agree on at least three areas of common experience:

1. their common experience of the vocabulary and grammar of English . . . along with understanding of rules which allow for and control verbal inventions
2. their common cultural experience and their agreement about its meaning and value
3. their common experience of literary genres, a potentially large (but almost certainly finite) number of shared grooves or tracks into which reading experience can be directed.

(p. 100)

For many African American students (and others whose community culture differs markedly from mainstream school culture), these areas of experience are not shared understandings, particularly when reading literature that does not reflect their common experiences with vocabulary and grammar, cultural values that are not part of their experience, and literary genres with which they are explicitly unfamiliar. On the other hand, in an act of signifying, it is safe to assume that a majority of African American students who speak AAVE will have a common understanding of language conventions and meaning, values around the import of the ritual of the act, and under-standing of the the rules of the game that I believe may be analogous to expectations regarding literary genres.

Booth (1974) distinguishes between the act of recognizing irony and the act of reconstructing the meanings of an ironic passage. Smith (1987) outlines five clues that Booth argues an author may use to signal irony in a work or passage:

1. "a straightforward warning in the author's own voice . . . in titles, in epigraphs, and in other direct clues."
2. "when an author has his or her speaker proclaim a known error. . . ."
3. "existence of a conflict within a work."
4. "a clash of style," as when the "language of a speaker is not clearly the same as the language of the author" or when the author uses understatements or exaggerations.
5. "a conflict of belief" between a speaker and the author or "behavior of a speaker that the author could not endorse."

(pp. 11–13)

Smith adds, "In each case the reader must bring to bear standards from outside the text onto the world of the text, proceeding from the belief that the author does not hold alien values" (p. 13). The clues identified by Booth and Smith may be classified as rules of notice, as defined by Rabinowitz (1987). Rules of notice are strategies and clues that readers of fiction use to deter-mine that something in a text requires additional and special attention. As framed in this chapter, attention signaling that the surface or literal meaning is insufficient is the issue of focus.

COMMON PROCESSES IN UNDERSTANDING IRONY AND OTHER TROPES IN LITERATURE AND SIGNIFYING IN SOCIAL DISCOURSE

In this section I provide examples of signifying. I argue that the rules for recognizing each example as signifying parallel the clues for signaling irony, as defined by Booth (1974). Considering that signifying in social discourse does not involve a printed text with such conventions as titles and epigraphs, it is reasonable to distill the following parallel steps in recognizing an act as signifying.

1. *When a speaker proclaims a known error*, as in the following example (Mitchell-Kernan, 1981, p. 317): [Relevant background information: the husband is a member of the class of individuals who do not wear suits to work]

Wife: Where are you going?
Husband: I'm going to work.
Wife: (You're wearing) a suit, tie and white shirt? You didn't tell me you got a promotion.

The surface meaning of the wife's final comment is rejected because of the rule of notice by which the speaker proclaims a known error. An ironic meaning in opposition to the literal one is constructed. In addition, both the husband and the wife recognize the husband as an unreliable narrator.

2. *Existence of a conflict*, as in the following example (Mitchell-Kernan, 1981, pp. 318–319): [Relevant background information: Grace hadn't told anybody that she was pregnant and was starting to show. The following exchange is between Grace and her sister.]

Rochelle: Girl, you sure do need to join the Metrecal for lunch bunch.
Grace: (Non-committally) Yea, I guess I am putting on a little weight.
Rochelle: Now look here, girl, we both standing here soaking wet and you still trying to tell me it ain't raining.

Again, this rule of notice, existence of a conflict, signals that Rochelle's final comment is not intended to be interpreted literally. The intended meaning is in opposition to the literal one, that is, they are not soaking wet. The statement "we both standing here soaking wet and you still trying to tell me it ain't raining" requires that we think analogically, and consider relationships between the tenor of the metaphor and the situation between Rochelle and Grace.

3. *A clash of style*: Smitherman (1977, p. 86) references a cartoon by Ollie Harrington. Two African American men are in what looks like a hotel room, which could be in Paris. One man, dressed in an undershirt and boxer shorts, with a cigar in his mouth, is looking at an open book. The other man, dressed as a dapper dandy in a 1940s-style fancy dress, says:

"That book ain't gonna teach you no French, Bootsie. You got to live it. Now s'posin' you just had a fine feed at some chick's pad. You bows and says, 'Bon soir mademoiselle, et cetera.' Now that means, 'Goodnight, Irene. Thanks for the fine scoff. The chitterlings was simply devine and I'll dig you by and by!"

Harrington, the cartoonist, as the author, is signifying on the men, affecting to be more sophisticated than they really are. There is a clash of styles between the men's attempt to be sophisticated speakers of French and their obvious working-class origins. The scenario is ironic because what we are to infer about the men is the opposite of what they purport to be. Besides being ironic, the cartoon is satirical.

4. *The speech behavior of the signifier could not possibly be one that the speaker would actually do or believe, analogous to Booth's conflict of belief.*

The dozens presents an excellent example. In the dozens, one ritualistically insults another's mother, usually, or another family member. Smitherman (1977) warns that in order for the dozens not to be offensive, the insults must have no basis in fact, as in the following excerpt from Richard Wright's (1963) *Lawd Today*, in which a group of Black men playing cards engage in playing the dozens (thanks to Smitherman, 1977, p. 127, for the example):

> "Yeah," he said slowly, "I remembers when my little baby brother was watching with slobber in his mouth, your old grandma was out in the privy crying 'cause she couldn't find a corncob. . . ."
>
> Slim and Bob groaned and stomped their feet.
>
> "Yeah," said Al, retaliating with narrowed eyes. "When my old grandma was crying for that corncob, your old aunt Lucy was round back of the barn with old Colonel James' old man, and she was saying something like this: 'Yyyyou kknow . . . Mmmiister Cccolonel . . . I jjjust ddon't like to sssell . . . my ssstuff . . . I jjjust lloves to gggive . . . iit away . . .'."

The rule of notice applicable here notifies the reader or listener to reject the surface meaning. This text of signifying is satiric and, in a sense, involves an unreliable narrator.

Booth makes an important point when he distinguishes between the strategies a reader uses to recognize irony from the strategies he or she uses to reconstruct meaning in the ironic passage. The reconstruction process is necessary because once the reader identifies the passage as ironic (or the speaker recognizes the first turn in the speech act as signifying), the reader (or listener) realizes that the surface meaning must be rejected. Smith (1987) recounts four steps that Booth indicates may be used in reconstructing meaning: "rejecting the surface meaning, trying out alternative meanings, applying one's knowledge of the author, and selecting among alternatives" (p. 13). Smith observes that in "the usual case of quick recognition" the alternative meanings of which Booth speaks may come "flooding in." However, Smith is concerned that Booth's explanation does not attend to what variables control a reader's selection of alternative meanings. Smith says that the variable cannot simply be knowledge of the author because readers "understand the irony of unknown authors" (p. 14). To account for this discrepancy, Smith offers his own four steps of reconstruction. Smith believes that readers

1. Reject the surface meaning
2. Decide what is not under dispute in the work
3. Apply their knowledge of the world to generate a reconstructed meaning and, if possible,
4. Check the reconstructed meaning against their knowledge of the author.

(p. 15)

Because Smith's reconstructive steps are more specific than Booth's, and because knowledge of the social world as well as knowledge of the signifier is crucial in reconstructing meaning within a signifying speech act, I will apply Smith's reconstructive steps in analyzing signifiying. One rarely signifies with a person about whom one has no personal knowledge and especially not with a person outside one's cultural community. There are also restrictions on what kind of signifying may acceptably occur across, for example, age cohorts. It would not be socially acceptable for an adolescent boy or girl to play the dozens with an adult or elder.

The extent to which a reader or listener may use these reconstructive steps as a conscious strategy depends on several key factors. However, Smith's (1989) study on the effects of direct versus tacit instruction of irony with high school students suggests that whether explictly conscious or implictly tacit, readers do seem to employ these strategies in reconstructing meaning in the ironic poems in his study. I agree with Smith that when expert readers read texts with which they are very familiar (familiar with the text, the author, and the author's other texts), it is possible that alternative meanings to the surface meaning may indeed come "flooding in," as suggested by Booth (1974). However, any of the following variables that must be considered in the interpretive process may sufficiently slow down processing to the point where a reader begins consciously to employ the steps identified by Smith: the skill of the reader, the complexity of textual antecedents needed to generalize meaning, knowledge of restrictions or possibilities brought to bear by the genre, and/or real-world knowledge of the reader. On the other hand, a participant in extended dialogue within a signifying speech event cannot possibly take time to employ such strategies consciously, but rather must be verbally and mentally quick enough to respond immediately.

The intensity of this intellectual challenge may differ according to the kind of signifying event taking place. Gates (1984, 1988) says that signifying is not primarily transmitting content, but rather rhetorical style. I agree with Gates when the signifying event involves something like rapping or playing the dozens, for in these instances truth is not the hallmark, but rather style. However, when the signifying event is meant to be directive or persuasive, and particularly when the event involves extended dialogue, quick interpretation of meaning (having rejected the surface meaning) is mandatory and ongoing throughout each speech turn. In such signifying events, the signifiers must be astute enough to process the reconstructed meaning immediately. I argue that expert signifiers have a richly embedded network of associations represented in signifying schemata that allow them to respond immediately. This embedded network distinguishes expert signifiers (of whatever signifying category) from novices and the ordinary folk. I consider myself among ordinary folk in the world of signifying discourse in that I can recognize signifying and interpret it accurately and quickly, but I am not adept at the quick verbal retort. This richly embedded network of associations may relate to ritualized themes (such as "yo mamma," or "what's happenin' baby?") or to rhetorical techniques such as exaggeration.

A pivotal inference that participants in a signifying dialogue must make concerns the motives of the signifier. What one interprets about motives determines the category of signifying being invoked and directs the kind of response that is appropriate. The second party in the dialogue (as the first speaker initiates the signifying event or "sounds out" the second party) must infer one or some combination of the following motives:

1. A challenge to a verbal duel
2. An attempt to persuade
3. Criticism
4. Praise
5. A reversal of an existing relationship

Failure to interpret accurately the motives of the speaker may result in dire consequences. The tale of "The Signifying Monkey" demonstrates such results. The monkey speaks metaphorically as a signifier, but the lion interprets literally. Kochman (1972) and others (Baugh, 1983; Gates, 1984, 1988; Mitchell-Kernan, 1981; Smitherman, 1977) argue that these two interpretive stances reflect fundamental differences between the African American speech community and the European American English-speaking community in terms of attitudes toward language.*

APPLYING STRATEGIES FOR PROCESSING IRONY AND RELATED RHETORICAL TROPES TO SIGNIFYING DISCOURSE

I will apply Smith's (1989) four steps in reconstructing the meaning of irony and the choices of motives to be inferred to an extended signifying dialogue

---

* I recognize that the European American English speech community is not monolithic. One European American English-speaking group demonstrating different discourse, syntax, and prosody features speaks Appalachian English. I use the term *European American English speech community* to represent what is institutionally captured in assumptions about mainstream standard English.

reported by Mitchell-Kernan (1981, p. 319). The researcher in the dialogue is Mitchell-Kernan. The dialogue occurred while she was conducting ethnographic fieldwork for her doctoral dissertation on language practices in the Black community. All comments in brackets are my analysis of the strategies used by both parties in the exchange to identify and reconstruct ironic meanings throughout the dialogue.

The following interchange took place in a public park. Three young men in their early 20s sat down with the researcher, one of whom initiated a conversation in this way:

I: Mama, you sho is fine.
      [Initiates a signifying event]
R: That ain no way to talk to your mother.
      (laughter)

[Researcher rejects the surface meaning of the statement. She decides what is not under dispute, i.e., the young man is not trying to offend or seduce her. She signals by her use of the reference to his mother that she recognizes that a signifying speech event is underway – in this case and at this point in the dialogue a challenge to a verbal duel – and that she is willing to participate in the ritual.]

I: You married?

[Since this is a signifying speech event, this question sets the stage for an unexpected turn by the interlocutor, something to be expected by an expert signifier. The interpretation of this request will then be held critically in abeyance until further information is available.]

R: Um hm.

[Researcher remains uncommitted in her response. Because of her "knowledge of the world" of signifying, it is important that she hold her options for response open.]

I: Is your husband married?

[An obvious case of signifying because, to use Booth's strategy for recognizing irony, the speaker in this instance (as opposed to the author's speaker in a written text) proclaims a known error. Obviously her husband is married.]

R: Very.

[The researcher accepts the statement as signifying. She recognizes that what is not under dispute is whether her husband is married or not. Using her knowledge of the world of signifying – i.e., the interlocutor's motives may now have changed to either persuade her to do something or to reverse an existing relationship, namely, to question the fidelity of her husband – and her knowledge of the rules operating around even the surface meaning of to be married – i.e., to be sexually loyal to one another – she infers that the interlocutor is asking whether her husband operates according to the same rules of fidelity as she, and if not, perhaps she needn't operate by them either. At the same time, this exchange at the level of inferences must be understood within the context of signifying, which means that neither the interlocutor nor the researcher takes these understandings as literal attempts to seduce. This, I think, is verified by the fact that the researcher does not get offended by the question; nor does she encourage the interlocutor to continue any serious attempts at seduction. In this case, she has checked her reconstructed meaning against her knowledge of the intent of the interlocutor.]

(The conversation continues, with the same young man doing most of the talking. He questions [the researcher] about what [she is] doing, and [she tells] him about my research project. After a couple of minutes of discussing "rapping" I [interlocutor] returns to his original style.)

I: Baby, you a real scholar. I can tell you want to learn. Now if you'll just cooperate a li'l bit, I'll show you what a good teacher I am. But first we got to get into my area of expertise.

[The interlocutor is now rapping, praising himself and the researcher. However, the signal statement in this exchange is the phrase "into my area of expertise." This statement signals an act of signifying and therefore calls for an ironic interpretation.]

R: I may be wrong but seems to me we already in your area of expertise. (laughter)

[In order to interpret the interlocutor's statement as continuing to signify, the researcher using Booth's clues for identifying irony must recognize a kind of clash of style, if you will, and a known error. That is, the interlocutor is not a teacher in the traditional sense, and whatever his area of expertise is, it is not likely to be one traditionally associated (surface meaning) with the profession or art of teaching. To reconstruct the ironic meaning, then, the researcher must again reject the surface meaning. She must decide that what is not under dispute is whether he has some area of expertise, but exactly what that area of expertise is. She applies her knowledge of the world of signifying and infers his motive to be both to persuade and possibly to reverse a relationship – namely, her relationship as the researcher/teacher/scholarly expert and his as the object of study. She must also check her reconstructed meaning against her knowledge of the interlocutor. He has proven himself to be good at flirting and at signifying. She then reconstructs the ironic or signifying meaning as a kind of double entendre, deciding that his area of expertise is in fact both. However, as an expert signifier herself, the researcher redirects the double entendre and redefines his area of expertise simply as signifying.]

I: You ain' so bad yourself, girl. I ain't heard you stutter yet. You a li'l fixated on your subject though. I want to help a sweet thang like you all I can. I figure all that book learning you got must mean you been neglecting other areas of your education.

[In the first two sentences, the interlocutor praises the researcher because she has played the game well. These sentences are meant to be interpreted literally as content, but within the play of the verbal game, they act as a setup for his redirection of her last verbal volley. In other words, he recognizes that he has been signified upon.]

II: Talk that talk! (Gloss: Ole)

[This is the response of a third party to the interchange. He is now *testifying*, a form of signifying in which a respondent praises and reinforces the verbal skill of the signifier. This response is a further indication by all parties involved that everyone recognizes this speech event as an act of signifying.]

R: Why don't you let me point out where I can best use your help.

[The researcher has accurately interpreted his redirection and has redirected his intent again. In order to recognize the interlocutor's last statement as continued signification, the researcher realizes that within his statement there is both a clash of styles and exaggeration. From what she surmises of the interlocutor from the circumstances of their meeting and from her real-world knowledge that middle-class Black scholars don't ordinarily carry on extended signifying with people they meet in the park, she concludes that there is some discrepancy between his concern about book learning and other areas of her education. This discrepancy, along with the recognition that this entire speech event so far has been an act of signifying, would lead her to recognize the statements as signifying and therefore ironic. In order to reconstruct the meaning of his last statements, the researcher decides that what is not under dispute is whether she studies the linguistics of signifying too much. She uses her knowledge of the world of signifying and infers his motives as a challenge to continue the verbal duel, possibly to persuade her still, and to reverse the relationship of teacher and object of study. She checks her reconstructed meaning against her knowledge of the past exchanges with the interlocutor, namely, his sly, gamish attempts to flirt with her and his prior rapping to establish himself as a lover – but only in the context of the verbal game of signifying. She thus interprets the other areas of her education with which he can help her as an intended double entendre, involving the area of love making and flirting, along with her formal education in linguistics. By making the response she does, the researcher redirects his verbal volley once again. At the same time, the researcher signals her willingness to continue the game because she maintains the metaphor established by the interlocutor.]

I: Are you sure you in the best position to know?

[The interlocutor accepts the challenge and volleys back. The elaborate metaphor has been maintained and redirected by each signifying participant.]

(laughter)
I: I'mo leave you alone, girl. Ask me what you want to know. Tempus fugit, baby.

[This response is very important in the interchange because it signals the end of the signifying event.] Mitchell-Kernan (1981) comments that "the interchange is laced with innuendo – signifying because it alludes to and implies things which are never made explicit" (p. 319). Mitchell-Kernan's analysis of the preceding speech event is quite informative and has influenced the analysis offered by this author to each turn in the exchange.

Having attempted to establish in some sense the parallel uses of strategy in identifying and reconstructing meaning in both signifying speech events and irony and other rhetorical tropes in literature, I can reasonably argue that signifying represents the special kind of concept that fits nicely into the possibilities of transfer suggested by Vygotsky's notion of the interchange of spontaneous and scientific concepts within a ZPD. That is, both concepts have enough common attributes to provide unique bridging possibilities for using knowledge in one arena to scaffold formal knowledge in the second arena. Because the two concepts require comparable mental processing, I argue that Vygotsky's construct of higher mental functions operates in both signifying and the interpretation of literary tropes.

SIGNIFYING AND AFRICAN AMERICAN LITERATURE

Besides sharing formal qualities with the literary constructs of irony, metaphor, symbolism, and point of view, signifying also serves well in a Vygotskian ZPD because it is widely used within African American literature. This context is important for several reasons. First, Booth (1974) and Smith (1987) both argue that knowledge of literary genres plays an important role in the act of recognizing and reconstructing ironic meanings in literature. Although the use of oral language traditions such as signifying and the use of AAVE are factors that help constitute African American literature as a unique literary tradition, African American literature also is constituted through traditional and postmodern Western literary genres. Thus in the context of literature, to bring the shared strategies of identifying and reconstructing ironic, meta-phoric, and symbolic meanings in oral signifying and in literature to a meta-cognitive level of explicit awareness is to strengthen the shared lessons of the two experiences. The advantage that African American literature potentially gives young, novice, African American readers is through their prior know-ledge of the social milieu, values, and issues addressed in such texts, as well as their familiarity, in many cases, with the language style and its import for meaning. Hynds (1989) has acknowledged the role of social knowledge in constructing meaning from literary texts. She accurately points out that knowledge of the social world is too seldom used to assist students in con-structing meaning from literary texts, an observation that she believes inten-sifies student alienation from literature. These observations, however, are not meant to imply that all African American literary texts offer such a privileged position to African American students, nor that there is a straightforward advantage that African American literary texts offer African American stu-dents. I have argued elsewhere that a close analysis of the interpretive demands of the text is required to understand how to prepare students to tackle such problems independently. In one sense, Vygotsky's conception of capacity as the relationship between what the novice can do alone and what the novice can do with the support of a more knowledgeable other (i.e., the ZPD) applies. A central premise of the conceptual framework on which this chapter is based is that when the capacities of underachieving African American students in terms of literary analysis in signifying dialogues are recognized, honored, and addressed in the design of supports for learning, the independent capacities of these students are powerful. What that support looks like is addressed in the next section of this chapter.

Gates (1984, 1988), Ishmael Reed (1974), and Zora Neale Hurston (1935) all talk about the talking book, the oral book. Such texts within the African American literary tradition give voice and tenor to the speech of ordinary Black folk. In a culture in which the African American has historically been viewed as the *Invisible Man*, in a Western literary tradition in which the Black voice is not heard, the speakerly text, as Gates calls it, resonates the choir's *Talkin' and Testifyin'* from the fields, the bedrooms, the parlors, and the bar rooms, from the church pulpits and the street corners. The Black talking book represents the oral tradition of the African American community. Jones (1991), Gates (1988), Baker (1984), and Smitherman (1977), among others, recount significant literary texts in which the oral tradition, and specifically signifying play important roles. Signifying, then, is not limited to the context of oral conversation, but is catapulted into the realm of rhetorical technique within the tradition of African American literature.

SIGNIFYING IN A ZPD: CLASSROOM APPLICATION

This section moves from a theoretical discussion of signifying as a bridge between spontaneous and scientific concepts to examine how the mediation occurs within classrooms. Because issues of culture and ethnicity are central to the argument of this chapter, I will illustrate how the culturally rooted prior knowledge of these African American students was used by the teacher to apprentice these students into a particular community of practice.

Scribner (1984) and Leont'ev (1981) argued that activity as a unit of analysis offers a useful way to understand thinking in context. I will describe the enactment of this instructional unit wherein spontaneous concepts guide the development of scientific concepts played out in a Vygotskian ZPD. The process of semiotic mediation is enacted between teacher and student, as well as among students with evolving levels of expertise. This semiotic mediation is rooted in a cultural foundation, just as the premise of signifying as a spontaneous concept linked structurally to literary tropes is cultural. This semiotic mediation also unfolds over time. Understanding its changes over time, changes in the reasoning processes of both students and the teacher, is important. The process of semiotic mediation demands a classroom culture in which the salient elements of the practice are assumed over time by the novice and monitored by more expert-like others. In the case of this class, this means students not only learning to see connections about what they know about signifying and how to attack problems of literary analysis, but also learning how to raise appropriate questions, how to attend to salient parts of the text, how to generate arguments using both textual and real-world knowledge, and how to monitor this understanding.

I have previously (1991, 1993, 1994, 1995a, 1995b, 1997) implemented an instructional intervention based on the conceptual framework described in this chapter. I have labeled this conceptual framework *Cultural Modeling* (Lee, 1994). In Cultural Modeling, explicit strategies for attacking problems of irony, symbolism, and point of view are modeled as students make public the strategies they invoke in interpreting such problems in signifying dialogues and other cultural data sets. Extending the analysis of signifying as a conceptual tool, such cultural data sets include not only signifying dialogues but also lyrics to rap songs, as well as rap and popular music videos. In order to illustrate the effects of this theoretical framework, I will draw from transcripts of several days of instruction in one classroom in which a unit based on Cultural Modeling is being carried out. Results of gain from pre- to posttesting provide evidence that the quality of reading and reasoning evident in the transcripts is not confined to these examples (Lee, 1993). Rather, the transcripts are used to provide a detailed view of the nature of expert-like practice into which these students had been apprenticed.

The student population included African American underachieving seniors in two urban high schools. A quasi-experimental design was implemented involving four experimental classes studying the short story "My Man Bovanne" by Toni Cade Bambara (1972) and two novels, Zora Neale Hurston's *Their Eyes Were Watching God* (1937/1990) and Alice Walker's *The Color Purple* (1982). I taught two of the experimental classes. The students in the experimental classes studied samples of signifying dialogue taken from Mitchell-Kernan (1981) and extrapolated the rules they intuitively used to generate the intended meaning for each turn of talk. They then applied those strategies to the interpretation of complex inferential questions based on the two novels. One control class in each high school studied its usual curriculum for world literature. The experimental group achieved a statistically significant gain from pre- to posttesting over the control classes (Lee, 1993, 1995a, 1995b).

In these transcripts students demonstrate the mental qualities of reasoning about literary problems, the same habits of mind that Vygotsky argued are required by scientific concepts: deliberate attention, comparison and contrast, and abstraction. Although not explicitly stated, Vygotsky implies that an understanding and use of scientific concepts involves expert-like activity in a community of practice. An analysis of how the ZPD plays out in this instructional unit involves a focus on the definition of what is to be learned, what the learner knows and what the teacher or more expert-like other wants the novice to learn, what the teacher understands about the task, and what the learner initially understands that is related to the task. Of interest in this instantiation of a ZPD is how the novice's knowledge of signifying is transformed over time. The observed transformation is from a spontaneous concept that is applicable in the students' minds only to the oral contexts of signifying talk to a more scientific representation of literary tropes, sometimes embedded in signifying examples in literary texts. The exploration of the links between the spontaneous concept of signifying and its scientific counterparts leads to a shared sense of the following: (1) what to value in literary texts and (2) what tools to use deliberately to construct the kinds of generalizations about works of fiction that are characteristic of more expert-like practice. Figure 11.2 provides a graphic representation of the features of reasoning about scientific concepts in the Vygotskian sense that come to be associated with signifying. In this framework, signifying is used as a mediational construct through which to apprentice these students into ways of reasoning about literary texts.

A pattern of classroom culture (Green & Dixon, 1994) provided a structure through which semiotic mediation took place:

1. Posing questions that require students to make inferences that draw on evidence from across the text.
2. Modeling through practice the reasoning processes required to approach such questions.
3. Constantly probing students to question their assumptions and to prove their claims, not only by evidence from the text but also by

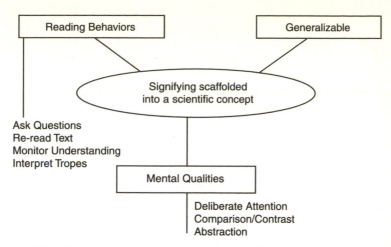

Figure 11.2 Reading strategies and habits of mind linking signifying to scientific concepts.

articulating the warrants based on values and beliefs that would make one accept the evidence as applicable.

4. Modeling and asking students what one point in a line of argumentation has to do with another point.

The unit began with analyses of signifying dialogues and then applied strategies gleaned from the signifying to analysis of "My Man Bovanne" (Bambara, 1972) and then *Their Eyes Were Watching God* (Hurston, 1990). By the time the class reached the second novel, *The Color Purple* by Alice Walker (1982), it had become clear that the intellectual culture of the class had drastically changed. In the Bakhtinian (1981) sense, the utterances of students were dialogically responsive to the prior conversations that had occurred in the class. One can begin to hear the earlier voice of the teacher resonating through the voices of the students. Bakhtin's question "Who is doing the talking?" is of interest here. A response to that question may provide insight into the importance of the role of the teacher as one who explicitly models, guides, and supports not only what students do but also how they think. In addition, there is a historical and cultural antecedent to the shared norms or intersubjectivity evident in these discussions. The content on which questions and reasoning processes were based consisted of linguistic knowledge and practices with which this group of students was very familiar.

The content of many of the discussions that occurred over the next 2 weeks focused on questions generated by the students. However, because the students and the teacher had come to think alike – in essence valuing and becoming interested in the same questions – the questions posed by the students were some of the same questions the teacher had been thinking about. Earlier discussions were very teacher directed, in part indicating the distance between the conception of the task held by the teacher and the conceptions held by the students.

ACHIEVING INTERSUBJECTIVITY: ENGAGING IN EXPERT-LIKE PRACTICE

In the transcript examples that follow, students demonstrate their participation as members of a community of practice. They exemplify some of the habits of mind that expert-like readers bring to the challenge of interpreting complex works of fiction. They consciously use metacognitive strategies like text reinspection. They make explicit statements that articulate what counts as questions worth asking, engage in analysis of point of view based on issues they have raised, and respond to questions by constructing mini-arguments with positions, evidence, and warrants.

In the first instructional episode, the teacher gathers questions from the students about *The Color Purple*. This lesson differs substantially from earlier ones because the entire lesson and many that follow are driven by student-initiated questions. The level of involvement in the intellectual issues of the unit is exemplified in the following exchange:

S: Mrs. Lee, before we get started . . . remember last Friday you told us that we were going to finish why we think God

T: We were going to do that at the very end of the period. Maybe we will stop by 2:30 so that you could finish that question on why *Their Eyes Were Watching God* is called that. . . .

The teacher passes out index cards on which the students can write their individual questions. One student says, "I need about thirty of them." Reiterating the kinds of questions that students should generate, the teacher says:

T: But it ought to be a question that you don't know the answer to, and preferably they should not be questions like how old was Celie or those kinds of questions. They should be things that you really worry about. For example, a question that

S: Why is Mister referred to as Mr.

T: Right. That was a good question that Calvin came up with last week.

This exchange suggests that a focus on this quality of question has become part of the norms of the class, because Calvin doesn't wait for the teacher to provide an example but interrupts and provides his own, one that he came up with the week before. It is common for the teacher to respond to students' questions, rather than to questions the teacher herself poses, and for students to interrupt the teacher's talk. In the midst of fielding students' questions, one student initiates a micro-episode by posing a question of interest to her:

1	S:	Mrs. Lee, look at this. This letter is typed to Nettie, right?
2	T:	Yes.
3	S:	So why does she refer to Nettie like she ain't writing to Nettie? It is like she ain't writing to Nettie.
4		It is like she is writing to somebody else. Then I look back to one of Nettie's letters (unintelligible).
5	T:	Because she hadn't sent it. She didn't know where Nettie is.
6	S:	She do. She had been reading Nettie's letters.
7	T:	When Nettie and Celie write the letters do they ever
8	S:	She, Nettie never got none of Celie's letters, but Celie got all of, well not all of them at first. She
9		got half of them and then Harpo made his father give her the rest later.

In lines 3–4, the student's question is asking implicitly about point of view. The student in line 4 uses a metacognitive reading comprehension strategy by selectively reinspecting an earlier letter sent by Nettie. After the teacher, who in the beginning lessons had been the primary source of authority, responds, the student in line 6 contradicts the teacher. In the next line (7), the teacher attempts to pose a probe question, but the student interrupts with evidence from the text. This micro-episode revolving around a student's question continues for 20 turns and ends with the teacher asking a student to explain a question the student had, when the student responds, "You know how my questions could be." This student seems to recognize something about her own learning style and thinking habits as they relate to the quality of the questions she asks. The responsibility for directing this intellectual activity has shifted to include much more student initiative. In response to a student's question, "It says that she had two kids, right?" the students exchanged 14 rounds of talk, working through the text to answer a question asked by a member of the group. After hearing the questions generated by the students, the teacher revoiced them:

> Let me share the questions that you all can come up with. And they are very good questions. Why did she start each letter off with dear God and then later on change it to dear Nettie? Don't try to answer, I'm just going to share with you what the questions are. We are going to take a few of these each day. Why didn't Nettie tell Corine and her husband the truth about being Olivia and Adam's aunt at first or in the beginning? Who told Celie they had sex with her and if is her husband, why would they say that to her? This was relative to a particular page. We will find that page. Why did Shug marry Brady if she loved Celie? Good question. Why does Celie act the way she does when it comes to sex? . . . What was Mister's reason for not giving Ms. Celie Nettie's letters? Why did it take

Celie so long to leave Mister? Why does Mister love Shug so? Interesting question . . . Why is Mister referred to as Mr. blank? Why did Celie stop writing to God? Why did Celie start bad mouthing God? Why do Celie and Shug always play with each other?

None of the questions posed by the students is limited to a single answer, and none of the answers can be isolated to a single page or paragraph in the text. The questions are authentic, complex, and intriguing. They formally initiate a new phase in the instruction that is truly dialogic. The role of the teacher is no less pivotal, but it is less directive. The second episode that follows on this day of instruction is in response to a student-initiated question.

In this second episode, the teacher decided that in order to respond adequately to the question of why Celie addresses her letters to God, a reader must infer some essential qualities of Celie's personality early on. For that reason, the teacher turned attention to the first letter that Celie writes. Not only were the class discussions marked by student-initiated questions, long turns of student–student interchange, and debate, but also the quality of students' responses to questions changed since the beginning of instruction. Students were more likely to offer responses that were longer and structured as mini-arguments with claims, evidence, and occasionally warrants. The question arose as to whether Celie recognizes that she has been raped and is pregnant. One student responded:

Cause she was crying. Most people, when it comes down to sex and stuff, they don't cry and do certain things. And then again when he started choking her and said she better get used to it and stuff. That in a sense makes me think that she don't know what she is doing.

The implicit claim is that Celie doesn't understand. The evidence is based on text, namely, that she was crying. The warrant is that most people don't cry when enjoying sex. The second source of evidence from the text is Celie's stepfather's choking her and telling her to get used to it. The warrant for that evidence is in the last two lines. The warrants are based on prior social knowledge.

In the continuing dialogue around the micro-question of whether Celie truly understood what was happening to her, another student introduces as evidence:

Because this never happened to her before. Cause he said that "you better get use to it" and then it later says "but I don't never get use to it and now I feel sick every time I be the one to cook."

This response was also a mini-argument with a claim, evidence, and a warrant. The exchange that followed introduced briefly a new literary concept and an interesting mini-debate of students over warrants. Several students introduced the fact that Celie says she gets sick at the smell of food as an indication that she is pregnant.

T: Alright, you are saying that when she says she feels sick every time she cooks that is an indication that she is pregnant. But does she know that? Does she say that I'm pregnant?

S^1:   No

T: So who is letting us know that she is pregnant?

S^2:   The letter.

S^3:   Nobody yet.

S^4:   We don't know she is pregnant.

S^5:   We know she is pregnant, but she don't.

S^6:   Because of the symptoms, the way she is feeling.

Implicit in the question of the teacher in line 4 is the concept of authorial voice. Although the focus was brief and abbreviated, the responses of Students 2 and 5 distinguished the point of view of Celie from that of the author implicit in the language Alice Walker chose to place in the letter. Several turns later, the discussion focused on a mini-debate among students over the warrants offered to support the claim that Celie was pregnant because she became sick at the smell of food:

S^1:   If you knew the symptoms of a woman being pregnant, certain smells make her sick.

S^2:   What if you were a man and didn't know nothing like that?

S^1:   If you are a man you should know that.

S^3:   It might be like that cause of the (inaudible) of the word. She might not be pregnant.

T: At least you know that it is a possibility.

S^3:   When I smell chitterlings, I get sick. That don't mean that I'm pregnant.

According to Toulmin, Rieke, & Janik (1984), the use of warrants in argumentation marks sophisticated forms of reasoning.

SIGNIFYING AS A SCIENTIFIC CONSTRUCT: GENERALIZING ACROSS TEXTS

In the transcript that follows, students demonstrate how they use their knowledge of signifying as a formal construct, as a heuristic through which to analyze formal properties across several texts. The participants in this transcript distinguish signifying in texts according to how the signifying functions. They distinguish its informal use just as a form of oral talk from its use in the texts as representational, symbolic of major shifts in the internal states of characters. They make these comparisons across the two novels and in this way use the concept as a generalizable construct. They work intentionally and deliberately to resolve the questions at hand.

Another final characteristic of the changes in student interpretive strategies and reasoning processes is exemplified in the following segment, where students demonstrate a cumulative understanding of relationships across the texts in the unit. The teacher initially revoices conclusions the students have generated about why Celie writes letters to God and then asks a probing question:

1	T:	Because when she writes them her writing is another way of her speaking and expressing herself in things that she can't do. This is an idea to keep in mind because talk does become important in this book, doesn't it? 'Cause does Celie begin to change along the dimensions of talking?
2	S^1:	Yes.
3	T:	Where?
4	S^1:	She starts signifying. There is a lot of signifying in this book.
5	T:	Was that important?
6	S^1:	What? The signifying? That depends on where it is at. In some places they were just sitting around joking. In other places, they were serious, like when he told her, you ugly, you can't cook and all of that, and she came back and crack on him.
7	T:	Does the signifying in that instance have anything to do with the signifying in *Their Eyes Were Watching God*?
8	S^2:	Nope.
9	S^3:	Yes it do. Because when they were in the store when Jody told Janie that she was ugly and that she was getting old and stuff. That is the same thing that he is telling her.
10	S^4:	No, he was just trying to front her.
11	S^5:	You know how Jody never did want her to say anything. He didn't want her to speak. In a way, Mister was the same way with Celie. She couldn't do nothing but what he told her. And she couldn't say nothing but what he told her to say. So in a sense, it is like the same.
12	S^6:	I think there is a little bit of similarity to it. They both are trying to front each other.
13	S^7:	Jody was trying to keep that control back. He was starting to lose it. Just like Mister was trying to get in this book.
14	S^6:	That is what I'm talking about.
15	S^8:	Jody lost his control until he snapped. He wasn't going around beating her like he is.
16	S^6:	Yes, it did.
17	S^9:	This broad gets beat everyday.
18	S^{10}:	Why she got to be a broad?
19	S^{11}:	No she not.

20 S^9: Why he got to be a Mister?
21 S^{10}: Don't use the name broad.

In line 6, the student reasoned conditionally, indicating that the significance of the signifying in the novel depends on the context. Students applied their linguistic knowledge to an interpretation of the two novels. When the teacher asked the students to consider links between the two novels in the unit, a debate began among them. Their level of engagement was evident in the interchange from lines 17–21, where a male student and a female student argued over the points of view implicit in the terms *broad* and *Mister* and demonstrated a personal identification with the characters.

In the final sections of this day's dialogue, the teacher stated that she would not be in class the next day. The students would work in groups the next day on questions they had generated. Because what was going on in this instructional intervention was so contrary to the culture of the school, the students recognized the difficulty they would have in conducting their own intellectual inquiry with a substitute teacher.

1 S: Could you leave a note because. . . .
2 T: I am going to leave a note.
3 S: Calvin is going to try to run the class.

Implicit in line 1 is that the teacher's authority will be necessary to allow the students to work independently the next day.

CONCLUSION

I have attempted to argue in this chapter that signifying as a form of social discourse within the African American community has attributes in common with the strategies used to identify and reconstruct the intended meaning of literary tropes, including irony, metaphor, symbolism, and point of view in literature. I argue that the strategies used in signifying made explicit and applied to examples within the African American literary tradition serve as a propaedeutic guide to the refinement and sophistication of knowledge in both the oral and literary arenas. Such an interaction of concepts in the oral and literary domains exemplifies Vygotsky's (1986) general genetic law of cultural development. That is, concept formation evolves from the social/ interpsychological level to the individual/intrapsychological level. This evolution from the social to the individual occurred in this instance within a classroom culture that honored the prior knowledge brought by these African American adolescents while carefully designing cognitive and social supports for their apprenticeship. The instructional framework based on cultural modeling (Lee, 1993, 1995a, 1995b) draws on the interanimation of spontaneous and scientific concepts, as described by Vygotsky. The assumptions about a

ZPD implicit in the instructional design take seriously the relevant prior knowledge that these African American students brought to the English class. The level of problem solving toward which the instruction aimed bridged the informal knowledge that students employed independently in circumscribed settings and formal literary constructs that were applicable across multiple settings. Studies of cultural modeling begin to address Vygotsky's claim that "Future studies should include concepts from various fields of school instruction, each set matched against a set of everyday concepts drawn from a similar area of expertise" (p. 20).

REFERENCES

Abrahams, R.D. (1970). *Deep down in the jungle: Negro narrative folklore from the streets of Philadelphia*. Chicago: Aldine.

Andrews, M., & Owens, P. (1973). *Black language*. Los Angeles: Seymour-Smith.

Baker, H. (1984) *Blues, ideology and Afro-American literature: A vernacular theory*. Chicago: University of Chicago Press.

Bakhtin, M.M. (1981). *The dialogic imagination: Four essays by M.M. Bakhtin* (M. Holquist, Ed.; C. Emerson & M. Holquist, Trans.). Austin: University of Texas Press.

Bambara, T.C. (1972). My man Bovanne. In T.C. Bambera (Ed.), *Gorilla, my love* (pp. 1–10). New York: Random House.

Baugh, J. (1983). *Black street speech: Its history, structure and survival*. Austin: University of Texas Press.

Booth, W. (1974). *A rhetoric of irony*. Chicago: University of Chicago Press.

Brown, R. (1969). *Die nigger die!* New York: Dial Press.

Cazden, C. (1988). *Classroom discourse*. Portsmouth, NH: Heinemann.

Cook-Gumperz, J. (Ed.). (1986). *The social construction of literacy*. New York: Cambridge University Press.

Cooke, M. (1984). *Afro-American literature in the twentieth century: The achievement of intimacy*. New Haven, CT: Yale University Press.

Delpit, L. (1990). Language diversity and learning. In S. Hynds & D.L. Rubin (Eds.), *Perspectives on talk and learning* (pp. 247–266). Urbana, IL: National Council of Teachers of English.

Ellison, R. (1964). *Shadow and act*. New York: Random House.

Gates, H.L. (1984). The blackness of blackness: A critique of the sign and the signifying monkey. In H.L. Gates (Ed.), *Black literature and literary theory* (pp. 285–322). New York: Methuen.

Gates, H.L. (1988). *The signifying monkey: A theory of Afro-American literary criticism*. New York: Oxford University Press.

Goodlad, J.I. (1984). *A place called school: Prospects for the future*. St. Louis: McGraw-Hill.

Green, J., & Dixon, C. (1994). Talking knowledge into being: Discursive and social practices in classrooms. *Linguistics and Education, 5*, 231–239.

Heath, S.B. (1989). Oral and literate traditions among Black Americans living in poverty. *American Psychologist, 44*, 367–373.

Hurston, Z.N. (1935). *Mules and men*. New York: Harper & Row.

Hurston, Z.N. (1937/1990). *Their eyes were watching God*. New York: Harper and Row.

Hynds, S. (1989). Bringing life to literature and literature to life: Social constructs and contexts of four adolescent readers. *Research in the Teaching of English*, 23, 30–61.

Jones, G. (1991). *Liberating voices: Oral tradition in African American literature*. New York: Penguin.

Kochman, T. (Ed.). (1972). *Rappin' and stylin' out: Communication in urban Black America*. Urbana: University of Illnois Press.

La Rocha, O.D.L. (1985). The reorganization of the arithmetic practice in the kitchen. *Anthropology and Education*, *16*, 193–198.

Lave, J. (1977). Cognitive consequences of traditional apprenticeship training in West Africa. *Anthropology and Education Quarterly*, 7, 177–180.

Lee, C.D. (1991, April). *Signifying as a scaffold to literary interpretation: The pedagogical implications of a form of African-American discourse*. Paper presented at the annual meeting of the American Educational Research Association, Chicago.

Lee, C.D. (1993). *Signifying as a scaffold for literary interpretation: The pedagogical implications of an African American discourse genre*. Urbana, IL: National Council of Teachers of English.

Lee, C.D. (1994). Cultural modeling in reading comprehension. Proposal submitted to the McDonnell Foundation, Cognitive Studies in Educational Practice.

Lee, C.D. (1995a). A culturally based cognitive apprenticeship: Teaching African American high school students skills in literary interpretation. *Reading Research Quarterly*, 30, 608–631.

Lee, C.D. (1995b). Signifying as a scaffold for literary interpretation. *Journal of Black Psychology*, *21*(4), 357–381.

Lee, C.D. (1997). Bridging home and school literacies: Models for culturally responsive teaching: A case for African American English. In J. Flood, S.B. Heath, & D. Lapp (Eds.), *A handbook for literacy educators: Research on teaching the communicative and visual arts* (pp. 330–341). New York: Macmillan.

Leont'ev, A.N. (1981). *Problems of the development of mind*. Moscow: Progress Publishers.

Major, C. (1970) *Dictionary of Afro-American slang*. New York: International.

Michaels, S. (1986). Narrative presentations: An oral preparation for literacy with first graders. In J. Cook-Gumperz (Ed.), *The social construction of literacy* (pp. 94–116). New York: Cambridge University Press.

Mitchell-Kernan, C. (1981). Signifying, loud-talking and marking. In A. Dundes (Ed.), *Mother wit from the laughing barrel* (pp. 310–328). Englewood Cliffs, NJ: Prentice-Hall.

Nunes, T., Schliemann, A.D., & Carraher, D.W. (1993). *Street mathematics and school mathematics*. New York: Cambridge University Press.

Philips, S.U. (1985). Indian children in Anglo classrooms. In N. Wolfson & J. Manes (Eds.), *Language of inequality* (pp. 311–323). Berlin: Mouton.

Rabinowitz, P. (1987). *Before reading: Narrative conventions and the politics of interpretation*. Ithaca, NY: Cornell University Press.

Reed, H., & Lave, J. (1981). Arithmetic as a tool for investigating relations between culture and cognition. In R. Casson (Ed.), *Language, culture, and cognition: Anthropological perspectives* (pp. 437–455). New York: Macmillan.

Reed, I. (1974, June). Ishmael Reed: A self interview. *Black World*, 20–34.

Rogoff, B. (1990). *Apprenticeship in thinking*. New York: Oxford University Press.

Saville-Troike, M. (1989). *The ethnography of communication, an introduction.* New York: Basil Blackwell.

Saxe, G.B. (1988). The mathematics of child street vendors. *Child Development, 59,* 1415–1425.

Scribner, S. (1984). Studying working intelligence. In B. Rogoff & J. Lave (Eds.), *Everyday cognition: Its development in social context* (pp. 9–40). Cambridge, MA: Harvard University Press.

Smith, M.W. (1987). *Reading and teaching irony in poetry; Giving short people a reason to live.* Unpublished doctoral dissertation, University of Chicago.

Smith, M.W. (1989). Teaching the interpretation of irony in poetry. *Research in the Teaching of English, 23*(3), 254–272.

Smitherman, G. (1977). *Talkin and testifyin.* Boston: Houghton Mifflin.

Toulmin, S., Rieke, R., & Janik, A. (1984). *An introduction to reasoning.* New York: Macmillan.

Vygotsky, L.S. (1978). *Mind in society: The development of higher psychological processes* (M. Cole, V. John-Steiner, S. Scribner, & E. Souberman, Eds.). Cambridge, MA: Harvard University Press.

Vygotsky, L.S. (1986). *Thought and language* (A. Kozulin, Ed. & Trans.). Cambridge, MA: MIT Press.

Walker, A. (1982). *The color purple.* New York: Simon and Schuster.

Wertsch, J.V. (1984). The zone of proximal development: Some conceptual issues. In B. Rogoff & J.V. Wertsch (Eds.), *Children's learning in the zone of proximal development* (pp. 7–18). San Francisco: Jossey-Bass.

Wertsch, J.V., Minick, N., & Arns, F.J. (1984). The creation of context in joint problem-solving. In B. Rogoff & J. Lave (Eds.), *Everyday cognition: Its development in social context* (pp. 151–171). Cambridge, MA: Harvard University Press.

Winner, E. (1988). *The point of words: Children's understanding of metaphor and irony.* Cambridge MA: Harvard University Press.

Wright, R. (1963). *Lawd today.* New York: Walker.

12 Social constructivist perspectives on teaching and learning

A. Sullivan Palincsar

INTRODUCTION

Recent chapters in the *Annual Review of Psychology* closely related to the general subject matter of teaching and learning (Glaser & Bassok 1989, Sandoval 1995, Snow & Swanson 1992, Voss et al 1995) have generally examined issues of cognition from an individualistic perspective. Voss et al (1995) indicated that the recent decade has witnessed the "sociocultural revolution," with its focus on learning in out-of-school contexts and on the acquisition of intellectual skills through social interaction (p. 174). In this review, I examine the nature and consequences of this revolution.

The review begins by intellectually situating social constructivist perspectives. Following an explication of the tenets of this approach, I explore issues of teaching and learning that are particularly salient from social constructivist perspectives. These issues are presented using institutional, interpersonal, and discursive levels of analysis. I then proceed to the application of social constructivist views to contemporary issues of importance to education; namely, the acquisition of expertise across subject matter, assessment practices, the education of linguistic and culturally diverse children, and school reform. The review concludes with a critique of this perspective and a discussion of future directions.

INTELLECTUALLY SITUATING THE SOCIOCULTURAL REVOLUTION IN INSTRUCTIONAL RESEARCH

Instructional research in the West was initially informed by behaviorist accounts of learning found in classic writings such as those of Thorndike (1906). Thorndike postulated that learning took place through the differential strengthening of bonds between situations and actions. Teaching, in turn, was a matter of shaping the responses of the learner through using instructional procedures such as modeling, demonstration, and reinforcement of closer approximations to the targeted response. From this perspective, academic tasks were analyzed to determine their component parts, and the curriculum was carefully sequenced to ensure that students were acquiring the necessary prerequisite skills before the introduction of more advanced material. The instructional model that best reflects the tenets of behaviorism is referred to as direct instruction teaching. The hallmark of direct instruction is the active and directive role assumed by the teacher, who maintains control of the pace, sequence, and content of the lesson (Baumann 1988, p. 714):

> The teacher, in a face-to-face-reasonably formal manner, tells, shows, models, demonstrates, *teaches* the skill to be learned. The key word here is *teacher*, for it is the teacher who is in command of the learning situation and leads the lesson, as opposed to having instruction "directed" by a worksheet, kit, learning center, or workbook.

The research regarding direct instruction suggests that while it is an effective means of teaching factual content, there is less evidence that this instruction transfers to higher order cognitive skills such as reasoning and problem solving, nor is there sufficient evidence that direct-instruction teaching results in the flexibility necessary for students to use the targeted strategies in novel contexts (Peterson & Walberg 1979). In addition to these practical concerns with the limitations of direct instruction, there are significant theoretical limitations of the behavioral perspective; namely, this perspective offers no satisfactory explanation of the mechanisms that account for learning.

With increased interest in human information processing in complex cognitive activity, the cognitive perspective assumed prominence. Bruner (1990) argues that the cognitive revolution was meant to do more than simply be an improvement on behaviorism; it was also meant to promote a psychology that focused on "meaning making." To explain meaning making, cognitive psychologists introduced cognitive structures (such as schemata and heuristics) as the representations of knowledge in memory. These cognitive structures are assumed to underlie such phenomena as problem solving and transfer ability. Virtually all cognitive science theories entail some form of constructivism to the extent that cognitive structures are typically viewed as individually constructed in the process of interpreting experiences in particular contexts. However, there are many versions of constructivism, suggesting a continuum anchored by trivial constructivism at one end, which stresses the individual as constructing knowledge but is concerned with whether or not the constructions are correct representations, to radical constructivism, which rejects the notion of objective knowledge and argues instead that knowledge develops as one engages in dialogue with others.

In this review, I consider research on teaching and learning that has been conducted from postmodern constructivist perspectives (cf Prawat 1996). What unifies postmodern constructivist perspectives is rejection of the view that the locus of knowledge is in the individual; learning and understanding are regarded as inherently social; and cultural activities and tools (ranging from symbol systems to artifacts to language) are regarded as integral to conceptual development. What distinguishes various postmodern constructivist perspectives is a bit murkier. For example, Cobb & Yackel (1996), distinguishing a perspective they call "emergent" from a sociocultural perspective, argue that while sociocultural approaches frame instructional issues in terms of *transmission* of culture from one generation to the next, the emergent perspective conceives of instructional issues in terms of the *emergence* of individual and collective meanings in the classroom. However, John-Steiner & Mahn (1996) argue that this is not an accurate interpretation of sociocultural theory which, in fact, has as its overarching focus the interdependence of the social and individual processes in the co-construction of knowledge.

While not wishing to trivialize differences among social constructivist perspectives, we also don't wish to become mired in them. Furthermore, given the fairly emergent state of this perspective—especially when considering its implications for teaching and learning, the revolution is perhaps best characterized as under way. Hence, the focus of this review is on the social dimensions of constructivism generally speaking. Where researchers have drawn distinctions among perspectives, these are identified.

Interest in social constructivism has been motivated by a number of factors, many of which were actually informed by cognitive perspectives on teaching and learning (cf Bruer 1994). As psychological research called attention to the strategic activity of experts (e.g. Flower et al 1992), intervention researchers investigated the use of think-alouds as a means of making problem-solving skills public and accessible to those with less expertise. An example is the research of Duffy et al (1986) in which they determined the value of engaging teachers in public modeling, via think-alouds, of the use of reading strategies such as using context for the purpose of figuring out the meaning of an unknown word. They determined that the children of teachers (in third and fifth grades) who were skilled in modeling the mental processing they were using when experiencing difficulty understanding text recalled more from the lessons and indicated a greater awareness of why they were learning particular strategies.

In another line of research, Palincsar & Brown (1984, 1989; Brown & Palincsar 1989; Palincsar et al 1993b) designed an intervention, called reciprocal teaching, in which teachers and children used discussion structured with four strategies—predicting, questioning, summarizing, and clarifying—to engage readers in constructing the meaning of a text and monitoring to determine that they were making sense of the text. While the teachers were encouraged to explicitly model the strategies, they were also urged to cede control of using the strategies to the children by asking them to take turns leading the discussion. As children led the discussions, the teachers provided whatever support each child needed to use the strategies. The intervention was designed for students who, while fairly adequate decoders, were very poor comprehenders. A program of research indicated that these discussions were a successful means of enhancing comprehension skills; furthermore, the research provided evidence of a relationship between the quality of the interaction between children and teachers, as well as among children, and the nature of the learning that occurred. For example, heterogeneous groups of children with diverse comprehension skills attained competence by using the learning dialogues more quickly than groups of more homogenous ability (Palincsar & Brown 1984). Furthermore, the children of teachers adept at providing specific feedback to children were able to extend children's contributions to the discussions by building upon their ideas. Consequently, these children made greater gains than those of teachers who were less effective at scaffolding children's contributions to the discussions (Palincsar 1986).

As cognitive research clarified the demands of expert reasoning and problem solving, interest emerged in distributing the cognitive work (Bruer 1994). Researchers hypothesized that by drawing upon a larger collective memory and the multiple ways in which knowledge could be structured among individuals working together, groups could attain more success than individuals working alone. Research in writing provides examples. Daiute & Dalton (1993) investigated how children aged seven to nine used diverse capabilities as they taught one another how to write stories. The peer collaboration resembled interactions between teachers and children, resulting in the generation of new story elements and more mature forms of writing than children had demonstrated alone. Furthermore, the researchers speculated that the peer interaction was more facilitative than teacher and child interactions, given the shared perspectives and life experiences that the children were able to bring to the collaborative writing process. This notion will be examined more fully below in discussions of Piagetian and Vygotskian perspectives on learning.

Another explanation for interest in the social dimensions of cognition is derived from awareness of the role that language production plays in promoting learning. Explaining one's thinking to another leads to deeper cognitive processing (Scardamalia & Bereiter 1989).

A final impetus to understanding how social and cultural factors influence cognition is the perspective that thought, learning, and knowledge are not just influenced by social factors but are social phenomena. From this perspective, cognition is a collaborative process (see Rogoff 1997), thought is internalized discourse, and the purpose of inquiry regarding cognitive development is to examine the transformation of socially shared activities into internalized processes (see John-Steiner & Mahn 1996). In the next section, we explore two perspectives on the mechanisms accounting for learning from social constructivist perspectives.

MECHANISMS ACCOUNTING FOR LEARNING FROM SOCIAL CONSTRUCTIVIST PERSPECTIVES

The sociocognitive conflict theory of Piaget

There are several theoretical perspectives that have been proffered, in fairly well-developed terms, as explanations of the mechanism by which social interaction leads to higher levels of reasoning and learning. The first, socio-cognitive conflict, is derived principally from the work of Piaget and his disciples: "Cognitive conflict created by social interaction is the locus at which the power driving intellectual development is generated" (Perret-Clermont 1980, p. 12). From this perspective, contradiction between the learner's existing understanding and what the learner experiences gives rise to disequilibration, which, in turn, leads the learner to question his or her beliefs and to try out new ideas. In Piaget's words, "disequilibrium forces the subject to go beyond his current state and strike out in new directions" (1985, p. 10). Piaget further suggested that the social exchanges between children were more likely to lead to cognitive development than exchanges between children and adults. This observation was premised on the belief that among age peers there is mutual control over the interaction.

Among studies that have investigated sociocognitive conflict theory is the research by Bell et al (1985). Using conservation tasks, they determined that children working with peers showed more cognitive growth than children working alone. However, there were particular conditions that were in place for children who derived the most from this opportunity. For example, the child had to be actively engaged in the problem-solving activity and not merely observing the more advanced peer. In addition, if the partner's cognitive level were too much in advance of the child's, the outcome mirrored that expected of interactions with adults: the partner's answer was merely accepted and did not stimulate the process of "strik[ing] out in directions."

In search of evidence that peer interaction provides greater opportunities for learning than adult-child interactions, Radziszewska & Rogoff (cited in Rogoff 1991) compared children's interactions with adults and peers, using one group of peer partners who had been taught to use an optimal strategy for completing an errand-planning task and another who had received no special preparation. When the children were later asked to plan without assistance, those children who had collaborated with adults were more successful than those who had worked with prepared or unprepared peers. In an effort to reconcile these differential outcomes of Piagetian studies, Damon (1984) argued that it is important to attend to the nature of the shift the child must make. For example, he suggested that development that requires giving up current understanding to reach a new perspective might best be attained through interaction with peers, whereas learning that does not require a transformation of perspective but rather is characterized as the accretion of a new skill or strategy might be best attained by working with more skillful and experienced partners, such as adults.

Suggesting that verbal interaction is the key to co-construction and cognitive change, Forman & Kraker (1985) cautioned that cognitive conflict may not be enough if there is insufficient verbal interaction or if the social structure permits passive compliance. The importance of considering social status within the group was demonstrated in the research by Russell et al (1990), who observed that social dominance influenced whether a child's conserving answer was adopted by the second child. Merely having the right answer was not consistently enough to persuade the other child.

The sociocultural theory of Vygotsky

The role of social processes as a mechanism for learning is usually identified with Vygotsky, who suggested: "The social dimension of consciousness is primary in time and in fact. The individual dimension of consciousness is derivative and secondary" (Vygotsky 1978, p. 30, cited in Wertsch & Bivens 1992). From this perspective, mental functioning of the individual is not simply derived from social interaction; rather, the specific structures and processes revealed by individuals can be traced to their interactions with others. Wertsch (1991) has proposed three major themes in Vygotsky's writings that elucidate the nature of this interdependence between individual and social processes in learning and development.

The first theme is that individual development, including higher mental functioning, has its origins in social sources. This theme is best represented in Vygotsky's "genetic law of development" (Valsiner 1987, p. 67):

> Every function in the cultural development of the child comes on the stage twice, in two respects: first in the social, later in the psychological, first in relations between people as an interpsychological category, afterwards within the child as an intrapsychological category. . . . All higher psychological functions are internalized relationships of the social kind, and constitute the social structure of personality.

From this perspective, as learners participate in a broad range of joint activities and internalize the effects of working together, they acquire new strategies and knowledge of the world and culture. Typically, this tenet has been illustrated by examining the interactions between individuals with disparate knowledge levels; for example, children and their caregivers or experts and novices. Illustrative is the cross-cultural research of Rogoff, who studied the supportive contexts in which Mayan children acquire knowledge and strategies (Rogoff 1991, p. 351):

> The routine arrangements and interactions between children and their caregivers and companions provide children with thousands of

opportunities to observe and participate in the skilled activities of their culture. Through repeated and varied experience in supported routine and challenging situations, children become skilled practitioners in the specific cognitive activities in their communities.

Perhaps as a consequence of these research contexts, contemporary critics of a sociocultural perspective argue that it is a "transfer of knowledge model" (e.g. Cobb et al 1993). However, scholars of this perspective have argued that this interpretation is simplistic and misinterprets the transformative nature of internalization that has been described by sociocultural researchers. For example, Leontiev suggested that "the process of internalization is not the transferral of an external activity to a preexisting internal 'plane of consciousness'; it is the process in which this plane is formed" (Wertsch & Stone 1985, p. 163).

In contrast with prevailing views of his time, in which learning was regarded as an external process and development an internal process, Vygotsky was concerned with the unity and interdependence of learning and development. For example, he was critical of Piaget's theory in which "maturation is viewed as a precondition of learning but never the result of it" (Vygotsky 1978, p. 80). In contrast, Vygotsky proposed that (p. 90):

Learning awakens a variety of internal developmental processes that are able to operate only when the child is interacting with people in his environment and with his peers. . . . [L]earning is not development; however, properly organized learning results in mental development and sets in motion a variety of developmental processes that would be impossible apart from learning. Thus learning is a necessary and universal aspect of the process of developing culturally organized, specifically human, psychological functions.

In support of this perspective, Vygotsky (1978) introduced the construct of the zone of proximal development (ZPD) as a fundamentally new approach to the problem that learning should be matched in some manner with the child's level of development. He argued that to understand the relationship between development and learning we must distinguish between two developmental levels: the actual and the potential levels of development. The actual refers to those accomplishments a child can demonstrate alone or perform independently. This is in contrast with potential levels of development as suggested by the ZPD—what children can do with assistance: "the distance between the actual developmental level as determined by independent problem solving and the level of potential development as determined through problem solving under adult guidance or in collaboration with more capable peers" (p. 85). The ZPD was regarded as a better, more dynamic and relative indicator of cognitive development than what children accomplished alone. In summary, productive interactions are those that orient instruction toward the ZPD. Otherwise, instruction lags behind the development of the child. "The only good learning is that which is in advance of development" (Vygotsky 1978, p. 89). Hence, from a Vygotskian perspective, cognitive development is studied by examining the processes that one participates in when engaged in shared endeavors and how this engagement influences engagement in other activities. Development occurs as children learn general concepts and principles that can be applied to new tasks and problems, whereas from a Piagetian perspective, learning is constrained by development.

The second Vygotskian theme that Wertsch (1991) has identified is that human action, on both the social and individual planes, is mediated by tools and signs—semiotics. The semiotic means include: "language; various systems of counting; mnemonic techniques; algebraic symbol systems; works of art; writing; schemes, diagrams, maps and mechanical drawings; all sorts of conventional signs and so on" (Vygotsky 1981, p. 137). These semiotic means are both the tools that facilitate the co-construction of knowledge and the means that are internalized to aid future independent problem-solving activity. Leontiev (1981), a colleague of Vygotsky, used the term "appropriation" to characterize this process (quoted in Newman et al 1989, p. 63): "[Children] cannot and need not reinvent artifacts that have taken millennia to evolve in order to appropriate such objects into their own system of activity. The child has only to come to an understanding that it is adequate for using the culturally elaborated object in the novel life circumstances he encounters." It is in this sense that the process of collaboration is at the same time the product of collaboration.

The third theme that Wertsch (1991) proposes from Vygotsky's writing is that the first two themes are best examined through genetic, or developmental, analysis (Vygotsky 1978, pp. 64–65):

> To study something historically means to study it in the process of change; that is the dialectical method's basic demand. To encompass in research the process of a given thing's development in all its phases and changes—from birth to death—fundamentally means to discover its nature, its essence, for it is only in movement that a body shows what it is. Thus the historical study of behavior is not an auxiliary aspect of theoretical study, but rather forms its very base.

There are four aspects essential to developmental analysis from a Vygotskian perspective, all of which are interwoven. *Phylogenetic* development is concerned with what distinguishes humans from other animals. Of particular interest in this analysis is human use of tools—especially the psychological tools of signs and symbols, including language (Vygotsky & Luria 1993). A second level of analysis, *cultural/historical*, calls attention to the profound role that the practices of particular cultures and of the same cultural group play, over time, in development. *Ontogenetic* analysis calls our attention to ways in which individual characteristics, such as physical or mental challenge, age, temperament, and the fruits of individual history influence development. Finally, *microgenetic* analysis deals with the actual processes of interaction between the individual and his or her environment; hence microgenetic analyses take into account the interplay of individual, interpersonal, and social/cultural factors simultaneously.

In summary, from a sociocultural perspective, learning and development take place in socially and culturally shaped contexts, which are themselves constantly changing; there can be no universal scheme that adequately represents the dynamic interaction between the external and the internal aspects of development. There is no generic development that is independent of communities and their practices (Rogoff et al 1995). Hence, it is with the use of genetic analysis that the complex interplay of mediational tools, the individual, and the social world is explored to understand learning and development and the transformation of tools, practices, and institutions.

In the next section, I explicate these tenets by examining research that enhances our understanding of social constructivist perspectives on teaching and learning. Given the highly interactive ways in which social constructivists view the world, the challenge in presenting this research is determining the appropriate grain size. From social constructivist perspectives, separating the individual from social influences is not regarded as possible. The sociocultural contexts in which teaching and learning occur are considered critical to learning itself, and learning is viewed as culturally and contextually specific. Furthermore, cognition is not analyzed as separate from social, motivational, emotional, and identity processes, and the study of generalization is the study of processes rather than the study of personal or situational attributes. Given these complexities, researchers are still developing research methods consistent with the assumptions of this perspective. Commonly used methods include: microgenetic analysis (described above), conversational analysis as opposed to protocol analysis, and the use of activity rather than the individual as the unit of analysis.

Rogoff (1997) suggests that "[t]he parts making a whole activity or event can be considered separately as foreground without losing track of their inherent interdependence in the whole. . . . Foregrounding one plane of focus still involves the participation of the backgrounded planes of focus" (pp. 2–3). In this spirit, the next portion of this review foregrounds institutional, interpersonal, and discursive levels of analysis in turn (cf Cobb et al 1993, Forman et al 1993), examining the literature to determine how research conducted from social constructivist perspectives might contribute to our understanding and improvement of teaching and learning.

ANALYSES OF SOCIAL CONSTRUCTIVIST PERSPECTIVES

Institutional analyses

It is interesting to consider the extent to which contemporary interest in social constructivist perspectives is propelled by recent educational reform efforts encouraging students to assume a more active role in their learning, to explain their ideas to one another, to discuss disagreements, and to cooperate in the solution of complex problems, while teachers participate in the design of these contexts and the facilitation of this kind of activity (cf Resnick et al 1993). All these notions have enormous implications for the culture of schools: "the meaningful traditions and artifacts of a group; ideas, behaviors, verbalization, and material objects" (Fine 1987; cited in Cole 1996, p. 302).

For example, given the tenets of postmodern constructivism, one of the challenges for those interested in its application to education is the development, among learners, of an *intersubjective attitude* about the joint construction of meaning; a commitment to find a common ground on which to build shared understanding (Crook 1994, Rommetveit 1974). This is a particular challenge in Western societies in which individualistic traditions have prevailed. For example, Ellis & Gauvain (1992) conducted cross-cultural research in which they observed that pairs of nine-year-old Navajo children who were asked to teach seven-year-olds to play a game were much more likely to build on each other's comments than were European-American children who more often gave parallel, unrelated lines of instruction. Furthermore, while the Navajo children stayed engaged observing their partners when they were not controlling the game moves, the European-American children lost interest when they were no longer in control of the game, sometimes even leaving the task.

The study of schooling as a cultural process and the school as a cultural system is a fairly recent endeavor. Illustrative is the research of Matusov et al (1997), in which they studied how children who were attending an innovative public school that was structured around collaboration throughout the day, and throughout the curriculum, approached decision-making and assisted younger children in problem-solving activities. Participants were 48 9–11-year-old children recruited from two public schools. One was an innovative school, and the second was a traditional school. The innovative school included activity-based learning, parent participation in the classroom, adult and child direction of the lesson plans, and a problem-solving curriculum. In addition, learning to work in small groups was an explicit part of the curriculum. Twelve pairs of children were recruited from each of the two schools. Working in same-sex pairs, consisting of one third grader and one fourth grader, the children completed a card sorting task and three math problems. The fourth grader was asked to help the third grader to solve each problem in such a way that the third grader would be able to solve the problem alone over time. The children's interactions were rated to provide global characterizations of prevalent approaches to (*a*) working together (which ranged from non-shared decision-making to working together through consensus), and (*b*) providing guidance (such as quizzing, directing actions with no rationale, pure instruction, and instruction embedded in collaboration).

Dyads from the traditional school used more quizzing in their interactions with their tutees, and instruction embedded in collaboration was more frequently used by the children from the innovative school.

While the researchers acknowledge the problems inherent in the fact that the children were not randomly assigned to the innovative school, they none-theless suggest that their work provides useful evidence about how schools must be considered not just in terms of different teaching methods but also in terms of different cultural systems, representing different educational, social, and communicative norms and priorities.

Research on *The Fifth Dimension* conducted by Cole, Griffin, and their collaborators (Cole 1996, Nicolopoulou & Cole 1993) examined institutional and cultural contexts for collaborative activity. The *Fifth Dimension* is a com-puterized play-world that is constituted by a system of rules. When children join the *Fifth Dimension*, they are provided the rules and embark on a journey through a maze of problems that involve increasing mastery of a sequence of activities. Nicolopoulou & Cole (1993) conducted "cross cultural" research investigating children's engagement in the *Fifth Dimension* across two sites: a Boys and Girls Club and a library. Striking differences observed in the cultures (e.g. norms for interacting, use of time and space) of these two contexts resulted in significant differences in the amount and kinds of learn-ing that occurred in the *Fifth Dimension*. In the Boys and Girls Club, there was no overall growth in the level at which the game was played, whereas in the library there was marked and sustained progress as shared knowledge regarding the game grew in that context.

Another line of research has examined the culture of classrooms. For example, Roth (1996) studied a fourth/fifth grade classroom in which children were using a curriculum entitled *Engineering for Children: Structures*. This program is designed to engage children in the practical application of science concepts as they work collaboratively on open-ended engineering problems. The study occurred over 13 weeks and involved using extensive data sources, including video, field notes, students' and teachers' documentation, as well as interviews. The focus of this study was on the diffusion of knowledge in the classroom; knowledge was represented in terms of resources, tool-related practices, and intellectual practices. Roth observed that facts and resources readily spread throughout the classroom, principally driven by the students. Tool-related practices also spread, though less readily, and again were princi-pally driven by students. However, intellectual practices (in this case the use of triangular constructions) were relatively slow to suffuse the classroom, and to the extent that they did they were largely promoted by the teacher. It is useful to draw upon constructs introduced in earlier descriptions of socio-cultural theory to understand this finding. Specifically, the failure of students to appropriate the use of triangular constructions may have been a function of the fact that their experiences were not sufficient to transform their understanding of the relationship between form and function. Support for this explanation may be found in the fact that some children did indeed appropriate the use of triangles in their constructions, but only for aesthetic purposes.

The critical role of the teacher was captured in another exemplary study of the culture of classrooms, conducted by Cobb et al (1991) as they explored the analogies between scientific communities and the social life in a second grade classroom in mathematics. Their work revealed how the teacher created a classroom where the children were validators of one another's ideas, including establishing norms such as persisting in the solution of personally challenging problems, explaining personal solutions to one's partner, listening to and making sense of the partner's explanation and attempting to achieve consensus about the answer, and a solution process. By the end of five months, these norms were in place, and the teacher had to do less to guide children toward these norms.

Interpersonal analyses

From social constructivist perspectives, interactions such as those achieved through classroom discussion are thought to provide mechanisms for enhancing higher-order thinking. There are a number of ways in which interpersonal interactions have been studied from this perspective. For example, Forman et al (1995) examined this issue in terms of the activity structures in place in a middle school mathematics class. Their analyses indicated that 71% of the two hours analyzed was spent in student-centered activity structures (15% devoted to student presentations and 55% devoted to pair or small group work). Furthermore, of the 29% of the time that was rated as teacher-centered, the teacher's interactions were facilitative rather than directive. These findings are a striking contrast with the use of time in more traditional settings. For example, Stodolsky (1988) reported that 40% of instructional time in a fifth grade math class was spent on independent seatwork, 29% was spent on whole class, teacher-directed recitations, and 1% was devoted to small group work.

Taylor & Cox (1997) were also interested in characterizing the learning of mathematics as a social enterprise. They hypothesized that children construct and invent mathematical competence rather than learn it through modeling or imitation. In their study, conducted with fourth graders, there were two peer interaction conditions (socially assisted learning and modeling) as well as a classroom control. The researchers selected word problems that would encourage students to focus on the underlying problem representation rather than to simply "graft numbers onto words." Included in the socially assisted learning were: (*a*) use of a reflection board in which members could share publicly their representation of the problem; (*b*) peer collaboration; (*c*) reflective questioning; (*d*) scaffolding; (*e*) shared ownership; (*f*) quizzes, feedback, and rewards; and (*g*) daily math lessons in the regular classroom. The modeling condition was identical but did not include reflective questioning, scaffolding, or shared ownership. Results indicated that the quiz scores for both interactive groups were superior to the control group, but the scores for the socially assisted were better than the scores of students in either the modeling or control conditions. Furthermore, children in the modeling group had difficulty linking the number quantities to the quantities of objects mentioned and in applying the appropriate operations; that is, they were not as adept at constructing a representation that linked numbers to world knowledge. Finally, in a microanalytic study of the interactions of the tutors with the groups, the researchers determined that the support offered by the tutor was not a function of the number of statements that the tutor made but rather that the statements came at the right time, when they would indeed serve to scaffold understanding.

In explaining the different outcomes, Taylor & Cox (1997) speculated that success with this type of learning was a function of the extent to which there was shared ownership of the learning, which discouraged the division of labor in favor of the negotiation of shared meaning. Instrumental to promoting the negotiation of shared meaning were expectations that: (*a*) all members of the group work on the same aspect of the problem at the same time, (*b*) members externalize their thoughts, including possible wrong procedures and answers, (*c*) members come to agreement among themselves before proceeding, and (*d*) as instruction moves forward, more of the regulative activity be transferred from the adult to children.

In the work of Taylor & Cox, there are integral relationships between cognitive and social processes. These relationships can raise a host of thorny issues. For example, social relationships can work against group sense making and the negotiation of meaning. O'Connor (1998) examined this issue in the research that she conducted as a participant observer in a sixth grade mathematics class over two years. Her close study of students' interactions revealed the ways in which ideas were often subordinated to social processes that arose from past interactions among students, suggesting ways in which learning opportunities were filtered through complex interpersonal contexts. Specific phenomena included: discounting or dismissing individual contributions and resistance to the spirit of the entire enterprise. Anderson et al (1997) reported a similar set of findings in their study of sixth graders engaged in collaborative problem solving. Research of this nature reveals the increased complexity for the teacher who must attend to socializing students into new ways of dealing with peers as intellectual partners, as well as new ways of thinking about subject matter learning (see also, Hatano & Inagaki 1991).

The research of Chan et al (1997) refines our understanding of conditions likely to enhance the effectiveness of peer interaction to promote learning. Students from grades 9 and 12/13 were randomly assigned to one of four conditions: (*a*) individual assimilation, (*b*) individual conflict, (*c*) peer assimilation, and (*d*) peer conflict. Assimilation in this research refers to the presentation of probe statements that were maximally congruent with the participants' conceptual understanding of the topic of evolution. Conflict refers to the presentation of probes that maximally contradicted the students' understanding. The presentation of probes was accompanied by the opportunity for participants to revise original ratings of agreement or disagreement with factor statements. In the peer conditions, the students had to negotiate and attain consensus on any changes in their ratings.

While there were a number of interesting findings, I focus on those most central to this review. Older students performed better in the peer condition, while younger students performed better in the individual condition. In addition, students in the conflict condition earned higher scores on quality of post-test knowledge building and experienced greater conceptual changes than students in the assimilation condition. However, conflict was instrumental only to the extent that the learner engaged in some form of knowledge building that aided the restructuring of understanding. Examples of knowledge building included: (*a*) treating new information as something problematic that needs explaining (such as constructing explanations that would reconcile knowledge conflict), and (*b*) using new information to construct coherence in understanding (for example, seeking connections among diverse pieces of information).

By examining the discourse that occurred in the peer conditions, the researchers contribute to our understanding of the differential effects of peer interaction. In discourse that the researchers identified as "[debilitating]," statements that should have caused conflict were simply ignored or treated superficially, whereas in "productive" discourse, there was careful uptake and problematizing of statements that were conflictual in nature.

Webb & Farivar (1997), extending Webb's program of research regarding peer interactions in cooperative learning contexts, used an experimental design to systematically examine the processes of preparing students to work in collaboration with one another. The components of the intervention included: (*a*) engaging the students in activities to ensure that they knew one another; (*b*) teaching communication skills, such as norms for interaction; (*c*) devising activities designed to develop students' abilities to help one another while working on problems, and (*d*) developing skills for generating explanations. The experimental program was implemented in six seventh grade general-math classes. Two teachers taught three grades each. In one condition, the classes received all the preparatory activities and worked in collaborative arrangements for a semester. In the second condition, the students did not receive preparation to develop skills of explanation. Students who received the three phases of preliminary instruction were more effective in using communication skills, helping behaviors, and explaining skills. Mirroring the findings of Chan et al (1997), Webb & Farivar (1997) found that while the level of help peers received was an important predictor of achievement, this was predicated on the help leading to constructive activity.

Furthermore, while there was some improvement in explanations over time, they were not explanations of a high level, raising the question about whether it is perhaps necessary to teach ways of supporting explanations that are specific to the cognitive demands of the domain in which the students are working [see Coleman (1992) and Palincsar et al (1993a) below].

Using a case study approach, Cobb et al (1993) investigated the extent to which children engaged in inquiry mathematics when they worked together in small groups. They also examined the extent to which small group collaborative activity facilitated children's mathematical learning. Stable groups' interactions were studied over 10 weeks to determine the relationship between learning opportunities and the different types of interactions in which the children engaged. Their findings suggested that the stability in the children's small group relationships across the 10 weeks of study was matched by the stability in each pair of children's cognitive capabilities relative to those of the partner. Children's cognitive capabilities and social relationships may have constrained each other in the sense of limiting possibilities for change. Furthermore, interactions in which one child routinely attempted to explain his or her thinking were not necessarily productive for either child's learning. Finally, harmony in a group's relationship did not appear to be a good indicator of learning opportunities. In fact, contentious relationships in which the children's expectations for each other were in conflict were often productive. What led to productive relationships was the development of taken-as-shared bases for mathematical communication and the routine engagement in interactions in which neither child was the authority.

Discursive analyses

From a social constructivist perspective, discourse is the primary symbolic, mediational tool for cognitive development. This notion is captured by Bakhtin (1981, p. 293): "[A]s a living, socio-ideological thing, language for the individual consciousness lies on the borderline between oneself and the other." For discourse to be an effective context for learning, it must be communicative. Much research has been conducted to understand the qualities of discourse that enhance its effectiveness. In this section I consider a subset of this research, drawing from various subjects. There are at least two approaches to the study of discourse. One is the investigation of naturally occurring instructional discourse to examine its patterns and opportunities, and the other is the systematic manipulating of features of discourse to determine the effects on learning.

We begin with Roschelle's (1992) inquiry on the processes by which individuals achieve convergence in collaborative activity. There is considerable research in science education examining the tendency of students to construct naive or alternative conceptions. Roschelle has argued that any serious account of science learning must provide an analysis of how convergence is achieved despite these tendencies. Toward this end, Roschelle conducted a microgenetic study of two high school students engaged in discovery learning with *The Envisioning Machine*, which is a software program that enables direct manipulation and graphical simulation of velocity and acceleration. His analyses of two one-hour sessions revealed how these students cooperatively constructed an understanding of acceleration that represented a significant conceptual change from their previous understanding and approximated the scientific meaning of acceleration.

Roschelle asserts that the students attained convergent conceptual change to the extent that, by the end of the session, important aspects of velocity and acceleration were shared, including: change of speed, change of direction, and the implications of these changes in application. Furthermore, the conversation revealed how the students responded to one another with mutual concern for shared knowledge, exerting a deliberate effort to create convergence and avoid divergence. How did this convergence happen? Roschelle suggests that it included the construction of situations at an intermediate level of abstraction from the literal features of the physical world, which was achieved through (*a*) the interplay of metaphors in relation to each other and in reference to the constructed situation, (*b*) iterative cycles of displaying, confirming, and repairing meanings, and (*c*) the application of progressively more stringent standards of evidence. Furthermore, Roschelle suggests that *The Envisioning Machine* played an essential role, simultaneously supporting individual reasoning and facilitating the negotiation of meaning.

The program of research by Raphael and her colleagues, studying elementary-aged students engaged in Book Club discussions (Raphael et al 1992), reveals the value of naturalistic study of discourse in another complex learning environment. The leading question of this research was: How do book club discussions influence fourth and fifth grade students' abilities to discuss literature? By studying children's conversations across time and across texts, we learn about the role of the constitution of the groups, literature selection, and assigned writing activities. For example, in the selection of a text, it needed to have the potential for controversy and the power to elicit emotional responses—in addition to high quality, the proper reading level, availability, and suitability for meeting curricular goals. Furthermore, writing activities that offered more flexibility in responses were more beneficial and led to more interesting discussions than did more carefully structured responses. Finally, the research speaks to the multiple roles played by the teacher in Book Club discussions: guiding students in using text comprehension strategies, modeling ways to articulate personal responses to literature, and illustrating interaction patterns that would promote improved interactions in Book Clubs.

The crucial role that the teacher plays in promoting the co-construction of knowledge in classrooms was also demonstrated in the research of Forman et al (1995). In the micro-analytic study of the discourse of middle school children and their teacher (introduced above), these researchers captured the dynamic role of the teacher in guiding classroom discussions in the context of mathematical problem solving. In addition to evaluating the frequency of teacher and student contributions, they analyzed the functions of these contributions. The scheme that they devised revealed a broad range of conversational turns. For example, there were *initiations* in the service of requesting an answer or explanation; *responses:* and *reconceptualizations* that included restatements, rephrasing, expansion, and evaluation. The research of Forman et al suggests the importance of moving beyond the traditional static treatments of I-R-E (initiation-response-evaluation) patterns in classroom discourse. While an initial pass at the discourse in this classroom might suggest it fit the I-R-E framework, the students rather than the teacher were engaged in significant evaluative activity, and the responses of the teacher expanded on students' contributions to the discussion. Forman et al also note another crucial feature of the teacher's role, which they refer to as "discussion orchestration," which served to focus student attention and facilitate negotiation in the interest of consensus building.

Lampert (1990), reflecting on her own teaching activity in mathematics, captures the role that she has played in this negotiation process (p. 41):

> The role I took in classroom discourse, therefore, was to follow and engage in mathematical arguments with students; this meant that I needed to know more than the answer or the rule for how to find it, and I needed to do something other than explain to them why the rules work. I needed to know how to *prove* it to them, in the mathematical sense, and I needed to be able to evaluate their proofs of their own mathematical assertions. In the course of classroom discussions, I also initiated my students into the use of mathematical tools and conventions.

In this manner, Lampert clearly joins the dialogue as a knowing participant, but she is not the arbiter of truth. The burden of mathematical judgment is distributed to the classroom as a community of mathematical thinkers.

Naturally occurring differences across four classrooms enabled Smagorinsky & Fly (1993) to determine how the discourse in teacher-led discussion groups influenced the nature of subsequent small group discussions. The discussions were in the service of interpreting short coming-of-age stories and took place in four sophomore high school classes. By examining transcripts of discussion across whole class and small group contexts, the researchers were able to determine that the skill with which students engaged in productive discussions during small group discussions was related to the experiences of the students in the whole-class work. Specific teacher moves in whole-class discussion that subsequently served to scaffold small group discussions included: posing questions that encouraged students to make connections between the text and their own life experiences, and stepping outside the discussion for the purpose of making analytic/interpretive procedures explicit (for example, the need to pose a question, the need to support a generalization with evidence).

Finally, we report on two studies of small groups engaged in peer-editing activities, unassisted by a teacher. Daiute & Dalton (1993) studied the inter-actions between 14 seven-to-nine-year-old children in an urban setting and the impact of collaboration on their abilities to write stories. The study traces how the children internalized the fruits of their collaboration by examining individually generated written work before, during, and following collabor-ation. This study was conducted in an urban school over eight weeks. The researchers found that the children brought diverse areas of expertise related to story structure knowledge, style, and schema to the story-writing activity. Furthermore, they described the writing processes in terms of initiating and contesting. Analyses of independent writing samples indicated that the participants used significantly more story elements following collaboration.

In another study of peer collaboration in writing, Nystrand (1986) found that students who worked in groups demonstrated greater gains than those who did not. Furthermore, students who had experienced group work came to think of revision as reconceptualization, whereas those who worked alone continued to think of revision as principally editing. However, he also found remarkable variability in the discourse across groups. For example, some groups felt they had accomplished their task if they labeled the problem, failing to examine the trouble source in any detail, while other groups would talk at length about ideas. Successful groups focused on issues of genre and the most successful groups engaged in "extensive collaborative problem solving," in which members joined together to address rhetorical problems in concrete, cooperative ways.

Next we turn to those studies that have been designed to manipulate features of discourse to learn more about how they operate to promote learn-ing. We begin with a study by Teasley (1995), which was designed to study *collaboration* and *talk* as separate variables. Questions driving this research asked: Does the production of talk affect performance? What kinds of talk affect performance? Does the presence of a partner affect the kinds of talk produced? Teasley used a microworld (designed by Klahr and his colleagues) to investigate scientific reasoning. The task required figuring out the effect of a mystery key and then designing experiments to test the hypotheses. The 70 fourth grade participants were assigned to work alone or with a same-sex partner for one 20-min session. Within each condition, half of the children were asked to talk as they worked and half were asked not to talk. There was a main effect for talk that was more pronounced for talk-dyads than for talk-alones. Talk-dyads produced more talk and more specific types of talk than talk-alones. However, neither simply having a partner nor talking a lot improved learning. What was crucial was that children produced interpretive types of talk; that is, talk that supported reasoning about theories and evi-dence. Furthermore, while dyads directed more of their talk to evaluating and explaining the program outcomes, students working alone simply remarked on the behavior of the spaceship without making any assessment of that behavior.

Teasley's findings are supported by research on reasoning indicating that children's performance on reasoning tasks is significantly affected by their ability to coordinate hypotheses and evidence (Klahr et al 1993, Kuhn et al 1988, Schauble 1990). Findings of this nature informed the design of an intervention study conducted by Coleman (1992), in which she sought to define the merits of collaborative learning more precisely; that is, to describe some of the specific mechanisms of group learning that appear to be more successful than others for promoting conceptual understanding.

Coleman's findings are mirrored in a study by King (1990) who did research altering group discourse to determine whether it would affect reading comprehension. The intervention was called "guided reciprocal peer questioning" and involved teaching students question stems (such as "How does ... affect ...?", "What would happen if ...?"). King reported that students who used this procedure generated more critical thinking questions, gave more high-level explanations, and demonstrated higher achievement than students using discussion or an unguided reciprocal questioning approach.

In summary, studies of discourse are generally quite supportive of the benefits of instructional conversation. However, the benefits depend upon the types of talk produced. Specifically, talk that is interpretive (generated in the service of analysis or explanations) is associated with more significant learning gains than talk that is simply descriptive. Furthermore, teachers play an important role in mediating classroom discourse by seeding the conversation with new ideas or alternatives to be considered that push the students' thinking and discussion and prepare them for conversation. Finally, it is important to attend to the structure of group activity so that responsibility is shared, expertise is distributed, and there is an ethos for building preceding ideas.

In the next section, I consider the contributions of social constructivist perspectives to selected contemporary educational issues; namely, acquiring expertise across domains, assessment practices, equity in education, and the transformation of schools.

THE APPLICATION OF SOCIAL CONSTRUCTIVIST PERSPECTIVES TO CONTEMPORARY EDUCATIONAL ISSUES

Acquiring expertise across domains

Writing from a traditional psychological perspective, Gallagher, in a 1994 *Annual Review* chapter on teaching and learning, wrote that "[E]ducators are increasingly viewing learners as bundles of knowledge structures that become increasingly sophisticated and hierarchical as they gain experience" (p. 172). In contrast, from social constructivist perspectives, expertise is characterized not in terms of knowledge structures but rather in terms of facility with discourse, norms, and practices associated with particular communities of practice (Lave & Wenger 1991). While from cognitive perspectives knowledge is generally represented in terms of cognitive structures that are acquired and organized in memory, social constructivists generally regard learning as the appropriation of socially derived forms of knowledge that are not simply internalized over time but are also transformed in idiosyncratic ways in the appropriation process. Furthermore, learning is thought to occur through processes of interaction, negotiation, and collaboration (cf Billet 1995, Hicks 1995–1996).

The influence of social constructivist perspectives has led to reexamining what it means to teach and learn across subject matters. From social constructivist perspectives, researchers have asked what it means to "talk science" (Lemke 1990) or to participate in the discourse of mathematics (Cobb & Bauersfeld 1995). For example, Lemke (1990) suggests that talking science means: "observing, describing, comparing, classifying, analyzing, discussing, hypothesizing, theorizing, questioning, challenging, arguing, designing experiments, following procedures, judging, evaluating, deciding, concluding, generalizing, reporting, writing, lecturing, and teaching in and through the language of science" (p. ix). Furthermore, drawing upon anthropological research (e.g. Latour & Woolgar 1986), it is clear that scientific practice in the world is heterogeneous rather than unitary to the extent that practitioners orchestrate a variety of means (tools, discourses) to construct scientific meaning.

In turn, educational researchers have pursued the connection between scientific practice in professional communities and in schools, testing out the implications of this view for curriculum and pedagogy. Illustrative is the research of Rosebery et al (1992) in elementary classrooms where science is organized around students' own questions and inquiries. Students design studies to explore questions that they find compelling; collect, analyze, and interpret data; build and argue theories; establish criteria and evaluate evidence; challenge assumptions; and take action on the basis of their results. Among the many outcomes that Rosebery et al report are: the generative nature of children's thinking in this context and the deepening of scientific thinking (for example, students came to understand that hypotheses are springboards for inquiry rather than explanations). Finally, the researchers report that participants became comfortable identifying with scientific activity and not simply attributing scientific activity to others.

Assessment

Assessment practices informed by social constructivist perspectives stand in striking contrast with assessment procedures informed by the psychological theory that prevailed in the 1960s, in which testing contexts (e.g. Wisconsin General Test Apparatus) were designed to reduce social influences (Brown

1994). Assessment informed by social constructivist perspectives is frequently referred to as "dynamic assessment" (Feuerstein 1979) and characterizes approaches in which the performance of the individual being assessed is mediated or guided by another individual to determine the individual's potential to profit from assistance or instruction.

Dynamic assessment provides a *prospective* measure of performance, indicating abilities that are developing and is *predictive* of how the child will perform independently in the future. Furthermore, the response of the child to the assistance is intended to inform instruction. In Vygotskian terms, while traditional static measures at best inform us about an individual's actual level of development, dynamic assessment is designed to reveal the child's potential level of development (Vygotsky 1986, pp. 203):

> The state of development is never defined alone by what has matured. If the gardener decides only to evaluate the matured or harvested fruits of the apple tree, he cannot determine the state of his orchard. The maturing trees must also be taken into consideration. Correspondingly, the psychologist must not limit his analysis to functions that have matured; he must consider those that are in the process of maturation . . . the zone of proximal development.

There are a number of models of dynamic assessment (Lidz 1987, Palincsar et al 1991) that vary in terms of the nature of the task, the type of assistance that is provided, and the outcomes that are reported. For example, the model pioneered by Feuerstein (1980), the Learning Potential Assessment Device (LPAD), is organized around tasks that Feuerstein argues require higher mental processes that are amenable to change, such as matrix problems, digit span tests, and embedded-figures problems. Hence, they bear a strong resemblance to the kinds of tasks used in traditional measures of IQ. However, when administering the LPAD, the examiner interacts in a flexible and individualized manner, anticipating where the child might experience difficulty and noting how the child uses reminders and other prompts. The outcome of the assessment is a cognitive map that is designed to specify the nature of the child's problem in terms of familiarity with content, strategies attempted in problem solving activity, and modifiability of the learner.

Test-train-test is another model of dynamic assessment that has been used in the research of Budoff (1987), Carlson & Wiedl (1979), and Campione & Brown (1984) and colleagues. Some form of guided learning occurs between pre- and posttesting. These programs of research indicate that dynamic assessment procedures do reveal a different picture of competence than do static measures, which typically underestimate many children's abilities to learn in a domain in which they initially performed poorly. The use of transfer tasks in dynamic assessment indicates that learning and transfer scores are better predictors of gain than are static measures.

It has been only recently that the principles of dynamic assessment have been explored within academic contexts. An excellent example is the research reported by Magnusson et al (1997). Magnusson et al were interested in children's conceptual understanding of the flow of electricity and devised a context that would allow the fourth graders in their research to test out their conceptions and then revise their ideas on the basis of the outcomes of their tests. They used the same basic circuit in three tasks, with each circuit differing only in the number of switches, which in turn determined which light-bulbs were lighted as well as the brightness of the bulbs. Hence the students had multiple opportunities to construct, test out, and revise explanations for the flow of electricity. The role of the interviewer in this assessment context was to elicit and probe predictions and explanations that would reveal the conceptions of the student participants. This dynamic science assessment proceeded by engaging the students in (a) predicting what they thought would happen, given a specific circuit, along with their reasons for making these predictions; (b) describing their observations; (c) comparing predictions with observations and discussing differences between them; and (d) explaining the result, focusing on underlying causes.

The use and outcomes of microgenetic analysis are illustrated by Schauble's (1996) research in which she examined the development of scientific reasoning as participants completed two experimentation tasks involving the use of fluids and immersed objects. Given recent calls for reexamining the usefulness of high-stakes assessment practices and questioning the extent to which these practices truly inform curriculum and pedagogy, these forms of dynamic and microgenetic assessment offer potentially powerful alternatives to traditional measurement procedures to the extent that they reveal not only what has been learned but also how and why learning has occurred.

Providing meaningful education for all children

It is hard to imagine a more significant challenge to social constructivism than promoting meaningful learning for all children, especially for those who are linguistically and culturally diverse. Moll (1992) speaks to this possibility when he argues that "[i]n studying human beings dynamically, within their social circumstances, in their full complexity, we gain a more complete and . . . a much more valid understanding of them. We also gain, particularly in the case of minority children, a more positive view of their capabilities and how our pedagogy often constrains, and just as often distorts, what they do and what they are capable of doing" (p. 239).

A number of sociocultural explanations have been tendered for the failure of schools to serve all children. Examples include: (a) discontinuities between the culture (values, attitudes, and beliefs) of the home and school (Gee 1990, McPhail 1996), (b) mismatches in the communicative practices between nonmainstream children and mainstream teachers that lead to miscommunication and misjudgment (Heath 1983), (c) the internalization of negative stereotypes by minority groups who have been marginalized and may see school as a site for opposition and resistance (Steele 1992), and (*d*) relational issues, such as the failure to attain mutual trust between teachers and students (Moll & Whitmore 1993) and a shared sense of identification between the teacher and the learner (Cazden 1993, Litowitz 1993).

These possibilities have been pursued both in describing the performance of children in schools and in prescribing appropriate instruction. For example, Anderson et al (1997) drew upon these explanations to explore how sixth grade students participated in collaborative problem-solving activities in science. For a prescriptive example, we turn to the research of Needles & Knapp (1994), who conducted a study comparing three approaches to the teaching of writing. The first approach was *skills-based*, as characterized by systematic exposure and mastery of discrete skills (such as spelling and sentence structure). The second approach was *whole language*, which advocates that language is best learned in the context of use, should not be broken into discrete skills, and prescribes a minimal role for the teacher. The third approach reflected a social constructivist perspective, which Needles & Knapp described using the following principles: (*a*) component skills are best learned in the context of the writing task, (*b*) the quality of writing increases when children are writing what is meaningful and authentic, (*c*) fluency and competence are influenced by the extent to which the task connects with the child's background and experience, (*d*) involvement increases when children are encouraged to interact while performing writing tasks, (*e*) children develop competence if they approach the task as a problem solving process, and (*f*) children need ample opportunities to write extended text. They found that writing instruction that reflected these six principles accounted for a substantial proportion of children's improved abilities to write, once initial proficiency was considered.

Educational reform

Exciting educational innovations are under way that draw generously upon (and are contributing generously to) the social constructivist perspectives introduced in this review. Perhaps the most striking example is a collection of efforts designed to reconceptualize classrooms—and schools—as learning communities. For example, the Computer Supported Intentional Learning Environments (CSILE), a project led by Scardamalia & Bereiter and their colleagues (Scardamalia et al (1994) places "World 3" knowledge at the center of classroom activity. As described by Popper (1972), World 3 knowledge refers to the public construction of understanding and stands in contrast to "World 2" knowledge, which exists in individual minds. The features of CSILE include a communal data base that students use to generate World 3 knowledge, a curriculum that permits the sustained pursuit of topics of inquiry, a classroom culture that fosters collaboration among peers, and a teacher who engages in instructional design work. The researchers note that the successful implementation of CSILE engages the teacher in moving flexibly between World 2 and World 3 knowledge, tacking between what is in children's heads and what is taking shape in the public domain.

In the project Guided Discovery in a Community of Learners, Brown & Campione and their colleagues (Brown & Campione 1990, 1994) engage children in the design of their own learning and encourage students to be partially responsible for the design of their own curricula. Working on assigned curricular themes, students form separate research groups to become experts on subtopics of the theme. The students conduct seminars in which they share their expertise so that all members of the group can master the entire theme. Essential characteristics of Community of Learner classrooms include individual responsibility coupled with communal sharing; the use of select participation frameworks that are practiced repeatedly and that are compatible with the work of these communities; classroom discourse that is marked by constructive discussion, questioning, and criticism; conceptions of classrooms as comprised of multiple zones of proximal development (explained above), which include both children and adults at varying levels of expertise, as well as artifacts (such as texts and tools) that support learning; and the expectation that learning occurs as individuals contribute to and appropriate ideas (Brown & Campione 1994). Multifaceted assessments indicate that children in these learning communities retain domain-specific content better than youngsters in control groups, are able to think critically about knowledge, and demonstrate significant progress with an array of literacy skills such as reading comprehension and oral argumentation.

The demands of the types of teaching and classroom organization described throughout this review have special implications for the professional development of teachers. This is an area that has been virtually neglected in earlier educational reform efforts, which may well explain the efforts' demise. An educational innovation of particular importance is the application of the tenets of social constructivism to the design of professional development contexts with teachers. For example, Englert and her colleagues (Englert & Tarrant 1995) have brought teachers together in learning communities to examine their own practices in literacy instruction. This community of teachers works to translate the tenets of a sociocultural perspective into curriculum and pedagogy for students with serious learning difficulties. The teachers, informed by this perspective, systematically try out new practices, conduct their own inquiry regarding the outcomes of these innovations, and share their accumulated wisdom with one another. Additional professional development research, conducted in a similar spirit, has been reported by Grossman & Weinberg (1997; working with secondary literature teachers), Schifter (1996; working with elementary teachers in mathematics), and Palincsar & Magnusson and their colleagues (1997; working with elementary teachers in science).

Future directions for inquiry

The major theoretical contributions to the social constructivist perspective described in this chapter were developed and applied in the 1920s and 1930s by Vygotsky and his collaborators. Based on the notion that human activities take place in cultural contexts, are mediated by language and other symbol systems, and are best understood when investigated in their historical development, this is a complex and multifaceted perspective. Moreover, Vygotsky died at a very young age, with many of his ideas only partially developed. John-Steiner & Mahn (1996) caution that because the theory is complex and breaks radically with traditional educational and psychological theory, there is the tendency to abstract parts of the theory from the whole, which results in distorted understandings and applications. One direction for future inquiry is to continue the development of this theory.

Toward this end, it will be helpful to coordinate constructivist perspectives, informed primarily by cognitive psychology and socioculturalism. How might these perspectives be coordinated? Where constructivists give priority to individual conceptual activity, sociocultural theorists tend to assume that cognitive processes are subsumed by social and cultural processes. Where social constructivists emphasize the homogeneity of thought among the members of the community engaged in shared activity, cognitive constructivists stress heterogeneity of thought as individuals actively interpret social and cultural processes, highlighting the contributions that individuals make to the development of these processes.

It is important that inquiry conducted within this perspective shares a dual orientation to theory and practice (Cole 1996), designed to deepen our understanding of cognitive development as well as to produce change in everyday practice. As the research reviewed above suggests, social constructivist perspectives, which regard schooling as a system rather than as a set of isolated activities, have been extremely useful to understanding and describing the complexities of teaching, learning, and enculturation into schools. However, they have had little influence on the practices of schooling.

The genetic levels of analysis suggested by this perspective, as well as the methodologies that are drawn from this perspective, offer powerful tools for advancing both theory and practice. However, many educational researchers are unfamiliar with these tools. Finally, just as this perspective has been developed through the contributions of many disciplines (psychology, semiotics, linguistics, anthropology, etc), it would seem especially fruitful to promote interdisciplinary collaborations in the quest to advance this scholarship so that it might realize its potential and make a difference for children.

REFERENCES

Anderson CA, Holland D, Palincsar AS. 1997. Canonical and sociocultural approaches to research and reform in science education: the story of Juan and his group. *Elem. Sch. J.* 97:357–81

Bakhtin M. 1981. Discourse in the novel. In *The Dialogic Imagination*, ed. C Emerson, M Holquist, pp. 259–492. Austin: Univ. Tex. Press

Baumann J. 1988. Direct instruction reconsidered. *J. Read. Behav.* 31:712–18

Bell N, Grossen M, Perret-Clermont AN. 1985. Sociocognitive conflict and intellectual growth. See Berkowitz 1985, pp. 41–54

Berkowitz MW, ed. 1985. *Peer Conflict and Psychological Growth*. San Francisco: Jossey-Bass

Billet S. 1995. Situated learning: bridging sociocultural and cognitive theorizing. *Learn. Instruct.* 6:263–80

Brown AL. 1994. The advancement of learning. *Educ. Res.* 23:4–12

Brown AL, Campione JC. 1990. Communities of learning and thinking, or a context by any other name. *Hum. Dev.* 21:108–25

Brown AL, Campione JC. 1994. Guided discovery in a community of learners. See McGilly 1994, 9:229–72

Brown AL, Palincsar AS. 1989. Guided cooperative learning and individual knowledge acquisition. In *Knowing, Learning, and Instruction: Essays in Honor of Robert Glaser*, ed. L Resnick, pp. 393–451. Hillsdale, NJ: Erlbaum

Bruer J. 1994. Classroom problems, school culture, and cognitive research. See McGilly 1994, 10:273–90

Bruner J. 1990. *Acts of Meaning*, pp. 1–32. Cambridge, MA: Harvard Univ. Press

Budoff M. 1987. Measures for assessing learning potential. See Lidz 1987, pp. 173–95

Campione JC, Brown AL. 1984. Learning ability and transfer propensity as sources of individual differences in intelligence. In *Learning and Cognition in the Mentally Retarded*, ed. PH Brooks, R Sperber, C McCauley, pp. 137–50. Baltimore: Univ. Park Press

Carlson JS, Wiedl KH. 1979. Toward a differential footing approach: testing the limits employing the Roman matrices. *Intelligence* 3: 323–44

Cazden C. 1993. Vygotksy, Hymes, and Bahktin: from word to utterance and voice. See Forman et al 1993, pp. 197–212

Chan C, Burtis J, Bereiter C. 1997. Knowledge building as a mediator of conflict in conceptual change. *Cogn. Instruct.* 15:1–40

Cobb P, Bauersfeld H. 1995. *Emergence of Mathematical Meaning: Instruction in Classroom Cultures*. Hillsdale, NJ: Erlbaum

Cobb P, Wood T, Yackel E. 1993. Discourse, mathematical thinking, and classroom practice. See Forman et al 1993, pp. 91–119

Cobb P, Wood T, Yackel E. 1991. Analogies from the philosophy and sociology of science for understanding classroom life. *Sci. Educ.* 75:23–44

Cobb P, Yackel E. 1996. Constructivism, emergent, and sociocultural perspectives in the context of developmental research. *Educ. Psychol.* 31:175–90

Cole M. 1996. *Cultural Psychology*. Cambridge, MA: Harvard Univ. Press

Coleman EB. 1992. *Faciliating conceptual understanding in science: a collaborative explanation based approach*. PhD thesis. Univ. Toronto, Can.

Crook C. 1994. *Computers and the Collaborative Experience of Learning*. London: Routledge

Daiute C, Dalton B. 1993. Collaboration between children learning to write: Can novices be masters? *Cogn. Instruct.* 10: 281–333

Damon W. 1984. Peer education: the untapped potential. *J. Appl. Behav. Psychol.* 5: 331–43

Duffy GG, Roehler L, Meloth MS, Vavrus LG, Book C, et al. 1986. The relationship between explicit verbal explanations during reading skill instruction and student awareness and achievement: a study of reading teacher effects. *Read. Res. Q.* 22: 347–68

Ellis S, Gauvain M. 1992. Social and cultural influences on children's collaborative interactions. In *Children's Development Within Social Context*, ed. LT Winegar, J Valsiner, pp. 155–80. Hillsdale, NJ: Erlbaum

Englert CS, Tarrant K. 1995. Creating collaborative cultures for educational change. *Remed. Special Educ.* 16:325–36

Feuerstein R. 1979. *The Dynamic Assessment of Retarded Performers: The Learning Potential Assessment Device, Theory, Instruments, and Techniques.* Baltimore: Univ. Park Press

Feuerstein R. 1980. *Instrumental Enrichment: An Intervention Program for Cognitive Modifiability.* Baltimore: Univ. Park Press

Fine GA. 1987. *With the Boys*, pp. 41–57. Chicago: Univ. Chicago Press

Flower L, Schriver KA, Carey L, Haas C, Hayes JR. 1992. Planning in writing: the cognition of a constructive process. In *A Rhetoric of Doing*, ed. S Witte, N Nakadate, R Cherry, pp. 282–311. Carbondale: South. Ill. Univ. Press

Forman EA, Donato R, McCormick D. 1993. *The social and institutional context of learning mathematics: an ethnographic study of classroom discourse.* Presented at Annu. Meet. Am. Educ. Res. Assoc., 75th, New Orleans

Forman EA, Kraker MJ. 1985. The social origins of logic: the contributions of Piaget and Vygotsky. See Berkowitz 1985, pp. 23–39

Forman EA, Minnick N, Stone CA. 1993. *Contexts for Learning: Sociocultural Dynamics in Children's Development.* New York: Oxford Univ. Press

Forman EA, Stein MK, Brown C, Larreamendy-Joerns J. 1995. *The Socialization of Mathematical Thinking: The Role of Institutional, Interpersonal, and Discursive Contexts.* Presented at Annu. Meet. Am. Educ. Res. Assoc., 77th, San Franciso

Gallagher JJ. 1994. Teaching and learning: new models. *Annu. Rev. Psychol.* 45: 171–95

Gee J. 1990. *Social Linguistics and Literacies: Ideology in Discourse.* Bristol, PA: Falmer

Glaser R, Bassok M. 1989. Learning theory and the study of instruction. *Annu. Rev. Psychol.* 40:631–66

Grossman P, Weinberg S. 1997. *Creating a community of learners among high school English and social studies teachers.* Presented at Annu. Meet. Am. Educ. Res. Assoc., 78th, Chicago

Hatano G, Inagaki K. 1991. Sharing cognition through collective comprehension activity. See Resnick et al 1991, pp. 331–48

Heath SB. 1983. *Ways with Words: Language, Life, and Work in Communities and Classrooms.* New York: Cambridge Univ. Press

Hicks D. 1995–1996. Discourse, learning, and teaching. *Rev. Res. Educ.* 21:49–98

John-Steiner V, Mahn H. 1996. Sociocultural approaches to learning and development. *Educ. Psychol.* 31:191–206

King A. 1990. Enhancing peer interaction and learning in the classroom through reciprocal questioning. *Am. Educ. Res. J.* 27:664–87

Klahr D, Fay A, Dunbar K. 1993. Heuristics for scientific experimentation: a developmental study. *Cogn. Psychol.* 25:111–46

Kuhn D, Amsel E, O'Loughlin M. 1988. *The Development of Scientific Thinking Skills*. New York: Academic

Lampert M. 1990. When the problem is not the question and the solution is not the answer: mathematical knowing and teaching. *Am. Educ. Res. J.* 27:29–63

Latour B, Woolgar S. 1986. *Laboratory Life: The Social Construction of Scientific Facts*. Princeton, NJ: Princeton Univ. Press

Lave J, Wenger E. 1991. *Situated Learning: Legitimate Peripheral Participation*. Cambridge: Cambridge Univ. Press.

Lemke J. 1990. *Talking Science: Language, Learning, and Values*. Norwood, NJ: Ablex

Leontiev AN. 1981. *Problems of the Development of Mind*. Moscow: Progress

Lidz CS, ed. 1987. *Dynamic Assessment: Foundations and Fundamentals*. New York: Guilford

Litowitz B. 1993. Deconstruction in the zone of proximal development. See Forman et al 1993, pp. 184–97

Magnusson SJ, Templin M, Boyle R. 1997. Dynamic science assessment of new approaches for investigating conceptual change. *J. Learn. Sci.* 6:91–142

Matusov EL, Bell N, Rogoff B. 1997. Collaboration and assistance in problem solving by children differing in cooperative schooling backgrounds. Submitted

McGilly K, ed. 1994. *Classroom Lessons: Integrating Cognitive Theory and Classroom Practice*. Cambridge: MIT Press

McPhail J. 1996. *The use of narrative methods to explore failure to succeed in medical school*. Presented at Annu. Meet. Am. Educ. Res. Assoc., 77th, New York

Moll LC. 1992. Literacy research in community and classrooms: a sociocultural approach. In *Multidisciplinary Perspectives on Literacy Research*, ed. R Beach, JL Green, ML Kamil, T Shanahan, pp. 211–44. Urbana, IL: Natl. Counc. Teach. Engl.

Moll LC, Whitmore K. 1993. Vygotsky in classroom practice: moving from individual transmission to social transaction. See Forman et al 1993, pp. 19–42

Needles MC, Knapp M. 1994. Teaching writing to children who are underserved. *J. Educ. Psychol.* 86:339–49

Newman D, Griffin P, Cole M. 1989. *The Construction Zone: Working for Cognitive Change in Schools*. Cambridge: Cambridge Univ. Press

Nicolopoulou A, Cole M. 1993. Generation and transmission of shared knowledge in the culture of collaborative learning: The Fifth Dimension, its playworld and its institutional contexts. See Forman et al 1993, pp. 283–314

Nystrand M. 1986. *The Structure of Written Communication: Studies in Reciprocity Between Writers and Readers*. Orlando, FL: Academic

O'Connor MC. 1998. Managing the intermental: classroom group discussion and the social context of learning. In *Social Interaction, Social Context, and Language: Essays in Honor of Susan Ervin Tripp*, ed. DI Slobin, J Gerhardt, A Kyratzis, J Guo. Hillsdale, NJ: Erlbaum. In press

Palincsar AS. 1986. The role of dialogue in scaffolded instruction. *Educ. Psychol.* 21: 71–98

Palincsar AS, Anderson CA, David YM. 1993a. Pursuing scientific literacy in the middle grades through collaborative problem solving. *Elem. Sch. J.* 93:643–58

Palincsar AS, Brown AL. 1984. Reciprocal teaching of comprehension-fostering and comprehension-monitoring activities. *Cogn. Instruct.* 1:117–75

Palincsar AS, Brown AL. 1989. Classroom dialogues to promote self-regulated comprehension. In *Advances in Research on Teaching.* ed. J Brophy, pp. 35–72. Greenwich: JAI

Palincsar AS, Brown AL, Campione JC. 1993b. First grade dialogues for knowledge acquisition and use. See Forman et al 1993, pp. 43–57

Palincsar AS, Brown AL, Campione JC. 1991. Dynamic assessment. In *Handbook on the Assessment of Learning Disabilities,* ed. L Swanson, 5:75–95. Austin, TX: Pro-Ed.

Palincsar AS, Magnusson SJ. 1997. Design principles informing and emerging from a community of practice. *Teach. Teach. Educ.* In press

Perret-Clermont AN. 1980. Social interaction and cognitive development. *Eur. Monogr. Soc. Psychol. 19.* New York: Academic

Peterson P, Walberg HJ, eds. 1979. *Research in Teaching.* Berkeley, CA: McCutchan

Piaget J. 1985. *The Equilibration of Cognitive Structures: The Central Problem of Intellectual Development,* pp. 36–64. Transl. T Brown, KL Thampy. Chicago: Univ. Chicago Press. (From French)

Popper KR. 1972. *Objective Knowledge: An Evolutionary Approach.* Oxford: Clarendon

Prawat R. 1996. Constructivisms, modern and postmodern. *Educ. Psychol.* 31:215–25

Raphael TE, McMahon SI, Goatley VJ, Bentley JL, Boyd FB, et al. 1992. Research directions: literature and discussion in the reading program. *Lang. Arts* 69:55–61

Resnick LB, Levine JM, Teasely SD, eds. 1991. *Perspectives on Socially Shared Cognition.* Washington, DC: Am. Psychol. Assoc.

Resnick LB, Salmon MH, Zeitz CM, Wathen SH. 1993. The structure of reasoning in conversation. *Cogn. Instruct.* 11:347–64

Rogoff B. 1991. Guidance and participation in spatial planning. See Resnick et al 1991, pp. 349–83

Rogoff B. 1997. Cognition as a collaborative process. In *Cognitive, Language, and Perceptual Development,* ed. RS Siegler, D Kuhn, Vol. 2, *Handbook of Child Psychology,* ed. W Damon. New York: Wiley. In press

Rogoff B, Radziszewska B, Masiello T. 1995. Analysis of developmental processes in sociocultural activity. In *Sociocultural Psychology: Theory and Practice of Doing and Knowing,* ed. L Martin, K Nelson, E Toback, pp. 125–49. Cambridge: Cambridge Univ. Press

Rommetveit R. 1974. *On Message Structure.* London: Wiley

Roschelle J. 1992. Learning by collaborating: convergent conceptual change. *J. Learn. Sci.* 2:235–76

Rosebery A, Warren B, Conant F. 1992. Appropriating scientific discourse: findings from minority classrooms. *J. Learn Sci.* 2:61–94

Roth WM. 1996. *Communities of practice and actor networks: an analysis of the diffusion of knowledge in an elementary classroom in terms of changing resources and practices.* Presented at Annu. Meet. Natl. Assoc. Res. Sci. Teach., Anaheim

Russell J, Mills I, Reiff-Musgrove P. 1990. The role of symmetrical and asymmetrical social conflict in cognitive change. *J. Exp. Child Psychol.* 49:58–78

Sandoval J. 1995. Teaching in subject matter areas: science. *Annu. Rev. Psychol.* 46: 355–74

Scardamalia M, Bereiter C. 1989. Intentional learning as a goal of instruction. In *Knowing, Learning and Instruction,* ed. LB Resnick, pp. 361–92. Hillsdale, NJ: Erlbaum

Scardamalia M, Bereiter C, Lamon M. 1994. The CSILE project: trying to bring the classroom into world 3. See McGilly 1994, 8:201–28

Schauble L. 1990. Belief revision in children: the role of prior knowledge and strategies for generating evidence. *J. Exp. Child. Psychol.* 49:31–57

Schauble L. 1996. The development of scientific reasoning in knowledge-rich contexts. *Dev. Psychol.* 32:102–19

Schifter D. 1996. *Reconstruction of Professional Identities*. New York: Teacher's College Press

Smagorinsky P, Fly P. 1993. The social environment of the classroom: a Vygotskian perspective on small group processes. *Commun. Educ.* 42:159–71

Snow RE, Swanson J. 1992. Instructional psychology: aptitude, adaptation, and assessment. *Annu. Rev. Psychol.* 43:583–626

Steele C. 1992. Race and the schooling of black Americans. *The Atlantic* 269:68–72

Stodolsky SS. 1988. *The Subject Matters: Classroom Activity in Math and Social Studies*. Chicago, IL: Univ. Chicago Press

Taylor J, Cox BD. 1997. Microgenetic analysis of group-based solution of complex two-step mathematical word problems by fourth graders. *J. Learn. Sci.* 6:183–226

Teasley S. 1995. The role of talk in children's peer collaborations. *Dev. Psychol.* 31: 207–20

Thorndike EL. 1906. *The Principles of Teaching, Based on Psychology*. New York: Seiler

Toulmin S. 1995. Forward. In *Rethinking Knowledge: Reflections Across the Disciplines*, ed. RF Goodman, WR Fisher, pp. ix–xv. Albany: State Univ. NY Press

Valsiner J. 1987. *Culture and the Development of Children's Action*. Cambridge, MA: Harvard Univ. Press

Voss JF, Wiley J, Carretero M. 1995. Acquiring intellectual skills. *Annu. Rev. Psychol.* 46:155–81

Vygotsky L. 1978. *Mind in Society: The Development of Higher Psychological Processes*, ed. M Cole, V John-Steiner, S Scribner, E Souberman. Cambridge, MA: Harvard Univ. Press

Vygotsky L. 1981. The instrumental method in psychology. In *The Concept of Activity in Soviet Psychology*, ed. J Wertsch, pp. 3–35. Armonk, NY: Sharpe.

Vygotsky L. 1986. (1934). *Thought and Language*. ed. A Kozulin. Cambridge, MA: MIT Press

Vygotsky L, Luria A. 1993. (1930). *Studies on the History of Behavior: Ape, Primitive, and Child*. Hillsdale, NJ: Erlbaum

Webb N, Farivar S. 1997. Developing productive group interaction in middle school mathematics. In *Cognitive Perspectives on Peer Learning*, ed. AM O'Donnell, A King. In press

Wertsch J. 1991. *Voices of the Mind: A Sociocultural Approach to Mediated Action*. Cambridge: Harvard Univ. Press

Wertsch J, Bivens J. 1992. The social origins of individual mental functioning: alternatives and perspectives. *Q. Newsl. Lab. Comput. Hum. Cogn.* 14:35–44

Wertsch J, Stone A. 1985. The concept of internalization in Vygotsky's account of the genesis of higher mental functions. In *Culture, Communication, and Cognition: Vygotskian Perspectives*, ed. J Wertsch, pp. 162–79. New York: Cambridge Univ. Press

Index